THE
COMPLETE
TRACKER

THE
COMPLETE
TRACKER

Second Edition

Tracks, Signs, and Habits of
North American Wildlife

Len McDougall

LYONS PRESS
Guilford, Connecticut
An imprint of Globe Pequot Press

To buy books in quantity for corporate use or incentives, call **(800) 962-0973** or e-mail **premiums@GlobePequot.com**.

Lyons Press is an imprint of Globe Pequot Press.

Interior photos by Len McDougall unless otherwise credited. Interior illustrations by Len McDougall.

Project editor: Heather Santiago
Layout artist: Mary Ballachino
Text design: Elizabeth Kingsbury

Library of Congress Cataloging-in-Publication Data is available on file.

ISBN 978-1-59921-858-8

Printed in the United States of America

10 9 8 7 6 5 4 3 2

CONTENTS

Chapter One

TRACK IDENTIFICATION

Watching a good tracker at work can be pretty amazing. Making sense of scratches and impressions left in the earth, bent grasses, and shed hairs is a skill few folks in the new millennium ever need to learn. But it wasn't always that way. Tracking and hunting skills were once the equivalent of today's college degree, and they were passed on to every youngster from early childhood. Like tanning hides and making soap, these skills long ago became obsolete in a world increasingly dominated by technology. The finer points of tracking became blurred with time, and myths sprouted up like toadstools on a fallen tree.

There is nothing instinctive about tracking; only intellect and education can enable a tracker to discern that this impression shows the right front and hind hoofprints of a white-tailed buck, impressed during a hard rain two days prior to when this photo was taken.

The first five chapters will help dispel superstition and exaggeration about tracking with solid empirical knowledge. We'll learn about the nuts and bolts of locating a species of animal by analyzing its environment, learning its routines by interpreting the sign it leaves, and by tracking it to a feeding, watering, or denning area where it can be observed. Also covered are the tricks and tools most valuable to avoid being detected as you stalk within visual range. Much of the information presented in this section is generic, making it applicable to species not covered specifically in this book, to diverse types of terrain, and even to exotic species on other continents. If you have talent for tracking cougars in Montana, you also possess the basic skills needed to track leopards in Africa.

A warning is in order at this point: Trailing wild animals is a fascinating pastime, but their meandering paths can lead to remote country. Tracking yourself back out is never a good gamble, because snow, rain, and even wind can erase your trail, sometimes in a matter of minutes. Get a quality map compass, a detailed topographic area map, and a solid working knowledge of both before embarking on any tracking exercise. *Always* carry these items with you in the woods.

Animals carry a magnetic neural compass in their noses, but humans get lost easily without a compass and a map of the area they're exploring. Carry a GPS if you like, but rely on a virtually infallible compass for navigation.

Reading Tracks

Reading tracks accurately requires a trained eye. Just as a seasoned forester can point out a blue spruce in a forest where most laymen see only trees, an expert tracker can detect and identify tracks invisible to others because he or she knows what to expect. A tracker knows how to recognize and mentally assemble partial impressions into complete tracks, and how to use the arrangement of those imprints to arrive at an accurate explanation of what the animal was doing when it passed through. A veteran tracker knows what species are likely to inhabit an area by the terrain, flora, and fauna that he sees—he doesn't expect to find beavers in a desert or tree squirrels on a prairie—and his eyes automatically search for spoor left by animals that have not been seen yet.

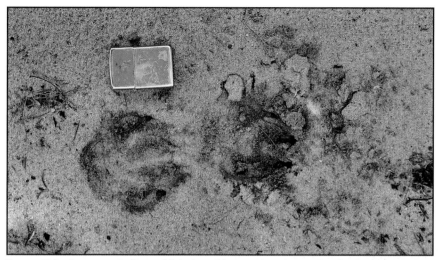

This pair of left-side coyote tracks (front on left, hind on right) were made just hours earlier, after dew-moistened sand had dried to a hard crust. Placement indicates an easy lope; hind food shows the animal made a slight turn to the right.

Example: A faint crescent-shaped impression in the ground below tall grasses is read as a whitetail's hoofprint. The sharpness of the corners in the print, along with the color, shape, and moisture content of crushed vegetation within it, reveal the age of the track with sometimes surprising accuracy. The depth of the track on one side tells if it is a right- or left-side hoofprint, and maybe even if the deer was pregnant, carrying extra weight.

While this book is intended to be carried afield as a reference, there are a number of small pieces of information that every tracker should commit to memory. For example, all cats, from African lions and Bengal tigers to South American jaguars and Canadian lynx, have four toes on each foot. So do canines, but cats have retractable claws that normally do not print, while members of the dog family have fixed claws that register at the front of every track. Bears have five toes with fixed claws on each foot, but their front paws are nearly doglike while the rear paws are shaped much like our own feet. In addition, black bears have short, sharply hooked claws, while a brown bear's claws are longer and straighter, designed for digging.

All weasels, including skunks, badgers, and wolverines, have five toes on front and back paws, but the size and other characteristics of their tracks make it possible to identify

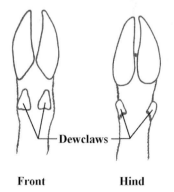

The hooves of a white-tailed deer are typical of ungulates in the order Artiodactyla, being cloven with paired dewclaws that may print on soft soils or snow.

individual species. Rabbits and hares have four toes on each foot, but their distinctive track patterns are similar only to those of tree squirrel, which have four toes on the front feet and five on the back, and are much smaller.

Another quadrupedal trait is that all species, hoofed or pawed, step down with most body weight on the outside of the soles, which maximizes stance width and stability, and makes the outermost toes largest—opposite the bipedal human design in which the big toes are innermost.

You'll still need a reference, however, because for every rule there are exceptions. The common muskrat, for instance, has five toes on each foot, while the closely related round-tailed muskrat has four on the front and five on the rear. The North American gray fox is unique among canids in having semiretractable claws that can be extended to enable it to climb trees. And while most quadrupeds have forefeet that are larger than hind feet because a running gait plants most force against the front paws or hooves, the stealthy bobcat possesses four equal-size feet that give it perfect balance when it freezes midstep while stalking prey.

TRACKS IN MUD

Trackers are seldom fortunate enough to find an obvious trail of perfect, complete prints, but wet sand, clay, or mud along the banks of lakes and streams will nearly always provide a few tracks distinct enough for positive identification, and for even a good plaster cast (explained later). Every animal in an area can be counted on to visit shorelines to drink or feed, or to escape predators—hares freely take to water when pursued because many predators break off pursuit rather than swim after them. Birds, reptiles, and even bats are among regular visitors to watering holes, while some animals, like beavers, muskrats, and nutria, live there full-time. Careful survey of a muddy bank can provide an accurate roster of almost every species within a mile or more, including birds, turtles, frogs, and even the clams that serve as food for numerous carnivores and omnivores.

In a few instances animals walking through mud leave a clear yet abnormal print. White-tailed deer typically leave split, heart-shaped prints on firmer ground, but on slippery mud and snow they tend to splay their hooves into a plowlike V to brake them against sliding forward or sideways. Cats also display insecurity when crossing mud, and often partially extend their retractable claws to maximize traction. Even with claws showing, feline tracks are different from those of the canines: Cat claws curve sharply downward and terminate in a keen weaponlike point, while the nonretractable claws of canines are thicker, more blunt (for digging), and have a less-pronounced curvature.

TRACKS IN SAND

Wet sand is usually an ideal tracking medium, another reason why shorelines are good places to scout for sign. An advantage of tracks found in wet sand is that they're fragile, easily washed away by waves and rain or blown apart by wind, while mud and wet clay can sometimes hold a near-perfect track for months. This fragility makes it easier to age tracks in sand, because few will survive intact for more than a day, and any clear print with sharp features is probably no more than a few hours old.

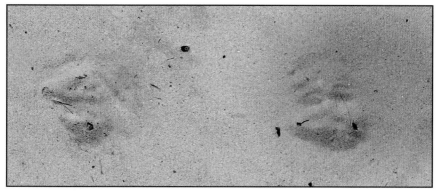

Even though dry powdery sand can make finer points of a track indistinguishable and blurred, track patterns, the environment, even the time of day are just some of the clues that help to identify these paired tracks as those of a river otter.

Conversely, dry sand can make track identification nearly impossible. Its powdery nature causes impressions to fill in partially as soon as an animal raises its foot, obscuring the details needed to make a positive identification. In dry, loose sand, prints are likely to be no more than bowl-shaped depressions, with the tracks of a deer being indistinguishable from those of a large dog, goat, or llama. In these cases you can get some type of idea as to an animal's species by gauging its stride, straddle, and gait; these will be explained in greater detail later.

TRACKS IN SNOW

Snow is a favorite tracking medium of biologists, because the right type of snow yields perfect prints. But, as indicated by each of the five Eskimo dialects, there are more than a dozen types of snow, with different densities, consistencies, and compressibility, and not all tracks in snow are the same.

First, consider the late-autumn "tracking snow" so wished for by whitetail hunters. This typically fluffy, large-flake snow falls atop earth that is still unfrozen, and it is very compactable, forming around foot contours with near perfection. In snow that's an inch or so deep, hoof- and paw prints may compress and melt the powder beneath them down to bare ground. These prints are obvious and easy to follow, but be aware that animals making them may spread their toes to maximize surface area and traction.

Even after the earth freezes, light, wet snow in temperatures just below freezing can hold ideal prints. But "warm" snow, further heated by compression and an animal's own body heat, tends to melt rapidly outward from a print, and especially when struck by sunshine. This phenomenon is responsible for reports of giant, exaggerated tracks made by gargantuan animals that no one ever sees.

Hardpack snow (several individual layers, compressed under its own mass), in temperatures below 20 degrees Fahrenheit, is another matter entirely. Hoofed animals passing over it during warmer daylight hours may sink in more than a foot, leaving prints at the bottom of a deep hole and limiting identification to measurements of stride and straddle. Lighter, wide-pawed species, such as bobcats and lynx, may leave distinct prints during daylight hours but they will begin to expand quickly, especially if the sun is shining. During the coldest hours, from about midnight to 4 a.m., pawed animals can travel along a frozen surface and hardly leave a mark; even the tracks of a large deer or elk may be faint, with only a dusting of crushed crystalline snow to tell of its passing.

Cutting the trail of a walking cat under such frozen conditions is nearly impossible, but this is where tracking devices and an ability to read sign come into play. Tracking conditions may also vary a great deal from one snowfall to the next. Warm, fluffy snow will hold a print well for a time, depending on the ambient temperature, but warm snowfalls are frequently heavy and may obliterate an existing trail completely. Cold, high-altitude snow, known as "powder" to skiers (it resembles dry laundry detergent), comes to earth as tiny balls of ice, and tracks in powder are frequently unrecognizable or badly distorted.

Every animal that walks must leave a track of some type, and most animals use regularly traveled trails for the sake of convenience.

TRACKS IN VEGETATION

Vegetation is the medium that defeats most trackers. Leaf-strewn hardwoods, grassy fields, and thick swamps pose a real challenge because prints there are seldom distinct. In these types of terrain, tracking consists mainly of looking for environmental disturbances that couldn't have been created by forces of nature alone, but must have been influenced by an animal.

Every creature that moves over the earth must leave some mark of its passing, however faint, and it's when a trail seems to just disappear that your entire arsenal of tracking techniques must come into play. Begin by identifying likely environments (here's where that detailed topographic map can be a useful

These tracks in dry reindeer lichen (aka reindeer moss) are not well defined, but they do show a flat, wide, elongated foot (bottom), and a more rounded front track (top), identifying the maker as a bear.

tool). Grassy meadows are good bets for finding herbivores and omnivores, as well as the carnivores that prey upon them. The grasses, clovers, and plantains that thrive in open spaces are favorites with many plant eaters. Sunny, open areas also provide space for wild cherries, strawberries, serviceberries, and, of course, the ubiquitous black and red raspberries, all of which are irresistible attractions to many birds and animals.

Tracking can be difficult in tall grass because ground vegetation cushions each step, distributing an animal's weight over a greater area (as a snowshoe would), and obscuring impressions made in the earth. There may be no real tracks to follow, but with patience, you can follow almost anything with enough body weight to break grass stems or press a plant to the ground.

The first step is to break the mindset of looking for tracks, and instead look for foot-

Tracking in tall grass and other vegetation can be challenging, but is not impossible.

prints—visible evidence that a paw or hoof was pressed downward. Twisted, broken grass stems and torn plant leaves at the bottom of a track impression in the grass indicate a change in direction, made as the animal turned with weight on that foot. A furrow of grasses pushed forward and aside by an animal's passing will remain obvious for half a day, particularly when the plants are weighted with morning dew.

Tracking can also be tough over the leafy floor of a hardwood forest, where years of dead leaves form a cushion of loose humus. Fresh trails left by hoofed mammals are fairly easy to follow because these animals leave sharp impressions; prints from pawed animals are less obvious. And the smaller the animal, the less noticeable its tracks. In this environment, tracking consists of looking sometimes very closely at the forest floor for unusual disturbances. You'll see for yourself that leaves are a slippery walking surface, and dry upper layers tend to slide over one another.

In lieu of footprints, small disturbances at regular intervals tell of an animal passing through on its way to a feeding, sleeping, or mating area. If such a regular trail can be found, the species of animal can often be determined by comparing to existing data its stride and straddle and the placement of its feet. A trail that looks as if the top leaves have been brushed forward and to either side, for instance, indicates that a porcupine passed through, sweeping the forest floor with its heavy tail as it lumbered along. Small sections of leaves pushed upward at short intervals denote the leaping gait of a squirrel.

Swamps are always interesting places to put your tracking skills to the test. Not only are they generally inhabited by an abundance of wild creatures, but the terrain is so variable that you can expect to encounter almost every type of tracking problem. One moment you're in water to your knees; a few minutes later you're on solid ground, or in shoulder-high sawgrass, or in a deadfall area so thick with fallen trees that normal walking is impossible.

Many species inhabit swamps for numerous reasons. The most obvious is that human beings avoid such places, which makes them wilder and more attractive to animals and people seeking to observe them. Another reason is safety: A typical cedar swamp is so thick with brush and foliage that anything more than 50 feet away may be out of sight. Animals whose principal sense is eyesight (like people) prefer to avoid such places, which defeat their main advantage, while those with keen hearing and an acute sense of smell can often locate and slip past would-be predators undetected. The pronghorn antelope, for example, is a creature of the open plains, where its sharp eyesight allows it to detect enemies from afar; the white-tailed deer inhabits thick cover, where its poor eyesight is more than offset by its keen nose. Swamps offer plenty of secluded spots to sleep in peace and also contain a variety of food plants.

The dense foliage of a swamp is both an advantage and a disadvantage for a tracker. Animals living there tend to follow regular, packed trails that allow swift, quiet travel, pursuit, or flight. And many different species are likely to use the same trail. Porcupines, raccoons, and bobcats use trails created by deer, and coyotes, cougars, and wolves may patrol those same trails routinely in search of carrion, fawns, or sickly adults. Bears also frequent deer trails in spring, hoping to catch a newborn fawn or a winter-weakened adult. Each of these creatures leaves its own spoor, and the advantage of scouting such a community trail is that many kinds of tracks lead to it. If you can determine where a certain species joined or left the communal trail, chances are good that the animal will pass there again come morning or evening.

TRACKS ON ROCK

The hardest medium to track over is rock (no pun intended), including asphalt road surfaces. No animal leaves footprints in stone (although I have seen ancient bear trails worn several inches into solid granite), but they will leave marks that can be followed. As any raw-fingered rock climber will attest, stone is abrasive; hooves, claws, and paws scraping over its surface leaves faint marks, like wood against sandpaper. Faint scrapes and light disturbances in the dust that invariably covers rocky areas also provide trails that can be followed, while patches of moss and lichen along the way may yield identifiable prints.

Roadways offer many of the same obstacles to tracking as bare rock, but with a few advantages. First, rural highways always have gravel shoulders. This loose stone and sand is easily disturbed by even something as small as a mouse or a sparrow, so almost any animal will leave a conspicuous trail. By studying the edges of a road you can determine whether an animal crossed, turned back the way it came, or traveled down the road a way before heading off.

Despite being too hard to imprint, asphalt can sometimes register near-perfect tracks on its surface, especially during early morning, when foliage is still wet with dew. Since most species are nocturnal and crepuscular (traveling mostly at dusk and dawn), the hours around sunrise are busy with animals returning to their dens after a night of foraging or hunting. If an animal crosses a road during its morning commute, chances are that it walked through grass heavily laden with dew. When that animal walks across the loose sand and gravel of the shoulder, its wet feet pick up grains of sand, leaving behind an outline in the shape of its paw or hoof. As it crosses over the pavement some of these particles fall away, leaving a kind of negative print in the shape of its paw or hoof.

The most common reason for losing a trail is simple impatience. If you find just one track of any animal that can't fly, there have to be more. In the case of powerful leapers like the whitetail, the next track may be as much as 20 feet from the first, but never doubt that it will be there; careful study of the last visible track will point you toward it. A change of direction is represented by a spiral twist against the earth, made as the animal spun on (usually) its hind feet. A sudden leap is indicated by hind tracks that are abnormally deep, especially at the toes, sometimes with a spray of dirt or debris behind them. You may have to drop to hands and knees to decipher what made the trail seem to disappear, but always remember that a trail doesn't actually simply disappear. It continues on because it has to; and all you have to do is find it.

Stride, Straddle, and Gait

When tracks are present but undefined, as they might be in loose sand, deep snow, or thick grass, you can get a good idea of an animal's species by measuring its stride, straddle, and gait. Different authors have used varying definitions of what constitutes a stride, but herein a stride is defined as the distance one foot travels in a single step. The distance in a stride depends on leg length—an elk will have a longer stride than a whitetail—but also on gait, or the speed an animal was traveling. Other factors affecting stride length include terrain, because all animals tend toward shorter steps on slippery ice or wet clay, and how deeply an animal is sinking into snow or mud. The length of the stride is also important to a tracker because it can reveal the mood of an animal; this will be covered in greater detail in the sections of this guide that address individual species.

Straddle is the distance between an animal's feet on either side, which is sometimes, but not always, determined by its body width. A phenomenon that every tracker should be aware of is the tendency for longer-legged animals to walk with their feet pointed inward. This is most pronounced in hoofed species, where the trail of a 200-pound whitetail with a 5-inch straddle may be used by a 1,500-pound moose with a 10-inch straddle. The purpose behind this characteristic is the need to use as little space as possible for walking, thus decreasing the amount of energy used for traveling through deep snow, mud, or sand, and minimizing the number of tripping and stumbling hazards encountered.

Gait is the pace an animal was traveling when it made the tracks. The three basic gaits are walking, trotting, and running, with minor variations between those. Among quadrupeds, these gaits result in distinctive "track patterns" that are largely generic to all species. The arrangement in which all four feet imprint as a set tells a tracker how quickly or slowly an animal was traveling, which in turn reveals the maker's disposition at the time. With practice, a tracker can use track patterns to determine whether an animal was relaxed, frightened, antagonistic, or purposeful.

Estimating Weight

Estimating an animal's size and weight from track impressions is an important skill for all trackers, especially guides and hunters. Knowing a species' average weight and size is important, because you will then have a frame of reference from which to extrapolate. The simplest method of gauging weight is to compare a print with the impression left by your own foot in the same medium. For hoofed animals, I step down hard alongside the track with just the heel of my boot, emulating the force and area covered by the existing print. By imprinting your boot heel over roughly the same area as a hoofprint, you can draw a conclusion about how much weight was on that foot. Bear in mind, though, that even at a casual walk, a quadruped's weight is supported on no less than two of its feet. Roughly speaking, a 200-pound man who impresses his boot heel over the same area as a walking deer's hoofprint, and sinks in to twice the hoofprint's depth, can estimate that the deer that walked there has a body weight of approximately 200 pounds.

For larger pawed animals, such as bears or pumas, I exert my full weight downward on just the ball of one foot. Most animals tend to walk on their toes, and the objective here is to mimic the animal's print as closely as possible. Again, use a two-to-one ratio to make your weight estimations: A cougar print registering 1 inch deep in mud, for example, indicates an approximate weight of 100 pounds if the toe print of a 200-pound man also sinks 1 inch.

Aging Tracks

In most instances, the tracks that most interest a tracker are the most recent, so knowing how to distinguish these from older tracks is a real help. Aging tracks can also provide important background information about an animal's habits. Comparing the time interval between each set of prints can tell you how frequently a trail is used, and this can cut the amount of time you spend waiting for an animal to appear. Remember, most wild animals are creatures of habit unless pressured. With a reliable timetable of its comings and going in hand, you can position yourself in a nearby hide literally within minutes of an animal's appearance.

The two factors that most affect tracks are temperature and humidity. Heavy rain can wash away a trail in minutes, and a hard snowstorm will erase the best trail. On the one hand, a track left in permanently wet swamp mud may stay sharp and fresh looking for weeks, while on the other hand a paw print made in wet sand may crumble quickly away under a hot sun. Sometimes you have to look closely to see everything a track has to tell.

All tracks become less well defined with continued exposure to the elements; the fresher a track, the sharper its features. Summer grass pressed flat against the ground by a bear's foot means you should keep your eyes open lest you run into the animal. An hour later, the grass stems in that same print will be slowly rising back to their upright positions. A day later, only a few broken, yellowed stems will mark the bear's passing.

Whenever possible, I like to hedge my bets by sweeping clean a sandy area where animal traffic appears regularly, in effect creating a clean slate on which fresh tracks will be conspicuous because there are no others. Surprisingly, wild animals seem almost oblivious to tracks or lack of them and even suspicious species will cross this prepared "litmus field" without apparent concern; so long as you take care not to disturb the surroundings or deposit foreign scent; never touch anything with bare hands if you can avoid it. By monitoring the swept area in the morning and afternoon and sweeping it clean again after each check, you can work out an individual animal's timetable precisely and quickly. In no more than a day or so, you'll probably be able to time your own arrival to within minutes of the animal's.

Chapter Two

READING SIGN

Reading tracks is only part of tracking. On most terrain, following a set of prints alone ranges from fairly difficult to darned near impossible. Fortunately, much of the information needed to trail any animal can be garnered from other marks left by its passing, known collectively as sign. We've all seen Hollywood movie trackers who can determine whether a fellow is wearing boxers or briefs from a blade of bent grass, but cinematic license aside, interpreting sign is among the most important skills any tracker can possess.

Trackers seldom have a clear trail of footprints to follow, but must extrapolate information about what an animal was doing from forensic clues. This photo shows the large scales of a carp that was eaten by a black bear (note heavily impressed hind footprint at lower left).

Environment

As my own tracking mentor, Amos Wasageshik, told me back in 1968, if you find a species' preferred food, you'll probably find those animals somewhere nearby. Fields of rich clover are irresistible to whitetails, but it's senseless to look for river otters on a dry mesa or fox squirrels on treeless prairie. These animals have each adapted to a specific environment and to the foods available within it. Some animals—bears and caribou—may wander hundreds of miles following seasonal foods, while others—white-tailed deer and porcupines—spend their entire lives within a square mile or so.

This deer trail passes through a smorgasbord of grasses, sedges, plantains, and other plants that are favored by herbivores . . . and where you find plant-eaters, you'll find meat-eaters that prey on them.

Vegetation is an important factor in locating any species, whether predator or prey. If you're looking for bobcats, begin by finding the grasses, willows, and other vegetation preferred by its primary prey, rabbits and hares. If there are bears in an area (reclusive black bears are more numerous than generally realized), among the best places to find one are areas where raspberries, serviceberries, or apples are ripening. Whatever species of animal you seek, its presence or absence hinges, directly or indirectly, on an area's plant life.

Water is a must for every habitat. Some small species, like rattlesnakes and mice, can absorb enough moisture from the foods they eat to function, and a few larger animals, like dromedaries and donkeys, can store water in their tissues. But for most, there must be a permanent source of water within any suitable territory, and trackers can anticipate that any creature living within reach of a stream, lake, or water hole will visit there once, maybe twice, each day—usually at sunrise and/or sunset.

Conversely, type of habitat also dictates which species will not live there. Deer are a timber wolf's natural prey, yet while whitetail populations have exploded across the country in recent years, wolf populations never will because people fear them and will either kill or drive them off. Canada geese have overpopulated city parks to the point of becoming a health risk, but coyotes and bobcats aren't welcome there because they are feared predators. These and other species, like rabbits, elk, and squirrels, are willing to live in close proximity to humans because people have proved willing to welcome cute little raccoons and bunnies into their backyards, but won't tolerate the presence of coyotes, bobcats, or bears. The inability of people to coexist with predators has created a safe haven for their prey, most of which seem to regard humans as the lesser of two evils. A gruesome yet fairly accurate way to determine how many predators are in an area is to note the number and type of prey animals killed by cars on nearby roads. A section of forest where roads are dotted with road-killed porcupines is a good indication that the fisher, a large weasel and the porky's most serious natural predator, is absent from the area.

Scat

Once you've found an environment and habitat suited to the animal you're looking for, the next step is to look for sign, the most prominent being scat, or feces. With the exception of beavers, even amphibious mammals don't normally defecate in water. This may stem from some instinct against polluting their own drinking water, but scat deposited on land also serves as a territorial marker, warning other members of the same species, or any competitors for the same foods, not to trespass. Territorial instincts are a natural safeguard against overpopulation, especially among predators, and the most effective means an animal has of broadcasting its claim to a territory is through scat, urine, and musk scents. Coyotes and bobcats patrol regular routes while hunting, and these will be dotted with scat deposits that are periodically freshened. The amphibious muskrat marks its territory by leaving its scat on a prominent log, and river otters declare their presence with scat deposited along stream banks.

Interestingly, prey animals like deer and rabbits may deposit scat anywhere within their chosen territories, unconcerned about using it to establish a defined territorial boundary. This random distribution of scat is a natural defense intended to flood an area with so much scent that predators will be confused about a prey's exact location. A pack of gray wolves that begins pursuit of a fleet white-tailed deer must catch it before it reaches the dense cover that deer are never far from; if the deer maintains a lead of even a dozen yards before leaping 20 feet or more into that maze of scent trails and random scats, the wolves will probably lose it.

Predators also tend to defecate directly on the remains of prey after everything edible has been consumed. I've noted this behavior in coyotes, bobcats, lynx, and black bears, and the practice is apparently common. Cached, partially consumed kills are not usually tainted with scat, only carcasses that have been picked clean; the act seems to be both a territorial marker and a boast of prowess. In most cases the tainted remains will have been marked by a strong, territorial male, but this behavior has also been observed among strong, dominant females.

Scat deposits can tell you a great deal if you overcome your natural aversion to handling poop and examine it closely. Feces can carry parasites dangerous to humans, so never handle scat with bare hands; latex or nitrile gloves, like those used in medical settings, provide the most natural feel, but less expensive polyethylene food-service gloves offer ample protection as well. Ziplock sandwich-type bags are very good for transporting samples out for closer inspection, and if maintaining the original shape is important, snap-lid plastic food dishes are ideal.

These red fox scats show various ages, with the white, crumbling specimens being the oldest.

Physical characteristics of a scat can reveal a great deal about its maker. Many of those characteristics are generic: Herbivores, from moose and white-tailed deer to rabbits and squirrels, tend to defecate clusters of pellets in oblong, spherical, or "acorn" shapes. Omnivores, like bears and raccoons, exhibit a "tootsie-roll" scat, with cylindrical sections of uniform diameter whose ends are squared flat and untapered. Predators, such as cougars, wolves, foxes, and sometimes bears, produce scat that is wrapped in a spiral sheath of prey fur, formed to encase sharp bones, teeth, or quills that could injure the intestines during digestion.

It can help to know the age of a scat deposit. Like ourselves, wild animals tend to fall into daily routines, and droppings left at 4 p.m. one day will likely be freshened at about the same time the following day. By observing changes in a scat due to evaporation, cooling, insects, and other elements of decay, it's possible to estimate how long a deposit has been there, and to extrapolate from that where an animal might be, and when it might return.

This collection of coyote scats, created periodically over the course of a winter, has decayed so far that only the indigestible deer and rodent hairs that encased them remain.

Temperature and humidity are key factors in how quickly moisture is lost from any type of scat, but there are a few rules of thumb: If it feels warm to the back of your hand, it's less than an hour old. If it's cold but still wet looking, it was left within the last 5 hours. If the outside is dry and hard but the inside is still moist, it's somewhere between 6 and 24 hours old. Scat that has dried throughout but still retains a dark color is from 1 to 3 days old. Deposits that have turned white and crumble when touched are at least 4 days old. You can see that aging scat becomes less precise the longer it has been exposed to the elements, and if it's raining or snowing hard you can probably toss these rules out the window. Still, they're fairly accurate for most scat types under most conditions.

Scent Posts

Scent posts are another way some species mark their territories. A scent post can be as simple as wolf urine on a tree trunk or as complex as the beaver's scent mound—a cone of mud, sticks, and grasses that may stand 1 foot tall with a base diameter of 3 feet or more.

Muskrat scent posts resemble those of the beaver but are about half the size. Cats, especially males, label their territories with a spray of strong-smelling urine on a prominent landmark.

Scent posts are refreshed periodically, usually every day or so, and because they're potent enough to warn off animal intruders or to attract potential mates from a distance, even relatively useless human noses can often detect one nearby. If you suddenly smell a musky odor on the trail, take a few moments to use both your nose and your eyes to determine its source. Once found, a scent post is a good place to wait quietly for its owner to return.

This old stump serves as an elevated feeding platform that enables the dominant red squirrel in this area to see all around, but also carries its owner's scent, with a warning to other squirrels that this piece of forest is claimed.

TERRITORIAL MARKS

Scent posts and scat are just a first line of defense against rival intruders, and many species complement these warnings with visual sign as well. The scent scrapes left by rutting (mating) males of the deer family serve not just to attract females but also as an obvious warning to rivals that these normally peaceful animals are prepared to fight for breeding rights. Bears leave long claw marks as high as they can reach on tree trunks to impress intruders with their size, and man-made structures such as wooden bridges, power-line poles, or even cabins frequently show the claw marks of a territorial bruin. The grizzly bear's "playful" shoving over of dead trees may actually be meant to advertise both its claim to a territory and the strength it possesses to defend that territory.

Some territorial marks are less conspicuous. Claw marks left on a tree trunk that a bobcat used for a scratching post are easy to miss since we have only our eyes to search with, but rivals spot them by scent. The feisty red squirrel, or chickaree, marks its territory with regular feeding stations littered with pinecone debris and droppings. Beavers sometimes mark trees at the outside of their working areas by gnawing off a small section of bark, possibly to identify the tree for future cutting, but certainly as a warning to other beavers not to trespass.

The remains of this predator-killed blue heron tell a tracker that there are large, fast, and stealthy carnivores in the area. But the lack of predator scat on the carcass indicates that the heron's fishy-tasting flesh was probably consumed by birds, not by the predator itself.

Trails

When you find an animal trail, you know that at least one animal uses it periodically, and it will doubtless use that trail again within a day or so. Four-footed creatures routinely establish regular trails for the same reason we use hiking trails: They beat fighting your way through the bushes.

But open trails are more than mere convenience for wild animals; they make possible high-speed escapes through dense cover, and through a chaos of confusing scents left by

This trail has been used by deer, raccoons, and other animals frequently enough to have become a rut, but it also has not been used for several weeks, as evidenced by an accumulation of pine needles that would have been displaced by heavy traffic.

themselves and other species. Snowshoe hares create well-packed runways in deep snow to save energy traveling to and from feeding spots; these narrow slots with hard-packed bottoms also give hares and rabbits a vital edge in speed when escaping predators too large to use such a trail themselves.

One problem with animal trails is that it isn't always easy or even possible for human trackers to follow them. Quadrupeds are more able (and willing) to scoot under half-downed trees, jump over logs, and wriggle through deep brush than humans. A raccoon's highway may be an impenetrable jungle to us, so it sometimes becomes necessary to skirt a difficult area and try to cut its trail on the other side. Be prepared to track on hands and knees when that becomes necessary, but once again the real secret is to know the species' habits intimately enough to make an accurate prediction about where your animal was going, and what it was doing.

The need for a good map and compass to keep from getting lost as your tracking skills lead you deeper and deeper into the wilderness was discussed in chapter 1. But a good compass and topographic map can also help you locate animals. The map contains geographical details that identify prairies, swamps, forests, and waterways that may be likely feeding or bedding areas, while a quality prismatic or lensatic compass serves as the navigational tool to help you find those places.

Since the first edition of this book was published, Global Positioning System (GPS) units have become a preferred method of navigation in both urban and wilderness settings. Reliant upon geostationary satellites, these electronic units are capable of fixing their users' positions within a few yards from anywhere, provided the user is versed in the Universal Transverse Mercator (UTM) coordinate system, is in possession of a map marked with a UTM grid, and has a working GPS receiver. The problem, which is stated in every GPS owner's manual, is that these battery-operated devices cannot deliver the almost absolute reliability of an old-fashioned compass. When Odawa tribal biologists and I worked together tracking gray wolves in Michigan's Lower Peninsula in the late 1990s, we used a compass and map for primary navigation, and the GPS for pinpointing precise coordinates of notable findings, which were then logged onto a larger map back at the office.

Bedding Areas

All animals need to sleep, and in most instances their sleeping and denning places are conspicuous. A large, oval-shaped depression in a field of tall grass says that a mule deer lay there to chew its cud and nap. Smaller depressions next to larger ones belong to fawns, which means that the animals who made the larger beds were mother does. Fawn-size beds that are far from larger deer beds could indicate that coyotes were lying in wait for the squeak of a rodent, or for a fawn to wander too far from its mother. In winter, a packed trail of cottontail rabbit tracks leading under a snow-covered brush pile or a fallen tree certainly points to a seasonal den. Sofa-size depressions pressed heavily into the leafy floor of a deciduous forest, or sometimes in a field or meadow, are the beds of elk, while bathtublike mud wallows on shorelines in wet northern forests tell of moose trying to escape the heat and biting flies of summer. A birdbath-size mass of twigs and leaves packed into the crotch of a limb overhead is a squirrel nest or "loafing platform."

Sleeping can be a dangerous proposition for wild animals, especially smaller ones, whose survival depends on resting with all senses alert for the first hint of predators. For this reason, bedding areas are always selected to give an animal the best odds for detecting predators before predators detect them, for making a quiet escape, or, as a last ditch, for mounting a defense formidable enough to discourage an enemy. The porcupine naps on a high tree branch, its tail facing the trunk, because few predators can get to it there and fewer still can negotiate the narrow branch without being slapped by the porky's spiny, clublike tail (one exception is the fisher, whose sharp claws enable it to clamber under the branch to emerge at a porcupine's unprotected head).

This blue heron was killed by a young adult wolf that hadn't yet learned that its oily flesh is unpalatable. Note perforations in its breast that outline the wolf's upper teeth, left when the probably sleeping heron was snatched by its left shoulder.

Deer make their daytime beds in heavy cover, where keen noses and sharp ears can detect enemies long before they come into view. Raccoons often elect to sleep in an abandoned fox den, where their own airborne spoor is greatly muted and they can mount a fierce resistance to attackers that must approach head-on. Bears and moose, whose size and power put them effectively outside of the food chain in most instances, sleep pretty much anywhere they choose, and that location is usually near a food source that they may choose to defend against intruders.

Chapter Three

TRACKING TOOLS

While it can be tough to say anything good about technology that has made sunblock a necessity, depleted entire oceans of fish, and enslaved us to conveniences of our own design, a few modern advances do benefit lovers of the outdoors. Many products developed for war, sport hunting, even daily urban life, also have applications in wildlife photography and animal observation.

Light-amplifying "Starlight" night-vision devices level the playing field between night-blind humans and nocturnal animals that see very well in the dark; handheld heat detectors can signal an unseen animal's location from its body heat; hunting calls can precisely mimic the sounds most likely to entice an animal into view; manufactured scent products can mask human odor or eliminate it entirely, while others can broadcast an illusion of food or sex. Had these modern hunting aids existed when our forefathers settled the New World, the number of species they hunted and trapped to extinction would doubtless have been greater than it is.

Scents

Artificial scents have come a long way since early trappers flavored beaver traps with casto-reum from the animals' own musk glands and Native Americans burned fleabane to attract deer. Even today, sport-hunting retailers find a ready market among deer hunters for tarsal glands cut from the knees of breeding does, the theory being that the aroma of sexual availability will override a buck's instinct for caution. The concept is sound, because most communication in a wild animal's life, whatever its species, is accomplished through widely varied odors that carry information about sexual readiness, gender, age, size, attitude, emotion, and a host of other data that science is still sorting out. The trick is to use what is known about scent communication to the best advantage, and, especially, to avoid using scents inappropriately, because it's also possible to scare off your prey with the wrong scent at the wrong time.

SCENT NEUTRALIZERS

Perhaps the most important scent breakthrough in recent years is the development of non-toxic sprays and soaps that break down odors at the molecular level—like "Scent Stop" from Buck Stop Scents & Lures. Initially developed for deer hunters, these scent killers have found applications among pet owners, homeowners, and in household air-freshener products. My own tests of these scent neutralizers have included using them to remove pet odors from furniture, plus a number of field trials that pitted them against the noses of several species of wild animals and one good tracking dog. I'm skeptical of a product that claims to do something I can't perceive, let alone measure, but I have to admit that these sprays do seem to at least muffle odors. I believe they've been at least partly responsible for my getting to within a few feet of deer, elk, and bobcats, undetected.

COVER SCENTS

Cover scents are intended to mask human odors (including sweat, aftershave, and petro-chemicals), and work by veiling those odors with a stronger smell. The most popular hunter's cover scent is fox urine, usually applied to boot soles to disguise a hiker's scent trail, and sometimes used on the ground around a blind or stand of trees. Raccoon urine is another overwhelming cover scent that can be used either on the ground or in a stand of trees without being out of place. Cover scents do work, but your own odors are mingled with the stronger odor of the scent, and it's difficult to say at what range or under what conditions animals will unscramble the confusion of smells. The most effective cover scent is skunk musk because its stench overpowers a victim's olfactory system, causing it to shut down, unable to smell anything. The obvious problem with skunk musk is that it also repels any animal that can smell it. Remember that older, more experienced members of any species got that way by being cautious. The spoor of a strange meat-eater—even a small one—may in itself attract attention.

Keen-nosed tattletales of the forest include scavenger birds like blue jays, ravens, and magpies, and especially squirrels like the chickaree, or red squirrel. Many species are keyed to the alarm calls of these smaller animals, and it's no exaggeration to say that many a trophy has been lost because a little bird told it that danger was lurking.

SEX SCENTS

While the majority of sex scents produced are for white-tailed deer, there are also scents for exploiting the mating urges of elk, moose, and black bears. Most used are estrus scents from sexually active females. Engineered to act on the powerful instincts of males that mate for just a few weeks each year, the intent of these products is to entice them into disregarding their own cautious natures to pursue the promise of sex. Since males are the sexual aggressors in most species, it's also in their nature to fall for this ruse.

Other sex scents are derived from hormone-laden male urine. Rather than encouraging an amorous reaction, these are meant to incite territorial males into jealous rages. Judicious application of these "piss-off" scents—as they were called off the record by one manufacturer—have at times brought males at a run, ready to defend their territories against an imagined usurper.

FOOD SCENTS

More constant and nearly as strong as the drive to mate is the need to eat. Food scents are attractive to animals in every season; all a tracker needs to do is match the proper aroma to the diet of the species he or she hopes to lure into sight. Apple and acorn scents appeal to deer, but acorn scent can also intrigue fox and gray squirrels, but apple scent is attractive to a variety of animals, from black bears to elk and porcupines. Many manufactured food scents also contain some essence of the species they're meant to attract—for example, Buck Stop brand's apple scent contains whitetail musk.

A time-proven alternative to manufactured food scents is to use a transportable form of an actual food. Many animals, including meat-eaters, are drawn to the odor of ripened fruit, because even the most carnivorous species require some vegetable matter to supply the vitamins and minerals not provided by a diet of flesh alone. One old hunters' trick is to dump a can of apple juice concentrate over a rotting stump or log; several species may then take part in the job of literally eating the wood down to the ground. Bears and raccoons are especially fond of maple syrup, honey, and molasses, and so are numerous other calorie-seeking creatures; pouring one of these sweets over a decaying stump will probably bring repeat visits from a variety of critters.

Some food scents can be found in your kitchen cupboard. Concentrated walnut and almond flavorings are attractive to squirrels, and many species will investigate the tantalizing odor of maple flavoring. A few old-timers swear that vanilla extract is just the thing for luring in both deer and bears, and problems I've had with bears raiding my cabin have convinced me that bruins have a real taste for the stuff, drinking it right from the carefully uncapped bottle and spilling almost none.

Bacon grease, known as "Indian butter" among backcountry chefs who use it to perk up modest cabin cuisine, definitely suits the palates of black bears, raccoons, and opossums. Blood collected from slaughterhouses attracts a host of sharp-nosed carnivores, including ravens, vultures, and magpies, who in turn signal larger meat-eaters. Blood carries a potent odor, but it has a short shelf life, and should be frozen until needed.

Or you might elect to use actual meat for carnivores. During a 5-year study of migrating wolves in Michigan's Lower Peninsula, Odawa tribal biologists and I transported hundreds of pounds of road-killed venison into the woods to use as bait. Fresh meat is especially effective in winter, when it remains detectable by carnivores that are probably anxious for an easy meal, but is kept from spoiling by freezing temperatures. We staked whole carcasses in open places—like on the frozen surfaces of lakes and beaver ponds—and suspended leg quarters from overhead branches, where wolves (and coyotes) would leap up to grab them, leaving tracks in the snow below. In some states officials from fish and game departments may give permission for photographers to lure carnivores with road-killed carcasses, but some states prohibit baiting of any kind. Always check with local officials before picking up any road-killed animal.

Salt and Mineral Licks

Salt is a necessary nutrient for mammals, and, like sugar, it's not widely available in the wild. Many a farmer has seen his cattle's salt block devoured by wild animals, and salt licks have proven so irresistible to wildlife that some states ban their use by sport hunters. Deer, bears, elk, and moose are among the more exciting visitors to salt blocks, but almost any mammal in an area may come by for a few quick licks sometime during the day or night. Mineral blocks are refined versions of salt blocks that provide not only salt but also other necessary nutrients. To enhance their appeal to wildlife, some mineral blocks are treated with food scents (usually apple). The downside is that toting a mineral block far into the wilderness can be exhausting, and in some places porcupines alone can devour a 25-pound block in days—then proceed to eat the salt-soaked twigs and leaves beneath it.

A simpler alternative to the salt block is a salt lick, made by dissolving a kitchen-size container of granulated salt in a quart of water. Pour the solution slowly over a dry rotting stump, allowing the absorbent wood to soak up as much of the liquid as possible. The odor of salt will be detectable by your own nose, and it's probable that the salted stump will attract, and actually be eaten by, a host of salt-loving creatures ranging from deer to porcupines.

The Tracker's Field Kit

A tracker gathering data in the field is, in effect, a forensic scientist acquiring data and deducing from clues what has happened in a particular area. And just like a police detective, he or she needs to have the specialized tools required to accomplish the tasks at hand. Some tools are generic: Measuring tools for recording the length of a stride or hoofprint are needed in every environment for any species of animal with feet. And casting tracks always requires water and plaster.

While most often thought of as the means to an end for hunters and biologists, wildlife tracking is an absorbing, often adventurous pastime in itself.

That said, there is no list of tracking tools that will be suited to every environment or season. In winter, you cannot mix plaster with frozen water, so casting tracks demands that a tracker have the means to keep water bottles warm. Determine what the objectives of your outing are and how accomplishing those tasks might be affected by the environment, then use the summaries provided in this guide to select the tools you'll need, subtracting from or adding to them as a situation demands.

EQUIPMENT BAGS

A working tracking outfit will fit into a large day pack, with room to spare for an ultralight bedroll, bivy shelter, mosquito net, and other tools that make working in a wilderness as comfortable as it can be. Commonly called a "day-and-a-half pack," suitable packs in this category have at least 2,000 cubic inches of storage, internal frame supports, padded shoulder straps and waist belt, and a sternum strap, and are comfortable enough to be carried all day. Models with lots of pockets help with organizing loose gear into dedicated kits that can be found quickly, even in the dark, and if more pockets are needed, there are add-on accessory pouches that fit any backpack with compression, or cinch, straps. Numerous small packs serve well as tracking kits, most costing well under a hundred dollars.

ANIMAL CALLS

Game calls have been used by hunters for centuries, and these can be valuable tools for trackers who hunt with cameras or binoculars, too. Never have there been so many types of game calls with so much sophisticated technology inside them, or so much hard science behind their designs. From traditional handheld, mouth-powered units to digital electronic playback devices that reproduce every known animal voice, modern calls enable humans to precisely mimic injured prey to draw in predators, or to emulate territorial adults and incite a protective response.

Success at calling wildlife depends not just on skill, but also on knowledge of the species being called. Varmint hunters know that the squeal of a wounded rabbit will interest most carnivores, but mule deer also respond to it (studies indicate that during times of starvation deer have become carnivorous). The soft calls of a nesting Canada goose emanating from a marsh at night are regarded as a dinner invitation by coyotes and bobcats, and the repeated squeaking of a squirrel call may bring around all sorts of predators to investigate. Bears loitering around deer trails in spring seeking a dinner of newborn venison may come to the low bleat of a fawn, as well as may cats and coyotes. And the repeated bleatings of an immature doe from the same place will sometimes bring in predators looking for a sickly deer. Actual animal calls recorded on cassette have also proven effective at luring different types of wildlife within gun, bow, or camera range, but their use is sometimes restricted by local laws, so check out the situation before using them.

OPTICS

John Wootters, the world's most famous whitetail hunter, once said that the average hunter will walk by ten deer for every one he sees. The trick is to utilize superior vision so you see the deer first. If you're tracking wild animals, you need a binocular; in fact, you need as good a binocular as you can get.

A scope or monocular won't cut it, because these instruments use only one eye. The reason humans, like most predators, have eyes paired at the front of the head is so twin images of the same scene, viewed from slightly different angles, can be constantly compared by the brain 60 times each second. The benefit of having a dual imaging system is that it gives predators an unmatched ability to precisely discriminate between objects at different distances or depths. Whether pouncing onto a prey's back or putting it down with an arrow, viewing the world three-dimensionally is critical to accurately estimating range, and that provides a baseline from which to calculate an optimum trajectory for achieving the most accurate strike possible.

Not only does a good binocular retain the stereoscopic ability to determine which of two distant objects is closer, it enhances that ability by magnifying viewed images from as low as 4 times (for "stadium" binocs) to as much as 25 times (for stargazing models). Today's precision-ground lenses deliver very good clarity at higher powers, but magnification is limited by other physical factors: The more an image is magnified, the more ambient light is required to illuminate it at the ocular (eyepiece) lens, so higher optical powers are generally less desirable for observations in low light. Increasing the diameter of the objective lenses permits more available light to be taken in and directed to a viewer's eye, but at the expense of portability.

A remedy for that dilemma is the metallic lens coating developed by Carl Zeiss just prior to World War II. Zeiss discovered that by applying the principle of a two-way mirror he could trap light gathered by the objective lens and

Modern binoculars endow human trackers with powers of vision that are superior to even the most sharp-eyed animals.

prevent it from being reflected back out, thereby intensifying light emitted through the ocular lenses and brightening the image seen through them. Modern lens coatings are also engineered to act as a selective light filter, blocking blues and greens that darken a viewed image while enhancing reds and yellows that brighten it (this makes deer and other brownish animals literally stand out from their surroundings). Probably the greatest advantage of optical coatings is that they enable a small objective lens to deliver the same brightness and clarity as a much larger uncoated lens, which means trackers can carry a more portable binocular.

Objective lens diameter and magnification also have an effect on "field of view" (FOV), which is the real diameter of a circular area that is visible through binocs at 1,000 yards (or meters). The higher the magnification, the smaller the field of view; the larger the objective lenses, the greater the field of view. Smaller field of view makes it more difficult to quickly find an object through the binocular, so squirrel hunters and deep-forest birders, whose viewing interests are relatively close-up, are most fond of wide-view models in the 4x to 8x range (4 to 8 times magnification). Lower magnifications require less ambient light, making them best for use in shadowed forest or twilight, and better models enhance sharpness and contrast beyond what the naked eye can perceive.

Size and weight have always been a concern with field binoculars. The large prisms responsible for giving traditional Porro prism models outstanding clarity and focus also make them heavy and bulky enough to leave behind when heading out to the blind. Continuing improvements in optical grinding have made possible very small but precise prisms that are also coated to enhance the best qualities of light refracted through them. Porro prism binoculars are the most bulky design, with their ocular and objective lenses offset to accommodate prisms in the viewing barrels, but this traditional configuration is still preferred by boaters and others for whom size and weight are less important than razor-sharp focus and maximum light-gathering ability.

Trackers and birders (and outdoor writers) want those same optical advantages, but people on foot tend to be conscious of weight and bulk, so most backcountry trekkers opt for a more streamlined roof prism binocular. Today's roof prism models provide nearly the same optical quality of a Porro prism, with the same magnification and lens diameters, but their prisms are contained inside straight viewing barrels that are more lightweight and compact to carry. The resulting "shirt-pocket" binoculars, generally in the 8x28 range (8 times magnification, 28mm objective lenses), have proven popular with hunters and especially backpackers, who typically resent every ounce of weight they must carry. With that in mind, I still take to heart the advice of Nikon's Greg Chevalier, who suggests, "Get big glass, and get the best glass."

When reading the specs on any bino, look for the designation BaK-4 in their description of its prisms. This cryptic identifier refers to a high quality prism design with the best visual fidelity available, as opposed to the lower optical quality of the less expensive BaK-7 prism. If you aren't sure which prism is inside, hold the binoc about 6 inches in front of your eyes and look through the ocular lenses; BaK-4 (barium-crown glass) prisms are revealed as a perfect circle, while BaK-7 (borosilicate glass) prisms show as fuzzy-edged squares.

Not all binoculars are waterproof. Casual-use "kitchen window" binocs aren't intended for exposure to wet conditions or subzero temperatures, and if moisture finds a way into the viewing tubes, prisms and internal lens surfaces may be fogged forever. Waterproof binoculars with sealed nitrogen-filled tubes will have that feature printed on their bodies, and are further distinguished by a higher price tag.

In fact, how well a binocular will perform in the field is linked to its manufacturer's suggested retail price, because rubber armor, precision lens coatings, and sealed construction add cost to the manufacturing process. It isn't reasonable to expect that a blister-packaged department store binoc costing $25 will give you the same brightness, resolution, and durability as more expensive model with more features. Among birders—a group that knows binoculars—the consensus is that it takes $200 to get a fieldworthy binoc, but sport hunters and campers can do well with a starter model in $100 price range. At the other extreme, there is little reason in the real world of dust, rain, cold, and hard knocks to spend $2,000 or more for a working binocular, and the few advantages offered by high-dollar models seldom justify their price tags. Based on Best Buy Awards awarded by *Consumers Digest* magazine, the most bang for your binoc buck will be priced at about $500.

However much you pay for your binocular, it should be treated like the valuable optical instrument it is. Most important is preserving optical lens coatings, identifiable as oily-looking swirls on the objective lenses. Treat these coatings gently; keep your lenses covered or your binocs cased when not in use, and use only soft glass cleaning cloths to wipe them. Never use spit to clean any coated lens (including rifle scopes and cameras), because enzymes in saliva are corrosive to them, and can seriously degrade optical performance over time.

Given proper care, even one of the less expensive binoculars sold today will remain serviceable beyond its buyer's lifetime. Springing for a higher priced model with more features enhances the likelihood that it will become an heirloom, and adds to its real value as tracking or hunting tool. Try to find a satisfying balance between price and performance, and get as good a binocular as your budget permits. Whether you're tracking a rare bird as it flits from tree to tree or picking out a motionless whitetail from tangled underbrush, having the super vision afforded by a quality binocular can pay a handsome dividend in the field.

TRACKING CAMERAS

A dying sun settled in the southwestern sky as I sneaked through a nearly impenetrable jungle of alder and river willow, trying hard to step silently on dry twigs and leaves that crackled underfoot like popcorn. Avoiding quick movements that might startle tattletale birds and squirrels into sounding an alarm, I eased down to one knee and lightly ran my fingertips around the edges of a deep hoofprint. The impression was sharp-edged and fresh, and the plant fibers that had torn under the hooves' tremendous weight were wet, crushed underfoot no more than an hour before. My prey, an adult bull moose, had to be very close.

Game laws prohibited hunting moose here, but I couldn't deny the excitement that accompanied tracking down this gigantic member of the deer family. So near my target, I was acutely aware of every sound, sight, and odor as my trigger finger caressed the shutter button of the digital camera that hung from my neck.

Different groups debate philosophical points, but the bottom line is that anyone actively seeking to observe wild animals is a hunter, whether individuals prefer to be called birders, naturalists, or photographers. The same knowledge and skills that make a bow or gun hunter consistently successful at finding game are needed for wildlife photography. And if you can maintain the calm needed to take a focused, centered photo of an animal, you'll doubtless do well at dealing with that jittery condition known as "buck fever." Better, there is no closed season for photography; any species can be hunted in any month of the year, and protected or nongame animals can be legally captured with a camera.

Despite lingering arguments over whether using film makes for a better photo, digital pictures are replacing shots on film as the standard for publications, and their quality is better than good. Trackers can take home images of animals, tracks, and sign, which makes the digital camera an excellent tool for recording sights, events, even sounds and video. If you don't like the picture you see in the preview window, simply delete it and try again.

Digital photos can be downloaded directly from camera to computer, where they can be enhanced with graphics software, made into frameable prints using photo paper and a color printer, or e-mailed to friends, family, or coworkers. Many department stores and pharmacies now have automated photo printers that will download images from your camera's

Using her own boot as a size reference, tracker Cheanne Chellis photographs a large moose track for her records.

memory card and print them onto photo paper, a compact disk (CD), or both. Memory cards can be erased and reused an indefinite number of times.

One problem is that even the best camera "sees" in only two dimensions, and cannot accurately reproduce depth or distances. Where this is likely to be a problem is in photos of tracks (which is why line drawings that accentuate desired features are often superior). Veteran trackers can relate the difficulty in pointing out nuances in a footprint, or even the footprints themselves, to novices, and even expert trackers can have a tough time discerning a track's details from a photograph. As a precaution—and because digital cameras permit large numbers of photos to be taken—I like to shoot a track from several angles to highlight every feature.

Suitable tracking cameras can be found at most department stores for under $100. Inexpensive 2.0 megapixel point-and-shoot cameras (which includes most camera-equipped cellular phones) are adequate for track photos, while 4.0 megapixel cameras offer as much resolution and clarity as a tracker will ever need.

TRAIL TIMERS

Where there are a lot of animals there will be, of course, a lot of animal trails, and if you plan to stake out one of them to wait for a sighting it pays to have some idea which one is most likely to be used. Animals sometimes change regular routes to follow seasonal foods, because part of a trail is blocked, to dodge a predator in the area, or because something has changed and the animal hasn't yet determined if that change is dangerous. Remember that no matter how you might feel about them, wild animals regard you as a dangerous predator; touch nothing unnecessarily when examining a trail, avoid leaving your scent, and disturb as little as possible.

A useful old trick for checking traffic on animal trails is to string a length of thread or light fishing line across a recently traveled path, then come back later to see if it has been knocked down. Tie off one end of

Trail timers with onboard digital cameras have become integral components of the tracker's kit in recent years.

the trip line to a tree on one side of the trail, and wedge the other end as tentatively as possible under a piece of bark or in a split twig on the other side. By setting a dozen or so trip lines on different trails, checking them twice a day, and resetting as needed, you can gather enough information to predict an animal's comings and goings with fair precision after just two days. You can even tell in which direction the animal was headed by which direction to string was dragged. You can also adjust the string higher up to help narrow which species used a trail—a string set at 3 feet above the ground will only be tripped by deer and larger animals, while smaller species like raccoons and porcupines walk under it.

Electronic Trail Timers

A modern version of the old thread-across-the-trail trick is a digital clock unit, like the trail timers made by the King Manufacturing Company of St. Paul, Minnesota. Like the thread timer, the Trail Timer uses a trip line, but it stores the date and time that the line was tripped, as well as the direction of travel. Units are mounted in their own weatherproof plastic cases and prices start under $20. More elaborate and expensive trail timing devices use an infrared beam to detect movement; some can use an optional camera, while some are in effect digital cameras.

One problem I've encountered with some trail cameras has been the lag time between when the light beam is broken by an animal and when the camera's shutter trips—sometimes taking a photo of trees, sometimes not taking the picture at all, even though tracks crossing the target area prove that an animal did pass. Another problem has been accumulation of snow in the unit's lens recess; in snow country you should try to take that into account when placing the camera.

HEAT DETECTORS

Handheld infrared heat detectors are a recent innovation that have earned a place in the twenty-first-century tracker's field kit, and have become a must-have tool in my own. Field tests with several models of the Game Finder units from Game Finder, Inc., of Huntsville, Alabama, have worked exceptionally well for detecting even very small heat sources in open terrain or woods. When a larger animal—like a deer or bear—is lying behind a downed log or earth knoll, these units even have the sensitivity to detect radiated body heat as it rises from behind the obstruction. Battery life can exceed 12 hours, depending on the model and how cold the weather is. Because they actually detect "thermal edges," where cooler ambient air is broken by a much warmer body, and vice-versa, the units work best in colder weather. But even in hot weather, the latest generation of heat detectors are triggered by temperature differences smaller than 1 degree Fahrenheit out to 600 yards in open terrain. A bar graph provides visual display of intensity—how large a temperature difference exists between the two objects at a thermal edge. Some units even have an earphone that provides different audio signals for how large a temperature difference exists—like metal detectors that emit different tones for different materials.

The Finder from Game Finder, Inc., can detect even minute traces of body heat, and signals their presence with either an LED bar graph or an audible tone through earphones.

PROTECTIVE GLOVES

Handling scat samples, collecting decaying bones, carcasses, and other organic samples, or even handling biting or stinging insects, are all made safer and more hygienic by having a protective layer of rubber or plastic on your skin. Thin latex (or non-allergenic nitrile) gloves, like the kind worn by medical workers, are ideal because they block infectious organisms or toxins while enabling the wearer to retain dexterity and tactile sensitivity. Good, less-expensive alternatives are the clear plastic gloves worn by food service workers.

Used gloves should be stripped off after use by pulling them from the wrist toward the fingers, turning the glove inside out as it's removed. Soiled gloves can be stored in a ziplock plastic bag to keep them from contaminating other items in your pack until they can be disposed of properly.

SPECIMEN CONTAINERS

Inexpensive disposable but reusable plastic storage dishes with snap-on lids are useful for transporting specimens and fragile track casts that you wouldn't want to touch or have contaminate other items in your equipment bag. These rugged, leakproof containers are available in the housewares aisle of most grocery and large retail stores. The dishes come in a variety of shapes and sizes, most are see-through to enable quick identification of their contents, and multicolored lids allow you to use color-coding to prevent putting your lunch in a container that once held scat.

Resealable plastic food bags are a convenient way to isolate scat and other organic samples for transport. They can also be used to protect cameras, casting plaster, and other equipment that might be harmed by exposure to the elements. Sealed bags can be labeled with permanent marker, left in the rain, or frozen without worrying that the contents will be contaminated or will contaminate anything else.

WATER

Casting a track in plaster requires water, and trackers need it to stay hydrated, too. Plaster can be mixed from any stream or pond, but people need water that is guaranteed free of harmful bacteria and parasites. A container holding at least one quart of potable water should be required equipment for any outing.

There are a number of good water bottles available, most made from rugged polyethylene or the less odor-absorbent Nalgene™, some with poppet tops, some with screw tops, and most priced low enough that you can afford more than one. Stainless-steel water bottles are recommended these days, because of the possibility of ingesting harmful chemicals from plastic bottles. Odorless, nonabsorbent, fireproof, and rugged, these are ideal for backwoods use. It's preferable for your bottles to have wide mouths in weather that can freeze water.

The most portable containers are collapsible water bladders, some of which are designed to be used with the hydration pockets and hoses found in many backpacks. Portability is one of the water bladder's big advantages, because it can be rolled up when empty and carried comfortably in a trousers pocket.

Whichever water container you choose, if you track in winter—the preferred season for many wildlife biologists—you'll need to keep the water you carry from becoming a block of ice. This was a chronic problem for Odawa tribal biologists and me when we were casting the tracks of migrating gray wolves during the notoriously cold and snowy northern Michigan winters.

Water is required for every plaster-casting kit, and potable water is required by trackers, so every tracking outfit should have a portable filtering unit.

The first rule is to never fill a container full, leaving space enough for the water to slosh from the movement of walking (or snowshoeing), because moving water doesn't freeze easily. Next, keep canteens and bottles close to your body, preferably under your parka waist. Finally, and most effective, you can duct-tape an air-activated hand-warmer packet directly onto the container.

CASTING KIT

At some point every tracker will want to take a track back home for further study, and that means "casting" it in a semiliquid medium that will flow into the impression's recesses, then harden into a negative copy of the print, resulting in a more or less accurate (depending on how clear the track) replica of the maker's foot.

Most tracks are cast in plaster of paris. This powder is an inexpensive commodity found in most arts and crafts stores, while the slightly more coarse—and more durable—patching plaster (such as Durabond), used by drywallers, is available at home improvement stores. One pound of either carried in a ziplock bag inside a snap-top plastic container will cast a half dozen or more tracks. The plastic bag helps to keep the plaster powder dry, while the plastic dish serves as a mixing bowl.

Casting a track in plaster isn't complicated: Dump about 4 tablespoonfuls of plaster from the ziplock bag into the dish that carries it, and add water a little at a time, always blending it well into the plaster before adding more, until the mixture has the consistency of cake batter. Some trackers carry stir sticks for mixing plaster, but most environments will provide one. When the plaster is ready, dump it into a track impression and wait until it sets up; this will take roughly half an hour (longer in wet conditions; less in very cold temperatures that freeze the plaster before it actually hardens). Don't press the wet plaster into the track depression, or you might deform its features; if your "batter" is the right consistency, it will flow into nooks and crannies on its own.

When the plaster has set, gently loosen it by cutting the soil or snow around it with a knife blade (never leave the beaten track without a working-class knife). Don't try to pry the cast loose, but rather lift it free by cutting around it, taking the entire track itself if necessary. When the plaster is fully cured, after a day or so, the cast will be a bit less fragile, but many a cast has been ruined before it ever got out of the woods. Place the cast, earth or snow and all, into a plastic dish lined with folded paper towels (or reusable cloths) that act as cushions, place another cushion on top, and snap the lid in place.

Making a plaster cast of a track

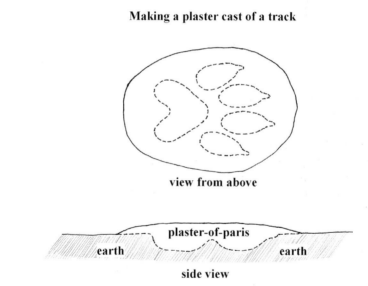

view from above

side view

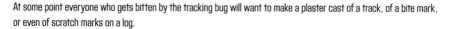

At some point everyone who gets bitten by the tracking bug will want to make a plaster cast of a track, of a bite mark, or even of scratch marks on a log.

In a few mediums, like hard-frozen mud or slushy snow that has since frozen to ice, it may be impossible to cut around a cast in the ground, and you'll be forced to lift it from the impression. For this delicate operation you'll need to first use a "mold release," typically an aerosol can of wax that ostensibly creates a soft, slippery film between impression and plaster. Wax sprays made for this purpose have not always performed well, sometimes spitting blobs of wax that can leave indentations in the cast that are not part of the track—and the problem worsens in freezing temperatures. Better—and cheaper—are wax sprays, like the Pledge brand. In either instance, aerosol cans should be kept warm, carried inside your jacket if necessary.

FIELD MICROSCOPE

Very close inspection of hairs, scat contents, vermin, and other sign can reveal important information that isn't visible to the naked eye. A magnifying glass is good for routine field inspections, but sometimes more extreme optical power is needed to see parasites and/or their ova, to identify insect parts in scat, to closely inspect hairs in shed fur, or to answer any number of questions than can best be approached from a microscopic point of view.

For these jobs, you'll need a good "pocket" microscope suited to fieldwork. About the size of a small flashlight, the best models are lightweight, have superb optical clarity, and provide enough magnification (25x to 50x) to be useful. The microscopes that I carry are also rugged, simple to use, and—as important as any other prerequisite—are inexpensive enough to prevent heartbreak should the instrument be lost or broken.

COMPASS

The popularity of satellite-linked GPS units has caused a waning interest in the old-fashioned compass. My own experience with both devices has convinced me that a compass is still the most reliable, most necessary navigational tool for those whose interests lead them away from the beaten path. That group would definitely include trackers.

Both the compass and a GPS unit provide navigational information, but in very different ways. A compass employs a mechanical magnetic indicator that is attracted toward Earth's magnetic North Pole—in simplest terms, it just points north, and all other orienteering information is derived from that single, reliable function. By knowing where north lies, a person facing that direction knows east is right, west is left, and south is to the rear. A tracker who enters even the most untracked wilderness by walking in a westerly direction knows that the way back must be to the east, 180 degrees (half the circle of a 360-degree compass dial, or bezel). And if his point of entry was from a road, riverbank, hiking trail, or another large, hard-to-miss landmark, it becomes almost impossible to get lost.

Unlike a GPS unit, a compass works well with any map, even road maps from filling stations. But you should use a good topographic map that shows the landmarks most important to a wilderness traveler. By orienting both map and compass to point north, you'll have a pictorial layout of the surrounding geography, and a virtual preview of the type of country you'll encounter long before you reach it. Being armed with this information enables you to avoid canyons, swamps, river rapids, and other obstacles before they force you to backtrack around them.

Most importantly, a compass gives you the ability to walk in a straight line, and there are few places left where a straight line won't lead to a road, railroad grade, or established hiking trail within a 10-mile radius, usually less.

A simple pocket compass will do the job, but a more sophisticated map compass, with prismatic or lensatic sights, map scales, and a clear base that permits features to be read with

Never hike—even in country you know well—without a reliable compass and a waterproof, laminated map.

the compass sitting on top of the map, is more versatile. Either compass should be liquid-filled, with strongly magnetized indicators that move easily, showing no sign of being sticky. Your compass should not have a bubble inside the indicator capsule, as this is a sign that the capsule has a leak.

GLOBAL POSITIONING SYSTEMS

Unlike a magnetic compass, GPS receivers use microwave signals from satellites in stationary orbit above the earth to triangulate their users' position on the planet surface. Today's GPS units can precisely fix, or "waypoint," the math coordinates of some point of interest—a bear den, for instance—within a perimeter of 50 yards. Those coordinates can then be transferred to a map to provide a visual representation of the surrounding terrain. If you're a tracker scouting animal habitats and habits, that data can be used to determine behavioral patterns and timetables of local fauna.

GPS units also feature a "trek" mode that records a hiker's location then remembers those waypoint locations to lead the hiker back out, then in again if desired, on a kind of connect-the-dots course. This can be handy, but do not rely on it to get you out of the woods. Some readers might remember that it was a GPS that led James Kim and his family onto a wrong, unmapped road in 2006. Their automobile became stuck in deep snow, and Kim later died of hypothermia while trying to find help. A GPS unit is only as accurate as the map from which it was programmed.

Other drawbacks of the GPS include the lack of reliability inherent to most battery-operated digital circuits when they're exposed to the environment. Battery life can be greatly diminished by cold, frost can form on contacts and prevent buttons from working properly, and getting the inside of the unit wet is virtually guaranteed to take it out of action until its circuit boards have dried completely.

Keep in mind that because GPS coordinates are taken from satellites, not the magnetic North Pole, the way they translate to a map is different than when they are plotted using a compass. For example, GPS coordinates cannot be applied directly to a conventional latitude-longitude map because those maps aren't sectioned and scaled using the relatively new Universal Transverse Mercator (UTM) grid system. Without the correct reference grid an orienteer has no point of reference from which to calculate everything else.

MAPS

While even a filling station road map is better than no map at all, good maps that are grid-ded for use with both compass (latitude and longitude in degrees) and GPS (UTM grid) are available. In mountainous or desert country, a detailed topographic map that shows elevations and depressions is essential. In dense forest or jungle, where visibility is measured in feet and distant landmarks can't be seen, an accurate trail and terrain map is more useful.

The United States Geographical Survey (USGS) offers detailed topographic maps that are marked with both navigational systems, and even trail maps from local chambers of commerce are being printed to work with both grid systems. Detailed topographic maps may be ordered online from www.usgs.gov for a reasonable price, plus shipping and han-dling charges (so it pays to order several at once).

Be especially wary in timber country. Logging companies use heavy equipment that can, in just a matter of hours, establish a road where there had never been one before, and by day's end logging trucks can make that road look as if it has been a thoroughfare for years. The danger this poses is that the next right or left turn your map (or GPS) says you should take might not be the right or left that you'll reach first, and it's not uncommon to turn onto a logging road that was made after your map was printed. Always expect that your map will be out of date, and keep track of distances traveled between points to help avoid wrong turns.

BUG PROTECTION

In the days when strong young men in the north woods grew up to try their hands at lumberjacking, there was an affliction known as "swamp madness" that struck mostly apprentice timbermen. The affliction was actually a nervous breakdown brought on by brutally hard labor performed in tormenting swarms of biting flies and mosquitoes, compounded by equally miserable sleepless nights filled with more bloodthirsty mosquitoes.

From spring until midsummer, and even longer in some habitats, biting bugs in sufficient numbers will make working among them unpleasant or even impossible. Most important is keeping clouds of blood-craving blackflies, mosquitoes, stable flies, and deerflies from getting into your eyes, nose, and mouth, and the most effective method so far has been to cover the head from hat to shoulders with a large mesh bag made from "no-see-um" netting.

Headnets are cheap and simple to sew from no-see-um material, or they can be purchased ready-made at most army surplus stores for a minimal price. You can see through the mesh well enough to wear it all day, and a good headnet, held away from the face by a hat brim or ball cap bill, can reduce bites to the head and neck to zero. That alone can make hours slowly stalking or sitting behind a camera amid swarms of bloodsuckers more tolerable. Added benefits of having this pocket-size necessity are that it camouflages the head very well, and even cuts glare to help prevent headaches or snow blindness when snowshoeing in bright sunlight.

WARM-WEATHER BOOTS

A tracker is, by definition, on his or her feet most of the time, and it would be hard to exaggerate the very real importance of wearing a comfortable, well-fitted pair of boots built for backwoods use. They should have shin-high uppers to guard and support the ankles, thickly cushioned insoles with firm arch support, flexible but aggressive lug soles, and waterproof internal bootie construction designed to "breathe" away moisture from perspiration.

Many boot makes and models can meet those criteria for under $100, especially if you shop around for discontinued models. When possible, try on a pair of boots before buying them, and always try them on while wearing hiking socks, because they're thicker than other socks. And never take to the woods in a new pair of boots until you've walked a few miles in them to crease the lowers, making the boot "break" where your joints flex and eliminating most pinch or rub points.

As I've had occasion to show some of my tracking and survival students, a stiff new pair of boots can be "speed-broken" to lessen or eliminate the rubbing that causes blisters by standing in water until the outer leather is saturated and takes on a darker color. "Walking-out" boots while they're wet and softened stretches tight spots, creases pinch points, and makes new boots fit as though you'd walked dozens of miles in them.

Tracking by definition means being on your feet much of the time, so trackers should have footwear that's light, comfortable, protective, supportive, and dry.

COLD-WEATHER BOOTS

Proper cold-weather footwear is routinely overlooked, even by field researchers, and frequently with tragic results. Snow is a favored tracking medium for biologists because it offers the best possibilities for finding cast-quality tracks, and trackers can expect to spend whole days—and maybe a few nights—walking and working atop frozen hardpack. Cold toes are a common complaint when there's nothing but snow underfoot, and cold feet mean heat loss that can lead to frostbite, which kills tissue much like a burn does and can eventually lead to gangrene. The journey through each of these stages is extremely painful—the old saw about freezing to death being painless is absolutely untrue.

No winter outdoorsman or woman need tolerate the unpleasantness of cold feet. For day-long outings with a return to warm housing at day's end, boots with integrated liners—that is, those with

Layered Cold Weather Outfit

hood

base layer

intermediate layer

windproof layer

base layer

oversock with liner sock

visored cap

glove shell with liner

windproof trousers

pac-boot

Whatever the season, latitude, or ambient temperature, every tracker should wear layers of clothing made from water-repellent synthetic fabric, adding to or taking from this system as needed to maintain comfort.

insulation built in and not removable—are the lightest and most comfortable choice. Many models are assigned a "comfort rating" that ostensibly tells buyers how low temperatures can fall before the boot can no longer retain enough body heat to keep a wearer's feet warm. Personally, I find 200 grams of Thinsulate™ to be adequate for temperatures that hover near the freezing mark. In freezing temperatures down to 20 degrees Fahrenheit, 400 grams of Thinsulate™ insulation is sufficient. From 20 degrees down to zero, I go with no less than 800 grams, and for temperatures below zero, I wear nothing less than full-blown pac boots rated to –100 degrees.

A winter tracker who cannot fly needs to treat his feet like the invaluable mode of transportation that they are, and a pair of good boots is beyond price.

Modern pac boots carry comfort ratings in excess of –150 degrees Fahrenheit, making them equal to the coldest environments on earth. Features to look for include removable liners that can be taken out and dried, or worn inside a sleeping bag. Boots should also have a cushioned foot bed that can be dried or replaced in the field, waterproof construction, lace-to-toe design for a custom fit between foot and boot, and an aggressive lug sole for traction.

Ideally, the boot should provide the walking comfort of a hiking boot, yet retain sufficient body heat to keep your toes warm during long spells of inactivity on snow—like when you stop to observe a carcass or photograph otters on a frozen lake. Name-brand winter boots in either of these categories can deliver the features recommended for under $150.

SOCKS

The wrong socks can make a good hiking boot feel uncomfortable, and a warm winter boot feel cold and clammy. The first rule: Do not wear cotton or cotton-blend socks of any kind, in any season (that advice applies to other garments, too). Cotton soaks up more water than any other fiber—that's why towels are made from it—and it dries very slowly, cooling the skin beneath it all the while. The key to insulation is motionless, "dead" air trapped within the weave, and when cotton gets wet, either from moisture without or perspiration within, the spaces for dead air between its fibers fill with water.

The best all-around combination for any season is a two-sock system consisting of a thick woolen or wool-synthetic sock worn over a friction-free synthetic liner sock that doesn't absorb moisture. The outer sock provides an insulating, cushioning layer, while the liner serves as both a friction barrier to prevent blisters and a wicking layer that keeps feet feeling dry.

HAT

In the wilderness a hat is more than an adornment for the head; it's a vital piece of equipment. A visored ball cap, or the more traditional brimmed "bush hat," is useful in all seasons for keeping rain and snow off your face or bright sun out of your eyes. They also keep deerflies from becoming entangled in your hair, and you can soak either type of hat in water to keep your head cool under a hot sun. A brim or visor also transforms a pocket-size bag of no-see-um mesh into an effective shield against bugs, and hats make handy containers for fresh-picked berries or for holding other small items.

In driving snow or freezing wind, a ball cap can be substituted for a balaclava that can be worn as a mask or hat as conditions require and can be rolled up and carried in a jacket pocket when not in use. A parka shell or jacket hood thrown over either type of hat provides an added layer of protection.

HAND WEAR

Gloves are important to field work in every season. In warm weather a pair of sturdy work gloves can protect hands from cuts, abrasions, and other injuries. Despite advances in synthetics, no material so far has proven more rugged and protective than

In warm or cold weather, trackers need rugged gloves that will protect their hands from injury and the elements.

old-fashioned cowhide—especially if the task at hand requires handling, or reaching into places inhabited by, scorpions, spiders, biting snakes, or even small animals.

In cold weather the same type of rugged insulated shell, sized one or two sizes larger than your usual glove size, protects hands from ice that can cut like glass, or snow that can abrade like sandpaper. For long exposure to very cold weather, glove shells insulated with Thinsulate™ provide added protection against frostbite. A synthetic woven fleece or knit wool liner, worn inside either type of shell, substantially increases a glove's warmth.

SNOWSHOES

If your tracking plans include going into high alpine or north woods snow country, where "hardpack"—that is, snow on the ground—can reach depths of a foot or more, you'll need snowshoes.

Snowshoes do not make it easy to walk over deep snow—they make it possible. If you've ever tried to wade through hip-deep snow, you know that it cannot be done for long. The effort alone is exhausting, but the real danger comes later, when spent muscles fail, evaporating perspiration cools the body, and there is no blood sugar left to feed the metabolic heater and ward off hypothermia.

When deep snow hampers every other animal, modern lightweight snowshoes can put human trackers at a distinct advantage.

Tough metal-frame, synthetic-decked modern snowshoes are required equipment for any northern tracker, and their stable crampon-equipped bindings enable wearers to safely traverse ice that would be dangerously slippery without them.

With snowshoes rated to carry the weight of the wearer, no snow is more than a few inches deep, regardless of how much might actually be on the ground. Like the snowshoe hare, a snowshoer has his or her body weight distributed over a broader area, meaning less downward force per square inch, which makes a person weigh less as far as the snow is concerned. The most popular size for all-around use is the 9x30-inch recreational model, which is rated to carry in excess of 200 pounds. The next step is the 10x36-inch model, which is rated for more than 300 pounds, and a favorite among winter backpackers.

Qualifications for becoming a snowshoer are simple: If you can walk, you can snowshoe. That isn't an oversimplification; virtually everyone who straps on a pair of snowshoes for the first time is able to set out as soon as their bindings are tight. Beginners should, of course, keep to well-marked trails until they feel comfortable enough to venture cross-country, and initial outings should be kept short—no more than a mile—until you have a feel for the demands snowshoeing places on your body.

An almost universal revelation among first-timers is that this gentle, no-impact workout is deceptively tiring. A man snowshoeing along a packed trail at just 2 miles per hour burns more than 700 calories per hour, according to studies done at Vermont State University, so plan to take breaks along the way. Always carry beverages on any snowshoe outing, because dehydration can quickly sneak up on you in winter. An air-activated hand-warmer packet (such as HotHands) duct-taped to water bottles keeps them from freezing, and a Thermos of hot cocoa is worth its weight.

You should also anticipate the increased consumption of blood sugar, and counter the probability of hypoglycemia with carb-rich snacks like cheese, granola bars, and dried fruits. These and other basic necessities are best carried in a small day pack, along with extra socks and shirt.

Which snowshoe model best suits your needs depends on where you mean to take them. Today's best crampon-equipped, metal-frame snowshoes are virtually unbreakable, provide insectlike traction on steep grades, and feature quick-release bindings that virtually make the snowshoe an extension of your boot. Avoid "sport" snowshoes with dimensions of less than 9x30 inches, because these do not provide enough flotation if you choose to leave the beaten path, especially while carrying a backpack laden with 15 pounds of tracking gear. Also avoid models equipped with "trail" bindings, which are too small to fit a thicker, serious, 100-below-zero pac boot.

Retail prices for working-class snowshoes begin at under $100, but the payoff is absolute freedom over deep snow.

Tracking Kit Equipment List

Following is a list of equipment that has proved to be most essential to gathering data and getting to know local wildlife while in the field. This list is comprehensive but generic; it cannot address every application, so it should be added to or subtracted from as needed. Brand names of equipment are given as examples only, meaning that these products are more representative of the level of quality and performance needed than an endorsement of particular models—which can be counted on to change or to be discontinued from one year to the next anyway.

For Observation and Data-gathering

❏ Binoculars (10x42 roof prism; Pentax DCF)
❏ Digital camera (at least 4.0 megapixel; Kodak EasyShare C713)
❏ Spiral notebook (pocket-size, with ink pen)
❏ Measuring scales
❏ Tape measure (25 feet, locking tape, both inches and centimeters; Stanley model 30-456)
❏ Ruler (6 inches, flexible, inches and millimeters; Empire stainless)
❏ Microscope (25x pen type packed inside a plastic toothbrush holder for protection; Edmund Scientific Co.)

Casting Kit

❏ Plaster (1 pound minimum, in a ziplock plastic bag carried inside a plastic snap-lid bowl)
❏ Plastic surveyor's marking ribbon (brightly colored for marking cast locations; 6 feet or more)
❏ Spray bottle filled with water (for spritzing an icy glaze onto tracks in snow before casting)

- ❏ Plaster mixing bowl with snap-down cover (2-cup capacity or larger; Gladware type)
- ❏ Resealable plastic dishes (at least 4x4 inches, for carrying casts; low-wall Gladware type)
- ❏ Paper towels (for cushioning casts in dishes; partial roll, flattened, carried in plastic bread bag)
- ❏ Belt knife (for loosening casts, skinning; 5-inch blade, sharp; Ontario Knives SpecPlus)
- ❏ Multitool with a variety of tools, marked with a scale (SOG PowerAssist)
- ❏ Gloves (for handling scat, carcasses; disposable medical or food-service type; 4 to 5 pairs)
- ❏ Air-activated hand warmer packets (HotHands brand [winter only])
- ❏ Duct tape (about 12 feet wound around a pencil)
- ❏ Small tube of disinfectant waterless hand soap

Generally speaking, the wilder the animal a tracker seeks, the wilder and more remote its habitat will be, so experienced trackers come appropriately prepared.

Orienteering
- ❏ Compass:
    Primary: prismatic-sighted map compass, liquid-filled (Brunton 8099)
    Secondary: pocket compass, liquid-filled, worn around neck (Brunton Tag-A-Long)
- ❏ GPS with 12 channels; AA-battery powered; lighted screen; replacement batteries (Eagle Expedition II)
- ❏ USGS topographic map gridded with UTM and latitude-longitude coordinates for use with both GPS and magnetic compass

Clothing

❏ Boots:

> Winter: waterproof, rated to at least –100 degrees F (Sorel Intrepid Explorer)
> Spring and winter hiking: waterproof; internal liner (LaCrosse Outpost)
> Summer: high-ankle; lace-to-toe; waterproof (Columbia Laman Peak)

❏ Socks (all seasons): Wool or synthetic sock worn over an acrylic liner sock (SmartWool)

❏ Base layer (winter/shirt and pants): synthetic fabric; matched to expected temperatures (Medalist X-Static)

❏ Parka shell (all seasons): hooded; large pockets; waterproof and breathable (Columbia Titanium)

❏ Trousers (all seasons): 6 pockets; ripstop weave; GI-type in a dark color or camouflage

❏ Gloves:

> Summer: leather or leather-and-fabric work gloves; gauntlet-length (Wells Lamont)
> Winter: shell gloves with liners (Grandoe Glove Component System)

❏ Snowshoes:

> Hiking: 9x30-inch aluminum frame with crampons (Tubbs Pinnacle)
> Heavy load: 10x36-inch aluminum frame with crampons (Redfeather Powder)

❏ Headnet made of no-see-um mesh, worn over a ball cap for bug protection, glare protection, and camouflage.

Equipment Bag

❏ Day pack: 2,500-cubic-inch capacity; outside pockets; internal frame; waist belt, sternum strap, and padded shoulder straps; hydration pocket (Exponent Otero by Coleman)

❏ Stuff sacks: Nylon; drawstrings with cord-locks; different colors for coding individual kits

At 32 pounds, this full-blown tracker's pack carries all the tools and gear that a tracker would need to spend a comfortable and productive three days in the wild.

Chapter Four

STALKING

The ability to stalk prey is instinctive in animals designed to eat meat. A house cat taken from its mother as a tiny kitten will still develop the stealth, speed, and agility that place *Felis silvestris* among the most efficient hunters on earth. Black bears, which are among the least successful hunters because their powerful physique isn't designed for pursuit, can demonstrate considerable sneakiness when attempting to catch young fawns in spring. Even human toddlers, with no outside instructions, quickly learn to sneak up on grasshoppers, butterflies, and frogs.

The author is shown hunting in the winter woods.

Nevertheless, predator mothers, and sometimes fathers, augment their offspring's inborn hunting instincts with lessons drawn from their own life experiences. Except for humans: On the whole, our species hasn't had to hunt to feed itself in a very long time, and as a species we're not very good at it. Anthropologists believe that *Homo sapiens* never possessed the heightened senses of lesser cousins, and that it was only through cunning and ingenuity born of intellect that humankind rose to the top of the food chain. Few animals have anything to fear from our physical strength or speed, but they have everything to fear from our abilities to devise tools and to manipulate situations to our own advantage. This intelligence can, with education and practice, make the Naked Ape as efficient a stalker as any in the world.

Camouflage

While most mammals are to some degree color-blind, nearly every species is as sharp-eyed as life in its habitat demands, and proper camouflage is necessary when stalking them. The more closely any hunter blends with the surrounding terrain, the less chance he or she has of being seen—not just by prey, but by tattletales whose cries are part of every ecosystem's web of life. Birds can see colors, typically have better eyesight than we do, and broadcast alarm calls that put every animal within earshot on the alert for a dangerous intruder. Just as bad are the chattering cries of an agitated red squirrel and the alarm "blow" of a deer. Sneaking up on a prey animal itself may be the easy part, because first you have to slip past many sentries. The less noticeable you are to birds, squirrels, and frogs, the better your chances of getting close to a deer.

Since we walk upright, humans are perceived as being larger—and more dangerous—than we actually are, and a standing human's shape seems to be the most frightening thing a wild critter could see. We need to make our silhouettes as indistinguishable from the surroundings as we can.

The trick is to effectively break up your outline with a camouflage in a pattern and texture that makes you look like many small parts of the immediate environment. Random spatters of color with shapes and hues that might be mistaken for leaves, branches, or other terrain features are best for breaking up the distinctive human silhouette. Animals may be color-blind, but there is a logical school of thought that holds that if an animal perceives a particular shade of green or brown in nature as a specific hue of blue or gray, it makes sense to have those greens and browns in a camouflage outfit.

Loose-fitting clothing, such as six-pocket military BDUs (Battle Dress Uniforms) printed with such a pattern, adds a three-dimensional effect with their rumpled, wrinkled appearance. As for camouflage patterns, there are many to choose from. I agree with veteran army sniper Major John Plaster (retired) that the old-fashioned green-brown-black Woodland pattern is best for all-around use in most environments, either in the original splotch pattern or the newer "digital" print.

The distinctive roundness of a human head is also out of place in nature, so a good hat isn't just the handy tool described earlier, but an integral part of any camouflage outfit. The military's cloth bush hat is probably the most effective warm-weather design; its full crown keeps horseflies and deerflies from biting your head, the floppy brim keeps rain off glasses and camera viewfinders, and the rumpled, misshapen look blends well into all types of terrain. Most bush-type hats also have a series of camouflage loops sewn around the crown to hold bits of foliage, which further breaks up your outline and helps you blend in with the environment. The washable bush hat is also one of the best places to apply cover-up scents. Mosquito headnets, mentioned earlier, also provide very effective camouflage for the head and face. So do "Spandoflage" pullover masks, made of stretchy material, relatively inexpensive, and found in army-navy surplus outlets.

Nor should you overlook your face and hands. A quick flash of contrasting skin may be enough to attract attention from wilderness tattletales who will alert every animal within earshot that there's danger afoot. Painting exposed skin with camouflage grease or creams is the traditional method for disguising uncovered body parts, but there are simpler, less messy alternatives.

Hands can be covered with a light pair of camo- or dark-colored cloth gloves. My own preference (temperature permitting) is a pair of uninsulated leather gloves that have been darkened and weatherproofed with petroleum jelly or cooking oil. Neither imparts an odor, but both darken leather, and a few drops of scent in the palm works well for intentionally leaving scent trails on tree trunks and branches.

In snow country, white military snow coveralls are ideal camouflage. A pair of white painter's coveralls and a white lab coat are equally effective. In snow-covered forests it isn't necessary, or sometimes even preferable, to be outfitted completely in white. White trousers and a camouflage jacket do fine, but avoid wearing a white overcoat over camouflage trousers, because this is opposite the natural appearance of the landscape, where the ground is white with darker colors elevated above it. In a pinch, you can make do with a white linen bedsheet draped around your shoulders like a cape—a quick-and-dirty winter camouflage that I've used to good effect many times.

For virtually disappearing in most types of wooded or grassy terrain, nothing matches the "ghillie suit." Named for the Scottish bond servants, or ghillies, who once patrolled their masters' lands as game wardens, this camo uses strips of colored rags tied or sewn onto an overshirt and pants to create an indistinct, tattered appearance that can make its wearer virtually invisible from just a few feet.

Manufactured ghillie camouflage is available but pricey. The plain camouflage netting used to make them is less effective than homemade ghillie material, and military snipers who bet their lives on their camouflage do not use them. The most effective ghillie suit is one made from a nylon mesh hammock or a badminton or tennis net that has been tied or sewn onto a camouflage-patterned shirt and trousers. Dyed burlap strips tied (not sewn, because you might want to remove them later) onto the netting complete the outfit. The strips can be cut from burlap bags that have been dyed to the proper colors, or you can buy predyed burlap ghillie stripping in roll form at army-navy outlets. Avoid the military's practice of using spray paint to blend together the colors of the burlap. This may work if you're tracking humans, but the powerful odor of ketones and enamel is guaranteed to announce your presence to any animal downwind of your position. If you need to color burlap, Rit clothing dyes, available inexpensively from crafts stores, do the job without leaving odors.

Burlap stripping is good camouflage by itself, but augmenting a ghillie outfit with ferns, fronds, pine boughs, even dead leafless branches stuck into the netting, can make it—and you—literally disappear from view. A ghillie-clad tracker camouflaged with juniper branches in a forest where junipers are all around will be difficult to spot at worst. At best, he will be invisible. Even if an animal detects your scent from several hundred yards—even if it hears you rustling as it draws nearer to investigate—it will likely not spook into taking flight if it cannot see you.

Stalking Techniques

After you've gathered the tools of a stalker, your next step is learning to use them in the field. To actively stalk all the time is impractical, because stalking is very slow, covering only about a hundred yards an hour, and may demand that you freeze instantly and hold position through several minutes of intense scrutiny. Maintaining such a heightened state of mental and physical control is both time-consuming and exhausting, so you should slip into stalking mode only when you're certain your objective is very close.

WALKING INDIAN

It is possible to walk quietly over most terrain and still move at a near-normal pace. Most of my own sightings occur when I'm walking quietly through the woods with a habitualized pace that my Ojibwa mentor Amos Wasageshik called "walking Indian." To walk Indian means abandoning the inherently off-balance heel-toe stride of a person accustomed to walking on smooth, predictable surfaces, and adopting the flexible, duck-footed gait of a hunter. Body weight is supported on the ball of your rear foot, most of it concentrated just behind the big toe.

The forward foot is brought down with toes pointing outward at about 30 degrees, landing initially on the outer edge of the heel. Body weight is then transferred smoothly to that (forward) foot as your rear foot is brought forward, and the process begins anew. The idea is to gently and evenly press twigs, stones, and other ground clutter that might make noise into the ground by rolling your foot over them as body weight is transferred forward, distributing your applied weight over as wide an area as possible.

Each time you bring your rear foot forward, make a conscious effort to raise it higher than normal, to clear sticks and other noise-making obstacles. Keep your knees slightly bent, never locked, your spine bent just slightly forward, and your hip joints loose to absorb the bumps and jars that are an integral part of walking on uneven terrain. This shock-absorbing walk is quieter, and it creates the springy step characteristic of folks who seldom turn their ankles on rugged terrain. Before long you'll be griping to your companions about how noisily they walk.

Adopt the style and gait of a hunter and stalker when tracking.

STALKING AN ANIMAL

Stalking is another matter, and for most people the hardest part is learning to slow down. Wild animals don't have schedules to keep, and most of their waking time is spent meandering in search of food. The steady two-legged pace of a human is unique, and few animals stick around for long when they hear it. The trick, therefore, is to not sound like a human being (the ultimate objective is absolute silence), and that means slowing down to about two steps per minute. Every step is taken slowly, and good balance is a must—a stalker needs to have an ability to freeze motionless midstep. The forward foot is brought down against the ground as gently as possible, always in the place where it's least likely to make a sound, and weight is transferred from one foot to another smoothly.

In places where silence is simply unachievable—an oak forest in fall, or among the "popcorn" twigs that litter the ground below aspens—bear in mind that slow, muffled noises are less alarming than quick, sharp ones. The low crunch of leaves as you bring your weight down on them may well go unnoticed, but the snap of a twig underfoot is good reason for a tracker to freeze for a full minute or two.

Quick, jerky movements are also sure to alarm your prey (remember the birds, squirrels, and other tattletales), so every motion of your body needs to be executed as smoothly as possible. One reason is to minimize noise; the zipping sound of a branch sliding quickly across the fabric of a field jacket is guaranteed to attract more attention than the lower-volume sound of the branch scraping across very slowly. The other reason is to avoid being seen. The human eye sees at a rate of 60 images per second—a figure that's more or less accurate for wild animals as well—so very slow movements are less likely to attract attention than quick ones. This is also a good argument for wearing long pants and mosquito headnets in bug country, because slapping a mosquito can scare off every animal within a quarter-mile: You slap a bug, which upsets a chattering squirrel, which sets a flock of ravens to squawking, and so on.

USING THE WIND

One element a stalker should be constantly aware of is the wind and its changes, which might reveal your presence via odor. Always begin any stalk into the wind; if the wind direction shifts, try to compensate by keeping the breeze in your face. In some places, most notably lowland swamps, air currents swirl like stream eddies and winds might blow from all directions in the space of a few minutes. While this might seem disadvantageous to a stalker, it's also confusing for an animal, which may get only a whiff of your spoor before the breeze changes direction again. In many such instances an animal will actually stalk the stalker, because it needs to know where you are for its own sake. If the animal is a deer or wolf, that curiosity to locate you can be exploited, but be very cautious if the situation occurs where there is fresh bear, cougar, or moose scat, because to suddenly surprise such powerful animals can be dangerous.

Windy or rainy days can also be advantageous for stalking because rustling foliage and creaking trees create a confusion of noise, and no animal upwind of you will detect your scent. With animals' two most powerful senses rendered largely ineffective, humans have a physical advantage with their superior eyesight.

Other sounds you can use to cover your movements include passing airplanes, distant traffic, rain, or noises made by animal activity. Regardless of cover noise, resist the temptation to move quickly, because quick motions might still alarm animals. When you do move, try to coordinate your motions with the breeze and the movements of foliage.

STALKING IN THE OPEN

Stalking in open country, with animals already in sight, requires good camouflage that matches and is augmented with natural foliage from the surrounding terrain, as well as steady concentration, and frequently a belly crawl to get within range. An old Native American trick for sneaking up on a lone grazing deer is to move while the animal has its head down in tall grass, blind to the world above it. Someone once determined that a deer keeps its head down to take a mouthful for roughly 5 seconds, and my own experiences support this. Advance on all fours while the deer has its head down, freezing after about 4 seconds, before the animal raises its head to look about. It may stare intently at you for 3 or 4 long minutes, aware that something has changed, but will probably be unable to determine just what that change is. If nothing that could be perceived as danger occurs after a few minutes of scrutiny, the deer (or elk, moose, or coyote) will almost invariably put its head down again for another bite, allowing you to gain a few more yards.

By keeping the breeze in your face and moving quietly only when the animal has its head down, you may be able to stalk within 50 yards before it sees you clearly enough to become alarmed. This trick works best with deer and other "prey" species (rabbits, elk, bison) because they are not only nearsighted, but have poor distance perception. These animals have eyes located at either side of their skulls; this endows them with an almost 360-degree field of view, but denies them the image-comparing binocular vision of predators, who have both eyes located close together at the front of their heads. A predator's narrow field of view is compensated for by a more necessary ability to precisely judge depths and distances in three dimensions, enabling it to deliver accurate killing strikes to its victims. Prey animals can get by just fine with a two-dimensional view of the world, so long as that view takes in as much of their surroundings as possible. As a result, a deer can't tell if a motionless "stump" has gotten closer since the last time it looked. A stalker may be scrutinized for several interminable minutes, but if he doesn't move, make noise, or smell like danger, he will probably be ignored.

Blowing in the Wind

Probably every experienced deer hunter has related sad stories about a trophy buck approached from behind or from the wrong side, sometimes stopping and staring at the hunter, who remained uncomfortably frozen in place because he was afraid of scaring off his prey. In most of these tales, the deer got away.

A solution that has proved itself for generations is "blowing in the wind." Rather than freezing in place, the hunter should begin to sway gently with the breeze (even if there is none). Gently swaying like a sapling in a breeze, not like a predator moving to strike, instills doubt in an animal's mind about the hunter being worth concern, and camouflages the fact that the hunter is slowly moving into shooting position with every sway.

Reading Wildlife Behaviors

According to Jim Williams, assistant director of the International Wolf Center in Ely, Minnesota, being attacked by a wild animal ranks as the greatest fear among outdoorsmen and women. The extreme drama accorded animal attacks has made many nature lovers afraid of the woods, and real or imagined animals moving unseen in the shadows makes every first-time camper afraid of the night.

That feeling of vulnerability isn't wholly unjustified: We can't see in the dark, our sense of smell is impotent, our hearing is limited, and, pound-for-pound, humans are physically inferior to wild animals. We run slowly, climb poorly, and lack natural weapons or armor. If some mean and nasty creature were waiting in the shadows, we couldn't know our peril until it was too late.

In the real world, the possibility of being attacked by a wild animal is almost none at all. Except under conditions of extreme starvation (situations in which even humans have eaten one another), land carnivores do not consider humans edible—not even people who are already dead.

Observations of radio-collared animals show that nearly all withdraw at the first scent of an approaching human, proving the maxim that a thousand bears will see you before you see one of them. Add to that many millennia of animals' learning to respect "Man, the weapon-maker"—even today whole prides of African lions will flee the long spears and shields carried by Masai tribesmen.

Recreational campers have lost some of the respect that our always-armed forefathers inspired in wild creatures, who equated humans with danger, but a few pointers about animal behavior and body language can still give you the upper hand in a chance encounter. For example, many predators have scared hikers by scrutinizing them from a distance—evaluating their threat potential—but eye-to-eye contact is abnormal. If you are facing a wild animal within 50 yards, it probably has possession of something worth defending—like food or offspring. A stare down does not indicate aggression, only assertiveness, but a proper response may be important to ensure that an encounter ends only as a treasured memory.

Bloody fights make good television, but conflicts between wild animals are normally resolved without violence because neither combatant wins in a knock-down, drag-out battle that inevitably injures both. Instead, challenges are made and met with body language and displays of strength. By understanding how an animal communicates through gestures and posturing, you can defuse a tense confrontation before the creature figures out that you aren't as dangerous as it might believe. Knowing how a particular species usually acts enables a person to react accordingly.

This cow moose in stare-down mode is no joke.

The universal response to any encounter in which an animal stands its ground is to back away slowly. Avoid sudden movements that might be construed as aggressive, and never turn your back on the animal until you're out of its sight. Some authorities recommend avoiding eye contact, claiming that could be perceived as a challenge; others maintain that eye contact instills doubt about how dangerous you might be, making you appear able to defend yourself, without demonstrating overt aggression. My Ojibwa mentor, Amos Wasageshik, maintained that a human must always exhibit dominance and look any animal straight in the eye, even while withdrawing. Old Amos's advice has always worked for me.

One absolute rule is: Never run from a wild animal, regardless of species. Fleeing labels you as the weaker animal, exciting the hunting instinct in carnivores, and giving normally peaceable omnivores a pleasurable feeling of territorial power—even marmots have pursued people who ran from them. Few of us can outrun even a raccoon, and the animal that inevitably catches you will be jacked-up on testosterone, so it is imperative that this situation never be allowed to occur.

Beyond these generics, it pays to know some of the behaviors that are unique to the species most likely to display aggression toward humans.

BLACK BEARS

This is the animal most feared by campers, even by noted brown bear researcher Doug Peacock, who points out that rare black bear attacks on people are usually predatory, for the purpose of nourishment. But healthy black bears do not usually eat people, not even corpses, and individuals who break that rule are often sickly and underfed, or old and arthritic (the token bear killed for such transgressions has not always been the guilty bear). Starving, unable to travel the long circuit required to keep abreast of seasonal foods, and too underweight to survive a winter in the den, aged bears may become desperate for nourishment.

Wildlife experts agree unanimously that a person should never show fear to a bear, even while withdrawing from a confrontation. Black bears are inherently peaceful, and it's imperative to make the animal believe you are dangerous. Most trackers nowadays carry a good modern canister of bear spray (something that can be useful in encounters with grizzlies, black bears, or mountain lions), but there are also other tactics you can use to protect yourself from an attack. Always stand upright, and try to make yourself appear as large as possible by holding your jacket open, or your arms wide. Never crouch or kneel, because in black bear language that position is a prelude to an attack. Should a physical confrontation occur, the recommended defense is to fight back enthusiastically, a strategy that has caused black bears to break off an attack.

GRAY WOLF

When geology student Kenton Carnegie was killed by an animal in Saskatchewan in November 2005, the incident was initially blamed on wolves. This caused a real stir, because never in history had a healthy wild wolf preyed on a human. A more expert examination of the evidence by biologist Dr. Lynn Rogers proved that the killer had been a black bear— probably old, sickly, and too undernourished to survive the coming winter. By then, three faultless wolves had been shot. But the fact that wolves do not prey on humans remains true.

Rarely seen even where they are abundant, gray wolves are highly intelligent, intently curious, and loath to risk injury to themselves. Hikers have been frightened to glimpse a wolf shadowing them through woods, sometimes "tasting" the air for spoor, with mouth open and teeth exposed. Again, it's important to never show fear to these hunters. Equally important with this species, according to veteran wolf handler Cheanne Chellis, is to avoid starting a fight. Never kick at a wolf, as that is an act of overt aggression. A long walking stick or branch struck against trees or the ground is frightening to wolves, which cannot comprehend the ability to transform objects into weapons.

COUGAR

On America's West Coast, the cougar is feared more than any other wild animal. The number of attacks on humans varies among official sources, as do population estimates and the cats' geographic range. But the bottom line is that these superbly adapted hunters are again ranging across North America.

Like all predators, the cats instinctively select prey that is unlikely to harm them. Horrific as it is to our sensibilities, the preferred human target is small-statured, including children, and usually alone. In many respects a cougar is like a house cat, easily excited, and possessed of the ultrasharp hunting instincts needed to survive without help in an unforgiving environment.

Avoiding a cougar attack begins with not looking like prey. A lone jogger or biker who is gasping for breath is, to a cat, an animal in distress; likewise small children running and shrieking at play, or a hunter or angler who smells like blood, or a camper running in apparent panic to seek shelter from hard rain. More than any predator in North America, it is imperative that a puma facing a human be convinced that this adversary is too strong to tackle. Never hike alone in remote country, avoid gasping for breath, and do not drop to all fours or lie down in the presence of a cougar. Most cats attack from hiding, and from behind, and the most recommended response is to fight back with any weapon available; if a victim can inflict pain on the cat, it will probably break off and flee.

In reality, few backcountry visitors will see a large carnivore in the wild, let alone be assaulted by one, but realizing that the possibility exists is enough to make most sensible adults fear shadowy woods. There's a balance between being unnecessarily afraid and being cautious. The intellect that causes fear is our greatest weapon, because only we possess the power to win a confrontation with stronger animals through intelligence and bluff. By knowing what is in the shadows, how it behaves, and how to respond to a face-to-face meeting, you take away the mystery that detracts from the joy of just being there.

Chapter Five

OBSERVING WILDLIFE

Stalking is a great exercise for becoming attuned to the sights, sounds, and smells of a natural environment, and frequently nets you a great photo. But it's sometimes necessary to get an animal to come to you. This can be accomplished with bait, scents, calls that imitate animal voices, or by staking out a well-used trail. Shooting from a blind, or "hide," is the preferred method of most hunters and photographers, however, because ambushing an animal is simpler than stalking it.

The first step, of course, is to use the strategies covered in the preceding chapters to determine where the animals you're looking for are most likely to be. Use a topographic trail map to identify types of terrain that are most likely to be frequented by them, to determine where the best feeding and bedding places are located, and to locate any mapped trails that are the most likely to get into and out of those areas. Once you've established an animal's route and destination, it's fairly simple to lie in wait for its return.

Remember that animals living near humans usually become nocturnal, because there are rarely humans afoot in the woods after dark. The advantage that this offers is one of surprise, because even the most alert animal is not on the lookout for a person hiding in a darkened forest. Many times I've taken an animal completely by surprise by hiding along a darkened trail where it wasn't expecting a human to be.

Be especially aware of how much better animals see in the dark. At twilight, when the world is balanced on the edge of day and night and features are getting fuzzy to the human eye, most animals can see close-up images (because most species are nearsighted) as well as we do at noon. Never think that just because you can't see your hand in front of your face, an animal can't see you move it there. We see well into the infrared end of visible light spectrum, while animals generally perceive more of the ultraviolet end of the spectrum. And because ultraviolet light is most prevalent in what we consider darkness, animals have much better night vision than we do. In daylight, we can discriminate between subtle colors to the point of nonsense, but most animals can run full speed through darkness that would have us colliding with trees. If animals do move about during the day, most confine their travels to within a secluded bedding or denning area where human activity is infrequent, typically in terrain we find difficult to negotiate.

Here's where the tracker who captures his prey on film has an advantage over hunters who kill game and then must, if they're worthy of the title, haul the carcass out of the woods. Bedding and denning areas are great places to set up a camouflaged tripod, and wildlife photography is a great way for gun and bow hunters to keep their skills sharp during the off-season. But such excursions typically reach far into rugged country. For sport hunters, a practical side of these exercises is that they can reveal intimate details about every animal in a given territory, and there's no better way to learn the habits of a trophy, or the best places to find meat for the pot.

Hides and Blinds

The terms *hide* or *blind* describe an artificial cave of sorts whose exterior is indistinguishable from the surrounding terrain, concealing its occupant while providing adequate interior space to move around inside. A blind can be as simple as a camouflage poncho draped over a photographer while he lies in wait at the edge of a game trail, or as complex as the heated plywood shacks used by deer hunters who want the comforts of home while in the woods.

The author's most used portable blind, this Mega Sola from Integral Designs is watertight, bugproof, low-profile, camouflaged, and opens from the front or from either side. It's one of numerous ultralight bivouac shelters that serve the camera or gun hunter well as a portable blind.

NATURAL HIDES

Traditionally, hides and blinds were constructed from natural materials taken from the surrounding terrain. Advantages included lessening the possibility that you might introduce foreign odors, or using a material during construction that could be visibly out of place. Disadvantages included disturbing the terrain, making it noticeably different than it had been to animals that know it intimately.

Even worse is that too-common practice of lopping down live foliage and tree branches to construct a blind. This is not only environmentally irresponsible, and illegal on public lands, but the odor of freshly cut foliage is a powerful olfactory signal to all wildlife in an area that something out of the ordinary has occurred there. The odor of a pine or cedar bough concealing wall, like those made by many deer hunters, is evident to a human nose even 5 months later, and even the most craftily contrived of these is more likely to keep wild animals away. If you must construct a hide from natural materials, use dead, dry foliage, and try to position concealing materials in a way that is not in contrast with the surroundings.

BIVOUAC SHELTER BLINDS

Better, in terms of portability and convenience are modern bivouac ("bivy") shelters. These ultralight single-occupant tents are about the size of a loaf of bread when in their stuff sacks, set up in mere minutes, have a low, unobtrusive profile, and are easily camouflaged. Some are made with camouflage print, others can be easily "disappeared" with a camouflage cover augmented with natural foliage. Best of all, these watertight, windproof, and bugproof shelters enable a tracker to set up behind optics, a camera, or a gun, and remain on station there in relative comfort until the job is done, regardless of weather.

One problem that is typical of all tents and shelters—especially when they're new—is a strong odor of plastic from the unit's polyurethane coating, and solvent smells from waterproof seam sealers. The odors diminish over time, but for the first several outings you might consider spraying the fabric with an odor killer, like Scent-Killer from Wildlife Research Center, Inc.

Fluorescent Dyes

The man with the brand-new orange camouflage hunting jacket drew stares from his neighbors when he took it from his truck and began kicking it around on the gravel road, scuffing it through the stones and dust, and wiping his dirty boots on it as if it were a rug. People stared in wonderment at the man's seemingly eccentric behavior, but a few of us just grinned, because we knew that he was just trying to subdue the brilliance of the "hunter orange" dyes that state law required every sport hunter to wear afield.

Just wearing contrasting garments is often enough to break up the distinctly human form, but tracking clothes should not be brightly colored, and never laundered with brightening detergents.

Probably every teenager learns that ultraviolet (UV) or "black" lights cause certain colors to fluoresce—to glow with a visible light that seems to emanate from the colors themselves. Some laundry detergents are even formulated to enhance that fluorescence, to make clothing appear brighter and less worn.

Almost ironically, there are laundry detergents designed for sport hunters who know that wild animals see best in the ultraviolet spectrum. Ultraviolet wavelengths—most of which are invisible to the human eye—are most prevalent light at night, and evolution has deemed night vision to be necessary for most wild species, so most animals see UV light very well. With that in mind, a tracker, stalker, or hunter should avoid laundering field clothing in color-enhancing detergents.

The Call of Nature

A situation that's sure to come up—especially for photographers who may shoot undetected for several hours even after their prey makes an appearance—is what to do when nature calls. Urine and excrement are powerful signs of human presence, and left in the open, either is sure to repel any wildlife within a half-mile or more.

The best way to dispose of urine with a minimum release of scent is to urinate into a resealable bottle. This has always been fairly simple for men, and now there are form-fitting devices for women too. A two-liter soda bottle is suitable, but more convenient is a two-liter water bladder, like Cascade Designs' Platypus, because these can be rolled up and carried in a pocket while empty. Barring that, urinating into a hole at least 4 inches deep, then covering it over with dirt, will hold scent to a minimum. A few drops of red fox scent on top of the filled hole helps confuse any residual odor.

Excrement should be deposited at least 100 yards from the blind in a direction downwind of the one from which animals are most likely to approach. Feces should be buried as deeply as the terrain and your tools permit, and the location well scented with earth, pine, or red fox cover scent. Never defecate within 100 feet of any body of water, and make sure that all traces have been completely buried. Nature will do the rest.

Chapter Six

DEER (CERVIDAE)

Deer are ungulates (hooved animals) of the order Artiodactyla (hooved animals that have an even number of toes). All four feet of all species have split hooves—actually a pair of heavily nailed toes—that leave a classic broken-heart track. A pair of smaller rearward-pointing toes, called dewclaws, at the back of each ankle, do not normally register in tracks unless the footing is soft enough to cause a deer to sink into it an inch or more. All deer are herbivorous grazers and browsers, and none have upper incisors, only a hard upper palate that enables them to pin plants between the lower teeth and palate before tearing them loose—in contrast to the neatly-snipped stems left by rabbits and rodents.

All deer possess extremely efficient digestive systems that can assimilate and metabolize the roughest vegetable fibers. Only caribou are known to migrate any great distance, largely because other deer do not need to migrate after seasonal foods.

From spring to autumn adult male deer—and roughly 15 percent of aberrant females—carry antlers. Antlers are covered with "velvet," a thin hairlike skin that nourishes and grows antlers until they mature in late October. The velvet is then shed by rubbing against trees. Polished antlers are used in ritual mating battles, essentially shoving matches used to determine which contender is strongest, and therefore most fit to breed. Males seldom injure one another, and never intentionally.

Cows or does, however, are territorial and possessive, and when there are mixed sexes, the dominant animal will always be female. Because they rear the young, and therefore require more resources, does and cows can be very territorial, and very violent about driving off other females that encroach on their domain. Whereas battles between antlered bulls and bucks seldom harm either contestant, the flailing hammer blows of two females battling with their front hooves can be bloody and injurious to both animals.

All cervids are herbivores, although there have been rare instances during which starving deer have eaten rabbits and rodents. They are also ruminants, like cows, able to eat hard-to-digest vegetation, then retire to a safe place where the partially-digested "cud" is regurgitated and chewed to a fine mash from which nearly all usable nutrients can be extracted by the digestive process.

Cervids are reproductively programmed to lose at least half of their populations annually, and need to have their numbers diminished by that much to ensure that food exists for all. The young, the old, and the sickly are prey for wolves, pumas, bears, and occasionally—if a victim is very small or sickly—bobcats or coyotes.

In an evolutionary response to predation, whitetails in particular have learned to associate human habitation with safety. The upsurge in whitetail numbers since World War II has been followed by a number of diseases that have not formerly threatened deer populations, like bovine tuberculosis, chronic wasting disease, and bovine spongiform encephalitis (mad cow disease).

New World Moose (*Alces americanus*)

The world's largest deer, the American moose is the same animal that was once known as the elk in northern Europe and Asia. The first New World explorers reported seeing huge elk— the animal we know as moose—but those who came later mistakenly gave that name to the first really large deer they encountered, the wapiti, which was thereafter known as the American elk. Today moose are known as moose the world over.

Adult moose require 10 pounds of plant material per day.
RYAN HAGERTY/USFWS

GEOGRAPHIC RANGE

Found throughout boreal forests in the Northern Hemisphere, from Siberia to Canada and the northern United States, and southward along the Rocky Mountains into Colorado.

HABITAT

Coniferous and mixed forests with permanent water. Summers spent browsing aquatic plants along shorelines; winters in "yards" of poplar, aspen, and other trees with tender bark that serve as winter food. Blackfly, deerfly, stable fly, and mosquito hatches cause moose to seek higher elevations and shorelines, where constant breezes keep biting insects at bay.

PHYSICAL CHARACTERISTICS

Mass: 1,400 pounds or more at maturity. Cows are roughly 10 percent smaller than bulls.
Body: Shoulder height is 5 to more than 6 feet. Body length is 8 to 10 feet; long legs, thick rump, broad back. Heads of bulls grow palmated antlers from spring to winter, when mature antlers that can span 4 feet are shed. Distinctive head, with a long thick muzzle, overlapping nose, drooping lower lip. A dewlap of loose skin under the jaw becomes longer as its owner grows older. Large, horselike ears.
Tail: Similar to that of a domestic cow but shorter, with a length of about 8 inches.

TRACKS

The massive moose leaves clear tracks in most soil. The split-heart hoofprint is unlike the more circular, concave elk track, and is very similar to a whitetail print, but twice the size at 4 to 7 inches long, discounting dewclaws. Moose walk weight-forward, and on packed trails only hoof tips register, leaving abbreviated tracks that look like those of a whitetail or mule deer; stride lengths of more than 25 inches (walking) and 45 inches (trotting) are more than double those of smaller deer species. Inward-pointing legs result in a straddle of only 12 to 15 inches, only slightly wider than the much smaller whitetail.

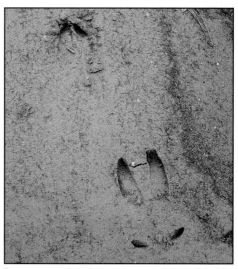

These moose tracks in damp sand are very similar to those of a whitetail or mule deer, but are three times as large.

SCAT

Normally brown pellets that are egg- or acorn-shaped, 1 to almost 2 inches long, or twice the size of a whitetail's. Variations include masses that resemble cow pies when foods have been especially rich—for example, after feeding at bait piles or in orchards. A unique scat

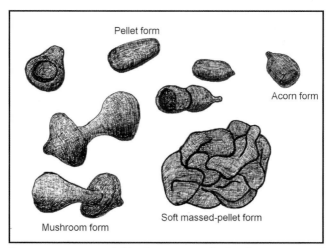

Pellet form

Acorn form

Mushroom form

Soft massed-pellet form

Most moose scats are typical of deer, being acorn- or pellet-shaped, sometimes massed but twice as large as that of smaller deer. One unique exception is the mushroom shape.

The large gray clumps in this photo are week-old masses of moose scat from a large bull that had been feeding at the bait piles of whitetail hunters; the darker and much smaller pellets are from white-tailed deer that use the same trail.

configuration is the mushroom-shaped dropping that seems most common when moose feed exclusively on green grasses.

COLORATION
Dark brown to nearly black, darkest along the spine, interspersed with gray in older animals.

SIGN
Moose leave identifiable marks on the environment, plowing paths through browsing thickets. Saplings are often broken by bulls polishing their antlers in early autumn, possibly leaving scraps of discarded velvet. Look for horse-size beds of grasses and plants that have been compressed under massive weight. Moose may wallow in mud to dislodge old winter fur, or to acquire a coat of mud as protection from biting flies. Entry/exit trails into mucky feeding places are marked by troughs as wide as the animal's body.

Winter sign of moose includes the gnawings they leave in the bark of poplar and aspen trees that serve as winter foods. Older, previously-gnawed trees will be scarred with scabs of rough black bark.

VOCALIZATIONS
Cows calling for calves issue a soft lowing sound, like the mooing of a domestic cow. Mothers also emit a sharp huffing sound or bovine grunt to warn intruders that they've approached too closely to calves. During the autumn mating season, moose become more vocal; males are boisterous and may grunt like hogs, huff and moo loudly, or bellow like a domestic bull.

LIFE SPAN
About 10 years in the wild; up to 27 years in captivity.

DIET

Adults require 10 pounds of plant material per day. In summer moose browse shorelines for pond lily, water lily, marsh marigold, horsetail, and rough grasses. I've also observed them eating jewelweed *(Impatiens capensis)* tops, a plant known best as a treatment for poison ivy. Long legs allow passage through deep muck, where preferred food plants grow thickest. In winter the moose diet is rougher, consisting primarily of willow and dogwood twigs, poplar and aspen bark, pine and cedar foliage. Long legs allow moose to wade through snows too deep for shorter deer.

MATING HABITS

Both genders are sexually mature at 2 years. Mating occurs from September through October. Cows are in heat for 30 days. Cows initiate rutting with strong pheromone scents in their urine and from tarsal glands inside the knees of the hind legs. Cows moo frequently while in heat to attract bulls.

Male moose become dangerously territorial during the rut. Increased testosterone levels cause muscles to swell, especially around the neck, and causes them to become hostile toward intruders. Trackers should be especially wary of bulls in autumn.

Cow moose undergo 8 months of gestation before giving birth to one or—if food has been abundant—two calves in April or May. Mothers that are not healthy may spontaneously abort fetuses, a natural phenomenon in nature, where offspring are more easily replaced than fertile mothers. Moose calves are born unspotted and grow quickly; they can outrun a man at 2 days old; at 3 weeks they can keep up with their mothers, and they're weaned at 5 months—in September or October. Calves stay with mothers until the next calves are born, which may be the next spring or the spring after.

BEHAVIORISMS

Moose are crepuscular (most active during the twilight of dawn and dusk), but may be active at any time, especially during the autumn rutting season. Bedding thickets will be close to or within feeding places, and never far from open water.

Adult moose are solitary, except for females with calves and infrequent incidents of usually related adults sharing especially lush feeding places.

Moose aren't normally migratory, but in Russia they've journeyed as far

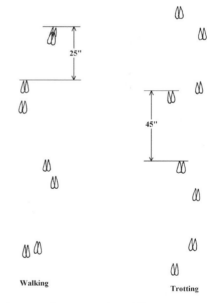

Track patterns of a moose traveling at different gaits.

The left front hoof print of this moose in the grass-covered mud of a dry marsh shows massive weight—about 1,200 pounds.

as 200 miles between summer and winter habitats. Adults are strong swimmers, and long legs help miles pass quickly.

Despite their solitary and cantankerous natures, moose have been domesticated for meat and milk, and some of those in Yellowstone National Park have been conditioned to be gregarious in winter because of handouts of food from local farmers.

Wapiti (American Elk; *Cervus elaphus*)

The world's second largest deer, elk were transplanted to the eastern United States from herds in the western states three times throughout the twentieth century, after uncontrolled hunting had decimated them. Native populations of the eastern woodland elk were hunted to extinction in Indiana (1830), Ohio (1838), New York (1847), and Pennsylvania 1867).

Today there are four subspecies in North America: Most common is the Rocky Mountain elk; then the larger-bodied Manitoban elk of Saskatchewan and Manitoba; the Roosevelt elk of Oregon, and Washington has an even larger body; smallest are the rare tule elk of northern California.

GEOGRAPHIC RANGE

Once common throughout much of the United States, today populations are found only in the western United States, from Canada through the eastern Rocky Mountains to New Mexico. Transplanted populations exist in Kentucky, Michigan, Wisconsin, Pennsylvania, and Missouri.

Elk prefer open areas where they can detect danger from afar. JIM LEUPOLD/USFWS

HABITAT

In general elk prefer open prairies and mature woodlands, where their good vision permits detection of impending danger from afar. But transplanted populations have learned to become comfortable in dense forests, too. Elk tend to travel more than whitetail or mule deer, but migrations are only as far as is required to find a suitable habitat.

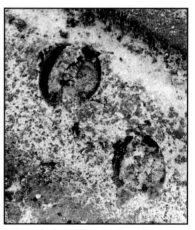

PHYSICAL CHARACTERISTICS

Mass: 900 to more than 1,100 pounds. Males about 20 percent larger than females.

Body: Shoulder height is 4.5 to 5 feet. Length is 6 to 9 feet. Stocky, with muscular humps at the shoulders and flank. Hind quarters are lower than the shoulders, giving elk a jacked-up silhouette.

Tail: Short, 6 to 8 inches, darker on top; normally held close to the rump.

TRACKS

4 to 5 inches long, discounting dewclaws. Cloven, but more round than those of moose or whitetails, and concave, resulting in tracks that are circular

Left front (top) and left hind wapiti tracks show the concave, caribou-like hoof shape that causes the outer edges of the hooves to imprint most heavily, maximizing traction for running on slippery ground.

and more deeply impressed around their outer perimeters than in the center. Stride is 30 inches at a walk; more than 40 inches at a run. Straddle is 10 to 12 inches.

SCAT
Dark brown pellets, sometimes acorn-shaped, 0.75-inch to 1 inch long. Sometimes massed and soft when feeding on succulent vegetation.

COLORATION
Wapiti means "white rump" in Shawnee, an allusion to the big deer's blonde rump patch, which serves as an easily seen beacon to following herd members. Cows and bulls have a dark brown head, neck, and legs, with a lighter body. This contrast is most obvious in winter, when animals grow a shaggy dark brown mane from head to shoulders.

This track pattern of a walking elk reveals long legs and a narrow straddle.

SIGN
One obvious elk sign is the species' signature mud wallow. These rowboat-size depressions are created when wapiti roll on muddy shorelines to dislodge old fur and biting bugs, or when rutting bulls scent themselves in urine- or feces-scented muck. Wallows can be positively identified by the presence of light-colored hairs and tracks.

Like moose, wapiti feed on smooth-barked poplar, aspen, and cottonwood trees during winter, leaving trunks scarred with their bottom-teeth-only scraping. Older scrape marks are covered with a rough black bark "scab."

VOCALIZATIONS
Most identifiable is the "bugle" of a rutting bull. Intended to be heard over long distances, the bugle starts as a low grunt, then becomes a hollow squeal that repeats two or three times. Bulls also issue coarse growling grunts that are similar to their bovine counterparts. The alarm call for either gender is a piercing squeal. Other voices include a soft mooing between cows and calves, and squeals from cows during infrequent territorial disputes.

LIFE SPAN
8 to 10 years; longer in captivity.

With no natural enemies as adults, and the safety of a herd as protection, wapiti were easy prey for the guns of early American immigrants.

DIET

The elk's herbivorous diet includes grasses and forbs, and bog plants like marsh marigold and elkslip. In winter the diet becomes rougher, including the bark, twigs, and buds of aspen, poplar, cottonwood, basswood, sumac, cedar, and conifers.

Elk are especially active during twilight hours at dawn and dusk, but human presence may cause them to become nocturnal. Left undisturbed, elk seem to prefer daylight grazing.

MATING HABITS

Mating season occurs in late August and September (earliest in the colder northern climes), peaking in October and November, when actual mating takes place. Both genders are sexually mature at 16 months, but competition from older, stronger bulls will likely prevent younger males from mating until age 2 or 3.

While they have adapted to lowland forest and high alpine habitats, elk are grazers and herd animals that prefer open prairies.

Cows initiate the mating period by emitting pheromones in urine and from tarsal glands inside the hind knees. Bulls are renowned for gathering harems, but in fact harems are maternal families consisting of a dominant female and one or more generations of her offspring. An average harem includes one bull, six adult cows, and four calves.

Courtship battles between bulls are shoving matches in which two males lock antlers and attempt to overpower one another. Injuries sometimes occur, but the intent is never to harm an opponent, and most matches end bloodlessly when one contender withdraws. Bulls mate as many cows as they can.

Gestation takes 8 to 9 months, ending when a single 35-pound spotted calf is born in April or May. Strong, healthy mothers might have twins, but this is unusual. Newborn calves and mothers live separate from the family herd for about 2 weeks, until calves are strong enough to keep up with the herd. Calves are weaned at 60 days.

Calves are preyed on by wolves and bears, but few lesser carnivores will brave the hammering hooves of a protective mother elk. Coyotes have been blamed for preying on elk calves because they've been observed feeding on already-dead carcasses, but only newborn calves that haven't yet joined the parent herd have need to fear them.

To prevent inbreeding, male calves are banished from the herd when they reach sexual maturity. Outside of the mating season, bulls of all ages band together in "bachelor herds," living amicably with one another but apart from female herds that are always dominated by a matriarchal cow. Females may stay with the family herd for their entire lives.

BEHAVIORISMS

The most social subarctic deer, wapiti spend all or most their lives in a herd. Outside of the mating season, they normally run in same-sex herds of males and females that may number from a half-dozen to several hundred. Bachelor herds are especially amenable to taking in wandering males, even those that may compete with them for mating rights in the rut. Together, wapiti of either sex enjoy the strength of numbers, presenting a formidable front to even the strongest predator, and an early-warning system that few carnivores have the stealth to penetrate unnoticed.

Cow and bachelor herds often share the same feeding and bedding areas, but the sexes do not socialize except in mating season. They might appear to be grazing or bedding together, but if startled the group will split into two same-gender herds.

White-Tailed Deer *(Odocoileus virginianus)*

The white-tailed deer—aka the Virginia or flagtail deer—is reputedly the most sought after game animal on earth. The wild popularity of deer hunting has made it an annual holiday event in much of America—some rural public schools even close for the first day of whitetail season in recognition of the fact that most students probably won't attend classes that day anyway.

Deer hunting has created an entire industry of clothing, tools, scents, weapons, and gadgets intended to help humans find and kill deer. As a result of the huge revenues generated from people who purchase licenses and equipment with which to hunt whitetails, no animal has ever been studied more thoroughly.

Despite being reduced by unrestricted hunting to just a few thousand individuals by the 1940s, whitetails have made a phenomenal comeback in the past half-century. Today there are between 11 and 29 million of them in the United States alone (depending on which official source you believe), and their range is more expansive than it ever was.

GEOGRAPHIC RANGE

Having expanded their range considerably in recent decades, white-tailed deer are found across the breadth and width of the United States, overlapping the western mule deer's range, and inhabiting all but the most arid regions. To the north, whitetails are found across southern Canada. To the south their range includes Mexico, Central America, and northern South America.

This white-tailed buck could weigh as much as 300 pounds.
N. AND M.J. MISHLER/USFWS

HABITAT

Whitetails are at home in any habitat that provides grazing and browse, water, and conceal-ment. Often seen grazing in open fields, they will never stray far from the dense cover that enables them to escape predators and sleep in safety. The least migratory of deer, a white-tailed deer will normally spend its entire life in an area of about 1 square mile, moving only between open feeding areas and bedding thickets.

PHYSICAL CHARACTERISTICS

Mass: 150 to 200 pounds, sometimes more than 300 pounds in the far north. Two sub-species, the Key deer of Florida and the Coues deer of Arizona, average 50 pounds and 75 pounds respectively.

Body: Muscular and more lithe than other deer species; 4 to 7 feet long. Shoulder height is 3 to 4 feet. Powerful hindquarters with strong, slender legs can launch them through dense brush faster than 30 mph. Whitetail antlers have a single main tine, or "beam," extending from the top of the skull on either side, from which single "point" tines protrude forward. Like all deer, whitetails have interdigital scent glands between the two halves of their hooves. When an animal is alarmed into flight, these glands exude a "smell of fear" that can be detected by other deer.

Tail: 4 to 5 inches long, brown on top, white below. Held erect when a deer is fleeing danger, exposing its white underside, it gives the whitetail its common name.

TRACKS

Cloven hooves normally make a split-heart impression, but may be splayed widely to act as a brake on slippery surfaces; length 3 to 3.5 inches, dis-counting dewclaws.

SCAT

Egg-shaped pellets, sometimes acorn-shaped, 0.5 to 0.75 inches long, dark brown color, lightening with age. Soft massed form when diet has been especially rich or succulent.

COLORATION

Red-brown coat in summer, becom-ing gray in winter. White chest and underside. Nose black with white band running encircling muzzle, white chin, white circles around the eyes.

More lithe and athletic than other deer, the whitetail can survive in most environments.

SIGN

Raggedly torn grasses. Saplings with bark "rubbed" from them by a buck's antlers in late summer. Patches of pawed-up, urine-scented earth, called "scrapes," seen prior to and during mating season.

VOCALIZATIONS

The alarm call, or "blow," is a forceful exhalation, like a sharp release of pressurized air. Does bleat softly to fawns. Injured deer bleat with a goatlike sound.

LIFE SPAN

8 years in the wild; up to 20 years in captivity.

DIET

Whitetails have crepuscular feeding patterns. Favorite summer browse includes grasses, alfalfa, clover, marsh marigold, and some aquatic plants. Winter browse consists of buds and tender twigs of evergreen trees, especially cedars, as well as the bark and buds of staghorn sumac, river willow, and hummocks of dead grasses found along stream and river banks. In deserts they can subsist on prickly pear, yucca, and other tough shrubs. Few plants are too tough for the whitetail's digestive system.

MATING HABITS

The whitetail rut begins in September and October (earlier in the colder north) with a pre-estrus period in which bucks 2 years and older polish their antlers against trees, spar in elimination bouts, and advertise themselves with urine-scented "scrapes" of pawed-up earth. When mating begins in mid-October, bucks will have established their places in the breeding hierarchy. Until the rut ends in late November (December in southern regions), adult males will be fixated on mating and little else and may be active at any time of day.

Does may breed in their first year, but play a passive role in mating. Driven by a need to feed and gain weight in preparation for gestation, does stop only momentarily at buck scrapes to scent them with urine, always allowing a few drops to dribble down their hind legs when they leave. A buck returning to check his scrape will detect her pheromone scent and immediately set off in pursuit.

Whitetail bucks are polygamous, mating with as many females as they can during the 30 to 45 days of rutting. A buck may remain with a female for several days, usually prior to her coming into estrus, but when she instinctively realizes that she is pregnant, she loses interest in mating, and the buck moves on to find another fertile doe.

Does are in estrus for a single day, which explains the urgency bucks display about mating. If a doe is not impregnated during her day of fertility, she will come into heat again 28 days later. Should this second heat pass with a doe still not pregnant, she will not come into heat again until the next mating season.

Gestation has a duration of 6 to 7 months. First-time mothers normally give birth to a single spotted fawn in April or May, with twins being the norm thereafter. Fawns are able to walk within hours of birth, and within a week they're eating vegetation. Mothers hide fawns in grasses or underbrush while grazing, checking on them regularly, licking them clean, and eating their feces to keep them scent-free. Should a carnivore wander too closely to a concealed fawn, the mother will try to lead it in the opposite direction, even feigning injury to lure the predator's attention away from her motionless off-spring. At 6 weeks fawns are weaned, but remain with mothers through the following winter, even though mothers will likely be pregnant.

BEHAVIORISMS

Whitetails are nocturnal and crepuscular, traveling from secluded bedding areas at dusk, and back to them from feeding places at dawn. They may move within the seclusion of bedding areas at any time during the day.

Whitetail fawns are easy prey for most predators in their first week of life; this newborn—probably just one day old—was eaten by coyotes after its mother was killed by a car. USFWS

When winter snows cover grazing places, whitetails move to protected yards where evergreen trees provide both a windbreak and browse. In most places winter yards will be within a mile of summer ground, permitting deer to use the same familiar trails year-round.

Does are the most dominant and territorial whitetail gender, because their survival and the survival of their offspring demands a secure habitat with sufficient resources to support rearing young. Bucks may be chased off without incident, but territorial challenges from other does are settled with blows from the front hooves, and may be violent.

Outside of forced cohabitation in winter yards, whitetails are generally solitary, but an abundance of food can cause them to be gregarious. Agriculture has caused overpopulation in farming regions where predators are unwelcome, with the result being an increase in disease and car-deer accidents.

Mule Deer (Odocoileus hemionus)

A western cousin to the whitetail, mule deer are arguably the second most popular large game animal in the world. Subspecies include the black-tailed deer of America's northwest coast.

GEOGRAPHIC RANGE

Mule deer range from southwestern Saskatchewan through the central Dakotas, southward into Nebraska, Kansas, and western Texas, with isolated populations in Minnesota, Iowa, Colorado, and Missouri.

HABITAT

Nearly as adaptable as the white-tailed deer, *O. hemionus* inhabits large portions of the western United States, covering a range of habitats that include woodland chaparral, desert, semidesert shrubland, mountain shrubland, prairie, and boreal forest. Most preferred is open grassland, and mulies are seldom found far back in the woods.

PHYSICAL CHARACTERISTICS

Mass: 110 to more than 400 pounds. Males about 25 percent larger than females.

Body: More barrel-shaped than the whitetail, mulies measure 4 to 6 feet from chest to tail. Shoulder height is 3 feet or more. Large mulelike ears, 4 to 6 inches long. Antlers up to 4 feet wide, with main beams that fork into points, rather than individual points like the whitetail. *O. hemionus* has keener distance eyesight than a whitetail.

Tail: 5 to 9 inches long; brown or black above and white below; tipped with a black or white tuft.

TRACKS

Cloven split-heart print, usually larger than a whitetail's at 3.5 inches long, discounting dewclaws.

Sometimes confused with the whitetails that overlap their range, mule deer are generally more barrel-shaped, with larger ears, forked antler tines, and a curious feet-together bouncing run.

SCAT

Pellet- or acorn-shaped, 0.5 to 0.75 inches long; pellets soft, massed together when browse has been succulent.

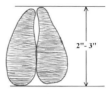

COLORATION

Reddish-brown in summer, gray in winter; white rump patch in younger individuals becoming yellow as the animal ages. White throat patch. Dark V-shaped mark, most conspicuous on bucks, extends between the eyes to the top of the head.

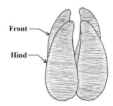

SIGN

Saplings with bark scraped by bucks rubbing antlers. Urine-scented buck scrapes during the rut. Both sexes wallow in mud like elk, but the depressions are smaller at 4 to 6 feet long.

Slightly larger than an average whitetail track, mule deer hooves may be indistinguishable from the whitetail's; trackers should not depend on hoofprints alone to make identification.

VOCALIZATIONS

Alarm call similar to the blowing of a whitetail, but usually more prolonged, ending with a whistle. Deer grazing in herds issue a variety of grunts, snorts, moos, and squeals.

LIFE SPAN

About 10 years in the wild.

DIET

A cud-chewing ruminant, the mulie appears to have a less efficient digestive system than its whitetail cousins. This helps explains why the whitetail has expanded into the mule deer's range, but not vice-versa. As a result, *O. hemionus* feeds with more urgency during summer to put on enough fat to sustain it through winter. Grasses, acorns, legumes, berries, and fleshy fruits are preferred foods.

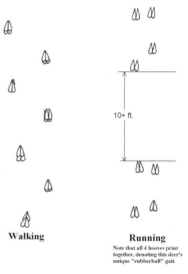

Walking   Running

Note that all 4 hooves print together, denoting this deer's unique "rubberball" gait.

MATING HABITS

The mule deer rut begins in October, peaking from November through December. Does initiate the rut with pheromone scents from tarsal glands and in urine. Bucks are most proactive in mating, creating urine-scented scrapes of pawed-up earth

A mule deer's walking track pattern is very similar to a whitetail's, but the bouncing "rubber ball" running gait shown at right is uniquely mule deer.

Mulie scat is often identical to whitetail scat, but with smaller pellets than moose or elk. Note the massed form at right, which indicates a rich diet of succulent plants.

that does urinate onto as they travel to feeding or bedding areas. When the buck finds its scrape has been scented by a doe, it sets out in pursuit immediately, because the doe is in heat for only one day. Unmated does come into heat again 4 weeks later, again for just one day.

Mule deer bucks are polygynous, mating with as many does as possible in a season, and remaining with a single doe only until she becomes pregnant. Bucks are sexually mature in their second year, but competition will probably keep them from breeding until age 3 or 4. Bucks engage in pushing matches by locking their antlers and shoving one another until the weaker opponent withdraws. Injuries sometimes occur, but the objective is to establish which is the stronger.

Does are less likely to mate in their first year than whitetails. First births usually produce a single fawn, with twins being the norm thereafter. Gestation is 29 weeks, with fawns born from mid-June to July. Fawns weigh from 6 to 10 pounds at birth; twins weigh less per newborn than singles, and males are a few ounces heavier than females. Fawns can walk within hours of birth, and begin eating vegetation at 3 or 4 days. Fawns are weaned at 4 months, and achieve full skeletal maturity at 3 years for females, 4 years for males. Does continue to grow until age 8, bucks until age 10.

BEHAVIORISMS

Mule deer prefer a small home range that provides for their needs in every season, but they are migratory when circumstances demand seeking out a more suitable habitat. Bucks are driven off at 2 years of age to prevent inbreeding, and typically travel 5 or 6 miles before finding territories of their own. Seasonal migrations may be prompted by biting insects, drought, and deep snows. Although mule deer prefer to bed in concealing thickets, they seem less shy of open places than whitetails because they have better long distance vision. Major predators include mountain lions and wolves. Mulies can see predators coming from as far as 400 yards, and with a head start their 30-miles-per-hour running speed gives them an edge. At close range, powerful hindquarters and the species' trademark "rubber ball" bouncing run enable the animals to instantly change direction, frustrating pursuers.

Female mule deer are territorial at all times, defending their home ranges against usurping does with pummeling blows from their sharp hooves. Bucks travel alone or in bachelor herds for most of the year, but don't engage in the fierce territorial fights that occur between does.

Odocoileus hemionus is victim to a variety of viral, bacterial, and parasitic diseases. Gastrointestinal nematodes (worms) can be deadly where overpopulation results in widespread malnourishment. Infection can cause fatal neurological complications. Livestock may infect deer that share free-range pastures with hoof-and-mouth disease and bovine tuberculosis.

Caribou *(Rangifer tarandus)*

Best known as the reindeer that pull Santa's sleigh at Christmas, caribou are the most northern of deer. They have been domesticated to pull sleighs and wagons, as well as for their milk, and they've always been an important source of food for northern aboriginal cultures.

Both male and female caribou are antlered, but males have the largest and most ornately-branched set. USFWS

GEOGRAPHIC RANGE

Caribou were once native to all northern latitudes, but sport hunting by humans—who have erroneously blamed gray wolves—has driven it to extinction over much of its original range. Large herds still exist in Alaska, Canada, Scandinavia, and Russia, but unrestricted hunting is now a thing of the past.

HABITAT

Caribou are most suited to life on arctic tundra. They migrate long distances in response to changing seasons and the availability of food. They have adapted well to temperate forest and rain forest, but require open plains and cold winters.

PHYSICAL CHARACTERISTICS

Mass: Bulls weigh from 275 to 600 pounds, cows from 150 to 300 pounds.
Body: Length is 4.5 to 7 feet. Shoulder height is 3 to 3.5 feet. Barrel-shaped with thick legs and large knee joints. Large nose pad. Both sexes antlered, but males wear the largest and most ornately-branched antlers.

TRACKS

Rounded cloven hooves leave broken-circle impressions that are 4 to 5 inches long. Feet are slightly broader than they are long, maximizing stability on icy terrain and spongy tundra. The pad between hoof halves expands in summer to increase traction against slippery, lichen-covered ground, shrinking again in winter to minimize heat loss.

3.5
Front

SCAT

Oval or acorn-shaped pellets, 0.5-inch long, sometimes clumped in a mass, can measure more than 3 inches long when the diet has been succulent browse.

COLORATION

Dense, wooly underfur is predominantly brown, with whitish chest, buttocks, and legs. Populations in Greenland and northeastern Canada have nearly white coats.

3.0
Hind

Caribou tracks are similar to those of elk but more rounded, with a distinct opposing-C design, and their ranges do not overlap.

SIGN

Browsed reindeer moss (*Cladina rangiferina*), actually a lichen that is a staple in the caribou diet. Shed antlers often found on open tundra.

VOCALIZATIONS

Grunts, squeals, and whistles, especially during seasonal migrations when large herds congregate. Cows moo softly to young calves. Caribou have thick tendons that snap across a bone in the foot when they walk, producing the loud clicking sounds alluded to in the Christmas carol lyrics, "Up on the rooftop, click, click, click . . . " This clicking can be heard from long distances when a large herd is walking.

LIFE SPAN

4 to 5 years in the wild; up to 13 years in captivity.

DIET

Herbivorous caribou can digest most types of vegetation, including leafy browse, evergreen buds and foliage, and fine twigs. When green plants are unavailable, caribou can subsist on their namesake reindeer moss, a hardy lichen that grows in carpetlike masses and is common to open, barren places around the world.

MATING HABITS

Mating season begins, and usually ends, in October, with northern populations typically rutting earlier than those in the south. Both genders are sexually mature by their second year, although competition from older bulls will probably keep males from mating until their third year. Cows are seasonally polyestrous, meaning that those not impregnated

These caribou, looking scruffy as they shed their thick winter coats, represent the northernmost members of the deer family. USFWS

during the first 10-day period of estrus will come into heat again ten to fifteen days later. Like elk, bulls gather a harem prior to mating; harem size is dependent on competition from other bulls, but may exceed twelve cows.

Despite appearances, the dominant animal in any harem or herd is always a matriarchal cow. In May or June, after a gestation of 8 months, cows birth a single calf. Twins may occur if populations are low and food is abundant, but this is uncommon. Calves weigh 12 to 19 pounds at birth; they can follow their mothers within an hour of birth, and can outrun a man by the end of their first day.

BEHAVIORISMS

Caribou are active during daytime (diurnal) and naturally gregarious. Herds can number more than one thousand individuals, increasing to as high as two hundred thousand animals during seasonal migrations. The most migratory of deer, herds may travel 1,000 miles between northern summer ranges to southerly winter habitats. Migrations begin abruptly, with family groups quickly combining to form herds that may number more than twenty thousand animals per square mile and travel more than 30 miles a day.

Caribou are the fastest runners in the deer family, reaching speeds of 50 miles per hour for short distances. A healthy adult can swiftly outdistance its most common predator, the arctic wolf. Bullets are another matter: Caribou had been hunted to extinction over most of their European range by the 1600s and nearly to extinction over much of their Canadian range by the latter half of the twentieth century. Today thirty wild herds are known to inhabit North America; the smallest are in Idaho and Washington, numbering about thirty animals apiece. The largest are in northern Canada and Alaska, and number more than fifty thousand individuals. Hunting regulations have helped populations to recover, but oil exploration and associated developments are a potential threat. Climate change may be a factor in recent findings (as of 2009) that overall caribou numbers have fallen 60 percent over the past 3 decades. Biologists are quick to point out that caribou numbers are and have always been highly cyclical—big herds strain habitats, suffer disease outbreaks, and attract large numbers of predators. These factors can in turn cause herds to diminish, forage to recover, predator numbers to fall, and the herds to eventually recover. But the recent findings of significant decline are a real cause for concern.

Thousands of animals migrating hundreds of miles leave millions of tracks that form an obvious trail. USFWS

Chapter Seven
ANTELOPE (*ANTILOCAPRIDAE*)

Antilocapra americana, the American pronghorn antelope, is the only species in its family. Fossil data indicates that the species originated in the Miocene epoch and is the sole surviving species of at least thirteen genera that existed in the Pliocene and Pleistocene epochs.

Classified as a goat, there has been speculation over whether the antelope might actually belong to the bovine family. Placement in family Antilocapridae stems from physical characteristics that set it apart from bovids, primarily the annual shedding of horn sheaths a month after breeding. Some biologists argue that horn-shedding is insufficient reason to classify pronghorns in their own family, because at least one species within each bovine subfamily sheds its horn sheaths. A point of contention between "splitters" and "lumpers" is that bovids shed the sheaths in pieces, while pronghorn sheaths are shed intact.

Pronghorn Antelope (*Antilocapra americana*)

Pronghorns are the fastest runners in America, reaching more than 60 miles per hour and able to maintain that speed for several minutes. Remarkably, pronghorns can sustain 30 mph for more than half an hour, making them the fastest long-distance runners on earth.

GEOGRAPHIC RANGE

Pronghorns are native to the western plains of North America, from southern Alberta and Saskatchewan in Canada, throughout the western United States, and into the western Sonoran Desert of Mexico.

Because it grows horns, not antlers, shedding them annually (as this animal has), there's some argument over whether the pronghorn is a goat or a cow. But everyone agrees that the species is unique in North America. USFWS

HABITAT

Pronghorns are best suited to prairies and savannahs. They won't be found in forests, deep snow, or on rocky broken terrain, where fast running is hampered.

PHYSICAL CHARACTERISTICS

Mass: 75 to 140 pounds, bucks 15 percent larger than does.

Body: Length is 4 to 5 feet. Shoulder height is 3 to 3.5 feet. Both sexes grow a pair of inward-curving smooth black horns, but the buck's horns are 12 to 20 inches long with a forward-facing tine, or prong; does' horns are about 4 inches long and have no prong. The head appears inordinately large for the body. Does carry 4 mammae, sometimes 6. A thick woolly undercoat is covered by coarser guard hairs.

Tail: Length is 3 to more than 6 inches, with a white underside and top, but with a brown stripe extending from the brown back and down the upper tail.

TRACKS

Cloven hoofs are deerlike, but hoof halves are narrower and there are no dewclaws. Prints are 2 to 2.5 inches long. Stride is 12 inches at an easy trot. Straddle is narrow, 4 to 6 inches.

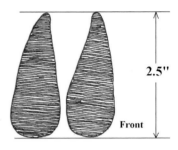

2.5"

Front

SCAT

Egg- or acorn-shaped pellets, 0.5-inch long. Massed when feeding on succulents.

COLORATION

Reddish-brown or tan above, white below. The neck has a short black mane and 2 white stripes across its anterior. The rump is white. Males have a black mask and black patches on the sides of the neck; females have no mask.

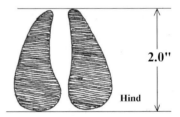

2.0"

Hind

SIGN

Raggedly torn browsed grasses. Areas of grassland tracked heavily where herds have fed, with body-size depressions where animals slept and ruminated.

Pronghorn tracks

VOCALIZATIONS

Calves bleat like goat kids. Mothers grunt to call calves. Males bellow like bulls during fights over females or territory. Adults blow through their nostrils when alarmed, much like whitetails. The white rump patch becomes fluffy and erect when its owner is upset.

LIFE SPAN

About 8 years in the wild; captive individuals have lived longer than 11 years.

DIET

One study estimates that two-thirds of antelope inhabit open grassland, while the remainder live in sagebrush and bunchgrasses, and about 1 percent occupy desert regions. A study of pronghorns in Kansas concluded that cactus constituted 40 percent of the species' diet, grasses 22 percent, green plants 20 percent, and woody browse about 18 percent. Antelope can dig through shallow snows with front hooves to reach ground plants, but avoid snows deep enough to impede running.

Antelope seldom drink from open water unless their foods are especially dry, being able to extract most of the moisture their bodies need from green browse.

MATING HABITS

Pronghorns in the species' southern range breed over a 3-week period between mid-September and early October; those in the northern range mate as early as late July. Females normally mate in their second year, but competition usually keeps bucks from mating until their third year.

Males gather harems prior to mating, and will sometimes lock horns with challengers in shoving matches. However, they are best known for facing off in almost comical bug-eyed staring matches, locking eyes until one of them relents and retreats. This nonviolent method of settling territorial disputes is unique in the animal world.

After mating, the fertilized ovum is stored in stasis (delayed implantation) for 1 month before it attaches to the uterine wall and the fetus begins to grow. If a mother is malnourished or in poor health, the egg will spontaneously abort before it can draw from the female's compromised bodily resources.

First-time pronghorn mothers birth a single calf after 7 months of gestation, with twins being the norm in following years. Unspotted newborns weigh an average of 6 pounds at birth and have a grayish coat until 3 months old. Fawns can run at the end of their first day, and all herd members protect them from predators. At 3 weeks fawns are feeding on plants, but suckle on their mothers' fat-rich milk for a month or more.

Track pattern of a walking pronghorn.

BEHAVIORISMS

Pronghorns may be diurnal or nocturnal, but their most active times are crepuscular, in the twilight hours of sunrise and sunset. Daily movements depend on need, and a herd may not travel at all so long as an area provides for its requirements. When browse is scarce they may range 2 to 7 miles each day, and pronghorns in regions of deep snows—the Yellowstone herds and others—make annual migrations of 150 miles or more to winter ranges where the wind blows the grass clear of snow, as in parts of Wyoming's Green River Valley. From post-rut in late autumn to spring, antelope congregate in loose herds of up to one thousand individuals of both genders and all ages. In spring these herds disperse into smaller same-sex groups. Both sexes travel peacefully together during summer migrations, although males 3 years or older spar in mock combat in preparation for the rut.

Upon reaching summer range, dominant animals establish territories that encompass about 2 square miles, bounded by mountains, fences, or other obstacles that males employ to keep female herd members close. Dominant males scent mark territories with urine to keep intruders from claiming females. Bachelor herds of young, nonbreeding males may wander freely, but mature males will be driven off by dominant males. After mating, horn sheaths are shed and pronghorns of both sexes become less possessive and territorial.

Pronghorns once numbered 35 million, but they were seen as competitors for grassland resources coveted by cattle ranchers, who shot them on sight. By 1920, only twenty thousand individuals were left in the United States. Today, legal protections have enabled pronghorn numbers to increase to over eight hundred thousand, although the numbers vary dramatically with the harshness of winters, the amount of rainfall, and access to habitat. Farming operations and cattle grazing also limit pronghorn numbers, and fences (pronghorns, because of a unique body structure that is built for sprinting, do not jump fences well), large highways, and other developments block the pronghorns' ability to migrate to better habitat in harsh winters, contributing to excessive mortality. More recently, the explosion in energy development across the inland West has resulted in numerous threats to the species.

The Sonoran pronghorn population has been in trouble for decades. The Sonoran pronghorns on the US side of the border almost disappeared in 2002, during a long period of drought, but have since recovered somewhat. The Sonoran pronghorn faces a storm of challenges—poaching, development that blocks migration to water sources, domestic livestock overgrazing in an arid land where forage is already scarce. Most recently, both the large numbers of illegal immigrants traveling from Mexico to the US, and the efforts to stop them with walls and roads, have further stressed and fragmented pronghorn habitat. In Mexico, the Sonoran pronghorn has dwindled to an estimated 500 individuals.

Chapter Eight

BOVINES *(BOVIDAE)*

Bovids are large, heavy-bodied, cloven-hooved mammals that are herbivores and ruminants. Like deer, these grazing animals possess large grinding molars but no upper incisors, having only a hard upper palate, or dental pad, against which plants are pinned using the lower incisors and torn off rather than bitten free. Both genders carry a pair of permanent horns on top of their heads at maturity, and unlike deer, these horns are the animals' primary weapons. All have relatively short, thick legs that are built for walking great distances, but not for running fast. For protection against predators, bovids find safety in numbers and individual size.

Members of the bovid family include Africa's Cape buffalo, Asia's water buffalo, the American bison, the arctic musk ox, and all domesticated cattle.

Still a prime source for dairy products, leather, meat, and soaps, large domestic cattle herds are grazed on public lands, sometimes to the detriment of wild herbivores that share those lands.

Domestic Cattle *(Bos taurus)*

First domesticated from wild Asian bovids about eight thousand years ago, domestic cattle have had a crucial role in the development of civilization. These powerful, easily trained animals had the strength to pull a plow or to be engines for gristmills and other primitive machines; leather tanned from their hides became the belts and harnesses needed to fasten the animals to those machines. The rich milk, cheese, and meat cattle provided were essential to preindustrial diets, in which fat and proteins were prized nutrients, while tallow served as an essential ingredient in making candles and soap. Even their manure was used as fertilizer and fuel. Cattle still provide all those commodities and more to the technology-driven culture of the twenty-first century.

GEOGRAPHIC RANGE
Worldwide.

HABITAT
Domestic cows live where humans can provide for their needs, and so can exist practically anywhere. Most large-scale beef or milk businesses incorporate large plots of grassy rangeland into their operations. In the western United States, large areas of public prairie lands are leased cheaply to cattle ranchers.

PHYSICAL CHARACTERISTICS
Mass: Varied, ranging from 600 pounds to more than 1,000 pounds.
Body: Domestic cows are large and barrel-shaped, with short, thick necks, short, heavy legs, and a pair of permanent hollow horns atop their heads. Shoulder height is 4 to more than 5 feet.
Tail: 12 to 20 inches long, tufted at the end, used for shooing away insects.

TRACKS
Cloven hoofs, 4 inches long or longer, proportionally wider than most deer.

SCAT
Typically semiliquid masses, known as cow pies, 8 to 12 inches in diameter; sometimes segmented when cattle are feeding on dry browse.

Cattle hooves are cloven, similar to that of deer, but proportionally wider.

COLORATION
Usually short haired, cattle may be shades of black, white, or brown, sometimes one solid color, often mottled. Spotted patterns are like a fingerprint, with no two cows having exactly the same arrangement.

SIGN

As herd animals, cows leave heavily trodden trails. Grasses and forbs are browsed short, torn free rather than clipped.

VOCALIZATIONS

Usually moos (lowing), sometimes punctuated with higher-pitched bellows. Alarm is a sharp exhalation, often followed by a snort. Bulls bellow loudly and snort to assert dominance.

LIFE SPAN

8 to 10 years.

DIET

Grazing cows feed on grasses, ground plants, and some tree leaves. Bovids, wild and domestic, twist long grasses around their rough tongues, then pin the spiraled mass between their lower incisors and toothless upper palates, ripping the plants free with a twist of the head.

All bovids are ruminants (cud chewers), with an elaborate digestive system that has four independent chambers: the rumen, reticulum, omasum, and abomasum. Food enters the rumen, where it's broken down by specialized bacteria. The food then moves to the reticulum, where digestive enzymes break it down further. Next, the partially digested cud is regurgitated back into the mouth, where grinding crushes remaining plant fibers. Upon being swallowed a second time, the cud passes into the omasum and, finally, into the abomasum, where nutrients are absorbed into the cow's body. The entire process requires between 70 and 100 hours, but it enables bovids to live on the coarsest vegetation.

MATING HABITS

Bovids live in herds dominated by a single polygynous bull that is mated to all mature females within that herd. Mating habits of wild bovids are seasonally predictable, but domestic cattle may mate at any time of year, birthing a single calf (twins are rare) after a 9-month gestation.

Newborns can stand and walk within 2 days. Calves suckle for 6 months. Both genders reach sexual maturity at one year; females remain fertile for up to 12 years.

BEHAVIORISMS

Like wild bovids, domestic cattle follow a hierarchy, with a lead bull that defends his herd and subordinate cows and calves that follow their own hierarchy. Alpha bulls maintain dominant status until usurped by a younger and stronger male. Calves inherit their mother's social status within the herd, and maternal care—including suckling—may be shared among other cows.

Alpha bulls may be fiercely protective of their territories. Mother cows are protective of offspring, but personal observations convince me that they will not risk their own safety against large predators, notably wolves.

Cattle ranching can have negative impact on the environment, especially where overgrazing by domestic herds that number in the thousands threatens the food supply of wild herbivores. More serious is the spread of domestic cattle diseases, some of which cows are inoculated against, but against which wild grazers have no defense. Bovine tuberculosis has become a common threat, spread in large part by sport hunters who bait deer with corn and other foods that are contaminated with the disease. Cattle feed has also been responsible for incidents of bovine spongiform encephalopathy, or mad cow disease, a fatal brain disease caused by feeding cattle processed foods that contain "prion" proteins from meat additives.

Bison (New World Buffalo; *Bison bison*)

The largest terrestrial species in North America, bison are the native wild cows of the continent, New World cousins to the water buffalo of Asia and the Cape buffalo of Africa. It's believed that bison migrated across the land bridge that once spanned the Bering Strait between Russia and Alaska about twenty-five thousand years ago. Those first immigrants weighed up to 5,000 pounds and had horns that measured 6 feet across.

Most at home on open prairie, these shaggy grazers are well adapted to cold, and once occupied almost all of North America, from Florida to Maine, across southern Michigan and Wisconsin to California, and northward from the Canadian plains to the Arctic Circle. By the 1700s their numbers were estimated to be as high as 200 million animals, and the tribes who relied on "Tatonka," the Spirit Beast, to feed and clothe them described herds that stretched as far as the eye could see in every direction.

GEOGRAPHIC RANGE

Prior to the nineteenth century, bison numbered as many as sixty million animals, and the species was abundant from Alaska to northern Mexico. After decades of wanton unrestricted

Its humped back and heavily muscled front shoulders give the bison a front-heavy appearance. KAREN LAUBENSTEIN/USFWS

slaughter that included shooting from trains, and an army of government-employed buffalo hunters like "Buffalo" Bill Cody, bison were nearly exterminated. By 1900, fewer than one thousand remained, and there was legitimate fear that the species wouldn't recover. Today more than thirty thousand live in Yellowstone National Park and Wood Buffalo Park in Canada's Northwest Territories. There are also numerous commercial herds that provide meat and hides for the consumer market, and many farmers breed bison with domestic cattle to create "beefalo."

HABITAT

Bison prefer to graze open prairie grasslands, although a long extinct subspecies known as the timber bison, or wood buffalo, once inhabited the mixed forest and prairie lands of mid-western states. Today the bison's recovering population faces many challenges, among them opposition from livestock interests, and simply the rapid expansion of human enterprises across bison country. The old Tatonka is an amazingly stubborn and powerful animal, walking through fences, shoving cattle out of its way, and leaving for the far horizons, seemingly, whenever the urge strikes. It may be a human-dominated world, but the bison does not readily recognize man's superiority.

PHYSICAL CHARACTERISTICS

Mass: 1,000 to more than 2,000 pounds, cows 15 percent smaller than bulls.

Body: Humped back and heavily muscled front shoulders give the animals a front-heavy appearance. Body length to 12 feet; shoulder height to 6 feet. Large shaggy head with short, heavy muzzle and large black nose pad. Both sexes carry black, sharp-tipped horns, larger on bulls, that curve forward from the brow.

Tail: Cowlike; 16 inches long with a tufted tip to shoo away flies.

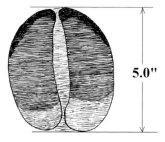

5.0"

Bison track

TRACKS

Cloven-hoofed; print 6 inches long for bulls, 5 inches for cows. Similar to the tracks of domestic cattle, but wider and more rounded at the sides. On hard soil the split between hoof halves may not show clearly, and can be mistaken for an uncloven horse hoofprint.

SCAT

Soft rounded mass with coarse plant fibers up to 10 inches in diameter; easily mistaken for the dung of a domestic cow.

COLORATION

Fur is dark brown to nearly black. Bulls are darker and shaggiest at the head, neck, shoulders, and back, with shorter, lighter-colored fur covering the rump and belly.

SIGN

Large mud wallows at shorelines, lined with shed fur. Scraped bark on trees and saplings from horn rubbing (and scenting). Shed fur might also be found on or around boulders and trees that serve as scratching posts, especially during the spring shedding season.

VOCALIZATIONS

Grunts, snorts, and mooing sounds, like domestic cattle. Bulls bellow when threatened or when competing for territorial rights.

LIFE SPAN

About 25 years in the wild.

DIET

Bison graze on grasses and forbs year-round, pawing through snow to reach them if necessary, and migrating as needed to reach suitable grazing areas. If plants are scarce, they browse the buds and ends of woody plants and shrubs, particularly sagebrush. A bison must consume 15 to 30 pounds of vegetation each day—roughly 2 percent of its own weight. As ruminants, they possess an elaborate and efficient digestive system, and can survive on a diet of coarse vegetation.

MATING HABITS

Cows reach sexual maturity at 2 years. Bulls are sexually mature at 3 years, but usually won't mate until they are at least 6 years old—or at all—because of competition from established herd leaders.

Mating season is long, starting in late June and lasting through September. A single dominant bull mates with all of the cows in its herd-harem. Other adult bulls may leave to seek out their own mates, usually challenging another bull for the position, or may join up with a bachelor herd of displaced males, or may just hang at the periphery of their parent herds. Mating peaks in July, when mature competing bulls engage in shoving matches, charging headfirst into one another using their massive skulls, not their horns, until the one withdraws, usually without injury.

Cows are in estrus for 24 hours and will experience 3-week breeding cycles (seasonally polyestrous) throughout the long mating season until they become pregnant. Gestation lasts 40 weeks, with a single calf, occasionally twins, usually born in mid-April or May. Cows give birth in brushy areas that offer concealment from predators. Newborns have a reddish coat and weigh from 30 to 50 pounds.

A bison newborn stands and nurses 30 minutes after being born, and in 1 or 2 days it follows its mother to rejoin the herd. Calves begin grazing within a week, but suckle several times a day for 8 months. Calves are not fully weaned until they are 10 months old. Bison mothers are fiercely protective of their young, but herd bulls seldom defend calves.

BEHAVIORISMS

Bison are gregarious, but herd composition changes with the seasons. Outside of the mating period, cows and bulls congregate in same-sex herds. Cow herds are composed of related females and males less than 3 years of age. Mature bulls join cow herds in mating season, but the lead animal in any herd will always be a dominant cow.

Adult males may live alone for short periods, but generally seek out safety in numbers by joining bachelor herds that number up to thirty animals during the nonbreeding season. Bachelors coexist peacefully, but with a clear hierarchy that ranks downward from a single alpha bull. Mock battles do occur, but these are essentially training exercises for young bulls.

Migrating bison tend to form a narrow line as they travel, an apparently instinctive habit that minimizes the damage their hoofs do to grazing land. These trails provided early explorers with a route through navigable mountain passes. Bison swim well enough, but old accounts from plains Indians describe how hundreds of drowned bison were scavenged from swollen rivers for meat and hides each spring.

Adult bison fear no predator, but small calves are threatened by most larger carnivores. Mothers defend calves by charging attackers, and calves may be shuttled to the center of a massed herd. Faced with multiple predators (wolves), the entire herd may run away at speeds of up to 45 miles per hour, which adults can maintain for only a few minutes.

Bison have poor long-distance eyesight compared to most plains animals, but they can distinguish large objects from more than half a mile, and detect movement at more than a mile. Their hearing is good, and olfactory senses can detect water from several miles.

Musk Ox (Ovibos moschatus)

This species was facing extinction due to overhunting by the start of the twentieth century, but was rescued from the brink by effective management programs. Many Eskimo tribes still depend on musk ox for hides, meat, and horns, and limited hunting permits are still granted to native peoples. Thick-furred musk ox hides were a commodity in Canada until 1917, when the Canadian parliament passed protective legislation.

GEOGRAPHIC RANGE

Native populations exist in the high arctic of Canada and Greenland, with introduced herds thriving in northern Europe, Russia, and Alaska. Worldwide, populations today are estimated to be as high as eighty-five thousand individuals, and introduced herds are actually increasing more quickly than had been anticipated.

HABITAT

Musk ox live only in regions of arctic tundra, but habitat varies with the season. In summer they prefer low wetlands like river valleys, marshes, and lakeshores. In winter they migrate to higher elevations where frigid temperatures help to minimize snowfall.

PHYSICAL CHARACTERISTICS

Mass: Males 600 to 900 pounds, females 400 to 600 pounds.

The shaggy dark brown fur and saddle-shaped patch on the back are typical of the species. TIM BOWMAN/USFWS

Body: Shoulder height is 3 to 5 feet; bulls are 30 percent to 50 percent larger than cows. Body length is 6 to 8 feet. Massive head with a thick, short muzzle. Short, thickly muscled neck. Very stout legs and large hooves. Shoulders humped, especially on bulls. Entire body covered with long shaggy fur.

Both sexes have large, black permanent horns at maturity, but bulls' are more massive, curving down and forward from the skull to end in sharp points at either side of the eyes. A cow's horns are shorter and straighter.

Tail: 2 to more than 6 inches long.

TRACKS
Cloven hooves with rounded sides. Prints appear much like the tracks of a bison, but hoof halves are more pointed at their fronts. Tracks average 5 inches long, nearly as wide.

SCAT
Cowlike, 6 to 8 inches in diameter, with plant fibers evident. Winter scats are smaller and drier, often segmented because most moisture comes from snow.

COLORATION

Shaggy fur is dark brown to black, with a whitish saddle-shaped patch on the back. There is a whitish patch atop the head of both sexes, a whitish patch around the muzzle, and whitish fur on the lower legs.

SIGN

Well trodden trails. In spring and early summer musk ox roll in mud to loosen shedding winter coats and to fend off biting flies, leaving wallows like elk.

VOCALIZATIONS

Bovine, including snorts, grunts, and bellows from excited bulls.

LIFE SPAN

Up to 20 years.

DIET

Summer foods include arctic grasses and sedges, horsetails, reeds, and almost any available plants. Winter diet changes with the availability of browse, consisting largely of reindeer moss (lichens). When snow covers the ground, musk ox clear large circular patches of tundra with their hooves to expose edible vegetation. These exposed patches are defended against other musk ox.

MATING HABITS

Musk ox bulls become sexually active at 5 years old; females at 2 years. Breeding season peaks in mid-August, after a herd's dominant bull has driven away other males and taken a harem. While rutting, the musky urine for which the species is named becomes especially pungent in the males.

Mating battles between bulls include head wagging, bellows, pawing the ground, and snorting. If these gestures fail to discourage a competitor, the bulls run toward one another, butting heads until one of them withdraws.

Cows normally mate every 2 years, but will breed sooner if a calf is killed. Gestation lasts 8 months, with a single calf being born in late April through May. Twins are uncommon, but may result from a mother who is remarkably healthy. As a result of growing up under such harsh conditions, musk ox calves are suckled for a comparatively long 12 months, but begin grazing on vegetation in as little as 1 week.

BEHAVIORISMS

Musk ox live in herds of ten to twenty animals, but sometimes more than one hundred. Herds include individuals of all ages and both genders, particularly in winter, but there is only one dominant bull among each herd, and the actual herd leader is always a dominant cow.

Musk ox are ideally suited to surviving 8 months of every year without sunlight in sub-zero temperatures. Their southern range is overlapped by that of moose, but only caribou can survive the extremes of cold and sparse tundra browse preferred by musk ox.

The name musk ox refers to the bovid's musky urine, which grows more pungent during breeding season. Unlike deer, musk ox lack external musk glands, but scents in their urine provide the same individual identification, and olfactory indicators of size, social rank, and mating status.

Although considered seasonally migratory, musk ox herds seldom range more than 50 miles, moving only as far as conditions demand to find sufficient food and water. If a habitat could provide for their needs year-round, herds would not migrate at all.

Musk ox are renowned for their unique defense against enemies. When threatened by wolves—the species' primary predator—the herd forms a tight circle, with the strongest members facing outward. Calves are kept to the inside, protected by the encircling wall of powerful adults. Predators that approach too closely are charged by a surprisingly fast and agile adult, which attempts to gore and toss the enemy with its powerful neck. Effective against wolves, this strategy made musk ox easy targets for rifles.

Chapter Nine

SWINE (SUIDAE)

Family Suidae includes sixteen species of pigs and hogs in eight genera. Suids originated in southern Eurasia, on large islands like the Philippines, and throughout Africa. *Sus scrofa,* the wild boar from which domesticated pigs were selectively bred, have been introduced by humans to numerous places where they didn't previously exist, including North America, New Zealand, Australia, and New Guinea. Suid fossils from the Oligocene epoch (30 million years BC) have been unearthed in Europe and Asia, and from the Miocene epoch (15 million years BC) in Africa.

Wild Pig *(Sus scrofa)*

The wild boar, feral hog, and domestic pig are essentially the same animal, but there are a few notable differences. True wild boars are lean, heavily muscled, fast, and potentially very dangerous to humans and to wildlife. The legs are longer than those of the domestic pig, and the forelimbs are powerfully built, with a hump of muscle between the shoulders; the snout is longer and better suited for digging up edible roots, or "rooting." The sharply pointed, self-honing canines begin as long and formidable piercing weapons, but, uniquely, grow outward and away from the upper and lower jaws with age, the upper canines curving 180 degrees upward, over the snout, to become formidable tearing weapons.

The wild pig's habitat includes marshes, forests, and shrublands where acorns, grasses, and roots are abundant.
STEVE HILLEBRAND/USFWS

Domestic pigs gone wild, and feral hogs that have lived in the wild for generations, also exhibit an arcing of their canines, but the teeth don't grow as long, and the curl is not usually so pronounced in their shorter snouts. Having been selectively bred for meat for some twelve thousand years, these pigs also have shorter, fatter legs, and longer bodies, with three more vertebrae than are found in the spines of true wild boars. Feral hogs also lack the "ridge back" of coarse fur that runs along the spines of their wild cousins, and their bodies are covered more sparsely with hair. It is suspected that feral hogs are mating with imported wild boars escaped from game farms, because typically multicolored farm pigs rarely have the reddish fur that is becoming common among feral hogs.

GEOGRAPHIC RANGE

Wild pigs, either domesticated hogs gone feral or Eurasian boars imported as game, are found throughout the world. Wherever wild pigs have been introduced, their presence has had a usually severe negative impact on native species. There were no significant populations of wild pigs in the New World until 1893, when fifty wild Black Forest boar were transplanted from Germany to a hunting preserve in New Hampshire's Blue Mountains. These were followed in 1910–12 by a release of Russian wild boar in North Carolina, near Tennessee, and another in 1925 near Monterey, California. A few were also released on California's Santa Cruz Island. Today, sources for *National Geographic* estimate there are more than four million wild boar in the United States.

HABITAT

Habitat includes marshes, forests, and shrublands where acorns, grasses, and roots are abundant. The species is poorly suited to deep open desert where hot sun burns their sparsely-furred skin and open water is unavailable for wallowing. Although wild boar tolerate moderately snowy climates, short-legged, heavy-bodied swine are ill-equipped for deep snow and subzero cold; temperatures below 50 degrees Fahrenheit are uncomfortable to pigs, and even Russian boar cannot negotiate or forage through hardpack snow.

PHYSICAL CHARACTERISTICS

Mass: 160 to more than 450 pounds. In May 2007, 11-year-old Jamison Stone killed a 1,051-pound preserve-raised wild boar, causing experts to rethink how large wild boar can grow.

Body: Stoutly muscled, 4.5 to more than 6 feet long. Shoulder height is 3 feet or more. Large head with short, massive neck and long muzzle terminating in a flat disc-shaped snout with large nostrils. Eyes are comparatively small in relation to head size. Ears erect and pointed in pureblooded wild boars, usually folded over in mixed breeds. *Sus scrofa* has a superb sense of smell, but its eyesight is thought to be monocular and weak at longer ranges. Canines are 3 to 9 inches long, arced in older animals; canines grow throughout the animal's life, and must be worn down to prevent malocclusions.

Tail: About 8 inches long on average. True wild boar have a straight tail with a tufted end, while domestic swine have coiled tails; hybrids may have either.

TRACKS
Cloven-hoofed with dewclaws printing to the rear and to either side; up to 4 inches long; shaped like a deep U. Dewclaws in front track longer and most prominent.

SCAT
Large pellets, 3 to more than 6 inches long, sometimes massed. Succulent vegetation or meat may cause scat to become soft and disc-shaped, like a cow pie. Content includes plant fibers, insect legs and carapaces, seeds, and small bones.

COLORATION
Wild boars are dark brown to nearly black, with a "razorback" of spinal fur, and often reddish areas. Feral pigs may exhibit the same sparse fur and splotched skin colors of domestic hogs, and rarely have red hairs.

SIGN
Well worn trails made by herds, called "sounders," of traveling pigs. Disturbed soil with grasses and roots torn up over large areas, unlike grazing herbivores.

VOCALIZATIONS
Grunting, oinking, squealing; some researchers believe that *Sus scrofa* speaks a rudimentary language.

LIFE SPAN
About 20 years.

DIET
Swine are primitive ungulates with a simple two-chambered stomach that processes plant cellulose less efficiently than cervids or bovids. That may explain their omnivorous diet of fungi, leaves, roots, bulbs, fruit, snails, insects, snakes, earthworms, rodents, eggs, and carrion—almost anything with nutritional value. They use their tough snouts, tusks, and forefeet to unearth food and plants.

Sus scrofa's broad diet enables it to survive in many environments, but brings it into competition with black bears; in some states—notably Tennessee—the species have killed one another.

Wild pigs are leaner than farmed hogs. Forced to live from the land, they're more active, and subsist on a less fatty diet. They will "pig out" if food is available, but the onus of gluttony is unwarranted, rooted more in the pigs' willingness to eat anything edible.

MATING HABITS
In northern regions, mating season runs from mid-November to early January, peaking in December. In snowless climes breeding may take place year-round. Both genders are sexually mature at 18 months, but only one alpha boar per sounder (herd) may breed. Other adult males, who will not achieve full physical size and strength until age 5, may leave family

herds to join bachelor herds, or try to establish themselves as alpha boars with their own harems of up to eight sows.

Mating battles between adult boars are among the most violent in nature, and they routinely inflict serious, even fatal wounds on one another. Extra-thick hide on the chest, shoulders, and belly offers some protection against tusks that stab and rip, but mating fights are often bloody.

Sows are in estrus for 3 weeks, but can copulate for only 3 days during that period. Those not impregnated undergo another 3-day heat before the rut ends.

Gestation is 4 months, with litters of 5 (sometimes as many as 16) piglets born in April. Because boars are notorious for eating their own offspring, mothers withdraw to a secluded grass- or leaf-lined nest a day before giving birth. Newborns are 6 to 8 inches long, with fine brown fur broken by nine or ten whitish longitudinal stripes on their backs. By 1 week piglets are able to travel with the group. The young begin feeding on solid foods almost immediately, but suckle for 3 months. The piglets' stripes have disappeared by 6 months.

BEHAVIORISMS

Wild *Sus scrofa* gather in sounders (herds) of up to one hundred individuals, but twenty or fewer is normal. Two or more dominant sows may join herds when food is plentiful. Sows generally coexist peacefully. Males 18 months and older form bachelor herds during non-breeding months. Although not especially migratory, wild pigs can travel 10 miles a day at a normal trot of 6 miles an hour; pigs seldom walk, but trot everywhere. A sprinting pig can run in excess of 20 miles per hour.

In medieval times pigs served as both food and farming tools; rough land was tilled for planting just by letting pigs root there. Early Egyptians used the hoofprints as planting holes for their seed, and pig dung is an excellent fertilizer.

Pigs have a superb sense of smell, arguably more acute than a bloodhound's, and this has been of great value to humans who gather the commercially valuable fungi known as truffles. In the United States pigs have been similarly employed for locating equally valuable morel mushrooms, and the animals have even been used to track down humans and locate cadavers, although surly temperament makes them less favored than dogs.

Chapter Ten

PECCARIES (TAYASSUIDAE)

Although not considered true swine, peccaries are New World cousins to Africa's warthog and the Eurasian wild boar. Peccaries have fewer teeth than pigs, and a two-chambered stomach that is evolutionarily transitional toward the order of ruminants. Peccaries are known alternately as "javelina," a reference to their long and sharply pointed straight canines, which do not curve like those of pigs. There are fourteen subspecies of peccary in North and South America. Like swine, peccary canines rub together when the jaws are worked, being constantly sharpened and worn to prevent malocclusions that could cause teeth to grow into the opposite jaw.

Collared Peccary (Tayassu tajacu)

GEOGRAPHIC RANGE
Collared peccaries inhabit warmer climates, from northern Argentina throughout Central America, and north into southern New Mexico, Arizona, and Texas.

HABITAT
In South and Central America, collared peccaries occupy rain forests and low mountains; in the southwestern United States and northern Mexico habitat includes deserts with prickly pear cacti. Peccaries have become fond of suburbs, where they've come to rely on handouts of food and human garbage.

PHYSICAL CHARACTERISTICS
Mass: 30 to 65 pounds.
Body: Stout, barrel-shaped body on short legs. Large head; long tapered muzzle tipped with a disc-shaped snout. Shoulder height is 20 to 22 inches. Body length is 35 to 40 inches. A distinct dorsal, or "precaudal," gland on the upper rump emits hormonal scents used in communication. Like swine, peccaries possess poor eyesight but good hearing, which contributes to the animals' very vocal nature.
Tail: Inconspicuous, 3 inches long, and straight.

Collared peccaries are found throughout Central America and in New Mexico, Texas, and Arizona. STEVE HILLEBRAND/USFWS

TRACKS

Cloven hooves on all four feet; tracks 1 to 1.5 inches long. Stride is 6 to 10 inches. Hind hooves usually register in front tracks. Peccaries comprise a unique Artiodactyl suborder by having 2 dewclaws on the forefeet, but only 1 on the hind feet; true pigs have 2 dewclaws on all four feet.

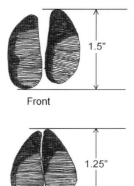

Front

SCAT

Large irregularly-shaped pellets, 2 to 3 inches long. Pellets may be flattened discs, similar to a cow pie, when feeding on especially rich succulents. Scat may contain small bones or insect parts.

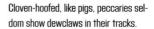

COLORATION

Grizzled, coarse-haired coat is gray to nearly black, with white guard hairs that lend a salt-and-pepper appearance. There are yellowish patches on the cheeks and a collar of yellowish hair encircling the neck just ahead of the shoulders. Males and females are identical in size and color.

Cloven-hoofed, like pigs, peccaries seldom show dewclaws in their tracks.

SIGN

Well-worn trails made by traveling herds; areas of disturbed earth, rooted up by tough snouts as peccaries dig for roots; chewed cactus, especially prickly pear. There will often be a strong odor of musk from the animals' urine and precaudal scent glands.

VOCALIZATIONS

Grunts, squeals, and growls. Peccaries are especially vocal because they have weak eyesight but good hearing, and often lose sight of one another in the brushy terrain where they forage. The alarm call is a sharp cough. Peccaries squeal like pigs, but only when terrified.

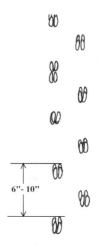

Peccary track patterns

LIFE SPAN

15 to 20 years; up to 24 years in captivity.

DIET

Collared peccaries are omnivorous, but primarily herbivorous, able to digest coarse plant material in their two-chambered stomachs. Prickly pear cactus leaves are a preferred food in desert habitats because

Pellets, sometimes massed, 1"-2" long. Some disclike, flattened, like very small cowpies.

Collared peccary scat.

the succulent cacti provide both food and water. The species also eats frogs, snakes, lizards, eggs, insects, and carrion, and frequently destroy vegetable or flower gardens.

MATING HABITS

Males become sexually mature at 11 months, females at 8 to 14 months. There is no set mating season, and rutting is initiated as a response to climate changes, particularly rain. Wet weather brings a greater abundance of food, ensuring that pregnant mothers will feed well, so most mating occurs during the rainy season. In years of drought, litters are smaller and fewer young are born. Peccary herds follow a rigid hierarchy; a single dominant male is the only male breeder in each herd. Subordinate males may remain with the herd during the rut, but will be driven off if they approach a female in estrus.

After a 4-month gestation, two to four piglets are born, with twins being the norm The ratio between genders is approximately equal, with males numbering the same as females in a given herd. Pregnant females withdraw just prior to giving birth, seeking out a sheltered location in which to deliver their young. If food is scarce, newborns risk being eaten by herd members, but after one day the mother rejoins her herd, where she provides fierce protection for her offspring.

Peccary young are yellowish brown with a black stripe down their spines. They follow their mother, but may be nursed by older sisters from a previous litter. Female peccaries have four teats, but only the hindmost pair produce milk, requiring mothers to nurse while standing and the young to suckle from behind, rather than from the side as with true swine. Young feed on vegetation within a week, but are not weaned until 2 to 3 months.

BEHAVIORISMS

Peccary herds consist of five to fifteen individuals of all ages and both genders. There is a defined hierarchy in which an alpha male leads and followers are ranked by size and strength. Old, sickly, or seriously injured members leave or are left behind by the group.

Peccary herds avoid contact with other herds, and will defend their territories against intruders. In large herds, subgroups of males, females, and young sometimes break away from the parent herd to establish their own territories. Territory size depends on herd size and the availability of food. Boundaries are marked by the herd leader, who rubs oily fluid from his precaudal rump gland onto rocks, trees, and other landmarks. Scats are also used to mark boundaries, especially at trail intersections, and these are refreshed at regular intervals. Herd members meeting one another after being separated rub each other head-to-rump, scenting one another with musk, and verifying that both belong to the same group.

Herd members defending their territories against intruders begin with a warning, laying back the ears, raising the hair (hackles) along the spine, involuntarily releasing scent from the precaudal gland, and chattering their teeth. If the intruder doesn't withdraw, the peccary charges in an attempt to knock the adversary off its feet, biting and sometimes locking jaws with its opponent. Fights may be bloody, but seldom are serious injuries inflicted before the weaker animal submits and runs away.

Sensitive and responsive to changes in precipitation, temperature, and daylight, peccary behavior changes with the seasons. In winter, when temperatures are coolest, foraging begins earlier in the evening and ends later in the morning, and herds that would normally seek shade to sleep through the heat of the day may forage for food at midday.

Collared peccaries have become habituated to residential areas, not just for the food found there, but because their major predators, coyotes, pumas, jaguars, and bobcats, avoid human habitation. The species is resilient and in no danger, although about twenty thousand are killed by hunters in Texas alone each year. More threatening to peccaries living in the tropics of South America is loss of habitat caused by destruction of the rain forest.

Chapter Eleven

HORSES *(EQUIDAE)*

The scientific name, *perrisodactyla*, of this taxonomic order of ungulates (hoofed animals) translates from the Latin as "odd-toed," a reference not so much to the number of digits as to the fact that the middle toe is largest, sometimes to the point of appearing to be the only toe. This order of horses, rhinoceroses, and tapirs was once the dominant order of hoofed animals, comprising fourteen families and numerous species. The rise of artiodactyls (even-toed ungulates), like deer and buffalo, is thought to be the prime reason for their decline to just three families and eighteen species today. Even so, the largest land mammal that ever lived, a rhinoceros that weighed more than a Sherman battle tank, was a perissodactyl.

Most perissodactyls are herbivores and many are grazers, but they differ from artiodactyls in numerous ways. Perissodactyls have both upper and lower incisors, as opposed to the lower incisors and the hard upper dental pad of deer and buffalo; this enables them to clip off grasses low to the ground, rather than just tearing them free. Most species have elongated jaws with forty-four teeth.

Perissodactyls have one large, single-chambered stomach, with an enlarged cecum that uses bacterial decomposition to complete digestion of tough cellulose. A few species—like the rhinos—have horns, but these aren't true horns with bony cores. Instead, they are dermal (skin) growths, and they are always sited in the middle of the skull or centered in the nasal ridge, rather than located at either side of the skull in pairs. Modern perissodactyls are native to Africa, Asia, and Central America.

The family equidae includes some of the most important animals in human evolution, including donkeys and horses. Mules are not a natural species because they are a hybrid of horse and donkey, and all mules are born sterile.

Domestic Horse *(Equus caballus)*

Horses were probably the third wild animal to be tamed for human purposes—after dogs and cattle—and these powerful beasts have been vital to the rise of civilization. By harnessing the muscle and speed of the horse and bending it to his will, a farmer had the engine to plow a field, to turn a gristmill, and to haul heavy loads to market. On horseback, a hunter or rancher could catch or kill creatures far larger and faster than a human, and when the need inevitably arose, horses became the first form of military transport. Human evolution would have certainly taken a much different path had it not been for this amicable beast of burden.

Today there exist small scattered populations of feral horses, but the only true wild horse, Przewalski's horse *(Equus caballus przewalskii)* is the root of every one of their family trees. Officially discovered on the Mongolian steppes by Russian naturalist Nikolai Michailovitch Przewalski in 1879, this miniature horse was too small for riding or working, and was

Although not native to the New World, several regions across the United States and Mexico today support thriving populations of wild horses and donkeys. STEVE HILLEBRAND/USFWS

hunted almost solely for meat. By 1968 Przewalski's horses were deemed extinct in the wild, although a few specimens still survive in zoos.

GEOGRAPHIC RANGE
Wild horses originated in the steppe region between Poland and Mongolia, where they were first tamed by humans. Now domesticated, horses are found throughout the world, while feral populations exist in Australia, Spain, and France, on the Outer Banks of North Carolina, and on the Great Plains.

HABITAT
Grazing animals, horses require large tracts of open grasslands. Suitable habitats include prairies, plains, and mountainous steppes. They can occupy elevations as high as 8,000 feet, so long as the habitat provides sufficient grazing and water.

PHYSICAL CHARACTERISTICS
Mass: 650 to more than 4,000 pounds.
Body: Length is 7 to 10 feet. Shoulder height is 3 to 6 feet. Long legs, barrel-shaped body, long and muscular neck with a mane of longer hair extending along the neck bone. Large head with long muzzle. Large, erect pointed ears.
Tail: Length varies, but actual tails are a relatively short (12 to 18 inches), with long brushy hairs that enable horses to shoo away flying insects.

TRACKS

Four to 8 inches long, U-shaped because horses have a single uncloven hoof on all four feet; rounded portion of the U points in the direction of travel. Stride varies with size, and straddle is always narrower than actual body width because legs point inward. Being poorly adapted for treacherous overgrown terrain, the tracks of a walking horse tend to print individually, rather than with the hind hoof registering in the front track.

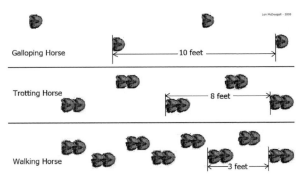

SCAT

Normally billiard ball–size segments, sometimes massed; green or brown, depending on browse, with plant fibers evident. When feeding on succulents, scats may be soft, flattened discs, 12 inches in diameter, similar to a cow pie or buffalo chip.

A horse hoof is concave, leaving a heavier impression around its outer perimeter, like the caribou and wapiti. But the hoof is a unit, uncloven, with a raised V-shaped "frog" that makes a distinctive wedge-shaped impression. Like those of dogs, equine tracks vary widely in size and dimensions, according to breed.

COLORATION

Highly variable, ranging from solid white to tan, brown, reddish, or any combination of these, depending on breed.

SIGN

Grasses and forbs neatly cut to near ground level, not ripped away raggedly as with bovines or deer. Trails are heavily trodden and obvious, usually impacted by the passage of numerous animals.

VOCALIZATIONS

Neighs, whinnies, and snorts. The alarm call is a blowing sound similar to that of the white-tailed deer, or a loud snort.

LIFE SPAN

20 to 30 years, occasionally longer.

DIET

Horses prefer to graze open grasslands, feeding on grasses, sedges, clovers, and alfalfa. They also like corn, wheat, and oats, as well as fruits like apples.

MATING HABITS

Horses are seasonally polyestrous; mares come into heat in April and keep coming into heat every 30 days thereafter until October, or until the female becomes pregnant. Mares attain sexual maturity at 18 months, but stallions will be kept from mating by older males until age 2 or 3. Stallions (studs) are physically capable of breeding throughout the year, but mares are not, and they determine when mating will begin by generating scent-borne pheromones.

Gestation for horses is a relatively long 11 months, with a single foal born in May or June. Size and weight of foals vary with the breed. Foals can walk within minutes of birth, and remain with their mothers constantly for at least their first week. Weaning occurs at 7 months, but older mares that do not breed in the coming season may suckle foals until they're 1 year old.

On reaching puberty, males leave the herd, usually chased away by their father, the lead stallion. Emancipated young stallions find mates of their own by enticing females from another herd. Even so, inbreeding is common among feral horses.

BEHAVIORISMS

Horses interact using a harem-type social system, where a single stallion controls a herd composed of sometimes numerous females and their offspring. The lead stallion drives off usurpers by rearing onto his hind legs, biting and pummeling a challenger with his front hooves until one of them retreats. Subordinate males may follow a herd, attempting to steal females with which to establish their own herd. Being plains grazers, horses avoid deep snows, migrating as necessary to find food and water, but rarely more than 50 miles.

Chapter Twelve

DOGS (CANIDAE)

Canids have pawed feet with a heel (plantar) pad and four toes, each tipped with a nonretractable claw. All are digitigrade, walking and running with body weight carried on their toes, causing plantar pads to print more faintly. Long tails are universal, as are long sharply pointed canine teeth. All species eat meat, but require some vegetables for vitamins and minerals. All have erect pointed ears that swivel to locate sounds, and all have an acute sense of smell.

Domestic Dog (Canis lupis familiaris)

Most researchers believe that dogs branched directly from gray wolves that learned to live with and work for people in exchange for food. Ironically, the free-living gray wolf has suffered centuries of persecution by humans, while dogs have been selectively bred to enhance the traits that are most important to humans. Modern dogs are so genetically different from the gray wolf as to be an entirely different species.

Dogs have become so reliant on human society that few can survive to reproduce in the wild like their ancestor, the wolf. ERIC GEVAERT/LICENSED BY SHUTTERSTOCK.COM

GEOGRAPHIC RANGE

Dogs are part of every human culture, but few can survive to reproduce in the wild (the Australian dingo is one exception). Homeless dogs can be found almost exclusively near human habitation, where they survive by scavenging garbage and from handouts.

HABITAT

Worldwide.

PHYSICAL CHARACTERISTICS

Mass: Varied.
Body: Dogs encompass a diversity of sizes, colors, fur types, and physiques, reflecting millennia of selective breeding.
Tail: Long, averaging about 50 percent of body length.

TRACKS

Prints are 1 inch to more than 5 inches for the largest breeds. Four toes in all tracks. Front heel pads have two or three rearward-pointing lobes; hind pads always have three. Claws always show in tracks.

SCAT

Because a dog's diet differs from that of wild canids, consisting of processed foods, its scat is easily identifiable, being generally cylindrical, segmented, and tapered at the ends. Similar to the scat of wild canids, but without fur or bone fragments. Outer texture is generally smooth, perhaps grainy from the cereals in commercial dry foods. Color varies from brown to black, depending on the foods eaten, becoming gray, then white and crumbly as organic materials decompose.

Size of a dog's scat generally matches the size of the animal, with larger dogs leaving larger deposits than smaller dogs. However, like most animals, diameter and mass can vary with content, the amount eaten at the animal's previous meal, and with the volume of water in its digestive system.

COLORATION

Varied.

SIGN

Scratch marks made by the animal's paws as it scrapes its feet against the ground after urinating or defecating. Dogs are also prone to chewing and gnawing, especially against softer materials like plastic and wood.

VOCALIZATIONS

Domestic dogs are far more vocal than their wild cousins. Barking is the most recognized form of communication among them, but they also growl, whine, and sometimes howl, although some individuals seem incapable of howling.

LIFE SPAN

About 10 years.

DIET

Primarily carnivorous, but dogs need some vegetation to acquire nutrients and sugars not found in meat. On average a dog needs 50 calories per pound of body weight each day for their first year, 30 calories per pound per day after reaching maturity.

Dogs like people foods, and exhibit a tendency to overeat, while wild canids seldom eat more than their bodies require, even in captivity. Dogs overfed with fat can contract pancreatitis, an often fatal condition in which the pancreas loses its ability to metabolize fats. Chocolate is toxic to dogs. Like wild canids, dogs are genetically predisposed to endure periods of starvation, and may lose up to 40 percent of body weight without permanent harm.

MATING HABITS

Dogs of either gender become sexually mature at 6 months, with smaller dogs typically mating sooner than large breeds. Unlike wild canids, whose testicles are normally retracted, male dogs are always prepared to breed. Females typically come into heat every 6 months, a characteristic described as seasonally monocyclic. The breeding cycle has four stages: anestrus, proestrus, estrus, and diestrus. The anestrus (nonbreeding) stage is 4 months, followed by the proestrus stage, when a bloody vaginal discharge appears, lasting from 9 to 28 days. Pheromonal scents emitted during the proestrus cycle attract mates.

Estrus is the stage at which females may copulate. Bleeding from the proestrus period may continue during estrus. Ovulation occurs within 24 hours of copulation, but eggs (ova) can remain fertile for four days, making it possible to have two or more fathers within the same litter.

If a female fails to become pregnant, the mating period ends with a diestrus stage in which swollen uterus and ovaries cause a female to appear pregnant. This "pseudopregnancy" passes in a few days, and reproductive organs return to normal.

BEHAVIORISMS

Like wolves, dogs are pack animals, which is why they can function so well as members of a human family. In an actual pack environment—like a sled dog team—there's always an initial struggle to determine which animal is most dominant.

Unlike wild animals, which are instinctively reluctant to seriously injure their own kind, dog fights are bloody, and sometimes to the death. The problem is worsened because team dogs are often not from the same family, while wild canid packs are nearly always related to one another. In the best case, battles end when one dog submits by rolling onto its back and averting its eyes.

A dog's body language communicates its intent, but be aware that the signals do not necessarily mean the same things among wild canids. A relaxed dog's tail is down, but not between the legs; ears are erect or loosely laid back. When meeting another dog for the first time, the ears will be laid back protectively, and the tail tucked between the legs to protect genitalia. Hackles (the fur along the spine) may be erected to make the dog look larger.

A stiff-legged gait and jerky, hyperalert body movements complete the picture of a wary sizing-up.

A dog on alert holds its tail erect, hackles raised, ears up to maximize hearing. Body movements are quick and fluid as the dog decides whether to flee or fight. The dog may bark in an attempt to frighten the object of its attention into taking flight itself, even though the object might sometimes be inanimate.

Any canid that feels threatened exposes as many teeth as possible in warning. Ears are laid tightly back, hackles are fully raised, and the tail is held stiffly up or down. Threat vocalizations include snarling, deep growls, and aggressive barking.

Pet dogs often learn from the way humans smile on meeting one another, and adopt the same mannerism, baring their front teeth and frightening people who don't recognize this reaction. Dog smiles are more easily misinterpreted from dogs that have learned to "talk," growling a greeting to people they regard as friendly. Clues to this behaviorism include a relaxed stance, a loosely held wagging tail, and unraised hackles.

Gray Wolf *(Canis lupus)*

Gray wolves are the original ancestors of all domestic dogs, including feral breeds like Australian dingos *(Canis lupus dingo)* and New Guinea singing dogs *(Canis lupus familiaris hallstromi)*. Genetic evidence indicates that gray wolves were domesticated by humans as many as five times.

Of the forty-one species of wild canids on earth, the gray wolf, or timber wolf, is the largest. All wolves in North America (except the red wolf, *Canis rufus*) are of the species *Canis lupus;* some "splitter" biologists believe there are as many as thirty-two subspecies.

The most impressive canine of all, the gray wolf ranges in color from a pale gray to almost jet black.

GEOGRAPHIC RANGE

Once the most prevalent wild canid, gray wolves occupied the Northern Hemisphere from the Arctic through central Mexico, North Africa, and Asia. Today there are an estimated nine thousand wolves living in the lower 48 states. Both Canada and Alaska permit wolf hunting, but at the time of this writing, in the contiguous United States only Idaho and Wyoming have imposed limited but controversial hunting seasons.

In Europe wolves were once common, but now there are only populations in Russia, Poland, Scandinavia, Spain, Portugal, and Italy, with a few in Japan. Wolves were exterminated from Great Britain in the sixteenth century, and nearly so in Greenland during the twentieth century, but Greenland's wolf populations have regained their original strength. Protected by law, wolves have thrived in the expanding human world.

HABITAT

Gray wolves are among the most successful animals in a broad range of climates, from arctic tundra and dense forest to prairie and high desert. Always preferring easy prey, large animals like musk ox, bison, and moose are within the scope of a wolf pack's abilities. The territory of a pack can include hundreds of square miles, but wolves range only as far as required to provide for their needs; in rich environments pack's territory may be no larger than a few square miles. Where prey is migratory, as with caribou herds, packs may travel hundreds of miles.

PHYSICAL CHARACTERISTICS

Mass: 60 to more than 135 pounds.
Body: Similar to a large dog, but with a much larger head, more massive muzzle, and heavier legs. Body length is 40 to 50 inches; shoulder height is 26 to 38 inches.
Tail: 14 to 20 inches long, bushy, darkest on top. The tail never curls, but is always held straight down (relaxed), straight back (trotting), or straight up (excited). All dogs, including wolf hybrids, curl their tails over their backs.

TRACKS

Front are at least 4 inches; hind are at least 3.5 inches. Tracks always

Wolf tracks on a snowy road show the animal's stride and gait.

A wolf on the move. Note its characteristic, hyperefficient trot.

show claws. Straddle is 4 to 6 inches. Walking stride is 26 to 30 inches. Plantar (heel) pads are shaped differently than those of a coyote, and are distinguished from those of a domestic dog by their larger size and longer stride. Hind heel pads have three distinct lobes to their rear, but the front heels show only two lobes, leaving a chevron-shaped imprint. Some husky breeds also display a chevron-shaped foretrack, but their feet are always about 20 percent smaller than those of a wolf of the same weight.

SCAT

Cylindrical, segmented, tapered at either end, typically 1.5 to 2 inches in diameter, 6 to 8 inches long. Often large bone fragments inside, with most fur wrapped spiral-fashion around the outside. Fresher scats are darker brown, black, sometimes greenish, becoming gray to white as organic matter decomposes. Gray wolf scat is identical to other wild canids' except for being proportionally larger, but may be confused with large cougar scat. An adult wolf can exert more than half a ton of jaw pressure to crush large leg bones to get at the

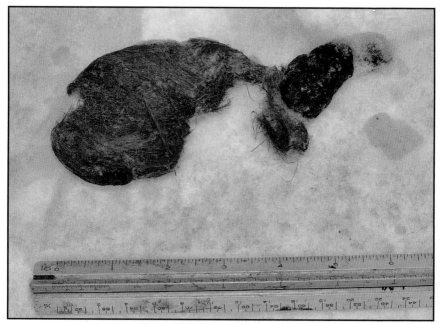

Note the masses of deer hair in this wolf scat.

fat-rich marrow that's inaccessible to smaller canids and felids, and thick bone chunks are characteristic of wolf scat.

COLORATION

Gray wolves display three distinctive color phases. The common gray phase consists of combinations of white guard hairs, with black, gray, red, and brown on the upper body and head. The back is usually darker (saddled), with most reddish fur occurring around the muzzle and ears. The belly is always lighter-colored, with a dark patch over the tail (precaudal) gland.

Color phases of wolves vary widely, even within the same pack.

The pure-black phase is a characteristic of young animals, and always lightens toward gray with age. Black wolves appear to always occupy a low place in the pack hierarchies. Completely white coats are most typical of arctic subspecies, where it works as camouflage. Even there, the gray and black phases are most common. Wolves in every phase tend to lighten in color with age.

Coyotes are often mistaken for gray wolves, especially the large northern coyotes, and particularly in winter when the coyote's seasonal coat is thicker and more gray. Even then, a 60-pound coyote is half the size of a wolf, with a much more pointed muzzle and proportionally longer, more pointed ears. Coyote tracks are rarely more than 3 inches long, and clear tracks reveal that a coyote's plantar pad has three rearward-pointing lobes, while a wolf's shows two in a distinct chevron shape.

SIGN

Digging for burrowing animals is one of the gray wolf's most obvious signs. Bears, coyotes, and badgers also excavate prey dens, but bears aren't active in winter, and loose soil from this activity usually holds a footprint that identifies the digger.

Scent posts are territorial advertisements and an indication of social status; males urinate as high up on a tree as possible to demonstrate their size. Dominant females may also urinate onto scent posts, sometimes actually cocking one leg almost like a male.

Wolves habitually carry larger prey away from the place where it was killed to secluded, usually elevated locations where they can eat in safety. I once found the bones of five deer that had been taken up onto a flat ridge by a wolf pack over the course of a winter. Look for traces of deer hair where the prey was scraped against a tree, or marks where hooves dragged. If prey cannot be carried whole, wolves dismember it, usually leaving blood trails.

VOCALIZATIONS

Howling is the wolf's most recognized sound. Prior to a pack hunt, the alpha males issue a "lone wolf" howl to gather pack members (mostly offspring) together. This monotonal howl, which humans often describe as sad, is heard in the early evening, usually coming from the same location. Gathering howls also warn other wolves that this territory is claimed.

Gathering howls work as pep rallies, getting pack members psyched up for a night of hunting. They are purposely varied to help convince predators and competitors that a pack's size is greater than it really is. Howls may be high- or low-pitched, some with a "woo-woo" wavering quality, but they never sound like the shrill yapping of coyotes. Wolves can bark, but never repeatedly like a dog; the alarm bark is a single "woof."

LIFE SPAN

About 8 years in the wild; up to 15 years in captivity.

DIET

Gray wolves are meat-eaters, but they require some vegetable matter in their diets. Wolves in captivity are fond of green beans, while those in the wild eat a variety of fruits and grasses for nutrition and as dietary fiber to keep their colons clean.

Best known for hunting large prey, a hunting wolf pack's drill-team precision is the stuff of stories. But in fact wolves avoid prey capable of injuring them because a flailing hoof can seriously harm the strongest wolf, thus weakening the entire pack. The prey of choice is always a small or sickly individual, and much publicized instances of packs bringing down young moose or elk are in fact acts of desperation. Deer that are starving are not eaten because toxins accumulate in muscle mass when it cannibalizes itself.

When a pack splits up in midwinter and the alphas leave to mate and dig a den, members regroup each night to hunt, but mature individuals may leave to find their own mates and territories. Lone wolves can't usually bring down large animals, so their diets typically consist of small animals, especially rodents, and even spawning fish in shallow streams.

MATING HABITS

Gray wolves mate between January and March, earliest in the south where spring arrives earlier. Only the parent (alpha) pair may mate within a pack, which is actually a family. Adult offspring must leave if they wish to find a mate, usually at 2 years old. Weaker "omega" wolves may remain with the pack for life. Female pups reach sexual maturity at 2 years, males at 3 years.

As with dogs, the female's breeding cycle has four stages: anestrus, proestrus, estrus, and diestrus. The estrus (copulation) stage lasts 5 to 14 days. Males come into heat at the same time, and only then do their normally-retracted testicles descend and produce sperm.

Wolf pairs separate from their packs 2 weeks before mating to find a den site, always near a source of water. Dens consist of a body-size tunnel, 18 inches in diameter and 10 feet long, that slants downward into a chamber 4 feet high by 6 feet long and 6 feet wide. Nursing chamber floors are at a slightly higher level than the tunnel to prevent flooding. Chamber floors are insulated with grasses and shed winter fur. A good den may be used repeatedly if left unmolested.

Adult offspring that do not leave to find their own mates while the alphas are denned teach younger siblings to hunt small prey. Only the alpha male is permitted at the den site until pups are weaned, but he may howl the pack back together at night for hunts. As the pregnant alpha female becomes more den-bound, her mate will bring her food.

Gestation lasts 60 days, with an average of six pups born between March and May, again depending on latitude. Pups weigh 8 ounces at birth, and are blind and deaf. They are completely dependent on the mother for nourishment and warmth for 2 months, and she will stay with them constantly for their first 3 weeks, except for infrequent outings to drink and to expel waste away from the fastidiously clean den. She will eat the afterbirth and the pups' excrement until they can leave the den. Pups grow fast, gaining 3 pounds of body weight every week.

At 6 weeks pups begin playing outside the den during daylight hours, and some pack members will be allowed to meet their newest siblings. Pups eat meat regurgitated by pack members returning from a hunt, stimulating them to throw up the predigested flesh by licking at the corners of their mouths. Predigested meat is easier to metabolize, and adults can carry more meat in their stomachs than in their mouths.

Pups are weaned by 9 weeks, freeing their mother to join in hunts while pups are guarded by a "babysitter," usually the weakest member of a pack. By 10 months the pups have grown to 65 pounds and hunt with the pack.

BEHAVIORISMS

Gray wolves are social; pack size may number from two animals—a newly mated pair—to thirty. Packs are family units that seldom accept unrelated adults, although orphaned pups are always adopted.

Each pack has a defined hierarchy. Alpha males are dominant, although packs have been led by a widowed alpha female, and all pack members are subordinate to the alphas. If one alpha is killed, the other may leave to seek out a new mate, leaving the beta—the strongest remaining male—in command. If the alpha female dies, her mate may take one of her sisters, who joined the pack when she did. Newly paired alphas often migrate with a third female, a sister of the alpha female, who helps to strengthen their ability to take large prey and serves as a secondary mate should the alpha female be killed. This sister wolf also serves as a babysitter for the first litter of pups.

Pack members almost never fight one another, because to injure a member of the team hinders its ability to hunt. An established eating hierarchy is strictly followed: Alphas and pups eat first, followed by betas and subordinates in descending order, and finally the omega, or lowest ranked wolf. Adults wishing to begin their own families must leave the pack to preventing inbreeding. Pack members are brought food if they become sick or injured, but these wolves often leave the pack voluntarily.

Wolves were once called "God's Knife" because these efficient predators take down the slow and the ill, keeping deer herds strong and healthy.

Wolf packs undergo yearly stationary and nomadic phases. The stationary phase is in spring and early summer, beginning when alphas establish a den and ending when pups are mature enough to travel. The nomadic phase spans autumn to late winter, when packs follow migrating deer herds. A hunting pack may travel more than 70 miles a day at an easy lope of 15 miles per hour, mostly at night.

Gray wolves are a keystone predator throughout the Northern Hemisphere. Like the lynx and the snowshoe hare, wolves and deer share a symbiotic relationship, each needing the other. White-tailed deer are genetically engineered to lose a third of their population each year, and Native Americans called the gray wolf "God's Knife" because wolf predation culled the weak and the sickly, leaving only the strongest and healthiest to reproduce.

The resurgence of wolves in America has been controversial. Ranchers and farmers argue that wolves prey on livestock, but actual losses have been negligible. More real are the fears of a citizenry that hasn't interacted with wolves in generations, and whose greatest frame of reference is rooted in fairy tales about talking pigs and little girls in red cloaks. In contrast, Native American tribes almost universally believed that wolves were a gift from the Creator, who promised them that wolves would never harm the people. Today, despite an occasional bite from young wolves that have been habituated to food handouts from campers, the aboriginal belief holds true: There has never been a single verifiable instance of a healthy wild wolf harming a human of any age.

Red Wolf (Canis rufus)

Little is known about the red wolf, because the species had been hunted, poisoned, and trapped nearly to extinction before it was studied. It was placed on the Endangered Species List in 1967. Biologists argue over the validity of classifying *Canis rufus* as a unique species: Some consider red wolves too different from coyotes and gray wolves to be members of either species, while others believe they are simply the product of wolves and coyotes interbreeding, which DNA testing has shown is more commonplace than previously believed. We do know that red wolves readily interbreed with coyotes, thus diluting their own bloodlines. Currently only about two hundred heavily protected red wolves exist.

GEOGRAPHIC RANGE

Red wolves once inhabited all of the southeastern United States, but today their range is limited to southeastern Texas and

Some believe that the red wolf is a product of wolves and coyotes interbreeding. JOHN AND KAREN HOLLINGSWORTH/USFWS southwestern Louisiana. Attempts have been made to reintroduce red wolves in South Carolina, North Carolina, and in Tennessee's Great Smoky Mountains.

PHYSICAL CHARACTERISTICS

Mass: 40 to 90 pounds.

Body: Slender and smaller than a gray wolf, 50 percent larger than a coyote. Shoulder height is 15 inches; body length is 60 inches. Nose pad broader than a coyote's, about 1 inch across. Pointed ears larger than a gray wolf's. Muzzle more blocky and heavier than a coyote's.

Tail: Bushy, 15 inches long, grizzled gray, reddish on top.

TRACKS

Four toes front and hind, claws show in tracks. All prints about 4.5 inches long. Two lobes on front plantar pad leave a chevron shape; three lobes on rear heel. Outermost toes are much smaller than center toes.

SCAT

Red wolf scat is similar to a coyote's, and much smaller than a gray wolf's; 3 to 4 inches long, segmented, tapered at both ends, 1 inch in diameter. Usually with small bones wrapped spirally inside preys' fur to protect the intestinal tract.

COLORATION

Grizzled gray back and flanks, red on shoulders and neck, with reddish ears and red on top of the muzzle. Legs are reddish.

SIGN

Deer carcasses with gnawed joint ends; excavated rodent burrows.

VOCALIZATIONS

Howling similar to a coyote's, yapping deeper-toned than the shrill barks of coyotes. Researchers describe the voice as between those of coyotes and grey wolves.

LIFE SPAN

Probably about 8 years in the wild; in captivity one individual lived to 14 years.

HABITAT

Originally native to any environment where coyotes or gray wolves live. Today there are only a few reintroduced packs living in the swamps and mountains of the southern United States.

DIET

Rodents and other small prey that can be overtaken by a red wolf's 40 miles per hour running speed. Often solitary, but family members may form packs to hunt larger prey. Like gray wolves, red wolves use their teeth to quarter larger prey. They then transport the prey to a secure location where they can eat in peace. These places are usually on high ground that lends a view of the surrounding area.

MATING HABITS

Female red wolves can mate at 2 years, but males will probably not breed until 4. Mates remain together for life. Breeding takes place from January to March. After a gestation of 2 months, litters of three to six pups are born between March and May, in dens ranging from undercut stream banks to hollow trees, or in existing dens appropriated from coyotes. Left unmolested, the same den may be used year after year. While a mother is den-bound with nursing duties, her mate hunts and brings her food. Both parents take an active role in rearing young. By 5 weeks pups are weaned and leave the den to play outside under their parents' watchful eyes. By late August pups will have grown to about 35 pounds, and are strong enough to hunt small prey.

BEHAVIORISMS

Red wolves are primarily nocturnal, although this is likely because humans are most active during daylight hours. Average territorial area is unknown, but red wolves probably travel no farther than is required to find the necessities of life.

Red wolf packs are made up of a mated pair of adults and their offspring. An average pack numbers eight members. Red wolves live harmoniously with their own pack, but are aggressive toward unrelated intruders.

Despite having smaller ranges, red wolves not in the static denned phase are more nomadic than gray wolves, moving on almost every week. With a diet of mostly rodents—whose own prolific reproduction has sometimes exceeded twenty thousand mice and voles per acre—red wolves simply stay in one spot until the pickings get slim, then move on. In a month the rodent population in that location will have recovered, and they can return.

Red wolves have been blamed for killing livestock, but reports of predation have been so grossly exaggerated as to be comical. They may kill small dogs and cats, but even this is unlikely because of the species' low population.

Coyote (Canis latrans)

The coyote gets its common name from the Nahuatl Indian word *coyotl,* meaning "the trickster." Never rare themselves, the elimination of other large predators made this little wolf the most successful carnivore in America. Subjected to the same poisons, traps, and prejudices that exterminated wolves from most of the continent, coyotes have thrived, even invading inner-city streets.

GEOGRAPHIC RANGE

Coyotes are unique to the Americas, ranging from Central America northward throughout Mexico, the lower 48 states, into central Canada, and up to Alaska.

HABITAT

Coyotes are adaptable to a broad range of environments and climates, from the jungles of southern Mexico to the desert Southwest, and into the bitter winter cold of northern boreal forests. They have learned to live in the vicinity of humans, and have come to recognize people as a potential food source, becoming pests by raiding suburban garbage cans.

Coyotes have adapted to living close to human habitation. GEORGE GENTRY/USFWS

PHYSICAL CHARACTERISTICS

Mass: 30 to more than 60 pounds in the far north.

Body: Lanky and slender, about half the size of a gray wolf and twice as large as a fox. Thick winter fur can exaggerate body size. Body length is 45 inches; shoulder height is 24 inches. Large pointed ears, narrow tapered muzzle, small black nose pad. Like most nocturnal hunters, the eyes have a yellow iris and round pupil. The molars are structured for crushing small bones, with scissorlike carnassials for cutting hide and long pointed canines for inflicting mortal wounds.

Tail: Bushy, 22 inches long, brush-shaped with a black tip. A precaudal scent gland is marked by a dark patch of fur on the upper base of the tail. The tail is normally held below the spine when running, while a gray wolf's tail usually points straight back.

TRACKS

Prints are 2.5 inches long for the forepaws, hind paws 10 percent smaller. In the far north tracks as large as 3.5 inches have been recorded. Three rearward-pointing lobes on the plantar pads of all four feet. Walking stride is 14 inches; straddle is 4 inches.

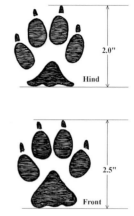

A gray wolf track is shown for comparison. A wolf track is much larger than any coyote track, and will often show the hairs that make the wolf so efficient in running on snow.

Coyote tracks

SCAT
Usually black to brown, growing gray to white as organic material decomposes with age. Length is 3 to 4 inches; cylindrical, 1 inch in diameter, segmented. May have a purplish or reddish color when berries are available, sometimes with seeds or cherry pits evident, but typically covered with fur spiral-wrapped around small bones of prey animals.

COLORATION
The coyote's pelage varies from gray-brown to yellow-gray on the upper parts, often with reddish patches around the neck, shoulders, and flanks, and grizzled black or dark gray on the back from shoulders to rump. The throat and belly are lighter, almost white. The forelegs, sides of the head, muzzle, and feet are often rust colored. The one molt per year begins with shedding the winter coat in May, and is usually complete by July. The new winter coat begins to grow in September.

SIGN
Tree trunks and stumps marked with urine by males to a height of 8 inches—half as high up as a gray wolf. Gnawed ribs and cartilaginous joints on deer carcasses; larger bones will not be crushed to obtain marrow, as with the gray wolf's far more powerful jaws.

VOCALIZATIONS
Shrill howling, with barking and yapping, especially at dusk and dawn. The scientific name, *Canis latrans,* is Latin for "barking dog," a trait that distinguishes it from the gray wolf.

LIFE SPAN
8 to 10 years.

DIET

Coyotes are broadly carnivorous: Their diets include lizards, fish, and even venomous snakes—coyotes appear to enjoy considerable resistance to venom. Most of the diet consists of squirrels, rabbits, mice, and voles. Skilled mousers, coyotes may often be seen standing in a field, cocking their heads and ears to pinpoint the exact location of rodents scurrying under snow or thick grasses. When one has been located, the coyote leaps upward with all four feet, coming down hard onto a victim with its forefeet. Stunned or killed rodents are swallowed whole.

Coyote scat

Coyotes eat carrion, especially deer, which are normally too large for even a family of coyotes to hunt. Coyotes are often seen by hunters, because they've learned to associate hunters with lost deer and bountiful meat.

Coyotes will often leave scats in the same place on habitually used trails.

Wintering coyote families may form packs to hunt deer, but only if smaller prey is in short supply. A sharp-hooved kick to the jaw is fatal if it prevents a predator from eating, so deer are never preferred prey.

Coyotes like blueberries, wild grapes, elderberries, and other sugar-rich fruits that help them put on precious fat for the coming winter. Where blueberries are plentiful, coyote scats are purple from August to October.

MATING HABITS

Coyotes are sexually mature by 12 months, but cannot mate until they leave their parents and find their own mates. Pairs are usually monogynist (mated for life), but occasionally "divorce" to find other mates, probably from an instinct to diversify the gene pool. Males attempting to usurp another's mate will likely find themselves run off by both members of the mated pair.

Mates retire to secluded dens in January, using the same site as the year before provided it is undisturbed. Dens are typically excavated into the side of a hill, sometimes under the roots of a large tree, and near to water but high enough to prevent flooding. Dens consist of a narrow tunnel, 12 inches in diameter, that slopes downward 5 or 6 feet to a nursing chamber 3 feet high, 3 feet across, and 4 feet long.

Males are infertile most of the year, their testicles retracted until mating season causes them to descend. Spermatogenesis, the production of sperm cells, requires 54 days of physiological preparation, occurring between January and February.

Coitus takes place between late January and March, and is initiated by the female pawing at the male's flanks. Females are monoestrous, remaining in heat for only 5 days, so they feel an urgency to become pregnant.

Gestation is 60 days, with one to nineteen pups born in April or May. Pups weigh 7 ounces at birth, and the mother remains with them constantly for the first 2 weeks, eating the afterbirth and licking up the pups' waste to keep the den free of contamination. At 10 days the pups will have doubled in mass and their eyes open for the first time. At 3 to 4 weeks pups begin emerge from the den to play, protected by their parents from the numerous predators that consider coyote pups a delicacy. While they are denned, the male brings food to his mate and offspring, feeding the young regurgitated meat and babysitting while the mother leaves to drink or relieve herself.

At 35 days the pups weigh 4 pounds and are weaned. By 6 months pups weigh 30 pounds and can fend for themselves. By 9 months most male pups strike out on their own, while females may remain for 2 years or more.

Although the coyote is an individual species, the red wolf *(Canis rufus)* is thought to be wiping itself out because it breeds readily with coyotes. Dogs with pointed ears and coyote-like traits have also mated with coyotes, producing a hybrid known as a "coydog." DNA testing has revealed that most gray wolves in Minnesota carry coyote genes in their bloodlines, proving that a wolf without a mate will sometimes accept a coyote.

BEHAVIORISMS

Being so efficient at catching rodents, coyotes do not normally form packs. When they do pack up, members are always relatives, usually parents and their grown offspring. Gatherings are initiated at dusk with a prolonged howl from the alpha male, which is punctuated by barks, unlike wolves.

The howl is repeated until it is joined by high-pitched yaps and barks from other members as they join with the alpha. Pack members may run together if they have an intended target, but may split up to discover more possibilities, communicating the find of a meal large enough to be shared with a prolonged, barking howl that is like the alpha's gathering howl. Nightly hunts encompass about 3 square miles.

Coyote territories are only as large as is needed, but usually range between 6 and 12 square miles. Territories include a source of water, especially near dens during whelping, along with fields where mice and voles live. Territories are marked by urine scent posts sprayed onto landmarks, and scat deposits left at intersections on regularly used trails.

An old myth claims that the coyote and the American badger *(Taxidea taxus)* hunt together, the coyote using its acute sense of smell to locate prey and the badger using its formidable claws to dig them out. This fable is half true; the coyote and badger do team against burrowed prey, but it's the coyote's idea. A badger's keen nose needs no help, and the two do not share meals. Instead, the intelligent coyote takes the position at the escape tunnel found in most burrows, knowing that a panicked inhabitant might try to escape past its lightning-fast jaws.

Gray Fox *(Urocyon cinereoargenteus)*

Gray foxes are native to North America, and they were the reason that red foxes were imported here from Europe. When English settlers in America attempted the noble sport of fox hunting from horseback, they found that the largest native fox had a unique ability to climb trees like a cat. That made for a short chase in the heavily forested New World, so the red fox was imported.

Note the rounded ears and the grizzled appearance of the outer fur on this gray fox. USFWS

GEOGRAPHIC RANGE

Gray foxes are found from southern Canada to northern Venezuela and Colombia. They are not found where there are no forests.

HABITAT

Deciduous forests, where the gray fox's unique ability to climb trees permits escape from predators. Gray foxes may sometimes be seen in fields, foraging for grasshoppers and rodents. They tend to avoid open agricultural regions, and are much less likely to be seen than red foxes.

PHYSICAL CHARACTERISTICS

Mass: 7 to 13 pounds.
Body: Foxlike; long bushy tail, short legs, long body. Length is 31 to 44 inches, shoulder height is 14 inches. Broad head with widely spaced temporal ridges unlike other American canids. Muzzle narrow and tapered, small black nose pad. Ears are shorter and more rounded than a red fox.
Tail: Bushy, black-tipped, 8 to 17 inches long.

2.0"

Front

TRACKS

Prints are 1.5 inches long, front and hind; front paws wider than hind. Claws partially retractable, but show in tracks. Three lobes on all plantar pads, but only the outer edges of the outermost lobes may show in hind tracks.

1.5"

Hind

SCAT

Scat is 2.5 inches long, 0.5 inch in diameter, with tapered ends. Probably encased in a spiral of fine rodent fur. Similar

Gray fox tracks

to red fox scat, but gray foxes eat a more vegetarian diet.

COLORATION

Sometimes mistaken for a red fox, especially red foxes that are in a "cross phase" of mottled red, gray, and black fur. The gray fox is grizzled gray and black on its back, neck, and the upper tail, colored much like a coyote. The upper head and muzzle are grizzled, with patches of white at the muzzle tip, the cheeks, and the underbelly. Sides of the neck, legs, body, and tail are rust colored.

SIGN

Food caches in shallow holes under loosely piled soil, or shallow holes left after caches have been excavated. Trees marked with urine at a height of 8 inches; yellow stains on snow. Gray foxes may den throughout the year under tree roots, in rock crevices, or in hollow trees, and may have several dens within their territories. Dens are much smaller than coyote dens (coyotes eat gray foxes).

VOCALIZATIONS

Shrill barks, yaps, and growls, like a small dog. Less vocal than red foxes.

LIFE SPAN

8 to 10 years.

DIET

Gray foxes pounce on mice in fields or catch rabbits in brush, but their diet has an added dimension because they can climb trees to snatch roosting birds at night, and rob nests of their eggs. They also eat frogs, grasshoppers, locusts, and carrion, and catch small fish.

Gray foxes eat more vegetation than other wild canids. Blueberries are a perennial favorite, and gray foxes can climb into fruiting trees to reach fruits that are beyond the reach of its cousins.

This gray fox scat has been bleached by weather.

Gray fox scat on a toadstool. The scat is darker due to the fox's diet of berries and green vegetation.

MATING HABITS

Gray foxes mate in March in the species' northern range, and in February in the warmer south (it is a rule of thumb that gray foxes mate 1 month after red foxes). Mated foxes are thought to be monogamous, although mating habits have yet to be researched.

Gestation spans 50 days, with up to seven pups born in secluded dens in April or May. Pups suckle for 3 months, during which the father brings food and babysits while his mate leaves the den to drink or relieve herself. He has no role in rearing pups, and doesn't enter the den.

Gray fox pups are precocious, and mature very quickly. Immediately after weaning they begin hunting with their mothers. At 4 months the pups have all of their permanent teeth, weigh about 7 pounds, and strike out to fend for themselves. The parents then resume a solitary lifestyle until the next mating season, when the pups will also be mature enough to breed. Radio telemetry data indicates that grown and separated family members remain within their own territories, and inbreeding is unlikely.

BEHAVIORISMS

Gray foxes are solitary outside of mating season, and a tracker who sees one should count himself lucky. The species is shy and the least vocal of the canids, retiring to secluded forest dens during daylight hours and hunting at night. Many larger predators, including raptors, consider these foxes prey.

But gray foxes are well adapted to their wooded environment. Their light weight permits them to pursue or flee across snow that heavier carnivores cannot, while sharp night vision, keen olfactory senses, and natural camouflage make them effective predators of small prey. The fox's most important advantage, however, is an ability to use its sharp, curved, semiretractible claws to climb trees and escape enemies that it couldn't outrun on the ground. This unique climbing ability also helps explain why gray foxes can run neither fast or far.

Occasionally gray foxes have been labeled as chicken killers, but instances where this rarely seen wild canid has actually been guilty of raiding a henhouse are few. Most often the real culprit is a red fox, if it was a fox at all, and in many instances farmers have simply presumed that the predator must have been a fox, without ever seeing it firsthand. Such erroneous leaps of logic are made all the more believable by adages like "a fox in the henhouse," and "sly as a fox." Meanwhile, skilled chicken and egg thieves, most notably raccoons, often go undetected.

Transplanted from Europe for fox hunting, the red fox has proven to be a sturdy and adaptable part of the North American ecosystem. USFWS

Red Fox *(Vulpes vulpes)*

The red fox was transplanted to North America from Europe so that gentle-born immigrants could continue to enjoy the nobleman's sport of fox hunting with hounds from horseback. The native gray fox, with its extendable claws and an ability to climb trees, was poorly suited to this pastime, so red foxes were imported. Before long the transplanted red foxes, whose adaptability to even the most hostile environments is equaled only by the coyote's, had escaped captivity to become firmly established as part of the American ecosystem.

GEOGRAPHIC RANGE

Although native to Europe and the British Isles, the red fox has thrived in almost every location where it has been transplanted, or simply escaped into, throughout the world. Today red foxes inhabit all of the continental United States, all but the coldest regions of Canada and Alaska, and can be found in Australia, Japan, and across Asia.

HABITAT

Red foxes occupy a wide range of habitats, including deciduous and pine forests, tundra, prairies, farmland, and suburbs. The species is becoming increasingly common wherever there are rats, mice, and other small animals that constitute most of its diet. Preferred habitats also have fruits and berries, especially blueberries, grapes, and cherries. Unlike the reclusive gray fox, red foxes are frequently seen in the open.

PHYSICAL CHARACTERISTICS

Mass: 7 to 15 pounds, largest in the far north.
Body: Slender, elongated body; short legs. Body length is 35 to 40 inches; shoulder height is 15 inches. Erect ears are long and pointed, with black backs. Long, slender muzzle, tipped with a black button nose. Eyes yellow.
Tail: Bushy, rust-colored, 13 to 17 inches long, white-tipped. Black scent gland patch on the dorsal base of the tail.

TRACKS

Larger than the gray fox's, but with smaller toe pads; 2.5 inches long, hind foot slightly smaller and narrower. Feet are heavily furred in snow country. All four plantar pads are two-lobed, leaving a chevron-shaped imprint, with a characteristic V-shaped ridge extending across the heel pad.

SCAT

Cylindrical, segmented, tapered at the ends, 0.5 inch in diameter, 4 inches long. Includes berry seeds and plant fibers when green foods are available. Often with an outer spiral of rodent fur encasing small bones.

COLORATION

Reddish brown on the upper parts, whitish on the underside. Lower legs black. Unlikely to be misidentified except in "cross fox" phases, when the fur is a grizzled mix of rust-colored and

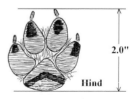

Red fox tracks

black that covers the upper body, head, and tail. The "cross fox" name derives from a black dorsal stripe extending the length of the back, and a perpendicular stripe across the shoulders, forming a T-shape. Also prized by furriers is the silver phase, in which the upper body is silver-gray with a black mask around the eyes, black ears, and dark gray to black legs. Either phase is too common to be a mutation: cross foxes constitute about 25 percent of a population, silver foxes about 10 percent.

Red fox scat

SIGN

Birthing dens excavated in hillsides, usually marked by a fan of soil outside an entryway that measures 12 inches across, and smaller escape tunnels radiating from the den chamber, 10 feet from the main entrance. Food caches are often found near the den.

VOCALIZATIONS

More vocal than the gray fox; calls include yapping and barking reminiscent of a small dog. The alarm call is a single sharp, high-pitched bark, almost like a shriek.

LIFE SPAN

8 to 10 years.

DIET

Rodents, rabbits, an occasional fish, and insects like grasshoppers, June bugs, and moths. When fruits and berries ripen, foxes may forego meat almost entirely. An adult red fox needs to eat at least 10 percent of its body weight daily, and the sugars in fruits are a valued calorie source.

Red foxes eat carrion, but are often forced to relinquish finds to larger carnivores. During deer hunting seasons red foxes have learned to associate gunfire with the nutritious liver, kidneys, and heart that most hunters leave behind.

MATING HABITS

The annual mating season varies by as much as 4 months from one region of North America to another. In the south, mating occurs in December and January; in the central states during January and February; in the north between late February and April. The estrus period of female, or vixen, lasts for 6 days. Ovulation is spontaneous; females signal their readiness through pheromonal excretions several days prior to coming into heat. Males compete for breeding status with usually bloodless fights. Males have an annual cycle of fecundity (fertility) in which they produce viable sperm, and are sterile the rest of the year.

Copulation lasts 15 minutes and is marked by barking and yapping, mostly from the male. Females may mate with more than one male to ensure impregnation, but pair off with only one at the end of breeding season. In a process called delayed implantation, the fertilized egg doesn't attach to the uterine wall for at least 10 days after mating, helping to ensure that only physically fit vixens will bear pups, while those that are not will spontaneously abort fertilized eggs.

Gestation lasts 49 to 56 days, with shorter terms indicating healthier mothers. Between February and May, depending on latitude, females birth litters of kits that typically number five, but may be as many as thirteen. Kits are born blind and weigh 3 ounces. By 14 days their eyes open, and at 5 weeks pups play outside, running back into the den when their mother issues a sharp alarm bark. Kits are weaned by 10 weeks, and the father who has provided food for his mate and regurgitated meat for his offspring leaves to resume a solitary lifestyle. Kits remain with their mother, learning to hunt and forage, until the following autumn. At 10 months pups disperse, and may travel 100 miles before establishing their own territories and taking a mate.

BEHAVIORISMS

Myths about red foxes abound, born of fairy tales about Brer Fox, metaphors about foxes in henhouses, and euphemisms about slyness. There have even been absurd exaggerations about red foxes that run in packs and prey on livestock. All are products of a less enlightened age in which every meat-eater represented a potential threat to a farmer's livelihood.

In fact red foxes are solitary, with a territorial range that depends on how fat the pickings are. Plenty of rodents will help keep a territory small, but the species' omnivorous diet includes berries and fruits as well. Generally territories range from 3 to 9 square miles. Territorial fights are rare but domains are defended, especially by females with kits. Even then, battles are usually just a nip and a chase, with the resident fox having the proverbial home field advantage.

A red fox habitually has several dens throughout its territorial range, interconnected by food caches and regularly patrolled trails. For vixens, one is a maternal den that will be used year after year, so long as it remains undisturbed. The others, all with escape exits, provide sanctuary if a fox is chased by predators that include coyotes, wolves, and bobcats. A healthy fox can run 30 miles per hour through thick terrain that hampers larger carnivores, usually reaching safety before being overtaken.

Red foxes have taken an occasional chicken from farmyards, but predations are limited to small animals, and simply having a dog discourages them. Good fencing and modern materials can reduce predation to zero.

Chapter Thirteen

CATS (FELIDAE)

According to paleontologists, the felids diverged from other mammalian groups nearly 40 million years ago, during the Eocene epoch. The felids became a diverse group of hunters, endowed with keen hearing, vision, sense of smell, and super-sensitive whiskers that detect faint air currents. All are armed with sharp retractable claws on all four toes, and a front dewclaw that can be used like a thumb to grip prey. They rank among the world's stealthiest and most effective hunters, possessing unrivaled agility, lightning reflexes, and daggerlike canine teeth that can kill instantly with a bite to a victim's brain stem. Impressive night vision and binocular eyesight gives them a distinct advantage over prey in the dark—most felids are nocturnal artists of the ambush. While cats will eat carrion during hard times, all prefer to hunt their food.

HOUSE CAT (FELIS SILVESTRIS)

Domestic cats are descended from a wild cat species, *Felis silvestris libyca,* that originated in Africa and southwestern Asia. Earliest records of cats as pets date to 1500 BC, when

Many house cats exhibit the "tabby" coloration of dark stripes or swirls on a paler background.
ECOPRINT/LICENSED BY SHUTTERSTOCK.COM

Egyptians used them to kill rodents that infested granaries. In AD 936, a law was passed in Wales protecting domestic cats—the first record of the animals' presence in Europe—and by the mid-1700s European sailors and settlers had introduced a thriving population of domestic cats to the New World and beyond.

GEOGRAPHIC RANGE
Domestic cats accompany humans throughout the world as pets and as tools to control rodents. One of the domestic species generally capable of survival in the wild, feral cats are also established around the world.

HABITAT
Domestic cats are found wherever there is human settlement. About 45 million cats are kept as pets in the United States, and about 2 million live in Canada. Feral house cats gravitate toward civilization, living in outbuildings, barns, and crawl spaces. The species can survive climates that range from tropical to temperate.

PHYSICAL CHARACTERISTICS
Mass: 4 to more than 10 pounds.
Body: Muscular and extremely powerful for its size; 10 inches at shoulder height; roundish head, short muzzle. Short triangular ears can swivel independently, and can detect ultrasonic frequencies up to 25,000 cycles per second. Females have four pairs of mammae. Eyes are close set at the front of the head, enabling the depth and range perception needed to make accurate strikes; large elliptical pupils provide exceptional night vision. Cats lack eyelashes, but have an inner eyelid, or nictitating membrane, that protects the eyeball. Teeth are specialized, with straight canines in the upper jaw and curved ones in the lower jaw to permit stabbing and holding prey. Molars are specialized for cutting (carnassial), like scissors, but cats lack the jaw strength to crush bones.
Tail: All but two domestic breeds have long tails equivalent to 75 percent of total body length (10 inches). The tail and whiskers are used the way a tightrope walker uses a long pole to amplify his own sense of balance.

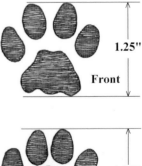

1.25"

Front

TRACKS
Cats have four toes with retractable claws at the front of each forepaw, with another thumblike clawed toe to the inside that provides a solid grip when climbing or holding prey, but does not show in tracks. Rear paws have four toes with retractable claws. Toes are nearly the same size, length, and usually oval-shaped, leaving a track whose overall configuration is nearly round. Hind paws only slightly smaller than front paws. Track lengths from 0.5 inch to 0.75 inch.

1.25"

Hind

Cat tracks

SCAT

Segmented, cylindrical, 1 to 3 inches long, 0.5-inch diameter, often with rodent fur spiraled around small bones. Insect parts, sometimes grasses, are evident on the outer surface.

COLORATION

Varies dramatically. Most house cats are black, gray, yellow, white, or "tabby," with dark stripes or swirls on a paler background. Tortoiseshell or calico markings are a mix of black, white, rust, and yellow seen mostly in females (calico males are rare and nearly always sterile). Eyes normally yellow (cats with blue or mixed eyes are often born deaf).

SIGN

Vertical claw marks on trees, posts (and furniture). Scratching posts deposit territorial scents from interdigital glands in the underside of the cat's paws, and show off their maker's size and armament. Cats urinate on scent posts, leaving an odor of musk and ammonia that cat owners will recognize immediately. Scratch marks in soil surround where a territorial—usually male—cat haphazardly buried feces. Mounded soil with a pungent urine odor is a territorial claim.

VOCALIZATIONS

Purring when content, but also when injured. Mewing for general interaction. Low growls when threatened or frightened. Yowling, likened to the wailing of a child.

LIFE SPAN

10 years or longer.

DIET

Domestic cats have retained the superb hunting skills of wild felids. While pet cats may enjoy a regular diet of processed foods, almost all will snack on fresh kills that include mice, birds, squirrels, and even frogs. Rural house cats take down prey as large as rabbits and muskrats. House cats are maligned for their irrepressible hunting instincts, but a need to hunt is part of a house cat's nature.

Although domestic cats, like their wild brethren, lack the crushing power of the jaws of a wolf or other canid, their unique teeth can scissor through hide and tendon to dismantle the largest prey, and the licking surface of a cat's tongue is covered with hooklike projections (papillae) that can efficiently rasp all meat from bones.

Cats may eat green grass, which is then vomited with indigestible bones and fur, or passed through the digestive system to scrub it free of lodged waste and parasites. A domestic cat's large intestine is comparatively bigger than those of wild felids, enabling it to absorb nutrients from vegetable matter more efficiently than its wild cousins.

MATING HABITS

Domestic cats mate any time of year. Males—toms—are sexually mature at 10 months, and a female cat may bear her first litter as early as 7 months of age. If a female doesn't mate

during her weeklong estrus period, she'll come into heat again within a month, and continues to come into heat until she becomes pregnant.

Male cats detect a female's sexual disposition by pheromonal scents, and when a female
comes into heat she will attract the attention of every unneutered male from more than a
mile away. Their nocturnal, yowling, wailing, and violent competition for a single female is
the stuff of urban legends.

Females have two to four litters of one to six kittens annually. Gestation requires 2
months. Kittens are born blind and deaf, and weigh 4 ounces. Kittens' eyes open after seven
days. Mothers provide good care until kittens are weaned at 8 weeks, then have little more
to do with them.

BEHAVIORISMS

Among felids, only the mighty African lions surpass the house cat as social animals.
Populations of half-feral "barn" cats on farms, ranches, and grain storage operations are
maintained or tolerated to keep rodent populations low, and these animals exist in relative
harmony.

While there is a defined hierarchy among groups, once a pecking order is established
through ritualized fights, the individuals tend to coexist peacefully. Males and females seldom exhibit animosity toward one another, even when meeting for the first time.

The body language of *Felis silvestris* has fascinated human beings since the dawn of their
partnership. A twitching tail, sometimes only the tip, is a clear sign of irritation or anxiety.
By flopping onto its side, relaxed, waving a paw, a cat indicates a desire to play. A stiff-gaited
strut, tail held straight up, is a cat showing dominance, and proving it by dispersing perineal
scents from its anal area. The unhurried, fluid walk of a cat at ease, tail hanging at a comfortable angle, is a portrait of calm.

Sleepy, lazy behavior is the trademark of all felids. A hunter's life is unpredictable, and
conserving calories when not hunting equals survival.

Domestic and wild cats are driven by their hunting instincts—watching a domestic cat
hunt a bird or mouse is to witness an animal in the grip of ecstasy. Such drive helps explain
the global success of the species.

Some naturalists fear that predation by house cats could negatively impact wild species.
Others believe house cats may play a positive role in urban and suburban environments
where the natural predators of rodents and other animals have been eliminated.

Mountain Lion (*Puma concolor*)

Known as cougars, pumas, painters, and catamounts, mountain lions are America's second
largest cat, next to the jaguar of the American Southwest and South America. There have
been a few instances in which a cougar, usually sick, has preyed on humans, but people
are not regarded as food. Most human victims have been small-statured people alone in
rural areas, and engaged in an activity that excites a cougar's hunting instinct the way a
wriggling string compels house cats to attack. To a cougar, a jogger or mountain biker who
is wheezing is an animal in distress, and this has led to tragic encounters—but victims are
rarely eaten.

GEOGRAPHIC RANGE

The cougar's range once spanned from Argentina to Canada, but because the big cats posed a threat to livestock they were trapped, poisoned, and shot on sight until only a few remained in the most remote locations. Today cougars are found in mountainous areas of the American West, with populations in South Carolina, Florida, Georgia, Tennessee, and Michigan's Upper Peninsula.

Not to be confused with native populations, an unknown number of cougars have been transplanted illegally from western states to areas east of the Mississippi River after bans on hunting them were rescinded in the 1990s. Animal rights groups reacted by live-trapping cougars, and by 1994 the cats were being reported in Pennsylvania, Wisconsin, and Michigan's Lower Peninsula—places where they had long been extinct. It was doubtful that the transplanted cats would propagate, but at least some have thrived and multiplied to become established populations.

Mountain lion, puma, catamount, or cougar: Whatever you choose to call it, it is one of the world's most impressive big cats. JOHN AND KAREN HOLLINGSWORTH/USFWS

HABITAT

Cougars are at home in a broad range of habitats, from jungles and northern evergreen swamps to alpine forests and desert mountains. Deep snows, craggy rock, and thick undergrowth are not limiting factors, and this species can thrive in any locale that provides water, cover, and prey.

PHYSICAL CHARACTERISTICS

Mass: 75 to 275 pounds.

Body: Muscular and lithe; length is 60 to 108 inches. Thick, muscular legs, longer in the rear, with powerful hindquarters that lend a jacked-up appearance. The skull is broad, with a short muzzle, a high, arched forehead, and a broad rostrum. Nose pad is large and shaped like a triangle. Ears are short and triangular. Short but powerful mandible, with long, stout, stabbing canines top and bottom; carnassial teeth are very sharp, but molars are not heavy enough for crushing bones.

Tail: Thick; one third of body length (21 to 36 inches long); brown with a black tip

TRACKS

More round than the elongated tracks of canids. Front tracks are 3 to more than 4 inches long; hind tracks 10 percent smaller. Four large toes show in tracks, but retractable claws do not register. Plantar pads of front and hind feet have three lobes, but front pads are blocky, less rounded. Walking stride is 20 inches; straddle is 8 inches.

SCAT

Segmented, cylindrical, tapered at one or both ends, 5 inches long by 1 to 1.5 inches in diameter. Deer hair usually predominant, wrapped spiral fashion around bones encased within.

COLORATION

The pelage is short and coarse, reddish brown in summer, becoming darker gray during in winter. The chest, underbelly, and mouth are white, turning yellowish in older individuals; backs of the ears are black. A dark stripe encircles the muzzle at either side of the pinkish nose. Newborn kittens have blue eyes; eyes of adults are yellow.

SIGN

Tree trunks used as territorial scratching posts; the span and thickness of claw marks are much broader than those of a bobcat or lynx, and higher up, at 3 or more feet. Scats dusted with soil show claw marks pointing in the same direction in which the cat was traveling.

VOCALIZATIONS

Mountain lions purr when content, and mew like house cats. Other voices include catlike hisses, growls, and the trademark snarl. Kittens mew, but have a loud chirping call when frightened.

LIFE SPAN

10 years in the wild; up to 20 years in captivity.

DIET

Pumas prefer to kill their own food rather than eat carrion. Superbly equipped in terms of stealth, speed, and weapons, a cougar can take down prey larger than itself, usually

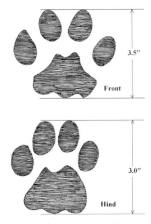

Cougar tracks—an unforgettable sight for the tracker.

Cougar track in soft sand

Cougar scat

by leaping onto the back of the prey and killing it with a bite to the brain stem. Smaller animals may make up the bulk of a cat's diet, though, because no predator willingly risks its own safety to obtain a meal. Annual food consumption for a single adult cat is 600 to 900 pounds.

MATING HABITS

Cougars are normally solitary, but when they breed it's a polygamous relationship, with both partners taking more than one mate. Both genders are capable of breeding at 30 months, but males must establish their own territories before mating, usually at about 3 years. Males remain sexually fertile for up to 20 years; females to 12 years. Mating is preceded by a courtship, but there is no fixed mating season, and the fact that most breeding occurs between December and March is determined by latitude. Males reply to pheromonal scents and yowling from females, which is an eerie caterwauling that has been likened to the wailing of a child.

Females mate every other year, devoting themselves to teaching offspring the skills of survival for the first full year of their lives. The estrus period spans 9 days, and if a female hasn't been impregnated in that time, she will undergo another 9-day cycle, usually within a month.

Males vying for the same female are relatively nonviolent, employing body language, yowling, and posturing to determine which suitor is the strongest. If males do fight, the contest is largely one of physical strength, and claws and canines are seldom used to draw blood.

Gestation is 82 to 96 days; mothers birth one to six cubs, weighing about 2 pounds each, in a secluded den within the father's territory. Kittens are blind and helpless for their first 10 days, and the father brings food to their mother, but takes no part in rearing offspring. At 40 days cubs are weaned and ready to accompany the mother on short hunting forays.

BEHAVIORISMS

A cougar's solitary, nomadic lifestyle is interrupted only by breeding and rearing young. Territorial ranges vary from about 9 miles to more than 60, depending on the availability of food and water. Territories may be in different locations in summer and winter, because the cats follow deer as they migrate from summer grazing to winter browsing areas. Both sexes mark their territories with urine sprayed onto trees and scats deposited at trail intersections.

Cougars are primarily nocturnal, with excellent night and binocular vision. Their main sense is that of sight, followed by smell, then hearing. Although able to pursue prey for short distances at speeds in excess of 35 mph, the cats are ambush hunters, leaping onto prey from hiding, and using stout claws to hang onto the animal while driving its canines into the prey's neck.

Cougars have been a threat to domestic animals and livestock, but tend to avoid human populations. There have been rare instances in which humans in cougar habitat have been attacked, nearly always while engaged in physical activities—like jogging or mountain biking—that caused them to pant, wheeze, and otherwise behave like an animal in distress, and therefore like easy prey.

Jaguar (*Panthera onca*)

Considered a forest god by pre-Columbian tribes in Mexico and South America, the jaguar's name means "kills in a single bound." There are eight subspecies, all of them threatened, and some are extinct except in zoos. The greatest threats to this largest American cat comes from the illegal fur trade and the clearing of virgin rain forest. Little research has been done on these disappearing felids; most of what is known has been learned from zoo captives.

GEOGRAPHIC RANGE

Native to warmer regions in the Americas to as far south as Patagonia, jaguars once ranged north into southern Texas, but are now rare, possibly extinct, in the United States. In February 2009 the only known wild jaguar in the United States was euthanized by wildlife authorities after suffering kidney failure as a result of old age.

HABITAT

Ideal jaguar habitat provides large prey, open water, and forest cover. Dense jungle and swamps are preferred, but historically jaguars have lived in scrub forest and rocky deserts.

Stealthy ambush hunter of the tropics and subtropics, the jaguar is at home on or in the water. RON SINGER/USFWS

PHYSICAL CHARACTERISTICS

Mass: Males weigh 120 to 300 pounds; females weigh 100 to 200 pounds.

Body: Very heavily muscled, with stout legs and a massive head. Body length is 4 feet; shoulder height is 2.5 to 3 feet.

Tail: Spotted with a black tip; 18 to 30 inches. The tail is proportionately shorter and thinner than a cougar's, probably because jaguars are less apt to pounce on prey from above and require a less acute sense of balance.

TRACKS

Forefeet measure 4 to 4.5 inches, nearly as wide as they are long, with widely-splayed toes that leave an almost circular paw print. Hind prints are slightly smaller, with toes closer together and pointing forward. Toes are smaller and plantar pads larger than a cougar's. Heel pads are all three-lobed, but the two outermost lobes in the front tracks are larger than the center lobe, whereas the three lobes in a cougar's foreprint are almost equally sized. Walking stride is 20 inches, depending on terrain; straddle is 8 to 10 inches.

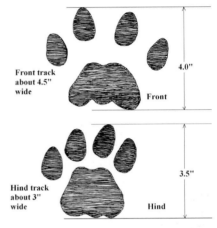

Front track about 4.5" wide

4.0"

Front

Hind track about 3" wide

3.5"

Hind

Jaguar tracks

SCAT

Cylindrical, segmented, tapered at one or both ends, 5 inches long by 1.5 inches in diameter. Positive identification is aided by the jaguar's tendency to prey on aquatic animals, including alligators, fish, and aquatic mammals.

COLORATION

Jaguars are yellowish with a mottling of black rings, many of which have a single black "bull's-eye" dot at their centers. Cheeks, throat, underbelly, and the insides of the legs are white. A few jaguars are black, with fur nearly as black as the spots it camouflages.

SIGN

Scat deposits at trail intersections; trees that have been clawed and marked with musky urine as territorial boundaries. Large cat tracks that enter and exit the water—a trait that is rare among felids.

VOCALIZATIONS

Jaguars are the only American wild cats that roar. The sound is a series of loud coughs rather than a single unbroken roar.

LIFE SPAN

Up to 22 years in captivity; life span in the wild is unknown, but probably 12 to 15 years.

DIET

Jaguars feed on terrestrial prey including deer, peccaries, and alpacas. The only wild felids that regularly hunt in water, they also prey on nutria, large fish, and alligators or caimans up to 5 feet in length. Like African lions, jaguars are powerfully built, and poor climbers that are more at home on the ground or in the water. Likewise, they are not pursuit predators, being built to overpower prey too strong for other carnivores to tackle.

MATING HABITS

Jaguars are sexually mature at 3 years. Those in tropical regions may breed any time, while those in colder latitudes usually mate in December or January. Females are believed to accept a single mate per breeding season.

Gestation is 93 to 110 days. Prior to giving birth the mother and her mate establish a secluded den in a cave or beneath the roots of a large tree. Jaguars are poor diggers, so dens are naturally occurring or appropriated from other animals.

Litter sizes are one to four cubs, born blind but furred, and weighing 1.5 to 2 pounds. Mothers remain with cubs almost constantly until they're weaned at 40 days, leaving only to drink or relieve herself while her mate guards the den. The father jaguar brings her food and protects his offspring, but does not enter the den.

Cubs can travel with their mothers at 2 months, when the father leaves to resume a solitary lifestyle. Cubs are skilled predators of small animals at 6

This jaguar kitten already displays the unique coloration of the species.

months. Males remain with their mother for the next year; female cubs may stay with the mother for 2 years.

BEHAVIORISMS

Jaguars are solitary except during the mating period. They are known to live within a territory as small as 9 square miles, but may travel 200 miles when prey becomes scarce. Jaguars are fast sprinters, but only for short distances. They can climb trees, but usually hunt on the ground or in the water.

Jaguars have killed domestic animals for food, but predation is usually the result of people moving into areas already occupied by the cats. Jaguars are reputed to be man-eaters, but Amazon tribes have coexisted with them for millennia, and the real danger seems to have been exaggerated. Amazonian Indians tell of jaguars coming from the forest to play with village children, and Mayans believed that the jaguar caused the sun to rise and set. Tales of humans being shadowed by lone jaguars are probably attributable to the cats' profound sense of curiosity.

Bobcat *(Lynx rufus)*

The most common wild felid in the United States, this adaptable cat occupies a broad range of habitats. Having been hunted, trapped, or poisoned to extinction in many places, bobcats are shy and are rarely seen anywhere. That shyness may be diminishing as development continues to bring humans into bobcat habitats.

GEOGRAPHIC RANGE

Bobcats occupy North America from southern Mexico to southern Canada. Populations are highest in forested regions. The species is rare or absent in the agricultural regions of southern Michigan, Illinois, Indiana, Ohio, and Pennsylvania.

The most common wild felid in the United States, bobcats are secretive and seldom observed. GARY KRAMER/USFWS

HABITAT

Bobcats can live in a variety of habitats, including dense forests, wet swamps, semiarid deserts, alpine mountains, and brushlands. These ambush hunters like lots of concealment, with trees large enough to climb. The species seems well adapted to snow, but isn't found in most of Canada.

PHYSICAL CHARACTERISTICS

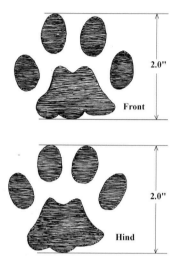

Mass: 14 to more than 68 pounds.

Body: Stout and well muscled, but built for agility; 28 to 50 inches long; shoulder height is 15 to 20 inches. Cheeks and ear tips are tufted, though not so heavily as in a lynx.

Tail: Short, black-tipped, 3 to 6 inches long. Rust with irregular black markings on top, whitish below.

TRACKS

Prints are 1 to 3.5 inches long, with four toes on each foot, no claws showing. Front and hind feet are the same size. Stride is 10 to 14 inches, straddle is 6 to 7 inches. Track patterns notable because hind prints register precisely inside front tracks at a casual walk, leaving a track pattern that appears to be two-legged. Front of heel pad, toward toes, is concave, and unlike any of the canids.

Bobcat tracks

Bobcat tracks in dry sand. They are too large to be confused with those of a house cat.

SCAT

Cylindrical, segmented, tapered at one or both ends. Length is 2 to 6 inches; diameter is 0.5 to 1 inch; rodent, rabbit, and occasionally deer fur are wrapped spiral fashion around the outside. Scats are easily confused with those of a lynx or coyote, except that canids

Bobcat scat is usually covered, with scratch marks all around it.

don't attempt to cover their scat with soil. Bobcats scratch soil over their scat from all directions, leaving sets of scratch marks all around the scat.

COLORATION

Variable and changes with the seasons. The summer coat is brown spots against a lighter coat of reddish brown. Winter coats tends to be darker, ranging from dark brown to gray. Insides of the legs, underbelly, and throat are whitish with brown spots.

SIGN

Scratches in tree trunks, about 2 feet high, often scented with pungent urine. Soft pines are often scratched, maybe because the sticky, scented sap masks the bobcat's own scent.

VOCALIZATIONS

Much like a domestic cat: mewing, purring, low growls, and childlike wailing during the breeding season.

LIFE SPAN

8 to 10 years.

DIET

Small rodents to rabbits to an occasional small deer; rarely eats carrion, preferring to kill its own food. Bobcats have an uncanny ability to sneak within striking distance of prey: Blue jays, grouse, turkeys, and waterfowl are often caught before they can take wing. Small deer may be taken by large bobcats perched on an overhead tree branch; when the deer passes below, the cat pounces onto its back, anchors itself with sharp retractable claws, and drives its sharply pointed canines into the base of its victim's skull, piercing the brain stem or the spinal cord.

Although "strictly" carnivorous, bobcats supplement their diets with fruits and vegetables. Blueberries and other sugary fruits help to put on fat against the cold of an approaching winter, as well as provide nutrients not found in flesh. Grasses are also eaten because their coarse fibers help dislodge hair balls, and help to clear the colon of undigested waste.

MATING HABITS

Bobcats in the northern range mate in February or March; those in the south mate throughout the summer; and in subtropical areas females may produce two litters per year. Breeding season is initiated by female pheromones, which may attract several suitors. Males compete with caterwauling, growls, and an occasional mostly bloodless scuffle. Mated pairs set off to find a birthing den in a rock crevice, under the roots of a tree, or in an appropriated fox or coyote den. Bobcats are not designed for excavating, so dens are existing shelters.

After a gestation period of 65 days, two or three blind kittens, weighing 8 ounces apiece, are born in April or May. After 10 days, they open their eyes and move about the den, nursing often.

The mother stays with her kittens constantly for their first 2 months, leaving only to drink and to relieve herself. The kittens' father doesn't enter the den, but brings the mother food and watches over kittens. Kittens are weaned in June or July, and the father leaves, taking no role in rearing his offspring.

BEHAVIORISMS

Bobcats are solitary except to mate, and during summer when mothers are training young. Females live discreetly, especially if they have kittens, but males advertise their claim to a domain of several square miles. Partly buried scats at trail intersections delineate boundaries, while pungent urine sprayed on tree trunks that may also be clawed warn intruders that they are trespassing.

The home range of a male bobcat overlaps the smaller ranges of nearby females. Occasionally the territories of two males—usually brothers—overlap, but this seldom causes conflict except during mating. Bobcats don't live in dens, but have several burrows throughout their ranges for escaping foul weather, or for eluding larger predators.

Some sport hunters have claimed that one or more bobcats attacked them, but none of the accusers has been so much as scratched by this cat, which could easily ambush a human. In nearly all of these alleged instances the bobcat was killed, sometimes along with kittens.

Lynx (Lynx canadensis)

This smaller cousin to the bobcat is one of the most reclusive species in North America. This cat is supremely adapted to life in dense forests and deep snows. Its thick, silky pelt presents considerable cash value to fur buyers since importation of exotic cat furs was restricted in the latter part of the twentieth century. Current low demand for furs, and the lynx's own reclusive nature, have protected it from over-harvesting.

GEOGRAPHIC RANGE

Never abundant anywhere, the largest populations of lynx exist in Canada and in northern Montana and Idaho, with smaller (or less studied) populations in New England, northern

Silent and solitary stalker of northern and high elevation forests, the lynx is a rare and thrilling sight for any wilderness traveler. ERWIN AND PEGGY BAUER/USFWS

Minnesota and Wisconsin, and Michigan's Upper Peninsula. An aversion to humans and a shrinking habitat make it unlikely that lynx will ever be common.

HABITAT

Lynx are occasionally seen on tundra or rock formations in the far north, but never far from old-growth forests and thick swamps. Superbly adapted to deep snow, lynx are very difficult to approach, and a tracker who sees one in the wild can consider himself blessed.

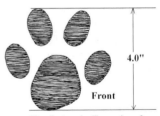

4.0"

Front

Like all cats, and unlike members of the Canine Family, claws are normally retracted, and don't show in tracks.

PHYSICAL CHARACTERISTICS

Mass: 11 to 40 pounds.
Body: Long legs; body is 29 to 41 inches long, shoulder height is 15 to 20 inches. Males are 10 percent larger than females. Pointed ears are tipped with long tufts of fur; cheeks are heavily tufted, giving the appearance of sideburns.
Tail: Shorter than a bobcat's; 2 to 5 inches long.

TRACKS

Four toes on each foot; no claws show in tracks. Paws are very large and well furred to provide flotation in

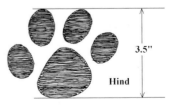

3.5"

Hind

Lynx tracks

deep snow. Heavy fur causes paw prints to appear overly large. Front tracks 3 to 4.5 inches long; hind prints 10 percent smaller. Front and hind paws have three lobes at rear of plantar pads, but the two outermost lobes of the front paws are larger, leaving a chevron-shaped impression unlike the three equal-size lobes of a bobcat. Stride is 14 to 16 inches; straddle is 5 to 7 inches.

SCAT

Cylindrical, segmented, tapered at one or both ends. Length 2 to 6 inches; diameter 0.5 to 1 inch. Scats are partially buried with soil or snow, and have a spiral casing of fine hair or rabbit fur wrapped over a core of prey bones.

Lynx scat

COLORATION

Varies somewhat with individuals, but the usual pelage is yellow-brown in summer, becoming grayish in winter. Some coats have dark spots, but generally lack the spotted appearance of a bobcat. Ear tufts and tip of the tail are black; the throat, underbelly, and the insides of the legs are whitish. Eyes are yellow with slit pupils.

SIGN

Smooth-barked trees that have been clawed and sprayed with urine. Partially covered scats at trail intersections. Large prey that cannot be eaten entirely will be camouflaged with forest debris or snow.

VOCALIZATIONS

Normally silent except at mating season, when males especially shriek or scream with an echoing wail that some have described as like the wailing of a woman.

LIFE SPAN

Probably 8 to 10 years in the wild.

DIET

Lynx are more carnivorous than most felids, although they too eat grasses to help clear their digestive tracts of hair balls and indigestible matter. As proficient a hunter as its larger cousin, the bobcat, the lynx can subsist on rodents, fish, and even small or sickly deer, but this cat's survival is linked to snowshoe hare populations. When hare populations decrease, as they do about every 9.5 years, lynx populations fall prey to starvation one year later.

Lynx do eat carrion, but only fresh carcasses. Deer wounded by hunters are favored, but road-killed animals are usually too close to humans.

MATING HABITS

Lynx come into heat in March and April, so females rear only one litter per year. Receptive females have several suitors that serenade them with caterwauling and an occasional fight marked by hissing, spitting, and growling, but not much bloodshed.

Females experience an estrus period of just 1 to 2 days, and are believed to accept only one mate. After mating, the pair establishes a birthing den in a secluded hollow log or rock crevice. After a gestation of 9 weeks, mothers birth two to five blind kittens, each weighing about 7 ounces, in May or June. Larger litters are the products of healthier and more well-fed mothers.

Except to drink, urinate, or defecate, mothers remain with kittens constantly for their first month, while the father brings food and guards against enemies. After 1 month kittens begin eating meat, but continue nursing for 5 months, and are weaned in October or November.

Weaned kittens are grown enough to learn to hunt, and the father lynx leaves them. Kittens remain with the mother until January or February before setting off on their own, with males usually leaving first. Mothers come into heat again about one month later. Female kittens reach sexual maturity at 21 months old, males at 33 months.

BEHAVIORISMS

Lynx are solitary, and adults avoid one another except for mating. Territories of females may overlap, and a resident male's range typically infringes on the territories of several females. Ranges encompass 7 to 200 square miles, depending on availability of food and resources.

Lynx are primarily nocturnal, with superb night vision and sonarlike hearing. They lie in ambush along a game trail, usually waiting overhead and often for many hours, then pounce onto prey from its blind rear. Long, piercing canines penetrate the base of a victim's skull, piercing the brain stem or spinal cord. Alternately, long-legged lynx may stalk to close range, then charge at speeds of 35 mph, even over rugged terrain, and sometimes kill by locking their jaws over a prey's windpipe, strangling it to death.

One unusual behaviorism is that lynx mothers sometimes hunt cooperatively, moving as a scouting unit through overgrown areas until one of them jumps a hare from hiding. The cat that catches the prey keeps it. This behavior appears to be more learned than instinctual, but it is a facet of the training that many kittens receive from their mothers.

Like bobcats, lynx shelter from foul weather and enemies under rock ledges, in caves, in hollow logs, or in appropriated dens, and there are typically several of these refuges throughout a lynx's territory.

Chapter Fourteen

WEASELS (MUSTELIDAE)

The weasel family is diverse, including skunks, wolverines, badgers, otters, and ermine. All weasels have five toes on all feet, each tipped with sharp claws on each paw; short, powerful legs; and perineal (anal) glands that emit musky skunklike odors. All are carnivorous (some are omnivorous), but none are fast runners. Some, like the badger and skunk, are amazing diggers who cannot climb trees, while the fisher and pine marten bound through treetops after squirrels, sea and river otters swim after fish, and the ferocious wolverine intimidates more capable hunters into surrendering their kills.

Sea otters are found all along the Pacific Coast of the United States from Alaska to Baja, Mexico. USFWS

Sea Otter (Enhydra lutris)
Earth's largest weasel, this Pacific Coast native plays an important role in controlling herbivorous sea urchins. Sea urchins eat kelp, and where otters are absent, they overpopulate and deplete an area's kelp forests. Where sea otters are present, urchins and benthic (sea bottom) feeders are controlled, and kelp forests are healthy.

Sea otter pelts were marketed from the 1700s to 1911, when populations had been depleted to less than two thousand animals and the International Fur Seal Treaty was agreed to by the United States, Russia, Japan, and Great Britain. The United States' Marine Mammal Protection Act of 1972 further reinforced that treaty. Population estimates made between 2004 and 2007 give a worldwide total of approximately 107,000 sea otters.

The California sea otter *(Enhydra lutris nereis)* population is estimated at 2,200, and will be listed as threatened under the Endangered Species Act until a population of 2,650 is recorded for 3 consecutive years. It is feared that another oil spill like the 1989 Exxon Valdez disaster, which killed five thousand sea otters, could make California sea otters extinct.

GEOGRAPHIC RANGE
Distribution once included Japan's Hokkaido Island, the Kuril Islands, the eastern coast of Kamchatka, the Commander Islands, the Aleutian archipelago, and the Pacific Coast of America from Alaska to Baja, Mexico. Natural boundaries include sea ice that limits the sea otter's range to 57 degrees north latitude, while availability of kelp keeps sea otters north of 22 degrees north latitude.

There are three subspecies *Enhydra lutris: Enhydra lutris lutris* is found along the Kuril and Commander Islands in the western Pacific; *E. lutris nereis* occupies the central California coast; and *E. lutris kenyoni* inhabits the Aleutian Islands and southern Alaska, and has been reintroduced to several locations from Oregon to Alaska's Prince William Sound.

HABITAT
Pacific Ocean kelp forests where sea urchins are abundant. Temperate waters with rocky or sedimentary bottoms less than 1 mile from shore are preferred; waters whose surfaces freeze are avoided in winter.

PHYSICAL CHARACTERISTICS
Mass: 25 to 80 pounds.
Body: Long and streamlined, similar to the smaller river otter. Body length is 30 to 71 inches. Hind legs are longer than front. Small rounded ears, blunt muzzle, long whiskers at either side of a broad nose pad. Males slightly larger. Females have two mammae. Sea otters are the only carnivorous mammals with just four lower incisor teeth.
Tail: Thick, heavily furred, 10 to 14 inches long.

TRACKS
Rare, because sea otters are in the water constantly. Five toes on all four feet; nonretractable claws on hind feet, retractable claws on forefeet. Hind feet elongated and webbed, leaving fan-shaped prints 5 to 6 inches long. Forepaws roundish, leaving circular tracks 3 inches long, often showing only four outermost toes.

Front

Hind

2.5"

6.0"

Sea otter tracks

SCAT

Cylindrical, like a cigar stub; 2 to 4 inches long and 1 inch across; with shards of crustacean and mollusk shells, fish scales, and bones. May be confused with the smaller regurgitations of sea birds.

COLORATION

Reddish to dark brown torso with yellowish head and neck that grays with age. Long whiskers; broad, black, triangular nose pad. Sea otter fur is the thickest on earth, with 250,000 hairs per square inch, because sea otters do not carry a layer of insulating fat like seals; this makes oil spills especially lethal to them because petroleum mats sea otter fur, stealing its insulative properties and exposing the animals to hypothermia.

SIGN

Sea otters seldom leave water, so little sign is left by them on shore, and the few scats or tracks they do leave are quickly erased by the elements.

VOCALIZATIONS

Most commonly heard among groups of foraging otters is a soft grunting that is repeated four or five times per call. Also heard is a clacking noise made when sea otters use a stone from the ocean floor to hammer mollusk shells until they break; this clacking can sometimes be heard for several hundred yards.

LIFE SPAN

Up to 23 years.

DIET

Sea otters live by hunting creatures in an ocean environment, and will eat most marine animals found in their kelp forest foraging grounds. The diet consists mainly of marine invertebrates and filter feeders like mussels, sea urchins, snails, and abalone, but sea otters will also eat crabs, octopus, squid, sea stars, and fish. Individuals may specialize in their choice of prey, with one otter preferring urchins or crustaceans, while another is partial to fish or mollusks. An otter must eat 25 percent of its body weight each day.

Sea otters are unique in their ability to use stones retrieved from the sea bottom as hammers to open mussels and shelled food animals. Floating on its back, an otter places a clam or crab on its belly. With its stone hammer clutched between its front paws, it then pounds the shell until it breaks. Stone hammers of the right size and shape are selected, and the same stone may be used many times. Otters also use an unusual method to crack a shell that is too large to be hammer-broken; the otter holds the shell tightly to its chest, then propels itself forward in the water to smash it against large rocks. Once a shell is broken, the otter rolls in the water, causing shards to fall away, then returns to a belly-up position to dine.

Most of the drinking water a sea otter needs is obtained from flesh, but the species also has a unique ability to drink sea water with no ill effect.

MATING HABITS

Female sea otters become fertile at 4 years; males at 5 to 6 years. Sea otters can breed any time, but delayed implantation causes fertilized eggs to be carried within the female until weather, food availability, and other conditions are right for pregnancy. Thus, gestation periods vary, ranging from 4 months under optimal conditions to 12 months if environmental conditions are poor. Births tend to peak in frequency in May and June among Aleutian Island populations, and from January through March in the California herds.

The estrus cycle for females lasts 72 hours, although females not impregnated during that period come into heat again soon after. Males breed with any adult females within their claimed territories, and try to steal mates from the territories of others. Battles between males are mostly splashing and body language, with little real fighting.

Mates remain together until the estrus period passes, copulating in the water, where the male grips his mate's nose in his jaws while holding her body with strong forelimbs. The breeding ritual is more violent than mating battles, and females that have mated can often be identified by scars on their noses and heads.

Females generally birth a single pup once per year; birthing happens in the water. Mothers that lose a pup come into estrus again within a few months. Twins are born about 2 percent of the time, but some biologists assert that mothers are able to rear only one pup at a time. Pups are born fully furred, with teeth, with eyes open, and weighing 2 to 4 pounds. Pups nurse while lying on their mother's belly as she floats on her back; when she dives for food, youngsters float until she resurfaces. If an orca, shark, or eagle threatens, the mother wraps her forelimbs around her pup and dives to the safety of kelp forest. Pups eat solid food within a month, and by 2 months begin foraging underwater. Weaning occurs at 5 months, but this varies according to the strength of individual pups.

BEHAVIORISMS

Sea otters claim territories, but live, feed, and breed in social groups. The social structure is herdlike, with males congregating and females remaining apart except when mating. Both genders spend their entire lives in water, but may come ashore when populations enable them to enjoy safety in numbers.

Sea otters swim using webbed hind feet for propulsion, adding thrust from undulations of their tails and bodies, with forelimbs tightly tucked against their chests. This technique is most efficient for the otter's streamlined body, enabling adults to swim at 6 miles per hour underwater.

Sea otters are active during daylight hours, with peaks in activity at dusk and dawn. They forage underwater for 50 to 90 seconds, but may remain submerged for more than 5 minutes. Foraging may require little more than half of an otter's day, depending on abundance of food.

Sea otter eyes are located in the front of the skull to provide binocular vision and good depth perception, and they see well underwater. Urchins and mussels are detached from their moorings with the otters' sensitive paws, and eaten on the surface.

Male sea otters steal food from smaller females, so females tend to forage apart from males, resting together while floating on their backs, combing their fur with their claws.

Sea otters rest and eat while floating on their backs, anchoring themselves in place by wrapping themselves with kelp, and sometimes with forepaws held over their eyes to block out sunlight.

Despite a moratorium on harvesting otter fur, as of 2010 populations were listed as stable or declining. A reduction in seals, the orca's *(Orcinus orca)* staple prey, may have increased the orca's predation on sea otters, and it is suspected that the great white shark *(Carcharodon carcharias)* and the sea lion *(Zalophus californianus)* might be responsible, too. Rebounding populations of bald eagles *(Haliaeetus leucocephalus)* also prey on young otters.

River Otter *(Lontra canadensis)*

River otters are a smaller, freshwater version of the sea otter, equally adapted to an aquatic life, but evolved to inhabit rivers, lakes, and streams, and better suited to cold environments.

River otters are rarely more than a few hundred yards from water. Their presence is a good indication that a river is clean.

GEOGRAPHIC RANGE

The American river otter ranges from Alaska across northern Canada to Nova Scotia, south to California, and down to rivers in Arizona. River otters were trapped nearly to extinction before laws were enacted to protect them in the twentieth century. Today the river otter is a success story of good wildlife management.

HABITAT

Rivers, beaver ponds, and lakes. Otters are rarely more than a few hundred yards from water unless migrating to a new territory. The species can withstand extremes of heat and cold, so long as a habitat provides a year-round supply of fresh water. River otter populations are an indicator that waters are clean, because the species isn't tolerant of pesticides, herbicides, or other chemical pollutants.

PHYSICAL CHARACTERISTICS

Mass: 11 to 30 pounds.

Body: Elongated and streamlined; body length is 35 to 51 inches. Legs short with webbed paws; wide, rounded head with short muzzle and small round ears. Nostrils can be closed voluntarily for diving. Long silvery whiskers droop from either side of the muzzle.

Tail: 8 to 12 inches long; well furred; thick at the base and tapering to a point. Used for propulsion and steering when swimming, enabling an otter to make abrupt changes in direction when pursuing aquatic prey.

TRACKS

Five widely splayed toes on all feet; toes bulbous, making almost round impressions ahead of plantar pads. Short, nonretractable claws register as points ahead of each toe. Front tracks are 3 to 3.5 inches long and nearly as wide as they are long; hind tracks are 10 percent smaller. Four lobes point forward on the heel pad of each paw, but usually just three register in hind tracks; a fifth lobe,

River otter tracks in soft sand.

separate and behind the others on the forefeet, may register as a round impression on soft surfaces. Hind toes are elongated and webbed; webbing may show in mud.

SCAT

Sometimes cylindrical, 2 to 6 inches long by about 0.5 inch in diameter. Often a shapeless mass of fish scales, fish bones, and crayfish shells. Always found along shorelines.

Aggregation of river otter scat.

COLORATION

Dark brown on top; belly, cheeks, and throat lighter brown to blonde.

SIGN

Opened mollusk shells and crayfish carapaces. Twisted tufts of grasses scented with a musky scent from the otter's perineal glands.

VOCALIZATIONS

Grumbling chuckles, loud whistles, growls, grunts, and screeches.

LIFE SPAN

8 to 10 years.

DIET

River otters are fast-pursuit swimmers that can remain underwater for about 8 minutes, catching frogs, clams, crayfish, panfish, suckers, or bullheads. Unattended beaver pups are taken, but adult beavers are much too large. In winter, hibernating frogs or small turtles are brought up onto the ice, where the heads and limbs are eaten. Whiskers are dragged along river or lake bottoms when hunting buried prey, and appear to be an acute sensory tool. Prey is brought to the surface to be eaten. On ice, otters are never far from an escape hole, because numerous other predators try to steal their catches.

MATING HABITS

Males 3 years or older seek out females 2 years or older for mating in March and April. Mating is initiated by scents that females deposit onto the same twisted grasses that males create as territorial claims. Mated partners remain together within the male's territory.

After an 11-month gestation—the result of delayed implantation—up to five pups are born in an excavated den in a riverbank. Den entrances are underwater, with an escape exit higher up on the bank. Mates remain together through the winter. Mothers give birth in February or March in leaf-and-grass-lined dens, and are provided for by their mates until pups are 3 months old. Males may not contact pups until they are weaned. Pups are weaned between May and July, depending on latitude. Fathers may remain after weaning, but pairs separate before summer's end. Pups can survive on their own by winter, and leave their mothers. Pups that don't leave voluntarily are driven off before mothers mate again the following spring.

BEHAVIORISMS

River otters are a solitary species, but families might stay together throughout summer and most of the winter, and there is seldom much territorial animosity between parents and adult offspring. Territories of males, especially, may exceed 60 miles of riparian habitat, but are typically 5 miles in length.

Otters seem playful, but they are such efficient hunters that they have time and energy to spare. Only half of an otter's day is committed to finding food, leaving the remainder open for swimming, diving, and frolicking that serve to hone hunting and survival skills.

One of the river otter's most recognized activities is its penchant for sliding on its belly. This is most notable along stream banks, where the practice creates troughs leading from shore to water in soil or snow. Sliding seems to be done mainly just for fun, but it can also serve as a quick escape; if a predator threatens, the otter can zip away, legs trailing under and behind its body. Slides are usually trough-shaped, but I found one that was actually a tunnel running under deep snow for approximately 10 feet before exiting at the waterline.

Fisher *(Martes pennanti)*

The fisher has always been a difficult subject, because the species is not numerous and individuals tend not to show themselves. More data needs to be established through field research before humans can really know the fisher, so the information presented here is limited to what modern science does know of *Martes pennanti.*

During months of snow most fishers are found near swamps and especially in white pine forests.
VISCERALIMAGE/LICENSED BY SHUTTERSTOCK.COM

Although only half as large as a river otter, it's obvious that the fisher shares a common ancestor with its aquatic cousin. Both species have elongated streamlined bodies, short legs, five-toed paws, and other physical characteristics shared by most members of the weasel family, and both are almost exclusively carnivorous.

Beyond those common physical traits, however, otters and fishers are distinctly different, because the fisher has adapted to make its living among the lofty branches of a mature forest canopy. In an arboreal environment, the same long muscular body that makes the otter such an excellent swimmer allows a fisher to demonstrate impressive agility when pursuing prey through the treetops. That the otter and fisher could be so physically similar, yet so different in habitat, is indicative of how well the weasel design can adapt to diverse environments.

GEOGRAPHIC RANGE

Fishers are native only to North America, and they can be found only in the most remote and vast of forests. The species ranges across the southern half of Canada, from Nova Scotia on the Atlantic coast to British Columbia on the Pacific coast, and north to southernmost tip of Alaska.

To the south, fishers can be found in New England, across Michigan's Upper Peninsula to the heavily forested northernmost tip of its Lower Peninsula, in the Sierra Nevada of California and in the Appalachians of West Virginia. The species is not found in prairie regions, or in most states south of the United States–Canada border. Populations have been in decline in the southern parts of the fisher's historical range in recent decades, mostly due to deforestation of its native habitat.

HABITAT

Fishers live only in large tracts of mature forest. The habitat may be hardwood or coniferous in the warmer months, but during months of snow most fishers are found near swamps and especially in white pines, where their staple winter prey, the porcupine *(Erethizon dorsatum)*, migrates to feed through the winter on buds and tender bark.

Fishers are designed to hunt in the treetops, and while an experienced individual might take an occasional hare or rabbit on the ground, their surefootedness and superb climbing ability make them efficient predators of squirrels, small birds and eggs, porcupines, and an occasional small raccoon.

Fishers often take to a den to wait out storms and blizzards, and their ideal habitat offers lots of hollow logs, where large fallen trees with less tough cores have rotted away to form a tunnel. Above-ground dens that once belonged to porcupines, found in large standing hollow trees, may be used as well.

PHYSICAL CHARACTERISTICS

Mass: Up to 18 pounds.

Body: Elongated and muscular, with short legs, a long bushy tail, a pointed snout that isn't so blunt as the otter's, and short rounded ears. The fisher might easily be mistaken for a tree squirrel as it bounds through the treetops, except that its body length of 31 to 41 inches is three or four times that of a large squirrel. Male fishers average roughly 10 percent larger than females.

Tail: Bushy, long, squirrel-like; 11 to 17 inches long. Functional for maintaining balance in the treetops, much the same as a squirrel.

TRACKS

Fishers have the weasels' trademark five toes on all four of their feet, but unlike most of their cousins, the fisher's sharply hooked claws are semiretractible, able to voluntarily extend into grappling hooks for treetop pursuits. Tracks are usually 2 inches or less in length, and typically wider than they are long, with widths between 2 and 2.5 inches. Front paws slightly larger than hind. The heel pads of both front and hind feet leave an irregular but roughly crescent-shaped impression that is also a trademark among long-bodied members of family Mustelidae.

Fisher tracks are usually 2 inches or less in length and wider than they are long.

SCAT

Cylindrical, tapered at one or both ends, 1 to 3 inches long, about 0.5 inch wide. Often with squirrel and rodent fur wrapped cylindrically around indigestible fragments of bone and, in spring, bird eggshell. Most notable in fisher scat is the species' penchant for making porcupines a regular part of their winter diet. This fact is made obvious by the number of mostly intact porcupine quills that are evident throughout the big weasel's winter scats. The fisher's digestive system can pass these sharp, barbed spears without suffering damage, and although a very hungry coyote or bobcat might take an occasional porcupine, only fishers are noted for making a habit of the practice.

COLORATION

The fisher's pelage ranges from medium to dark brown, with grizzled head and shoulders. Legs and tail are usually darker, often black. Some have a minklike whitish spot on their chests. Fur color and patterns may vary with the individual, the season (darker fur is more common in the winter coat), and possibly the sex or age of an individual.

SIGN

Porcupine skins with most quills intact, but meat-bearing limbs eaten or carried away from the carcass. Porcupine kills are usually found well away from hiking trails, and often under the large trees from which a fisher pushed them.

VOCALIZATIONS

Nearly always silent. If threatened a fisher may snarl, bare its teeth, and hiss like a cat.

LIFE SPAN

Life span in the wild is unknown, but fishers have lived in captivity for more than 10 years. The species appears to have a remarkable resistance to disease.

DIET

Fishers are efficient predators. The typical diet includes small rodents, squirrels, rabbits and hares, and roosting birds. Bird eggs are stolen from nests during the spring brooding season, and snakes and frogs are eaten as well. The fisher is not noted for catching fish, however, and it seems likely that the fisher's common name came after it was mistakenly ascribed skills that rightfully belong to the similar but much smaller mink, which is a proficient predator of small fish.

Fishers are agile hunters, with ferocious weasel-like personalities, but while they are capable of tackling hares nearly as large as themselves, they prefer smaller, more easily handled prey. A persistent but erroneous belief that fishers even take small white-tailed deer stems from exaggerated accounts by people who have seen them scavenging a deer carcass.

Fishers are also fond of fruits and berries. Their weasel-like metabolisms demand large amounts of calories, which can be found in the raw sugars of fruits. Blueberries are a seasonal favorite, as they are with so many carnivores.

The fisher's best known prey is the porcupine. Few predators are able or willing to tackle the porky's spiny defenses, but when porcupines take to the white pines in deep winter snows, the arboreal fisher follows. The porcupine's habit of sleeping the day away on a thick branch in a tree where it might feed for a month, heavily quilled tail toward the trunk, is protection against most climbing predators. But the squirrel-like agility of the fisher allows it to climb around, in front of the treed porky. There, face to face, the porcupine's unprotected head is an easy target for the fisher's sharp teeth and claws, and the fisher typically knocks the hapless porcupine to the ground, where it dies from the impact or is injured sufficiently to be easily dispatched.

MATING HABITS

Fisher females breed at the end of their first year, usually in March or April, and once every year after. Males, who probably mate in their second year, after establishing their own territories, become sexually aroused in response to pheromonal scents from the females' perineal scent glands. Mated pairs may remain together for a short time after mating, but most evidence suggests that they part company as soon as the female is sure she's been impregnated.

Like many female mammals, female fishers enjoy the advantages of a reproductive process known as delayed implantation, which allows them to mate in spring when the warming world makes life easier, but carry the fertilized egg dormant inside their wombs until early autumn. If a female hasn't put on enough fat, or if she's otherwise physically unfit to bear young, the egg will spontaneously abort so that she can reserve bodily resources for her own use. Delayed implantation causes females, who generally breed every year within two or three weeks after giving birth, to appear as if they're always pregnant or nursing.

Actual gestation, in which the fertilized egg becomes implanted on the uterine wall and begins to draw nourishment from the mother and grow, most likely occurs in November or December. Just before giving birth to a litter of up to five blind pups in February or March, pregnant females retire to a secluded den, usually up high in a standing dead tree. A hollow log or rock crevice may also be employed as a birthing den, but the fisher's habitat provides preexisting elevated dens that were created by porcupines. If a porcupine returns from a nightly forage to find its den occupied and scented by a birthing female fisher, its most dangerous natural enemy, the den will be given over to the fisher without a fight.

Fisher pups nurse within the den for about a month, but it isn't known if the father or older pups take part in bringing the mother food or watching the den while she's away to drink. Field researchers should note that denned fisher mothers are easily disturbed, and will move their entire litters to a different den if made to feel uneasy.

By the time pups are weaned in May or June, they will have become proficient climbers of the den tree. By the onset of winter, pups will have grown sufficiently to strike out on their own, leaving the mother, who is most likely pregnant, free to birth another litter, then breed again immediately.

BEHAVIORISMS

Like most weasels, fishers are normally solitary, quietly hunting high up in the shaded canopy where their agility equals that of the squirrels they pursue. Males appear to be territorial, judging from aggressive behavior toward intruders of the same sex, with territorial ranges averaging between 6 and 12 miles in diameter. Most of what little communication passes between fishers is through scents and scats deposited at regular places along a boundary trail, particularly at intersections.

In good weather fishers may sleep among tree branches, but the weasels are known to take shelter in hollow logs, porcupine dens, or in rock crevices during rain or snow storms. In winter they sometimes sleep in snow dens—essentially long tunnels hollowed through hardpack snow—and may take possession of fox dens or other excavated dens used the previous spring. Tree nests of sticks and branches constructed high up in the canopy are used year-round.

Fishers are active both day and night. Frontal eye placement gives them good binocular vision and the depth perception needed to catch prey, and the species apparently has good night vision as well. Nested or roosted birds and their eggs, sleeping squirrels, and most rodents become easier prey at night, so the fisher has learned to hunt day and night.

In the past, overtrapping of the fisher for its fur depleted populations in some areas to near extinction, but harvesting regulations and good management practices have ensured that the species as a whole was never endangered. In fact, recent upsurges in populations of both fishers and the humans who develop their habitats have led to a few rare instances in which wild fishers surrounding residences have taken chickens, attacked pets, and frightened children. Fishers react aggressively when startled or cornered, or if a mother's den is approached too closely, so proper care and respect should be exercised when observing this species.

Pine Marten *(Martes americana)*

The pine marten, known variously as the American marten or American sable, is a smaller cousin of the fisher. Like fishers, martens are weasels that took to the trees somewhere in their evolutionary process. But while fishers prefer tall deciduous forests, pine martens are best adapted to coniferous forests.

As its common name implies, the pine marten's preferred habitat is coniferous forests. USFWS

GEOGRAPHIC RANGE

Throughout the northern forests of North America, across Canada from Newfoundland to British Columbia, and north through most of Alaska. Martens are found in most New England states, across Michigan's Upper Peninsula to northern Wisconsin and Minnesota, and a few populations live southward in the Rocky and Cascade Mountain ranges.

HABITAT

As its common name implies, the pine marten's preferred habitat is coniferous forest, where its rusty-colored fur provides good camouflage against dead pine needles, and small tree squirrels like the red squirrel provide good hunting. Like the larger fisher, martens require expansive tracts of relatively unbroken forest, and like the fisher they spend much of their time in the treetops, where observers often mistake them for fox squirrels. The species is not found in plains areas or other environments that lack coniferous forest and snowy winters.

PHYSICAL CHARACTERISTICS

Mass: 1 to 4 pounds, about the same size as a fox squirrel.

Body: Elongated and muscular; short legs, long tail, long shiny fur. Forward pointed eyes, pointed snout with catlike whiskers, small rounded ears. Body length is 19 to 27 inches.

Females are slightly smaller and lighter in color than males. **Tail:** 5 to more than 9 inches long; fluffy, especially in winter; much like the tail of a fox squirrel.

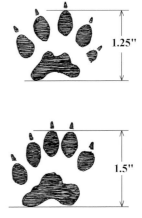

Pine marten tracks

TRACKS

The pine marten has five toes on all four feet. Tracks in soft soil show curved, sharp claws. Heel pads print in the U-shape distinctive of the weasel family, and tracks are easily mistaken for those of the slightly smaller mink in places where their ranges overlap, or for those of the larger fisher. Front track is about 1.25 inches long; rear about 1.5 inches. Tracks are approximately as wide as they are long.

SCAT

Irregularly cylindrical, tapered at one or both ends, 1 to 3 inches long, less than 0.5 inch in diameter. Dark brown or black when fresh, graying with age. Differs from mink scat by having more berries and vegetation in evidence. Scats are often deposited at regular places, especially as territorial markers at trail intersections, and are refreshed periodically.

COLORATION

Thick reddish pelage. Head is whitish to gray; legs and tail are darker, with reddish fur grizzled with dark brown to black fur. A small patch on the front of the throat is grayish white to orange.

VOCALIZATIONS

Normally silent. Can hiss and snarl if threatened, with that behavior usually accompanied by a pungent skunklike aroma from the marten's perineal scent glands.

LIFE SPAN

Probably 6 to 8 years in the wild.

DIET

Although as much an arboreal acrobat as its larger cousin, the fisher, the marten appears to be a more opportunistic hunter, preying on just about every small animal that it can find in its coniferous environment. Mice and voles, red squirrels, birds, eggs, snakes, rabbits, and an occasional small porcupine make up most of the marten's diet.

The marten is ideally matched against its main prey, the red squirrel *(Tamiasciurus hudsonicus),* able to scamper up tree trunks and scramble from tree to tree through intersecting branches with an ease that equals the most nimble tree monkey. When the prey is finally run to exhaustion, or cornered in a den into which the lithe weasel can follow, a death blow is delivered by driving the upper and lower canines into the base of the victim's skull, piercing its brain stem or spinal cord.

Pine martens are more omnivorous in their diets than minks or fishers. The carnivorous diet is regularly supplemented by whatever fruits and berries are available, seeds and other signs of which are evident in scats.

MATING HABITS

Pine martens reach sexual maturity at 15 months to 2 years of age, with females typically reaching puberty before males. Mating occurs during the period between June and August, when receptive females advertise their availability through skunky-smelling scent posts left on branches in a tree, or stumps and rocks on the ground. It appears that the normally solitary marten takes only one mate for the duration of courtship and mating.

After mating, the fertilized eggs are carried in a state of delayed implantation within the female's body, where they will remain until they attach to the mother's uterine wall and begin to develop in February and March. The embryos may be spontaneously aborted if she's physically unfit to bear a litter.

After becoming implanted to the uterine wall, the embryos develop quickly. After a brief gestation of about 30 days, as many as five young pups (or kits) are born blind and helpless in a leaf-lined den. The father may have already gone his own way by that time, and takes no part in the rearing of his offspring.

After nursing for roughly forty days, the pups are weaned and leave the maternal den to learn the skills of survival from their mother. The young learn and grow fast, and by June they begin to wander off in search of their own mates and territories.

BEHAVIORISMS

Except for their brief late summer mating season, martens are normally solitary. Mothers with young might also be seen from spring through summer, but in general the species is very shy of humans, and seeing one in the wild seldom happens to anyone but a dedicated observer.

Pine martens may be active at any time of day. Most tree squirrels are active during the daylight hours, so a marten in search of red squirrels must, by necessity, hunt during the day. Likewise, voles and most mice are active throughout the night, so a marten hunting small rodents must be nocturnal. The species' typical active times appear to be more crepuscular, with most hunting and mating activities being conducted in twilight hours at dawn and dusk, and sometimes on cloudy days.

Martes americana is territorial, especially males and females rearing young. Depending on prey densities, the availability of drinking water, and competition from other pine martens, a typical home range can vary from 5 to 15 square miles. The claimed territories are marked by musky scent deposits, which are often left among upper tree branches and undetectable by humans.

Like the fisher and mink, the marten is active throughout the year, as is the red squirrel. The animal has warm fur and can lay up for several consecutive days in a hollow tree or appropriated den during periods of harsh cold.

Although not quite as aquatic as its smaller cousin, the mink, pine martens are at home near, and occasionally in, water. Being such versatile hunters, they can forage along shorelines for crayfish, clams, and small fish, or in nearby pine forests for rodents on the ground, or among the treetops in search of red squirrels and birds.

Marten pelts are luxurious, and in the past they've fetched as much as $100 for a prime specimen, but today sell for less than $20. In a few places overtrapping has threatened local populations, but the species in general has never been threatened. When left alone, this efficient predator has shown that it can overpopulate and become a threat to its own food resources, although the species' natural aversion to humans usually keeps it away from chicken yards.

Wolverine *(Gulo gulo)*

The largest of the terrestrial weasels (only the sea otter is bigger), the wolverine epitomizes the characteristics that distinguish weasels from other animal families. A carnivorous hunter and scavenger, the wolverine demonstrates an almost unnatural feistiness, backed up by powerful musculature, sharp teeth, and strong claws, that evokes respect from predators many times its size. Before being properly classified, the species was known variously as "bearcat," because its physique and demeanor resembled both those animals, and as "skunk-bear," because its bearlike body is striped like that of a skunk, and it can emit a strong skunklike odor from its perineal glands. The wolverine's scientific name, *Gulo,* which means "glutton" in Latin, is probably more descriptive.

The wolverine is a fierce denizen of the wildest places. STAYER/LICENSED BY SHUTTERSTOCK.COM

The North American wolverine has also been referred to as *Gulo luscus,* as opposed to *Gulo gulo,* the Eurasian wolverine of northern Scandinavia and Russia's Siberia. In fact, they appear to be the same species, and most wildlife biologists now probably agree that the minor differences between them are no more than regional adaptations.

GEOGRAPHIC RANGE

Although generally thought of as a North American species, the wolverine's present range extends across northern Europe and through Siberia, as well as into the northern wilderness areas of the United States and Canada. The species' distribution was once more widespread, encompassing the Rocky Mountain range down through Colorado, the forests of Indiana, Ohio, and Pennsylvania, and the Great Lakes region in general.

In recent years there has existed a controversy over whether wolverines ever lived in Michigan, once known as "the Wolverine State," and defended by a winning college football team known as the Wolverines, from Michigan State University. The controversy was spawned by a graduate thesis in 1987 that challenged whether wolverines would live in any part of Michigan, based on terrain, habitat, and food requirements.

In fact, wolverines did once inhabit the Upper Peninsula of Michigan (and possibly still do, at its western end), and in 2005 an individual was found and photographed several times in forests of the Lower Peninsula's "thumb" area.

HABITAT

Wolverines essentially require a wilderness in which to live and procreate. The aggressive nature of this species, and its tendency to roam throughout its life, make it unwelcome anywhere close to civilization. Its willingness to meet a confrontation head-on soon reduced wolverine numbers at the hands of gun-wielding settlers.

Given a large territory where it isn't likely to be trapped, shot, or to interact with civilization, wolverines can inhabit nearly any northern or high-altitude environment where there is snow in winter, vast tracts of forest, drinking water, and an abundance of small prey. Dens used by nursing mothers, or for weathering storms, consist of leaf- or grass-lined rock cracks, existing coyote or badger dens, and burrows excavated under the roots of large trees. In winter a nomadic wolverine might also wait out a blizzard inside a snow cave made by tunneling into a large snow drift, a job made easy by powerful muscles, large paws, and strong claws.

PHYSICAL CHARACTERISTICS

Mass: 18 to more than 45 pounds. Females are on average 10 percent smaller and 30 percent lighter in weight than males.

Body: Second in size only to the sea otter among mustelids, the wolverine's body is wide and powerfully built, with longer legs than most weasels for traveling constantly and over long distances. Body length is 31 to more than 44 inches. The head is large with a wide skull, short powerful muzzle, short rounded ears, and teeth designed for rendering animals from prey to food. Eyesight is thought to be poor at distances beyond 100 yards, but the wolverine's sense of smell is excellent.

Tail: 6 to 10 inches, bushy.

TRACKS
Proportionally large wide paws, with five widely splayed toes on each paw, each toe tipped with a heavy, semiretractible claw that makes the wolverine nearly as good at climbing trees as the fisher and marten. Foreprint is 4.5 to more than 7 inches long, and as wide as it is long. Hind feet are slightly smaller than forefeet, with a heel pad shaped roughly like the outline of Lake Superior. The smallest inside toe often fails to print, leaving an apparently four-toed track that can be mistaken for that of a gray wolf.

SCAT
Wolverine scat is easily confused with that of a mountain lion, wolf, or coyote. Like the scats of these other predators, a typical wolverine scat is cylindrical, tapered at one or both ends, 4 to 6 inches long by 1 to 1.5 inches in diameter, and composed primarily of bones and bone fragments wrapped inside a spiral twist of fur from prey animals.

COLORATION
Wolverines have a long, thick coat, the color of which is largely a mottling of black guard hairs against predominantly dark brown. A lighter brown to blond band extends from the shoulders to the rump along either side of the spine, leading to the moniker "skunk-bear." The top of the head and cheeks are light gray, with a dark mask extending from around the eyes to cover the entire muzzle.

SIGN
Skunklike scents emanating from the remains of larger animals that have been fed on, or carcasses that are in the process of being consumed. (Never, ever approach a carcass you suspect belongs to a wolverine). Excavated rodent burrows are also common, but easily confused as the work of a badger.

VOCALIZATIONS
Wolverines are normally silent unless agitated, with most vocalizations occurring during mating season. Voices include a low grunting sound that repeats, as well as snarls, and screams.

LIFE SPAN
Wolverines have lived up to 17 years in captivity, but the life span in the wild is usually between 8 and 10 years.

DIET
The wolverine is a strong, well-armed predator with a willingness to fight that makes it more trouble to attack than it's worth, even to large carnivores. Despite being a third the weight of a gray wolf, a single wolverine has been known to drive several wolves away from a deer carcass, and even bears have relinquished kills to an aggressive wolverine that was too quick to get a grip on, and too violent to ignore. Ownership of any prey too large to be carried away

will probably be challenged by a passing wolverine. Once claimed, the wolverine urinates on the carcass, leaving a pungent skunklike scent that won't stop it from consuming the meat, but repels other carnivores.

When carcasses aren't available to steal, the wolverine is a capable hunter in its own right. It can excavate ground squirrels from their burrows nearly as well as its cousin, the badger, and it has little trouble catching small rodents, snakes, or frogs.

Wolverines are also capable of taking down deer-size prey. Some biologists have estimated that a wolverine can successfully tackle an animal five times its own weight, and while this might seem a bit arbitrary, there's little doubt that an adult has the means to kill a small yearling whitetail. Able to climb trees and pounce from overhead branches, capable of running at speeds up to 30 miles per hour, and strong enough to outmuscle large prey while inflicting mortal injuries with powerful teeth and claws, the wolverine is a capable predator that seldom goes hungry.

MATING HABITS

Wolverines become sexually mature at 2 years for females, 3 years for males. Females are monoestrous, coming into a prolonged heat once each year between the months of May and August. The long mating season allows time for these normally solitary and nomadic weasels to find one another. When a pair does mate, they remain together for only a few days before their natural animosity causes them to separate. Both may mate again before summer's end, a natural adaptation that helps to ensure that a female is impregnated with the strongest genes available.

Although female wolverines come into heat and emit sexual pheromones to attract mates, they don't actually ovulate until release of a fertile egg is triggered by copulation. Females that don't mate simply don't ovulate, which means they lose none of their body's resources. Females that do mate successfully carry the fertilized egg in a state of diapause (delayed implantation) for up to 6 months to ensure that the female is healthy enough to carry young through the coming winter—if she isn't, the egg spontaneously aborts. When the eggs take root on the uterine wall between October and January, gestation takes 30 to 50 days.

Just prior to giving birth—during a period between January and April, depending on geographic location—females excavate a den in snow if that medium is available, or enlarge an existing coyote or similar burrow, or sometimes take refuge in a rock crack. After insulating the birthing den with grasses and dry leaves, mothers retire inside to birth up to six cubs, some of which may have had different fathers.

Wolverine cubs nurse continually for about 9 months. After weaning, the cubs learn the basics of life from their mothers during their first year. Then the males begin to wander off to find their own way, followed by female cubs shortly thereafter. By their second spring, all cubs will have gone, leaving the mother free to mate again.

BEHAVIORISMS

Wolverines are all-terrain hunters. They can travel up to 10 miles at a loping gallop of about 15 miles per hour, and cover 30 miles in a day, enabling them to move nomadically to a more suitable habitat whenever resources grow scarce. They swim well enough to cross swollen rivers, and they climb and move about the treetops with nearly as much agility as a fisher or marten. Few smaller animals are beyond the wolverine's predatory abilities, and even an occasional yearling deer can fall prey to this ferocious weasel.

Wolverines are notorious for patrolling traplines, stealing whatever animals they find caught, and incurring the ire of fur trappers for whom a prime pelt might represent a substantial increase in their next paychecks. In some cases the wolverine itself has been used as fur, but mostly for parka hood linings and boots. Because while it has water- and frost-repellent qualities, it isn't a silky coat. Market demand for wolverine pelts has never been high enough to justify trapping them, but trappers from the sixteenth century through the first quarter of the twentieth century tended to shoot them on sight, and most residents of the countryside applauded them for doing so.

Wolverines have also earned a little hatred from gold panners, trappers, and folks who depend on a food cache to ensure that they'll get through a hard winter in relative comfort. Strong and able climbers, the animals can scramble up a pole to get at an elevated cache like those used in Alaska, and they're both powerful enough and smart enough to get locks open. There have also been instances of wolverines breaking into vacant seasonal cabins, usually by breaking a window, to get at the food stores inside. Aside from the damage incurred, marauding wolverines tend to add insult to injury by defecating and spraying the cache with a skunklike scent that claims it as territory.

Unfortunately, the wolverine's bold fearlessness and its instinctively aggressive reaction to confrontation with potential enemies place it at a real disadvantage when facing humans. A wolverine that dares stand its ground when surprised in a chicken yard by a farmer toting a large-bore shotgun is seriously overmatched; the ferocity that serves to frighten off larger adversaries is of no use against an enemy that could kill with a single blow from a great distance. That is why, within a few generations, farmers in the New World had all but eliminated wolverines from any but the wildest and most remote areas.

Depending on your perspective, an adult wolverine has either a huge territory or no territory at all. Left to itself the species appears to be nomadic by nature, wandering from one place to another throughout its life. There are no hard-and-fast rules concerning how long a wolverine might stay in one location, but a typical adult may range more than 500 miles in its lifetime.

Except for nursing females, wolverines aren't likely to den longer than overnight, and individuals have been observed going about their business in severe weather conditions. Some wolverines will take shelter from inclement weather to sleep in a dry place or to escape a howling wind, but shelters are rarely used for more than a single day.

American Badger *(Taxidea taxus)*

Second largest of North America's terrestrial weasels, the American badger is also the largest of its close cousins in the Old World. The common name refers to the medieval sport of "badgering," in which a squat and powerful dog, typically a dachshund or basset hound, was trained to crawl into a badger burrow and pull its resident out into the open. There, the two natural enemies would put on a spectacular show of fighting for human observers. The larger, more powerful, and definitely short-tempered New World badger soon made it

The American badger is a common weasel found in the western United States. GARY STOLZ/USFWS

obvious that no dog could enter its den without sustaining serious to fatal injuries, and the practice was abandoned.

GEOGRAPHIC RANGE

The badger is a very adaptable weasel. Its range covers nearly all of the United States from the west coast to Texas, Oklahoma, Missouri, Illinois, Ohio, Michigan, and Indiana. It is also found in southern Canada in British Columbia, Manitoba, and southern Saskatchewan. The species is absent throughout the eastern United States and Canada, although it appears that Michigan badgers are migrating northward into Ontario.

HABITAT

Left alone, badgers prefer open spaces. They were once common throughout the Great Plains region, where prairie dogs provided a ready supply of food and winters were usually warm in the lowlands. Prairie-dwelling badgers were especially feared by riders on horseback, because passing too closely to a den, or surprising one of the big weasels in the open, frequently led to snarling encounters in which horses sometimes threw their owners.

But badgers can also thrive in woodlands, deserts, low mountains, and even swampland, so long as the terrain provides enough high ground to accommodate the mice, chipmunks, and ground squirrels that make up most of the badger diet.

In times past badgers were trapped, their coarse fur used as bristles in shaving brushes. They were typically killed on sight. Today, badgers are making a comeback.

PHYSICAL CHARACTERISTICS

Mass: 8 to 25 pounds.

Body: Length is 20 to 34 inches from head to tail. Short legs and a flat, heavily muscled back give the badger's wide, powerfully built body a flattened appearance. Short snout, somewhat upturned black nose pad, muzzle black on top, white below. Broad, flat-looking skull with short, rounded ears at either side.

Tail: Short, 3 to 6 inches long, covered with fur.

TRACKS

Badgers have five toes on each paw. All toes are heavily clawed, but front toes are tipped with unusually long, almost straight claws designed for digging, reminiscent of a brown bear. Front claws are usually more than 1 inch long, the three inner claws longer than the outer claws. Foreprints are 1 to more than 2 inches long, usually with all five toes and claw tips showing, although the innermost small toe prints more lightly. Hind prints are slightly narrower but equally long, discounting shorter claws; all five toes usually show in tracks. Stride is 6 to 12 inches; straddle is 5 to more than 7 inches. Walking track pattern exhibits an extremely toed-in stride with the forefeet, leaving a unique trail in soft soil or snow that can be identified by inward pointing claw marks that may increase a track's overall length to 3 or more inches. Hind feet print on top of front tracks, usually at the same inward-pointing angle, making tracks appear longer because overall length of a paired track can exceed 5 inches.

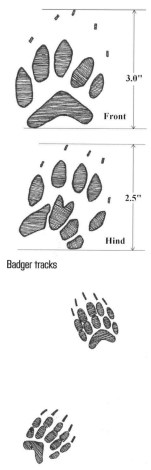

Badger tracks

The shuffling, odd gait of the badger leaves a distinctive track pattern.

SCAT

From 4 to 6 inches long, cylindrical, segmented, about 1 inch in diameter. Usually wrapped in a spiraled layer of rodent, rabbit, or sometimes deer hair. Often indiscernible from scats of a bobcat, coyote, or other medium-size predator.

COLORATION

The badger's most outstanding and identifiable feature is its masked face, which is actually whitish but broken by a pair of wide black stripes that run parallel to one another down the skull to the muzzle, leaving a white skunklike stripe between them. Interestingly, this white dorsal stripe ends at the shoulders in larger northern populations, but extends to the tail in badgers that live where winters are mild. Both cheeks have a black stripe that extends from the ears to under the chin. Fur on the back and flanks is a brindled coat consisting of a thick underlayer of whitish fur covered by coarser black, or sometimes auburn, guard hairs that are arranged in a way that gives the body a striped appearance, from auburn to gray, in older individuals.

SIGN

Excavated burrows, sometimes extending several feet underground, where the badger tried to corner a ground squirrel or other rodent. Excavations, including badger birthing dens, reflect the size and shape of the digger's body, being elliptical, wider than they are high, and usually 10 inches or more wide.

VOCALIZATIONS

Normally silent, but quite vocal when the animal feels threatened. Voices range from hissing to a grating snarl that most folks find unnerving.

LIFE SPAN

Probably 6 to 8 years in the wild.

DIET

Like most carnivorous species, badgers eat a variety of usually sweet berries and fruits when they come into season throughout the summer months, but the bulk of a badger's diet always contains meat, in every season. Carcasses of larger animals may be fed on, especially during the lean winter months, providing the formidable badger can take possession from another, often larger, predator. But *Taxidea taxus* is well designed to dig out mice, squirrels, and rabbits from their dens. No other species can excavate a tunnel so quickly, actually throwing a rooster tail of soil that also serves to keep an adversary at bay while the badger disappears underground, plugging the tunnel behind itself as it goes deeper.

With such tremendous digging speed, a badger can sometimes corner a ground squirrel before it can get away via its burrow's escape tunnel, but suckling litters are the more efficient prize. In winter, ground squirrels, marmots, and other hibernators may be dug out while they sleep, so long as the earth isn't frozen too deeply.

An old legend has it that the badger and the coyote hunt cooperatively, then share the results of their efforts. In fact, coyotes have, at some time in the history of these two species, learned to exploit the badger's efforts, stationing themselves at the escape burrow of a prey animal's den while the single-minded badger bores through the main entrance. If an adult squirrel tries to escape, the coyote is there, waiting to snap it up. If the den contains a litter of young, both predators can win an easy meal, but neither shares its catch with the other.

Other foods eaten by badgers vary with the environment and terrain, but include frogs, grasshoppers and other insects, fat-rich grubs dug from rotting stumps in the style of a black bear, turtle eggs, the eggs of ground nesting birds, and an occasional snake.

MATING HABITS

Badgers mate in late summer, beginning in late August and ending when all females have been impregnated, usually by October. Yearling females have normally reached puberty by 5 months, and may breed in their first year of life. Males will probably not be mature enough to mate until their second or third years, after they've established their own territories. Pairs of normally solitary adults join for a brief courtship before mating, then go their separate ways, often to mate with another partner, thus helping to ensure that a female is carrying the strongest genes available in her environment.

Like other weasels, badger females carry fertilized eggs in their wombs until autumn, a process called delayed implantation. The eggs will implant on the uterine wall in late December through February, providing the female is healthy enough to bear a litter of young; if she isn't, the fertilized eggs will spontaneously abort.

Actual gestation occurs over a period of just 6 weeks after implantation, with litters of up to five well furred but blind young born in a leaf-lined den in March or April. Dens are typically about 3 feet below the ground, with a 3- to 4-foot elliptical body-shaped tunnel leading into an enlarged sleeping and nursing chamber, and one or more additional tunnels serving as escape exits.

Badger cubs nurse frequently until June, when they're weaned, and the mother takes them out into the world to teach them the skills of badger survival. By August, when the mating season begins, the young will have grown sufficiently to live on their own, and they disperse to seek out their own territories.

BEHAVIORISMS

Badgers are solitary, with small home territories that range from 1 to 2 square miles, the larger territories usually belonging to adult males. Since most of the badger's diet consists of prolific breeders like mice and ground squirrels, territorial ranges can be kept small, permitting population densities of five or six peacefully coexisting adults per square mile. Territories are marked at trail intersections by scat deposits that are regularly refreshed, and often accompanied by a pungent odor of skunk musk. Despite exhibiting territorial behavior, badgers are quick to find a new territory should drought or other phenomenon result in limited resources.

Badgers are most active at night, when their keen sense of smell and good night vision give them an advantage over squirrels that have retired to their burrows for the evening. The species is also active by daylight hours in places where they don't encounter humans, the most frightening of daytime predators.

In snowy or very cold weather, badgers maylay up in a den for several days at a time, but not actually hibernating. The animals are quite capable of unearthing enough food to survive during harsh weather, but have adapted to taking long rests as a means of conserving energy. In a severe blizzard a badger may wait for better weather in a shelter it has excavated in a snowbank, but there are usually sufficient existing dens within a badger's territory to provide good shelter.

Known for its aggressiveness and seemingly terrible temper, the badger will nearly always shy from a confrontation, and if pressed will dig itself out of sight. Tales of its ferocity in a fight stem from incidents in which the animal was cornered by dogs, or involve a female with young.

The badger lives up to its image as digger to a sometimes surprising degree, emerging from tunnels it has dug upward through even asphalt-paved roads and driveways. Aside from creating road hazards, badger burrows are feared by horseback riders, and by ranchers whose cattle could be injured by stepping into them. In one case, a local bounty on badger carcasses was raised after a prize stallion stepped into a badger hole and had to be shot.

Long-Tailed Weasel (*Mustela frenata*)

Except for its notably longer tail and larger body, the long-tailed weasel in its summer coat is nearly identical to its close cousins, the short-tailed weasel (ermine), and the diminutive least weasel. This is the weasel of most cartoons, in which the species is depicted as very energetic, fearless, and always hungry, and it has frequently borne out those caricatures by slipping into henhouses to eat eggs and an occasional small chicken.

GEOGRAPHIC RANGE

The range of the long-tail weasel includes most of North America, encompassing all but the most arid regions of the southwestern United States and the Florida peninsula. It extends north into southern British Columbia, Alberta, and Saskatchewan, and southward through Mexico to Bolivia. This species ranges farther south and less north than the ermine and least weasel, and it has the largest distribution of any mustelid in the Northern Hemisphere.

A long-tailed weasel can survive in almost any habitat where it can hunt for mice and voles. JODY/LICENSED BY SHUTTERSTOCK.COM

HABITAT

Long-tailed weasels can survive in almost any temperate to subtropical habitat that provides water, dry ground, and vegetation in which to hunt its main food, mice and voles. Fortunately, that habitat is also good for the rodents, and predator and prey exist more or less harmoniously. These weasels tend to avoid dense forests, where the ermine and least weasel do well, and they tend to avoid very snowy and cold environments.

PHYSICAL CHARACTERISTICS

Mass: 3 to 9.5 ounces.

Body: Long and slender but agile and muscular; 11 to 21 inches long; males about 25 percent larger than females. Short legs lend a squirrel-like appearance, and like squirrels, the long-tailed weasel runs by bounding, leaping from one point to another through the air. The skull is slender, with short rounded ears and a short but almost sharply pointed muzzle tipped with long horizontal whiskers. Small eyes set into the front of the head denote that this animal is a hunter, with sharp eyesight, a good sense of smell, and the depth perception needed to swiftly strike a death blow to prey that is sometimes larger than itself.

Tail: 5 to more than 10 inches long, measuring proportionally to about half its owner's body length. The tail is bushy and warmly furred, and probably serves as a balancing aid when running along branches.

TRACKS

The weasel has five toes on all four feet, usually with claws showing in tracks. The smaller innermost toe may print lightly or not at all on firm ground. Like other weasels, *Mustela frenata* has an elongated hind foot that defines it as a plantigrade, or flat-footed, walker. But like other weasels, this one tends to walk weight-forward, on its toes, and the entire, somewhat human-looking pad might not print except on soft ground or snow. Hind prints average almost 1 inch wide by more than 1 inch long, up to 2 inches if entire heel pad prints. Foreprints are slightly longer than hind (unless entire hind foot prints), averaging a bit longer than 1 inch, and are noticeably wider than hind tracks. The heel pad, just behind the toes, prints in a typically weasel-like U-shape, with the ends of the U pointing rearward.

Like all of the long-bodied weasels, long-tails move in leaps, shoving off with their hind feet to travel 12 inches at a normal gait, and up to 20 inches when in pursuit of prey. Straddle may reach 3 inches. Tracks tend to be paired when leaping because the animal's short legs move in unison: It jumps forward with the hind legs, lands on the paired forefeet, and brings the hind feet forward to plant them for another leap.

SCAT

Dark-colored; brown or black. Long and slender, cylindrical, often unsegmented, averaging 2 to 4 inches long by 0.5 inch or less in diameter. Plant fibers and berry seeds are common in summer, but scats are predominantly covered with rodent fur wrapped around bones. Scats of the long-tailed weasel are often difficult to differentiate from those of other small weasels, and may be impossible to discern from those of the ermine or least weasel.

COLORATION

Long-tailed weasels are interchangeable with short-tailed weasels, or ermine, in what exists of the fur market today because both have nearly identical fur, and both shed their summer coats each autumn to grow a silky white coat that is strikingly beautiful. The white tails of both species are tipped with black. Long-tailed weasels in southerly climes, where winters are all or mostly snowless, don't experience this photoperiodic response to the coming of winter and maintain their summer coloration year-round.

The long-tail's summer coat consists of an upper and outer pelage of brown to cinnamon, with white fur inside the legs, under the belly, and below the chin. In this seasonal coat they are nearly identical to the ermine and least weasel, except for their larger size and comparatively longer tails. Another difference is that long-tailed weasels in their summer coats have brown feet, whereas ermine have white feet.

SIGN

Except for their scats and a faintly skunklike aroma left at territorial boundaries and emitted during mating season, long-tailed weasels leave little sign. Scraps of rodent skin or bone, broken eggshells under a bird's nest, and bird feathers scattered about, often with the feet left uneaten, are common clues left by the long-tail, but these may be tough to discriminate from other species of small carnivores.

VOCALIZATIONS

Long-tailed weasels are normally silent as they go about their business, but are known to be noisy when threatened. Voices include chattering, short alarm barks, and screeching.

LIFE SPAN

No data available, but probably 4 to 6 years in the wild.

DIET

Like other terrestrial weasels, the long-tail is an efficient hunter of prey even larger than itself, and like its cousins, its main prey consists of mice, voles, birds, and sometimes roosting bats. A long, stereotypically weasel body allows it to slip into almost any crevice that a small rodent might hide in, where a fast bite to the base of the skull from needlelike fangs ensures a quick kill with little struggle.

Long-tailed weasels are known to take larger prey, including adolescent cottontail rabbits more than twice their own mass, as well as tree squirrels and snakes. They've also been guilty of killing a chicken from time to time, and of eating eggs, but farmers generally like having weasels around because they keep mouse populations in check, and modern materials make it simple to weasel-proof a henhouse or rabbit hutch.

Like most weasels, the long-tail is a high-energy creature with a fast metabolism and high calorie requirements, all of which means that it takes advantage of the raw calories in fruits and berries whenever these seasonal fruits become available. Blueberries are a perennial favorite, with blackberries, grapes, and portions of apples favored as well. Scats will often show seeds and other evidence.

MATING HABITS

Long-tailed weasels mate in midsummer, usually late June through August. Courtship and breeding last only a few days before these normally solitary hunters separate, and often find another mate. After mating, females experience delayed implantation, carrying the fertilized eggs of perhaps several males within her womb, but in a state of hibernation, neither growing or dying. If the female survives the winter in good health, the eggs will implant on the uterine wall in late February or March. If she reaches spring malnourished or sickly, the eggs will abort without draining her resources.

If the eggs implant successfully, embryos develop quickly, and a litter of up to six pups is born about 30 days later, usually in April and May. Birthing dens are often taken over from ground squirrels after the residents have been killed and eaten, but may also be in hollow logs or rock crevices. Young are born blind and covered with white fuzz, but grow quickly under their mother's protection, nourished by her rich milk.

At about 35 days the young weasels are weaned and learn to eat prey brought back to the den for them by the mother. At this point she also begins bringing her offspring wounded prey, to give the pups valuable training in making kills (a trait seen with many carnivore mothers). After 2 months the youngsters have grown enough and become skilled enough to hunt and kill rodents on their own. At this point the family unit begins to break up, as male pups, then females, strike out to establish their own territories. Their mother may mate again after her broods leaves, and the females she gave birth to the previous spring are likely to birth their first litters the following spring. Males will probably not mate until their second spring.

BEHAVIORISMS

Like all weasels, long-tailed weasels are not social animals; the sexes live apart except for a brief interaction during the mating season, and same sexes never tolerate the presence of one another. A male's territory may overlap the territories of several females in an area, but there are defined boundaries separating his range from those of other males, and males never socialize without fighting. Intruders are driven away aggressively, with females exhibiting at least the same amount of territorial defensiveness seen in males.

Although often active by day, long-tailed weasels are primarily nocturnal hunters, with acute night vision and binocular eyesight that permits them to accurately judge distance and depth when attacking prey. They possess olfactory senses keen enough to detect a bird roosting in a tall tree, the stealth needed to sneak up on it, and the natural weapons with which to dispatch it quickly and with as little fight as possible.

Although sometimes accused of being a chicken thief, a title the long-tailed weasel sometimes earned, farmers have always tended to favor having the species around because it's one of the best rat and mouse catchers in the animal world. Especially with today's materials, it is fairly simple to keep the proverbial weasel out of the henhouse, but weasels in the corn crib help to ensure that rodents are not.

Long-tailed weasels in the north, where snowy winters cause them to grow a white coat of silky fur each December, are considered by trappers to be ermine, and there is still some demand for white weasel furs. The species has never been endangered, and populations are at least stable.

Ermine (Short-Tailed Weasel) *(Mustela erminea)*

Often confused with the larger long-tailed weasel, especially in snow country where both species wear a beautiful silky white coat until spring, the ermine has long been coveted among both fur trappers and consumers, even in today's depressed fur market. In Europe the black-tipped white tails of ermine were once used to trim and adorn the robes of royalty when they held court.

Despite its popularity as a pelt, the ermine has never been endangered. It has been accused of raiding a henhouse or two, but such accounts are typically overdramatized, because an average chicken is five times the size of an average weasel.

An ermine wearing its summer coat. STEVE HILLEBRAND/USFWS

GEOGRAPHIC RANGE

Unlike the larger, but very similar, long-tailed weasel, ermine prefer an environment that offers snowy winters, and they range much farther north. This species has a circumpolar distribution, and can be found in the Northern Hemisphere around the globe, including Asia, Europe, and North America. Ermine live throughout Canada, except for the Great Plains, throughout Alaska, and well above the Arctic Circle. To the south their range covers the northern East Coast west to Minnesota, southward along the Rocky Mountain range from Canada to Utah, and westward to northern California.

HABITAT

Ermine prefer northern mixed forests of coniferous and deciduous trees. The ideal habitat is riparian, or riverfront, with a year-round source of water, grasses, and brush through which to hunt rodents, and higher terrain that allows ground squirrels and other burrowers—a group that includes the ermine—to dig deep dens. They appear to do well in cedar swamps and marshlands, but are never found in prairie or desert regions.

PHYSICAL CHARACTERISTICS

Mass: 2 to 7 ounces.

Body: Typically weasel, with an elongated, somewhat squirrel-like body, relatively short legs, and a long bushy tail. Muzzle is short and pointed; horizontal whiskers extend from either side of the nose; ears are rounded and small; dark eyes face forward in the skull. Body length is 7 to more than 13 inches.

Males are roughly twice as large as females. The ermine falls between the larger long-tailed weasel and the much smaller least weasel in size, but aside from a few minor physical and color differences, the three are nearly identical.

Tail: Typical length equals about 35 percent of total body length, measuring 2 to 3.5 inches. Tail is bushy, especially in its white winter phase, and always tipped in black, as are the tails of the least weasel and long-tailed weasel.

Short-tailed weasel (ermine) tracks

TRACKS

Five toes on each foot, each toe tipped with claws that might be difficult to see even in snow or mud. Hind prints are plantigrade, or elongated, usually less than 1 inch long; front prints are about 0.5 long. Innermost toe may not print on firmer ground. Heel pad just rear of the toes on all four feet leaves a forward-pointed chevron impression. Except in instances where size distinguishes them from one another, ermine tracks are very easy to confuse with those of the long-tailed weasel or least weasel, but differ from the more U-shaped impressions left by the heel pads of the mink's front and hind paws.

Typical track patterns are paired front and hind prints. At a casual gait with leaps of about 10 inches, the two front tracks print side-by-side ahead of the paired hind tracks. At a fast run with leaps of 2 feet or more, the hind feet come far forward, pivoting past the planted forefeet to land ahead of them on either side, the rocking-horse running gait common to nearly all four-legged animals. Another feature of the casual, opportunistic gait is that it tends to meander back and forth in a kind of zigzag pattern, stopping at

Leaping   Running

Ermine track patterns, leaping and running.

holes and dens to sniff out possible prey before moving forward and in the opposite direction. The advantage of this zigzag is that it allows a hunting weasel to search as much ground as possible within its territory.

SCAT
Typical of the scats left by long-tailed and least weasels, and sometimes minks. Dark colored to black, 1 to 2 inches long, less than 0.5 inch in diameter, cylindrical, often segmented, tapered at one or both ends. Similar to the scat of a small domestic cat, except usually with a sheath of rodent fur.

COLORATION
In its summer coat the ermine is light brown to reddish on its back, from the back of its neck to its black-tipped tail. The underparts from the throat to the tail, as well as the insides of the legs, are white, becoming more yellow in older animals. The feet are white, in contrast to the similar, but usually larger, long-tailed weasel, which has brown feet in its summer coat.

In winter the ermine's thick, silky fur is white and the tip of the tail is black, although populations in the southernmost part of the range, where winters are not snowy, may retain their summer colors all year.

SIGN
Holes in fresh snow where an ermine dove in and burrowed below the surface for perhaps several yards before popping up again in an explosion of snow that spreads outward from the exit hole. Kills too large to be eaten at one sitting are cached under a loose spray of soil or snow, and scented with the ermine's skunklike perineal scent glands to discourage other predators from eating them.

VOCALIZATIONS
Generally solitary and silent, but vocal when faced with a threat. Agitated voices include screeches, hisses, and snarls. A quick barking chirp, similar to that of the red squirrel and possibly used as a ruse for hunting them, indicates curiosity.

LIFE SPAN
Average lifespan of an ermine in the wild has been estimated at 2 years or less, with females typically surviving longer than males. Maximum life span in captivity is about 7 years.

DIET
Ermine are almost strictly carnivorous, although it appears that they consume some berries as part of their diets, as well as a few fibrous grasses to keep the excretory tract scrubbed clean. Most of the ermine's diet consist of mice, voles, chipmunks, and an occasional red squirrel, pounced on by the fast and aggressive ermine as they pass an ambush point. Others are surprised inside their own burrows by this efficient hunter, whose streamlined body allows it to enter almost any place a mouse can. Small rabbits are taken opportunistically, sometimes from nursing dens, but adult rabbits or hares are too large and strong to be taken.

Ermine are thought to be mostly nocturnal, but they might also be seen bounding about during daylight hours in wilder places. At a wilderness cabin I lived in for a year, there were numerous wild species that simply got used to my presence, and one of them was an ermine, probably drawn to the cabin by mice, who were themselves drawn to the cabin by the odor of human food. Ermine are also attracted to rural barns and corn cribs for the mice and rats living there.

Typical of the weasel family, ermine are high-energy predators with a ferocious approach to hunting that gives them an ability to take down prey larger than themselves. Long needle-like canines drive into the base of the victim's skull, piercing the spinal cord or brain stem, sometimes repeatedly, and killing it quickly in most cases.

Ermine are good swimmers, and may forage along the same shorelines as their larger cousins,the minks, for crayfish, small fish caught in shallows near shore, and small freshwater clams. Frogs and small water snakes are on the menu as well, but larger snakes may make a meal of an unwary ermine, as will eagles, owls, and hawks.

MATING HABITS

Ermine mate from June through July, when the normally solitary hunters are drawn together by pheromonal scents emitted by receptive females. Pairs remain together for only a few days, and both sexes may mate with several partners over the course of the breeding period.

Mated female ermine carry the fertilized eggs inside them in stasis, where they neither grow or die, until the following spring. After about 8 months, usually in February or March, the fertilized eggs either implant onto the uterine wall and begin to develop, or, if the female is in poor health, spontaneously abort to conserve bodily resources for the female's survival.

Once implanted the eggs, which may have been fertilized by different fathers, develop quickly. After an active gestation period of roughly 35 days, females give birth in April or May to litters of up to eighteen pups, although seven is average. Females outnumber males by roughly two or three to one, although that ratio may fluctuate in environments that are more or less than ideal. Birthing dens are similar to those of the long-tailed and least weasels, consisting of cracks in rocks, hollow logs or trees, or the burrows of past victims.

Young are born blind and covered with fine white fur broken by a mane of darker fur around their necks, the purpose of which has yet to be determined. Some researchers believe that the father helps by bringing food to a birthing female, but it appears that a male attending a denned female is most likely courting her, and the male may not always be the father. This may be a natural response by males to both ensure themselves a healthy mate, or mates, as soon as the present litter is off on its own and the next breeding season begins.

Whether a male is present or not, ermine mothers nurse their young constantly until they're weaned at about 2 months. Females are able to mate about the same time their litter is weaned, sometimes even before, and will probably breed in their first summer. Male young are driven off soon after weaning to prevent inbreeding, and will probably not mate until their second summer, after establishing a territory for themselves.

BEHAVIORISMS

Mustela erminea is possessed of a constant, sometimes explosive physical energy, acute curiosity, and a short attention span, all of which combine to make it one of the most hyperactive creatures in nature. Although generally shy of humans, and especially pets, ermine have been known to scrutinize quiet humans in remote forests from close range. But they are almost never seen in civilization or rural areas where they might encounter a dog or house cat.

Being smaller than males, female ermine spend more time hunting in rodent tunnels and burrows, while larger males pursue chipmunks and red squirrels aboveground. This difference in preferred hunting environments probably explains why most of the ermine trapped are usually males. Both sexes can run in bounding leaps across the surface of snow to catch mice and voles, and either can lithely run up a vertical tree trunk after ground squirrels.

A typical ermine's range encompasses only about 5 acres, depending on the availability of good water and foliage, and whether or not an area supports a good prey base. Where numbers exceed ten thousand mice and voles per acre in an average habitat, there may be an ermine per acre, even though the rodent bounty is always shared with larger carnivores, from foxes to bobcats.

Ermine are subject to a usually fatal disease in which a nematode (terrestrial parasitic worm) infects the ermine's nasal passages, causing excruciating pressure on the sinus cavities until the skull eventually cracks and the animal dies from a brain hemorrhage.

Striped Skunk *(Mephitis mephitis)*

This weasel's most enduring image comes from the cartoon character Pepé Le Pew, whose moniker describes the intolerable stench emitted by this most odorous of North America's native weasels. All weasels have paired perineal scent glands that exude a musky scent used for marking territory and advertising for mates, but in the skunk these glands have been modified to actually shoot a stream of powerful smelling fluid from under the tail into the face of an adversary.

An odor might not seem like much of a defense against large predators, but skunks generally go about their daily lives unmolested once they've achieved a size too large to be targeted by eagles and owls. In one videotaped experiment, a rather silly researcher clad in a full-face grinder's shield and ankle-length rubber apron tormented a striped skunk until it pivoted around on its forefeet and sprayed him dead in the face. The aim was uncanny, and despite being

Skunks are generally solitary creatures, with most of their activities taking place at night. JOHN COLLINS/USFWS

protected from the spray's full force by his face shield, the volunteer victim immediately fell to his knees, vomiting and blinded by the fumes alone.

A skunk's spray can reach accurately to 15 feet, and a choking mist from it can drift more than 30 feet outward from the target on all sides. The odor can be smelled by humans from more than a half mile for several days afterward, and a typical skunk can fire up to five times before exhausting its supply of scent. Field researchers are advised to keep a distance of at least 50 feet between themselves and skunk subjects, to avoid having scent sprayed onto their clothing and equipment should the skunk decide to spray a warning perimeter while being observed.

If you are sprayed by a skunk, probably the most effective and available remedy for at least minimizing the stench is to wash both your body and clothing in a mixture of soap and tomato juice. Never wash affected clothing in a machine without hand-washing it first, or the plastic tub found in many washing machines may take on the odor of skunk permanently. If tomato juice is unavailable, good results have been obtained using a hand wash of turpentine, gasoline, or kerosene.

GEOGRAPHIC RANGE

Striped skunks occur throughout the United States, their range extending from the Pacific to the Atlantic, southward into Mexico from Texas and New Mexico, and northward through Canada's southern provinces. The species does not range as far north as Alaska.

HABITAT

Mephitis mephitis prefers a mixed habitat of forest, sheltering brush, and open water. It can tolerate all but the coldest places, holing up for days at a time in excavated dens during blizzards, but is most abundant in regions that have mild winters.

Just as striped skunks have proved adaptable to most temperate habitats in the United States, so too have they learned to view human habitation as a source of food. In rural areas they raid garbage cans, in subdivisions they go into garages in search of mice and pet foods, and on the outskirts of major cities you might find skunks that make up a large part of their diets with food scraps scavenged from dumpsters.

PHYSICAL CHARACTERISTICS

Mass: 6 to 14 pounds, with a few individuals in the far north exceeding 20 pounds.
Body: *Mephitis mephitis* is normally about the size of a domestic cat, and a few of its unfortunate encounters with humans have resulted from mistaking a skunk for a cat in the dark. The body is less elongated than that of most smaller weasels, with a humped back and short legs. The head is proportionally small, with small rounded ears, a long pointed muzzle, and the forward-facing eyeballs of a predator. Body length is 20 to more than 31 inches. The skull is easily distinguished from that of any other carnivore because it has upper and lower canines, with just one squarish-shaped molar on either side of the upper jaw, and two molars on each side of the lower jaw.
Tail: Bushy, usually held erect or straight back, 7 to more than 15 inches long.

TRACKS

Hind feet are plantigrade, almost human-shaped, 1.75 to more than 2 inches long, with five partially webbed toes, each tipped with a strong claw. Forefeet are shorter, 1 to 1.5 inches long, with five toes and long, almost straight claws that extend 1 inch or more from the toe tips.

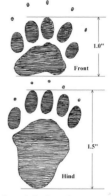

The striped skunk's walking track pattern reveals a waddling gait, illustrated by hind feet that print farther to the outside than the forefeet, and a trail that may be lightly brushed by the skunk's bushy tail. Straddle is 3 to 4 inches; walking stride is 4 to 5 inches. At a run, all four feet print in an almost straight line, alternating with a hind print in front and a foreprint at the rear, with short leaps of 5 to 6 inches between groups of tracks.

Striped skunk tracks

SCAT

Cylindrical, segmented, tapered at one or both ends; 2 to more than 4 inches long, about 0.5 inch in diameter. As individual sizes of skunks can vary greatly, so too can their scat sizes, and skunk scat is easily mistaken for that of other mustelids.

COLORATION

Striped skunks are easily recognized by their characteristic black-and-white color scheme, which is thought to be a visual warning, visible day or night, to potential enemies that they should keep their distance. The striped skunk is essentially black, with a distinctive triangle of white fur covering the top of the skull that extends in a thin white line downward along the top of the muzzle to the nose pad. At the rear of the skull the white cap separates at the neck into a pair of wide white stripes that extend to the tail along either side of the spine, then merge again atop the tail.

SIGN

Mephitis mephitis is a digger, its powerfully muscled back and long, strong front claws designed by nature to tear through tough masses of roots in forest humus to catch rodents in their burrows, to excavate turtle eggs in spring, or to find grubs in mostly rotted logs. Each of these foraging activities leaves unearthed debris and a spray of soil around the excavation that might be mistaken for the diggings of other small animals, and getting a positive identification will probably require reading tracks left at the site. Note, however, that a skunk seems to be very precise about where it digs for food, often leaving neat little holes, as opposed to the necessarily wider holes made by foxes or badgers. Look also for stones and small logs that have been rolled over in search of insects or earthworms.

VOCALIZATIONS

Skunks are normally silent in daily life. Forceful exhalations appear to be an alarm, like the blow of a white-tailed deer. Hissing, often accompanied by a partly open mouth to display the teeth, is an early warning to keep away. Snapping together the jaws (a behavior seen in bears and numerous other species) is a sign that the animal is nervous and expecting a confrontation.

LIFE SPAN

No established data, but pet skunks have lived more than 8 years in captivity, and it's likely that a striped skunk fortunate enough to reach maturity would live about the same number of years.

DIET

Striped skunks are the most omnivorous members of the weasel family, and probably most of their success as a species can be attributed to being able to subsist on a diet that can include grass roots, ants and grasshoppers, rodents, excavated turtle eggs, the eggs of ground-nesting birds, snakes, frogs, berries, and carrion. Although not as skilled at fishing as the otter or mink, skunks frequent riverbanks and the shorelines of ponds to drink, catch crayfish, and to harvest freshwater clams, which the powerful mustelid can pry open using its front claws. In winter, skunks feed on carrion, watercress, rodents, and sometimes appropriate kills from larger carnivores.

Striped skunks have also learned to regard humanity as a source of food, and in the twentieth century especially skunks began making a nuisance of themselves by digging through garbage cans and dumpsters for table scraps. Today striped skunks have become common nighttime scavengers in not just rural areas, but in suburbs, subdivisions, and within the outlying areas of major cities.

MATING HABITS

Female striped skunks usually mate in their second year of life, after spending a year with their mothers learning the skills of skunk survival. Males, which wander off to establish their own territories at the end of their first year, probably won't mate until their third year.

Female striped skunks are considered monoestrous, coming into heat only once each year between late January and March. It does appear, though, that receptive females not successfully impregnated during their first heat will experience

Skunk kits are raised primarily by their mothers until they are ready to exist on their own.

a second heat within a week or two. No data has yet been established, but it seems likely that females undergo a period of delayed implantation, carrying viable fertilized eggs but not growing embryos until late March or April, when the eggs implant on the uterine wall or abort, depending on the mother's fitness.

Actual gestation is about 45 days, with most striped skunk cubs born in litters of up to six during May. Although born blind and helpless, the young emerge already patterned with the distinctive black-and-white markings that give them their common name. Their defensive scent glands don't begin to fully develop until after weaning at about 7 weeks. Males will have left their partners soon after mating, probably to seek out another of the females whose territories overlap his own. All parental care comes from the mother.

After weaning, young skunks begin to leave the den for short periods of play and exploration, always under their mother's very protective eye and always prepared to rush back inside should a large hawk or eagle fly overhead. Skunk kits remain with their mothers through their first winter, learning from her how to exist on their own. Prior to the coming spring, usually in January or February, the young strike out on their own, leaving the mother free to mate again at the height of breeding season.

BEHAVIORISMS

The striped skunk's defensive spray is known throughout the world; the critter has been popularized in cartoons and caricatures, and is always portrayed in a somewhat frightening light in movies. In fact, this species is one of the easiest for humans to socialize with because adult skunks appear to be afraid of nothing. But neither are they aggressive without provocation—a mother is very protective of her brood, and the presence of a dog virtually guarantees that a skunk will spray—but there are numerous reports of people passing by wandering skunks (even on sidewalks), or surprising a skunk in a garage, without being sprayed. Like a rattlesnake or porcupine, *Mephitis mephitis* uses its defensive capabilities only when it feels mortally threatened.

And like the porcupine, skunks face danger with their rear ends. The first warning to an adversary may be a head-on chorus of hissing and snapping its jaws together, but if the skunk is pressed, for example by a curious domestic dog, the skunk plants its front paws together and quickly pivots its rear 180 degrees to face the threat. A fully erect tail and arched back, usually accompanied by a short spurt of scent to help get the point across, are the final warning.

As a last resort, the skunk plants its forefeet in something of a handstand and lifts its rear end off the ground, tail raised and spraying organs pointed at the enemy's face. Twin streams issue from scent sacs just inside the skunk's anus, merging together a foot or so beyond to blend into a widening cloud of thick, visible mist. The ensuing fog of choking scent is usually directed with sufficient accuracy for most of it to hit its victim in the eyes from more than a car-length away.

Even large animals that receive a faceful of skunk spray immediately lose their ability to be a threat. Typically, targets will panic because the spray has blinded them temporarily; they'll be unable to smell because the skunk scent literally overwhelms the olfactory centers and causes the nerves to shut down; and they'll begin rolling almost convulsively on the ground in an effort to get the scent off their bodies. On human victims the spray causes temporary blindness, nausea, vomiting, dizziness, and physical collapse to at least the knees.

Skunk scent also serves more conventional purposes, warning intruders that a territory is already claimed, advertising for mates, and making large caches of carrion unpalatable to other carnivores. Human manufacturers use skunk scent as a base for some perfumes because of its lingering qualities, and some human hunters use skunk scent to disguise their own odors when in pursuit of game.

Skunks are generally solitary creatures, with most of their activities taking place at night. They hole up to sleep the daylight away in an excavated den, a hollow log, or, increasingly, under the floors of barns and in the crawl spaces of houses. Because skunks are carriers (hosts) of sylvatic rabies, and sometimes become infected with the disease themselves, as well as because a resident skunk can be counted on to tear through any garbage left outside—and just because they smell bad—varmint removal has become a thriving business in many residential districts. Not surprisingly, most varmint removal professionals are fur trappers who have adapted their skills to this new industry.

Striped skunks are not hibernators, but neither are they well adapted to very cold weather. In the northerly portions of the species' range, individuals of both genders tend to become very lethargic during winter, particularly from late November through January, laying up in a sheltered den for a week or more at a time, especially during stormy weather. Like raccoons, striped skunks prepare for this contingency by eating almost gluttonously from late summer through autumn, accumulating a layer of insulating fat that equals 15 percent or more of its body weight. Females are especially reliant on body fats during the winter months, and may remain denned for longer periods than the males, which leave their dens periodically to forage.

Skunks have definitely been indicted as marauders of chicken coops, although their main objective, at least during the summer laying season, appears to be the eggs, not the chickens. Still, a single skunk can do a great deal of damage inside a henhouse, and leave it less than fragrant long after its departure. In a past era, farmers almost routinely trapped and killed marauders, but today an increasing number are opting to simply eliminate the problem by using modern, inexpensive materials, like sheet metal, steel mesh, and fiberglass panels, to predator-proof livestock enclosures.

Mink *(Mustela vison)*

At least as popular as ermine for making coats, stoles, and muffs, mink fur is silky and fine, and garments made from it are still considered a symbol of social status for ladies, although the trend toward wearing furs has diminished on the whole in recent years. Most minks that become fur are today raised on commercial mink ranches, and the musky skunklike scents produced by their perineal glands are collected for use as a lingering base in colognes and perfumes.

GEOGRAPHIC RANGE

Mink require a habitat that contains open and, preferably, flowing water, and the species can be found throughout the United States from the entire Atlantic coast to the northern, forested portions of the Pacific coast. Despite having been reported as living in every

The mink's fur is soft and thick, with oily guard hairs that provide waterproofing, and it doesn't change color with the seasons. H. HÄRING/LICENSED BY SHUTTERSTOCK.COM

state except Arizona, mink are not commonly found in the arid southwestern states or the southern Great Plains, and are never far from a water source. To the north, mink are found south of the Brooks Range in Alaska, and range eastward just south of the Arctic Circle, through Canada's Hudson Bay, on to the Atlantic coast, including an introduced population on Newfoundland. American mink have also become established in Great Britain, where animals being raised on fur farms in the 1960s escaped their enclosures and successfully adapted to their new environment. Strong and aggressive, the mink has today become a fairly serious pest on the British Isles, where it has overpopulated and threatens to decimate native prey species that native predators rely on for food.

HABITAT

Mink are never found far from a source of fresh water, most often a flowing stream or river that provides habitat for crayfish, minnows, frogs, snakes, rodents, and other small prey that makes up most of a mink's diet. Thick brush and tall grasses that typically line stream banks provide plenty of places to hunt or hide, and exposed riverbanks are good places to excavate or appropriate a den that allows for fast escape to the water. Mink are superb swimmers, able to dive underwater to forage for snails and crayfish like river otters, but also patroling local rodent habitat on nearby dry ground where long-tailed weasels hunt.

PHYSICAL CHARACTERISTICS

Mass: 1.5 to 3.5 pounds.

Body: Typical of long-bodied weasels like the ermine, fisher, and otter: long and slender with short legs, a long bushy tail, short round ears, forward-facing eyes, and a short pointed

muzzle with long whiskers extending from either side. Body length averages 19 to more than 28 inches. Males are often substantially larger than females.
Tail: Nearly as long as the mink's body, 15 to 20 inches, covered with long fine fur.

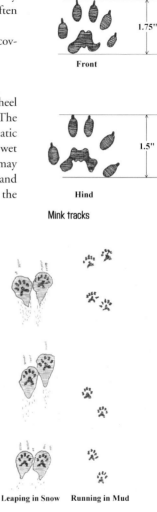

Front

TRACKS
Typically weasel, with five toes on each foot, multilobed heel pads that print in a U shape, and semiretractable claws. The toes are partially webbed, revealing the mink's semiaquatic nature, but webbing seldom shows in tracks except on wet snow or soft mud. The innermost smallest toe, which may fail to print on firm ground, is located farther to the rear and extended more to the inside, like a thumb, than it is in the tracks of other mustelid species.

Hind

Mink tracks

SCAT
Very similar to that of the river otter, but smaller, consisting of fish scales, small bones, and bits of crayfish carapace, sometimes wrapped inside rodent fur. Cylindrical, dark brown to black, tapered at one or both ends, segmented, sometimes more than 5 inches long.

COLORATION
Chocolate brown with white patches on the chin, chest, and throat. The fur is soft and thick, with oily guard hairs that provide waterproofing. Mink doesn't change color with the seasons as do weasels and ermine.

SIGN
Mink leave small scent posts of musky-smelling twisted grass stems along shorelines, smaller than those made by a river otter. Accumulations of crayfish carapaces, fish bones, and fins are left at favorite feeding spots.

Leaping in Snow   Running in Mud

Tracks left by mink leaping and running in snow and mud.

VOCALIZATIONS
Normally silent. Chatters, squeals, and hisses if threatened.

LIFE SPAN
Maximum life span has been estimated at about 10 years.

DIET

Mink are almost strictly carnivorous, and their semiaquatic habitat provides a diversity of prey animals in every season. The diet changes slightly with the seasonal availability of some prey species, but generally includes frogs, mice, crayfish, young muskrats, small rabbits, water snakes, snails, and hatchling turtles. Other prey includes the eggs and young of waterfowl, including larger species like geese and mallards, although raids on the nests of large birds that are potentially dangerous to a mink are always conducted surreptitiously and with urgency.

MATING HABITS

The mink breeding season coincides closely with that of most other mustelids, peaking in February and March when females born the previous spring and males born the spring before that come together to mate. As with most species, females outnumber males, and a single male's territory may be overlapped by the ranges of several females.

Like most weasel species, both mink genders are promiscuous, spending only a few days with one mate before going off to find another. It appears that at least some mink pairs remain together throughout the summer, but the male in a pair isn't always the sole father of the fertilized eggs carried in a state of delayed implantation within the female's womb. He takes no fatherly part in the relationship, but occasionally brings the female food when pregnancy or nursing duties restrict her ability to fend for herself.

Depending on the latitude, and counting the delayed implantation period before eggs begin to actually grow into fetuses, total time between mating and birth can number 40 to 75 days. True gestation time, from when the eggs implant to the time of birth, is more like 35 to 40 days. As with mated females of other species, this delay gives a female in the northern range a buffer of time in which to become extra healthy so that she can gestate and birth a litter of offspring. If she isn't, she can conserve bodily resources for her own survival by spontaneously aborting the fertilized eggs.

Mink mothers typically give birth in April and May. Litters may number up to six blind and helpless pups, each weighing 8 to 10 grams. The birthplace is usually a grass-, leaf-, and fur-lined den excavated into the side of a riverbank, and preferably opening onto year-round access to open water. It seems probable that the dens of other species might also be used, but a den excavated by mink is identifiable as a round hole, about 4 inches in diameter, located just above, and sometimes below, the water line. The hole marks a tunnel leading upward through the bank for a distance of 2 feet or more, finally opening onto a dry, enlarged maternal den deep within the earth.

After suckling for about 3 weeks, the fast-growing mink pups open their eyes and begin to move about the den and play. By 6 weeks the youngsters are weaned and can hunt for themselves. All are born with the swimming and hunting instincts of a mink, but the entire litter remains with its mother until November or December to learn about hazards like fast water and hungry owls. Both sexes reach puberty at 10 months. When the litter disperses in early winter, males are usually first to set off on their own, followed by their sisters, who may themselves give birth the following spring. The mother, too, will probably mate again after her offspring leave. Male pups probably won't mate in their first mating season, but those that successfully establish a territory of their own will mate in the second season.

BEHAVIORISMS

Like all weasels mink are solitary animals, and this species is well known for its aggressive behavior toward those of its own kind and, especially, gender. Males are extremely territorial and particularly intolerant of one another, fighting in a screeching, chattering, flurry of sharp teeth and claws. No real harm usually comes of territorial battles, which typically end as soon as it becomes apparent which mink is the strongest.

A tracker can use the mink's extreme territorial habits to advantage because minks, like otters, leave scent posts of twisted grasses whose blades have been wiped with a strong, musky secretion from the weasel's perineal glands. These scent posts are much smaller than an otter's, consisting of only a few blades of grass spiraled together, and have an even more potent odor of skunk about them. Scent posts are often accompanied by scats nearby, which are not likely to be mistaken for those of an otter.

Although considered nocturnal, it isn't unusual to see mink going about their business in daylight, especially in winter when increased calorie needs and the mating season add motivation. Apparently confident in their ability to escape into the water, into a burrow, or by scrambling up a tree using their sharp semiretractable claws, mink often make good subjects for photography. In every season and latitude the species tends to display crepuscular tendencies, being most active during the twilight hours at dusk and dawn.

Among mustelids, the mink is second only to the otter in terms of aquatic agility. Its webbed toes provide the power to paddle easily through river currents, to swim up to 100 feet underwater in pursuit of fish or crayfish, and to dive to depths of more than 10 feet in search of bottom dwelling prey.

Mink pelts, although small, have historically been considered one of the most luxurious furs on earth, and as such were once in high demand, especially during the early and mid-twentieth century. Trapping never put native populations in danger (largely because mink are wily and tough to catch), but it was deemed financially expedient to meet the strong demand for mink garments with pelts taken from farm-raised animals. The first mink ranches were established in the 1950s, and a decade later there were more than seven thousand of them turning a profit throughout North America. By 1998 the number of mink ranches that had withstood the continuous campaigns from antifur organizations had dropped to 439. In 1999 the existing mink ranches produced nearly 3 million pelts, valued at $73 million in US currency.

More than trapping, mink are in danger from loss of habitat. Most damaging is the tendency of humans to build along the natural river- and stream fronts that a mink considers ideal habitat, and pets kept by humans usually guarantee that existing mink populations will try to find new habitat. Some minks have learned to survive along developed riverbanks in municipal parks, which may be a heartening sign that humans and minks can coexist. One drawback is that more urban environments include waterways that are polluted by toxic runoff from highways and other sources during rainstorms—sometimes by sewage overflow—and mink tend to birth smaller and less healthy litters in places where the water is less than clean.

Chapter Fifteen

BEARS (*URSIDAE*)

Bears are native to the Northern Hemisphere; they are found in Europe, Asia, and India, but the three best known species are native to North America. All are large and powerfully built, ranging in weight from up to 600 pounds for a mature black bear to more than 1,700 pounds for a large Kodiak brown bear. All have five toes on each foot, each toe tipped with a stout, functional claw. The hind feet of all species are elongated, almost humanlike, denoting the flat-footed (plantigrade) walk of a strong but comparatively slow-running animal that has few natural enemies.

Until the latter part of the twentieth century it was commonly believed that bears hibernated, like ground squirrels, through the harsh months of winter. Today we know that bears don't enter the comalike torpor experienced by true hibernators, and sometimes leave their sleeping dens to wander during unseasonal midwinter warm spells.

Perhaps most interesting to humans are the bears' physiological attributes. Despite putting on about 25 percent of their body weight in fat each year, bears exhibit zero arterial blockage from cholesterol. Denned bears neither defecate or urinate for months at a time, and have a remarkable renal system that not only doesn't become toxified from a buildup of nitrogen urea, but converts this normally lethal waste product to useable amino acids. A bear also recycles the water from its urine for use in bodily functions. If modern medicine could figure out how a bear can reprocess its own urine, the positive implications for humans suffering from kidney failure would be enormous. The National Aeronautics and Space Administration (NASA) is also keenly interested in how a bear can remain motionless in a deep sleep for several months without experiencing the progressive loss of calcium and bone strength suffered by human astronauts in zero gravity conditions.

Black Bear (*Ursus americanus*)

Smallest of North America's three native bear species, the black bear is also the most abundant, and the most amenable to living in close proximity to civilization. Being a natural prey of the much larger brown bear, which tops the food chain with no natural enemies, black bears are driven instinctively to withdraw from conflict with other large carnivores, including humans. This innate shyness means that people living in black bear country seldom see one, and *U. americanus* never incurred the same wrath from people as the brown bear, whose instinct is to attack when surprised. The black bear was the original inspiration for the teddy bear, named after a young treed bear that outdoorsman and president Theodore Roosevelt refused to kill during a hunt. Smokey the Bear, fire prevention icon of the USDA Forest Service, is also a black bear.

Shy but powerful, the black bear is an icon of American forests.

GEOGRAPHIC RANGE

Black bears were once common throughout North America, But the presence of such a powerful carnivore near human habitation is rarely tolerated, and now, in the twenty-first century, the species' range is roughly half what it once was, restricted to woodland areas where bears can survive without coming into contact with people.

Today black bears can be found south of the Arctic Circle, throughout Canada and Alaska from the Pacific Ocean to the Atlantic coast. Populations also range from northern California east to the Rocky Mountains, and southward along the Rockies into central Mexico. In the eastern United States, black bears exist in healthy numbers from northern Minnesota to the north Atlantic states, with a few found along the Atlantic shoreline from New England to Florida. Black bears are not found in the Great Plains of the United States or Canada.

HABITAT

Black bear habitat is always wooded, always within close proximity to a source of fresh water, and usually contains thickets or swamps where an animal can doze the day away without being disturbed. Depending on geographic location, suitable forests and thickets range from hickory woods in North Carolina to the Everglades of Florida, and from the alpine forests of the Rockies to the fringes of the prickly pear and saguaro desert.

PHYSICAL CHARACTERISTICS

Mass: 200 to more than 600 pounds; males about 20 percent larger than females. The largest black bear ever recorded was an individual named Tyson at Oswald's Bear Ranch in Newberry, Michigan, which weighed 880 pounds.

Body: Stout and powerfully muscled, covered by a thick coat of fur; looks especially large in late autumn when the animal may be carrying up to 25 percent of its total weight in a layer of body fat. Total body length, from base of tail to nose, ranges from 4 to more than 6 feet, with males only slightly (about 5 percent) larger than females. Head is large and round, with a short rounded muzzle and small rounded ears standing erect on either side. Although some black bears have brown fur, especially in the western part of the species' range, they're distinguished from *Ursus arctos* by their smaller size, lack of a shoulder hump, and a rounded rather than upturned nose.

Tail: Short and heavily furred; no obvious purpose except covering the anus against insects; length 3 to 7 inches.

TRACKS

Five forward-pointing toes on each foot, each toe tipped with a thick, curved claw that's surprisingly sharp, enabling the black bear to escape its only natural predator, the brown bear, by scaling even limbless trees. Claws always show in tracks.

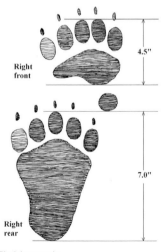

Black bear tracks

Front tracks are 4 to 5 inches long, 6 to 7 inches if the rear of the heel pad prints, usually as a round dot to the rear of the print. Hind prints average 7 to 9 inches long and are 5 inches wide at the toes, and very much resemble the bare footprint of a human, except that the largest, most heavily impressed toe is to the outside, opposite our own, and usually obvious claw marks extend 1 inch or more ahead of each toe.

The normal walk is a shuffling gait, with a stride of about 1 foot and a straddle of 10 to 12 inches, and hind feet printing on top of front tracks. Running gait is the "rocking horse" pattern used to achieve maximum speed and agility by most four-legged species, where the forefeet are planted together as the hind feet come forward on either side. When the hind feet hit the ground, the forelegs and back are extended fully forward as the animal makes a powerful leap, coming down again on paired forefeet . . . and the gait repeats. As is common with this pattern, stride lengthens to 3 feet or more, and the pattern is paired fore-feet planted side by side, bordered ahead of and to either side by the more elongated hind prints.

SCAT

From this scat, it's clear that the black bear who left it fed on berries or chokecherries.

Typically massive, reflecting the size of its maker. Usually cylindrical, dark brown to black when fresh. Smooth and unsegmented with flat, untapered ends when the animal has been feeding mostly on berries, vegetation, and insects; ant, beetle, and grasshopper legs often apparent in scat. Deposits become more like those of other predators when a bear has been feeding on deer-size kills or carrion: tapered at one or both ends, with small bones and fragments sheathed within a spiraled outer layer of fur. Length may range from seg-ments of about 2 inches to scats as long as 8 inches; diameter from 1 to

Here's what the scat looks like when the bear has fed on deer carcasses or other furred game.

more than 2 inches, with larger diameters indicating larger bears.

Black bear scat

COLORATION

Black bears are usually coal-black in color, with long, shiny fur. In the normal color pattern, the only contrasting markings include brown patches covering either side of the muzzle, bordering a black stripe that extends from the brow along the top of the muzzle to the nose pad. Each brow may be marked by a single small brown spot above each eye, much the same as the markings seen in rottweiler and some other dog breeds. Young bears especially may have a spot of white fur on the chest.

There are several variations in the black bear's color pattern, nearly all of them seen around the Pacific coastline of North America. Black bears living west of the Great Lakes are often brown or cinnamon in color, and are occasionally misidentified as larger, humped brown bears. A blue-gray phase occurs near Alaska's Yukatat peninsula, and black bears on Alaska's Gribble Island have a coat that may be almost completely white. Both of these color phases are found in British Columbia.

SIGN

Older boar (male) black bears are usually well established and can be very territorial toward intruder bears. Dominant males, usually 400 pounds or more, use regularly refreshed scat deposits to mark the intersections of trails that bound their territories, and often employ a nearby, usually smooth-barked tree as a scratching post. These trees are obvious to passers-by who look upward, because they will have five usually deep gouges extending downward along the trunk for a foot or so from a height of up to 7 feet, or as high as the individual bear

Black bears in a scuffle, showing color variations in the species.

could reach to leave a visual record of its physical size for intruders to see. Green trees, especially poplars, aspens, and cottonwoods, are often the most obvious sign because their shredded fibrous bark tends to hang down in curled strips, but standing dead and barkless trees are also used as territorial markers, and sometimes seem to be preferred for their softer, decaying texture. Man-made landmarks, usually wooden, may also be used as scratching posts, including bridges, fence posts, and power poles, where a demonstration of height may not be possible but a signature scent is applied through interdigital glands on the paws.

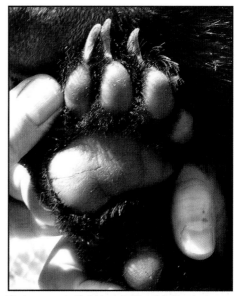

Sows (females) rearing cubs may also be territorial, although they appear to rely more on scent than visual markers to signal their territories. Large boars have been known to kill cubs to bring a female into heat earlier than normal, although

The front paw of a black bear cub. When he's older, this bear will do a lot of digging and marking with these claws.

this is more rare among black bears than among their larger cousins, the brown bears, so it behooves females with young cubs to be less blatantly territorial than bachelor males. Most of the obvious territorial sign a tracker finds will have been left there by males.

Other easily spotted black bear sign includes holes in meadows and knolls that almost appear to have been excavated by a shovel, but were actually dug in pursuit of rodents. Turned-up stones and rotting logs that have been rolled over and sometimes ripped apart are a common black bear sign, especially in spring when vegetation is scarce and fat-rich grubs are abundant. In late summer, fruiting wild cherry trees are often split apart at their crotches by bears trying to reach bunches in their upper branches, a foraging practice that has not endeared them to orchard farmers.

VOCALIZATIONS

Black bears are normally silent, but can use several voices that are similar to those of brown and polar bears. A clacking or chomping of teeth, frequently accompanied by a white froth of saliva at the corners of the mouth, indicates anxiety, and a human close enough to witness this is well advised to withdraw immediately. A loud huffing, usually issued from behind cover, is another warning against coming closer, and sometimes an invitation to leave the area. Low bawling sounds are used by mothers to communicate with cubs, while cubs tend to call back in louder, higher-toned bawls. Boars also bawl loudly during territorial fights, which are usually mostly bloodless wrestling matches.

LIFE SPAN

Black bears can live as long as 30 years in captivity, but the average life span in the wild has been estimated at less than 15 years.

DIET

Black bears are the most omnivorous of North American bears. Grasses make up a large part of the bear's diet throughout the species' range during its annual period of activity, and a black bear's digestive system can break down and assimilate the rough fibers with nearly the same efficiency as a deer's. In early spring, when the forests are warming but edible vegetation has yet to sprout, much of the bears' diet typically consists

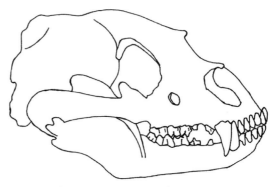

This drawing of a black bear skull shows the formidable teeth and heavy bone structure of this adaptable and intelligent creature.

of the fat- and protein-rich larvae of moths and beetles that have wintered inside rotting logs and stumps. They sometimes dig through the tops of large anthills, deliberately agitating the occupants, then insert a forefoot into the mass of panicked insects, which attack the paw until its owner pulls it away to lick off the ants clinging to its fur. Exactly which foods constitute a typical black bear's diet can vary widely from season to season and from one region to another, and it's this omnivorous diet that allows black bears to be the most successful species in family.

With a relatively slow running speed of about 30 miles per hour and a bulky body, bears are poorly designed as predators. They will appropriate deer and other kills from smaller, more skilled hunters if an opportunity presents itself, and are well equipped to excavate rodents and ground squirrels, but can seldom chase down larger prey. One exception is in late spring, when black bears prowl the thickets in search of fawns still too small to outrun them.

The territorial range of a black bear may encompass more than 150 miles, but most travel less far as they follow seasonal foods from place to place as they become available. However broad or narrow a territory, it must provide sufficient nutrition to enable its owner to put on a quarter of its body weight in fat for use in the winter denning period.

One dietary phenomenon that anyone researching black bears should be familiar with, especially in spring when the animals are emerging from winter dens, is the anal plug of mostly rough grasses that physically blocks the lower colon during the winter sleep. Just prior to denning, both black and brown bears eat a last meal of rough, mostly indigestible sedges, grasses, and sometimes pine needles, which then mass together and form a plug in the lower intestine. A similar intestinal blockage could be fatal for humans, but bears use a plug to ensure that no excrement can foul their dens during sleep, especially not birthing dens. In spring, after having been awake a few days, the anal plugs are expelled, usually along territorial boundary trails. A tracker will find them easy to identify: They are nearly cylindrical, 2 to 3 inches long, and comprised almost completely of long grass blades and probably pine needles, coated with a mucuslike fluid when fresh. Since bears tend to stay close to their dens for the first week or so after waking, a freshly expelled anal plug is a good indication that a bear den, and probably its owner, are nearby.

Also note that black bears have a penchant for leaving behind the feet of squirrel-size and larger prey, biting them free of the carcass as they feed and leaving them where they fall. The purpose of this behavior is to remove the very sharp climbing claws of squirrels and other large rodents to prevent them from abrading the convoluted intestines of a bear's complex digestive system, which are unlike the straighter, less winding intestines of most carnivores.

MATING HABITS

Like all bears, black bears are solitary except for the midsummer mating season. Males older than 3 years pair up briefly with females older than 2 years in June and July for roughly 2 weeks of courtship followed by mating, then go their separate ways—males to mate again should a receptive female become available. By this time females with grown cubs that have reached their second summer will have abandoned them, and will be ready to take another mate. Breeding sows will probably take just one mate.

After mating, both genders resume almost identical habits, traveling sometimes long distances over well worn bear trails that may be centuries old in some places to find the berries, nuts, and other high-carbohydrate foods needed to gain a layer of fat sufficient for denning. There's no animosity between mates, but a sow who senses she's pregnant will ward off further advances from a male with hard slaps and nips, because bears are designed by nature to fend for themselves.

Most black bears den in November and December, just before the permanent snows fall in the northern parts of their range, and only then do the fertilized eggs a sow has been carrying in a state of dormancy within her womb implant on the uterine wall and begin to develop. If the sow is sickly or otherwise too unhealthy to gestate and nurse young, the eggs will spontaneously abort. Conversely, if a fertilized female is well fed and strong, her litter size may increase from twins, which is the norm, to as many as five cubs. As with every species, large litter sizes are often a warning sign that bears are overpopulating, and that disease, famine, and other troubles are likely to follow.

Black bear dens are less conspicuous than would seem likely for such a large animal. Den sites are always located in a remote place where the bears won't be disturbed, especially by humans. Locations may range from excavations under the roots of large trees to burrows in the sides of a hill to large dry culverts under remote two-track roads. Den entrances are smaller than might be expected, just large enough for the occupant to squeeze through into a larger sleeping chamber. A small space is less drafty and loses less warmth than a more voluminous area, so den sizes are small and efficient.

Most black bear litters are born in January and February, after an actual gestation period of about 10 weeks. The naked 8-ounce cubs are usually born without waking the mother, and each of the blind, helpless newborns instinctively makes its way to a nipple. Once attached to a nipple, the cubs will remain there most of the time until spring, taking nourishment and growing rapidly. Not being a true hibernator, the mother's body temperature remains almost normal during the winter sleep period, keeping her offspring warm while she sleeps.

When mother and cubs emerge from the den in April or May, the youngsters will have grown to as much as ten times their birth size, weighing from 2 to 5 pounds. Youngsters begin traveling with their mother on her annual migration to follow available foods, learning the foraging, hunting, and watering places that they may continue to visit throughout their own lives. By 8 months the cubs will have been weaned and will weigh 25 pounds or more. They can forage for insects and grasses, and catch an occasional rodent or frog, but are still too immature to survive on their own.

By the end of their first summer the cubs will have grown to as much as 75 pounds, and the white blaze that most carry on their chests will have faded to black. Typical of all bears, the cubs' mother will not mate in their first year of life, instead devoting all her time and energy to teaching and protecting her young. When she dens at the onset of winter, the cubs, which have also been putting on a thick layer of fat, will den with her. When mother and cubs awaken in spring, she will continue their educations until June, when the youngsters, now approximately 18 months old and weighing 100 pounds or more, are either abandoned or chased off to allow the mother to mate again.

Newly emancipated female cubs may breed in the coming mating season, but males will wander in search of their own territories, and will probably not mate until they've found one, usually at age 3 or 4. Females will continue to breed every other year until about age 9, while males may remain sexually active until they are 12 years old.

BEHAVIORISMS

Black bears are most active at dawn and dusk (crepuscular), although seasonal breeding and feeding activities may alter the normal pattern of sleeping through the day in secluded thickets. In places where they aren't disturbed by humans, bears may forage day or night.

Excepting the distractions of mating season, the overriding motivation in a bear's life is to eat, and they feed almost continuously from the time they awaken in spring until they den again in early winter. This seemingly gluttonous behavior is an evolved response to sleeping through the lean months of winter, when plant foods are scarce or nonexistent and only the sleekest and fastest predators can catch enough prey to sustain themselves. A bear trying to forage or hunt in deep snows would have little chance of survival, but sleeping away the winter months requires taking enough nutrition into the den with them to live on until the return of warmer weather. A 200-pound bear requires 50 pounds of fat to remain healthy during the winter sleep period, so in the summer months a bear must consume enough food to not only keep well nourished, but to get fat.

The solitary lifestyle of black (and brown) bears appears to depend largely on the amount of food available. Actually better equipped to catch fish with their sharply curved claws, black bears frequently come together along stream and riverbanks where suckers, trout, and salmon are spawning, and even nonrelated individuals tolerate the presence of one another.

Similar congregations may be found in rich patches of ripening berries, in abandoned apple orchards, at land fills, and sometimes at campground dumpsters. During the latter half of the twentieth century it was an almost traditional pastime to drive to municipal dumps in the evening to watch black bears, sometimes more than twenty of them, rummage through human refuse. The dump bears seemed to get along well enough once a hierarchy was established, but the humans tended to get themselves into trouble, so today the city dumps and landfills are gated and locked after business hours.

Black bears have been known to kill small, easily caught livestock, like calves and sheep, for food, but their predations are rare and usually overdramatized. More real is the damage they inflict on corn crops, apple and cherry orchards, and bee yards. With their natural drive to feed bolstered by good intelligence, keen curiosity, and pound-for-pound physical strength roughly twice that of a strong man, black bears can do a great deal of damage to crops. Ripping down grape arbors, breaking the branches of fruit trees, and trampling sweet corn crops are some of the reasons farmers dislike them.

Black bears play an important role in the trophy hunting industry. Approximately thirty thousand are killed by sport hunters in North America each year, but with little demand for bear fur, the species is in no danger from overharvesting. In fact, black bear numbers may prove to be too high, as housing and other development projects occupy land that was previously black bear territory. There have been numerous recent cases of young black bears—nearly always recently emancipated cubs—wandering onto the streets of rural towns in search of territory and attracted to odors emanating from restaurant dumpsters. In a few instances the trespassing animals have been shot dead, but public uproar has caused local authorities to adopt less lethal means of removing wandering bears.

Researching black bears in the field is less risky than it might sound: In the past 109 years, only sixty-three people have been killed by black bears in the United States. Unlike the larger and more aggressive brown bear, which instinctively charges toward a threat, black bears are generally quick to withdraw from confrontations with humans. Mothers with small cubs are likely to send them up a tree, then climb up after them, until a potential enemy passes. Because of the species' keen sense of smell, only a few of the hikers detected by black bears will ever get a chance to see them.

In a few isolated cases black bears, usually dominant males in excess of 300 pounds, have stood their ground, or even approached a human. The most unbending rule in the event of such an encounter is to never, *ever* run from the animal. No human can outrun the 30-mile-per-hour sprint of a black bear, and fleeing identifies you as the weaker adversary. Running away excites the bear's predatory instincts, often causing it to give chase. Conversely, standing your ground in the face of even a large bear typically reveals that aggressive behavior, including charges that sometimes stop within a few unnerving feet, are nearly always a bluff. A person who appears unafraid and strong is not likely to be bullied by a bear.

In the rare instances where *Ursus americanus* can legitimately be accused of attacking a person, the motivation has usually been food. An old or sickly bear that faces starvation because it can no longer make the sometimes long seasonal trek to follow its food supply might be tempted to prey on a small human.

Brown Bear (Ursus arctos horribilis)

Measured by weight, the brown bear is the largest land carnivore in the world, sometimes reaching twice the size of a black bear, and being slightly heavier than the taller polar bear. Brown bears have no natural enemies except other brown bears and humans, so individuals are relatively fearless as they go about their business. Based on the accounts of field researchers like Doug Peacock, author of *Grizzly Years,* and a number of salmon anglers who share river shorelines with brown bears each year in places like Alaska's Denali National Park, this species is neither afraid of or hungry for humans. As with the normally harmless black bear, there have been instances where an old or sickly brown bear preyed on a human because it was starving, but in general these bears seem to regard *Homo sapiens* almost as they would a skunk—as both repulsive and annoying to have around, and not really worthy of much interest.

This photo shows the brown bear's distinctive large hump that extends upward from the spine to between the shoulders. USFWS

GEOGRAPHIC RANGE

Brown bears are thought to have once roamed most of the globe, and probably all of North America from the Arctic Circle to Central America. Unfortunately, this largest of carnivores has always evoked fear in humans, the weapon-making species, and today brown bears are gone from most of their original range. An estimated population of one hundred thousand can still be found in northern Eurasia, with about seventy thousand of those living in Russia. Isolated sightings have also been reported in the Atlas Mountains of northernmost Africa, and possibly on Japan's Hokkaido Island. Brown bears were extirpated from North America's Sierra Nevada mountains, the southern Rocky Mountains, and from northern Mexico during the twentieth century, when populations in the lower 48 states fell from more than one hundred thousand animals at the turn of the century to a current low of less than 1,200. Brown bear populations in Alaska and western Canada remain fairly stable at an estimated fifty thousand individuals.

HABITAT

Brown bears are at home in a variety of habitats, but in the North America the species seems partial to open areas like arctic tundra, alpine meadows, and coastlines. Brown bears were a common sight on the Great Plains when the first European immigrants arrived. With a digestive system that can metabolize rough foliage and grasses nearly as well as a deer's, the bears are at home on the plains, but never venture far from a thicket in which to sleep without being observed. In Siberia, brown bears are more creatures of the deep forest, while European populations are confined to mountain woodlands. So long as a habitat provides vegetation, nuts, fruits, rodents, fresh water, and a secluded place to rest, *Ursus arctos* can live there.

PHYSICAL CHARACTERISTICS

Mass: 400 to more than 1,700 pounds, with the larger individuals in the north. Males are approximately 10 percent larger than females.

Body: Very large and powerfully built. About twice the size of a typical black bear, with a distinctive large hump of muscle extending upward from the spine between the shoulders. Shoulder height is 4 to 4.5 feet; body length is 6 to more than 7 feet; standing height is 10 feet or more. The head is large and broad, with small, round, furry ears at either side. Facial profile is almost concave, giving the impression of an upturned nose, and unlike the rounded muzzle and profile of a black bear.

Tail: About 3 inches long, well furred, and the same color as the pelage.

TRACKS

Tracks are similar to those of the black bear, but often much larger and with longer, more obvious claw

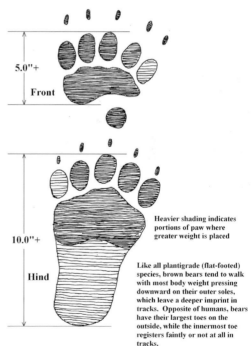

5.0"+

Front

10.0"+

Hind

Heavier shading indicates portions of paw where greater weight is placed

Like all plantigrade (flat-footed) species, brown bears tend to walk with most body weight pressing downward on their outer soles, which leave a deeper imprint in tracks. Opposite of humans, bears have their largest toes on the outside, while the innermost toe registers faintly or not at all in tracks.

The tracks of the mighty brown bear have brought fear to the strong hearts of many a wilderness lover.

marks showing in tracks. Five toes on all four feet, with almost straight claws extending from the front toes to a length of 3 inches or more. Forefeet are 5 to 6 inches long, discounting the dot-shaped impression that may print 3 or 4 inches to the rear of the forefoot heel pad; forefoot width is 8 to 10 inches. Hind feet are 10 to 16 inches long, 7 to 8 inches wide, elongated and flat, almost human-shaped, and tipped with much shorter claws.

SCAT

Similar to a black bear's but often much larger and with more mass. Shape is generally cylindrical, often segmented, and dark brown to black when fresh, with evidence of seeds, grasses, and berries in most samples. Diameter may exceed 2 inches. A single scat may be broken into several segments of 2 to 4 inches in length; when feeding on rich meats, it might be coiled and in a single piece. Rodent and sometimes deer hair may be in evidence, wrapped spiral fashion over bones and protruding objects, much the same as scats of other predatory species.

COLORATION

Fur is usually dark brown, but varies from blond to nearly black in some individuals. The common name of grizzly bear stems from the white-frosted, or grizzled, appearance of the bear's shoulders and back. The brown bear's muzzle is the same color as or darker than its pelage, but never lighter colored like the black bear's muzzle.

SIGN

Large excavations in hillsides and meadows where ground squirrel burrows have been dug out in search of prey. Large rocks and downed logs overturned. Bathtub-size depressions in the humus of brushy thickets where a bear slept.

VOCALIZATIONS

Grunts, growls, huffing, bawling. The clacking of teeth, often accompanied by a froth of saliva around the mouth, indicates anxiety, and researchers who witness such behavior should withdraw immediately . . . but slowly, never turning their backs to the bear.

LIFE SPAN

Up to 47 years in captivity, but normally less than 35 years in the wild. Some brown bears in Yellowstone National Park have remained sexually active until 25 years of age. Potential life span has been estimated to be as long as 50 years.

DIET

Like the black bear, brown bears have a highly efficient digestive system that allows them to subsist mostly on vegetation. In spring, before many food plants have sprouted, grasses, sedges, roots, and lichens may make up the bulk of a newly awakened bear's diet. As the warm season progresses and more plants mature and fruit, a bear's diet and range will change to match available foods. Calorie-rich berries, nuts, and fruits are preferred, and several types of fungi are eaten as well.

When they're available, insects in their various stages of development are eaten. Rotting logs and stumps are home to the larvae of beetles and other insects, whose grublike bodies are comprised mostly of fat. Spiders are eaten as they hang in their webs, and ants are gathered by sticking a big forepaw into anthills, then licking the clinging insects off with a raspy tongue.

Brown bears will eat carrion when they can find it or appropriate it from smaller carnivores. The seemingly instinctive hatred that exists between wolves and bears probably stems from the brown bear's practice of stealing carcasses brought down by hunting packs. Brown bears also prey on wolf pups if they can find a den guarded by only an omega wolf babysitter while the rest of the pack is away to hunt, but even a pair of wolves is usually sufficient to deter a large brown bear.

Like black bears, brown bears are poorly equipped to hunt prey compared to more lithe and speedy predators. In the far north, big Alaskan brown bears frequent fur seal and walrus colonies during their summer mating seasons, seeking out newborn calves, males seriously wounded in mating battles, and individuals weak from advanced age. A brown's 35-mile-per-hour run is too slow to threaten healthy deer, but brown bears may follow caribou herds during their annual migrations, waiting for those most easily preyed on to reveal themselves by falling behind the herd.

In spring, right after the bears emerge from their winter dens but before the summer growing season gets underway, most of the meat eaten by a brown bear consists of small rodents and ground squirrels dug out of their burrows by its massive, powerful forepaws. With mice and vole numbers typically numbering thousands per acre, rodents can make up most of a bear's diet in spring. Marmots and ground squirrels may escape through one of several exit tunnels that typically branch outward from their burrows. Like badgers, brown bears digging for denned prey may be shadowed by a coyote, which is itself too fast and nimble for the bear too catch. The coyote is there to exploit the bear's excavating power by guarding the prey's escape route, snapping it up if it pops out. This system appears to be mutually beneficial for both carnivores, because a trapped rodent's sense of smell makes it aware that a coyote is waiting at the back door, and the prospect of certain death in both directions may cause it to flee in blind panic toward either predator.

Salmon fishing is probably the best known of a brown bear's hunting skills, even to the point of becoming a tourist attraction in places like Alaska's Denali National Park. During their spring and autumn mating seasons (depending on the species), mature salmon and trout (family Salmonidae) migrate by the thousands, traveling upstream in the same rivers that they were born in to spawn the next generation of their kind. Waiting to ambush the usually large fish at narrows, rapids, and shallows are brown bears of all ages and sizes, all of which learned to come to this particular place at this time of year from their mothers, who in turn learned to fish from their mothers, ad infinitum.

Spawning runs are perhaps the only time and place where normally solitary, antisocial, and extremely territorial brown bears are found in close proximity to one another. Fatty fish flesh has been a critical part of the bears' diet since before recorded history, and the animals have learned over many generations to tolerate the presence of one another so that all can share in the abundance of rich food. Sows with cubs will keep their distance from adult boars, though, and even fight with one if it approaches too closely; boars have been known to kill, and sometimes eat, yearling cubs to induce their mother, who wouldn't normally breed until the cubs' second or third summer, into sexual readiness a year or two early. When the spawning run ends, the bears leave to resume a solitary and territorial lifestyle.

MATING HABITS

The mating habits of brown bears are very similar to those of the smaller black bear. In the summer months between May and July, sexually mature sows at least 3 years old begin involuntarily and voluntarily advertising their receptivity through pheromonal scents and hormones contained in their urine. Boars 5 or 6 years of age are attracted to the prospect of sex, and seek out females in heat, advertising their own availability through scat and urine deposits on trails that overlap a local female's territory. After roughly a week of courtship, depending on how quickly the female reaches a state of readiness, the pair copulate frequently for about 3 days, or until the sow realizes instinctively that she's been impregnated. Once her eggs are fertilized, the female will tolerate no further advances from the boar, and will drive him off (possibly to find another mate) with hard slaps and bites whenever he comes within reach. Females probably take only one mate per mating season.

Mated sows carry the fertilized eggs alive but dormant within their wombs until October or November, just prior to the winter denning season. At this time the eggs will implant on the uterine wall if the female is healthy and has put on 25 percent of her own weight in a thick layer of body fat—or they will spontaneously abort so that the female can conserve bodily resources for her own needs. Implanted eggs grow rapidly, and in late January to early March, two—and occasionally as many as four—cubs are born inside a snug excavated den. Although bears are not true hibernators, based on the facts that their body temperatures drop only slightly and they can be awakened easily, the birthing mother may sleep through her offsprings' delivery.

Weighing about 1 pound at birth, each of the blind and naked cubs will make its way to a nipple and nestle into its mother's warm belly fur to nurse almost continuously until she awakens in April or May. At this point the cubs are fully furred, mobile, and able to travel with their mother as she begins the same annual foraging trek to seasonal food sources that they will make as adults, and teach to their own offspring.

At 5 months, in late June to early August, the cubs are weaned and begin to forage for themselves on grasses, forbs, and insects. Mothers share kills with the cubs, but they soon learn to catch rodents, frogs, and other small animals without help. At the end of their first summer, the cubs will weigh 50 pounds or more, and most smaller mammals will have become potential prey to them. Yearling cubs accompany their mothers to rivers where fishing bears congregate to feed on spawning fish, but keep their distance from males that might kill them to drive their mother into an early estrus.

Cubs den with their mothers the first winter of their lives. When she emerges the following spring they remain with her until June or July, when she abandons them or drives them away. At this time the cubs weigh upward of 150 pounds, and aren't easy prey for any carnivore. Mother brown bears are less likely to breed every other year than black bears, and some sows go unmated for up to four years between litters. Emancipated cubs establish their own territories, sometimes traveling more than 100 miles to find suitable habitat not already claimed, and continue to grow until they reach 10 or 11 years of age.

BEHAVIORISMS

With no enemies except man, and no fear of anything, *Ursus arctos* may be active at any time of the day, but the species' foraging habits are generally crepuscular. After feeding during the cool early morning hours, warm days are spent sleeping in dense thickets. Researchers should be exceptionally careful in such occluded environments, and should always bear in mind that the instinct of a surprised grizzly is to charge, not retreat.

Carcasses of large animals are also to be avoided, observed only through binoculars, and never approached more closely than 200 yards—preferably you should stay farther away and downwind. Brown bears, black bears, cougars, and wolverines make a habit of camouflaging carcasses too large to be eaten in a single sitting with a partial covering of leaves and debris. Each of these species is likely to defend that food source from any large competitor, including humans, and it's a sure bet that the owner of the carcass is nearby.

The overall territory of a brown bear may encompass more than 1,000 miles, but the average is usually less than 200 square miles, and territories seldom cover more area than is required to meet the bear's needs. The territories of males average seven times larger than those of females, and will normally overlap the territories of several females that are potential mates.

The concept of territory doesn't apply to bears in the same sense that it does to most territorial carnivores, because most of a bear's time is spent following ripening foods from one location to another. An individual might spend several weeks in a place where blueberries and other fruits are plentiful, but when available foods are gone from an area, so are the bears. This system works well because the bear's omnivorous diet and nature's own diversity ensure that a number of food sources are available every month of its waking period.

Adult brown bears can't normally climb trees because their claws, which were more sharply curved to give them that ability when they were cubs, have grown out straight and long so that they are more useful as digging tools. This adaptation reflects the brown bear's typically open habitat, as opposed to the heavily forested environment preferred by black bears, whose sharp, curved claws permit them to climb even smooth-sided trees. This does not mean that climbing a tree is always a good way to avoid a brown bear, though, because there have been instances in which a bear used the branches of a large pine as ladder rungs to clamber up after a treed human.

Brown bears have frequently been observed pushing against dead standing trees until they topple. This seemingly idle behavior has a real purpose, which is to stun prey animals that might be holed up inside. Once down, the trunk can be torn apart in search of grubs, ants, and sometimes the honey of a wild beehive.

Although this species is sometimes temperamental and often petulant, traits that do nothing to endear them to humans, accounts of brown bears preying on livestock or threatening rural Americans generally range from exaggerated to fabricated, most of them presented merely as justification for killing a bear.

Polar Bear (*Ursus maritimus*)

Polar bears are the most carnivorous of family Ursidae, largely because of the lack of vegetation in the species' arctic habitat. Because polar bears regard virtually every other species as food, it has a definite predatory bent, and is one of the few terrestrial carnivores on earth that considers humans prey under normal conditions. Norwegian fur hunters in the twentieth century have reported that some or most of the ten polar bears a hunter was permitted to harvest each year were not hunted, but shot in defense of themselves or their sled dogs.

Because they spend their entire lives around and in the ocean, polar bears are categorized as marine mammals by some biologists. SUSANNE MILLER/USFWS

GEOGRAPHIC RANGE

Polar bears have a circumpolar distribution, albeit only at the top of the globe. The species ranges throughout the arctic region surrounding the North Pole, the limits of their range determined by the ice pack of the Arctic Ocean and of surrounding coastal areas. Polar bears have been reported as far south as the southern tips of Greenland and Iceland.

During the winter, polar bears range between the southern edge of the ice pack and the northern edge of ice formed off continental coastlines. In summer bears remain at the edge of the receding ice pack or on islands and coastal regions that remain ice-covered year-round.

Six individual populations of polar bears are presently recognized: (1) Wrangell Island and western Alaska, (2) northern Alaska, (3) the Canadian arctic archipelago, (4) Greenland,

(5) Svalbard–Franz Josef Land, and (6) central Siberia. Individual sightings have occurred as far south as Maine in the United States.

HABITAT

Because they spend their entire lives around and in the ocean, polar bears are categorized as marine mammals by some biologists, and the scientific name *Ursus maritimus,* or "seagoing bear," reflects this species' penchant for open water. Preferred habitat is the pack ice of the Arctic Ocean, where pressure ridges and buckled surfaces leave areas of open water in which foraging seals, a mainstay in the polar bear diet, find plenty of fishing opportunities.

When pack ice breaks up in spring, most polar bears migrate northward to stay with it, sometimes floating along on ice floes, and sometimes by swimming 20 miles or more to a colder, more suitable summer habitat. The spring breakup of pack ice leaves some polar bears stranded on solid ground in comparatively warm weather, unable to migrate north to permanent ice. In some of these places, like the little village of Churchill on Canada's Atlantic coast, polar bears have learned to feed at landfills, and a few of these appear to be voluntarily missing the annual migration northward in order to remain with a steady supply of people food.

PHYSICAL CHARACTERISTICS

Mass: Adult males are typically much larger than females, with males weighing between 800 and 1,100 pounds, and females between 350 and 700 pounds. The largest polar bear reported was a male weighing 1,760 pounds.

Body: The body of a polar bear is large and stocky, but longer and sleeker than that of the more thickly built brown bear, with longer limbs that provide a longer and more efficient swimming stroke. Polar bears lack the large muscular shoulder hump of brown bears. Height at shoulder is about 4 feet; body length is 7 to 11 feet. The polar bear's head is proportionally small compared to other bears, with a slightly longer muzzle and an elongated neck.

Tail: Heavily furred, white to cream-colored, 3 to more than 6 inches long

TRACKS

Polar bears have large feet designed for swimming long distances, with five widely splayed toes on all four feet. Heavily furred soles may obscure or blur print details. Foreprints are 6 to 8 inches long, longer if measured from dotlike heel print; toes are heavily clawed, but much

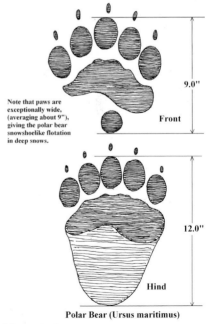

Note that paws are exceptionally wide, (averaging about 9"), giving the polar bear snowshoelike flotation in deep snows.

9.0"

Front

12.0"

Hind

Polar Bear (Ursus maritimus)

Polar bear tracks

shorter than the long, almost straight foreclaws of a brown bear. Hind prints are 10 to more than 12 inches long, almost human-shaped, indicating a flat-footed (plantigrade) walk. Heel is much narrower than that of a brown bear; tracks are much larger than the black bear's. Bear tracks on pack ice or ice floes are always from a polar bear.

SCAT

Similar to a brown bear's: cylindrical, often segmented, 2 or more inches in diameter, often more than 6 inches long. Dark brown to black, often with seal fur in evidence. Polar bears also eat small amounts of vegetation, mostly lichens like reindeer moss, and plant fibers might also be apparent.

COLORATION

The pelage is generally all white, contrasting against a black nose pad, and making the brown eyes appear to be black. In summer the coat may take on a yellowish hue, supposedly from oxidation in the warmer air, and polar bears that have been digging in soil or frequenting landfills might be a dirty gray. The polar bear's skin is black.

SIGN

Seal carcasses from which all fat and larger pieces of meat have been chewed. Hides of these carcasses will be shredded from the bear's sharp claws. Regularly packed trails in snow around seasonal hunting grounds, marked at intervals, and especially at intersections, by scat and urine deposits.

VOCALIZATIONS

Polar bears are normally silent. Huffing and grunting sounds are the most common noises made, but polar bears can growl and bawl like other bear species.

LIFE SPAN

In the wild polar bears may live to be 30 years old. One captive female at the Detroit Zoo, in Detroit, Michigan, reached 45 years in 1999.

DIET

Polar bears are the most carnivorous species in family Ursidae, largely because their icy snow-covered habitat prohibits being a vegetarian. In this streamlined and fragile ecosystem, plankton eat algae, small fish eat plankton, large fish eat small fish, seals eat large fish, and polar bears eat seals. Nothing preys on a polar bear except humans.

The polar bear's most common prey is the ringed seal *(Phoca hispida),* followed by the bearded seal *(Erignathus barbatus),* the harp seal *(Pagophilus groenlandicus),* the hooded seal *(Cystophora cristata),* and an occasional small walrus *(Odobenus rosmarus).* They will generally eat any animal they can catch, including seabirds, and often scavenge on the carcasses of dead whales and other large animals.

Polar bears are especially predatory of seals when the flippered mammals gather in large colonies along open shorelines to mate in January and February, and during their birthing periods in April and May. The usual technique is simply to stalk unseen as closely as possible to a crowded colony, then charge into its midst with sharp claws and teeth, hoping to mortally injure one or more seals before they can escape underwater.

In winter, polar bears lie in wait on the pack ice at a seal's breathing hole, moving into position while the seal is underwater. When the seal resurfaces to take air, the bear slaps it with a powerful sharply clawed paw, killing or mortally wounding the animal, which is then dragged onto the ice and consumed.

Blubber (seal or whale fat) is the most preferred staple in a polar bear's diet, and well fed bears will often eat only the blubber of their kills. More important than meat protein in the polar bear's frozen habitat is fat, which provides the necessary proteins and nutrients its body needs, as well as adding to its own layer of insulation. Arctic foxes have learned to make a practice of shadowing bears on the hunt to get the red meat they leave behind.

Polar bears aren't known to cache large kills that can't be eaten all at once, but partially consumed carcasses are always being guarded, and will be defended if approached too closely. As with other bears, never venture closer than 200 yards of a carcass.

MATING HABITS

Polar bears tend to mate earlier in the year than other bear species, with normally solitary males and females coming together to mate in April and May. After a brief period of courtship and mating that normally lasts about 3 days, the mates go their separate ways; both may mate again with another partner. Mating is terminated by the female, who seems to know when she's pregnant and wards off further advances from males with hard slaps and bites.

As with other bear species, mating fights between males of breeding age are rare, brief, and seldom injurious to either opponent. Physical size and body language are usually sufficient to determine which is the stronger animal, and when contentious males do battle, the contest is more of a wrestling match that ends as soon as it becomes apparent which bear is more powerful.

Polar bear females undergo a period of delayed implantation after mating successfully, carrying fertilized eggs dormant within their wombs until October or November, when the eggs

Cubs and mothers remain together for 2 to 3 years—up to a year longer than black or brown bears and their offspring. Larger size at birth, a faster rate of growth, and a longer period of maternal care all contribute to a young polar bear's chances of survival in the harshest environment on earth. Even with the best care, mortality for polar bear cubs is estimated to reach as high as one out of three.

implant or abort, depending on the female's state of health. At this time mated females migrate to ocean coastlines where banks and dunes provide places to excavate a birthing den, and nearby seal colonies allow for good hunting. Along Canada's Hudson Bay, the largest polar bear denning region on earth, dens may be excavated in dirt along the banks of both the ocean and the rivers feeding into it. In other places dens are excavated into snowbanks.

While no species of bear truly hibernates, polar bears are the most active during the winter months. Mothers may lay up in their dens for several days at a time, but will remain active until they give birth in December or January. Twins are the norm, with each cub born blind, fully furred, and weighing about 2 pounds (twice the birth weight of a brown bear newborn). After giving birth, often in her sleep, the mother remains inside the den, sleeping and reserving resources for her nursing offspring. She emerges from her den in April with her now 20- to 30-pound cubs, and begins their education.

Male polar bears reach sexual maturity at 4 or 5 years, and will mate every year if they can. Females become sexually active at 3 or 4 years, but may not mate for up to four years between litters.

BEHAVIORISMS

Polar bears are solitary, carnivorous, and the most predatory of family *Ursidae*. Living in an environment where almost every meal means killing another animal has caused *Ursus maritimus* to regard all other creatures as potential prey, including humans. Unlike brown bears, polar bears that attack people normally perceive them as food, and *Ursus maritimus* can legitimately be considered a man-eater. Fortunately, humans are scarce or absent throughout most of the polar bear's range, so encounters are rare.

Polar bears may be active at any time of day or night, especially in the continuous daylight of the arctic summer. To conserve energy, the animals spend an estimated 66 percent of their days either sleeping or lying in wait for a prey animal to present itself.

As its species name implies, the polar bear is an excellent swimmer. With a swimming stroke unique among mammals, the bear paddles with its forefeet only, letting the hind feet simply trail behind. Despite the seeming ungainliness of this stroke, polar bears can swim in excess of 6 miles per hour, and they've been observed swimming in open ocean more than 20 miles from pack ice.

Polar bear pelts were once an important commodity in the fur trade, with skins fetching as much as $3,000 apiece. The species has never been endangered, but fear that demand from the fur-buying public might change that prompted passage of the United States Marine Mammal Protection Act in 1972, which prohibits all sport hunting of polar bears. In 1973 those protections were also adopted by Canada, the Soviet Union, Norway, and Denmark. The U.S. Fish and Wildlife Service estimates that the polar bear population is currently at twenty thousand to twenty-five thousand bears.

A real worry—not only for polar bears—are the extensive arctic habitat alterations associated with global climate change. Climate change may place the species in more jeopardy than the fur trade ever did.

Procyonids are a diverse family that includes the lesser pandas of Asia, the ringtail and coati of the southwestern United States and Mexico, and the familiar raccoon. Despite the real diversity within this group, all have five toes on each foot, all are excellent climbers, and all have an omnivorous diet.

Raccoon *(Procyon lotor)*

Few animals are better recognized than the raccoon, with its distinctive bandit-masked face and striped tail. Cartoons and caricatures of the raccoon usually depict it as a thief, an allusion to both the animal's bold penchant for stealing from humans and to its masked face. Although considered prey by raptors and larger carnivores when they're young, an adult coon is ferocious when cornered, and only the largest predators are willing to tackle one. This aggressive nature, which is also seen in the wolverine and badger, is a good defense against larger predators whose objective is to kill their prey with little effort and with as little danger to themselves as possible. Unfortunately, that nature also makes raccoons willing to invade rural and residential areas to raid gardens, knock over garbage cans, and steal an occasional chicken.

Aside from causing property damage, raccoons are harmless to people unless cornered. One danger they do pose is rabies, a disease that some of them contract and die from each spring, especially when local populations are too high. Raccoons can also be hazardous to pets,

Playful wanderer of forests, streams, and river bottoms, the raccoon is common throughout North America. BILL BUCHANAN/USFWS

inflicting sometimes serious wounds to dogs, and the species is well known for drawing hunting dogs into deep water, where the coon then climbs onto the dog's head and drowns it.

GEOGRAPHIC RANGE
Excepting the treeless Great Plains and the desert Southwest, raccoons are found throughout the United States, ranging from the Pacific to the Atlantic. To the north their range extends only a little north of Canada's southern border. To the south raccoons range far into Mexico.

HABITAT
Raccoons are among the most intelligent and adaptable of mammals, but their preferred habitat always includes trees large enough to climb in search of a good observation point or to escape predators—especially domestic dogs, which are more likely to attack a raccoon than are wild carnivores like coyotes or bobcats.

Raccoon habitat will also always have a source of open water. The animals are superb swimmers, able to easily outdistance most enemies across lakes or rivers. But more importantly they require a water source that provides small prey like crayfish, clams, small fish, and frogs.

PHYSICAL CHARACTERISTICS
Mass: 12 to 48 pounds, with an occasional individual reaching 60 pounds or more in the far north.
Body: Built much like a bear—stocky, muscular, with a humped spine and thick fur over a layer of insulating fat. Males are generally larger than females, but the largest individuals reported have been old females. Body length is 23 to more than 38 inches, with an arched back 8 to more than 12 inches high. Head is proportionally small, with a short pointed muzzle tipped by a black nose. Ears are erect, large, and rounded at the tips.
Tail: Striped with alternating bands of darker fur, 7 to more than 14 inches long, roughly half as long as the animal's body.

TRACKS
Easy to identify; with five toes on all four feet, each toe tipped with an elongated fingernail-like claw. Toes are long and fingerlike, with four pointing forward, and a shorter, thumblike toe extending to the inside, making it look very much like a human hand. Tips of the toes leave a bulbous impression just rearward of the claws. Forefoot length is 2 to 3 inches. Hind feet are flat-soled and elongated, indicating the plantigrade walk of a slow runner that has little to fear in its daily life. The general outline is somewhat human-shaped, like all plantigrade mammals, but has uniquely raccoon features, including four fingerlike toes pointing forward, each terminating in a bulbous tip and fingernail claw, and one shorter thumblike toe well to the rear of the others and pointing inward. Length is 3 to 4 inches.

Procyon lotor's normal gait is a shuffling walk, much like a bear's, in which the soles of especially the hind feet tend to scrape the earth as they're brought forward, leaving scuff marks to the rear of the hind track. Hind prints generally register separately and beside front tracks at a relaxed walk. The bushy tail may brush over tracks on sandy or dusty soils. Stride is up to 2 feet between paired sets of front and hind prints, depending on terrain and an individual's size. Straddle is 3 to 4 inches, but can reach 6 inches in large old animals, indicating the species' wide, powerfully built physique.

At a fast run that can reach 15 miles per hour on flat ground, the raccoon gait changes to the almost universal "rocking horse" pattern, in which forefeet are planted side by side to act as a pivot while the hind feet are brought forward on either side. When the hind feet make contact with earth, the coon springs forward, forefeet extended, and the gait repeats anew. At a fast run, the distance between sets of all four tracks may reach 3 feet.

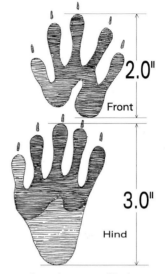

Raccoon tracks are distinctive, and familiar to any tracker who spends time along wooded creeks.

SCAT

Distinctive and easy to identify. Cylindrical and usually unsegmented; 2 to 3 inches long by up to 0.5 inch in diameter; the same diameter throughout its length. Ends usually untapered and flat.

COLORATION

The most obvious characteristics of the raccoon are the black mask around its eyes and its bushy tail, with up to ten black rings running circumferentially along its length. The pelage is grizzled, with fur color that varies from gray to reddish.

SIGN

This scat is from a blueberry-eating raccoon.

Shells of turtle eggs that have been excavated from buried nests along sandy lakeshores and eaten. Crayfish carapaces and empty clam shells along the banks of rivers and ponds.

VOCALIZATIONS

Most common is a chirring sound, sometimes described as cooing, made when the animal is curious or generally relaxed. Territorial and mating sounds include screeches, snarls, and growls.

LIFE SPAN
Raccoons have lived up to 16 years in captivity, but in the wild most don't make it past 4 years because of predation by birds of prey, land predators, and automobiles.

DIET
Like bears, raccoons are omnivorous and opportunistic, able to subsist on a broad variety of vegetation, insects, and small animals. Most foods are obtained along or near shorelines, where the majority of scat and sign are found. As with bears, raccoons are particularly fond of calorie-rich berries, nuts, and fruits of all types, and in many habitats and seasons vegetation might make up most of the foods a raccoon eats.

To the consternation of gardeners and farmers, raccoons are very fond of corn, and the normally solitary animals are known to descend on corn fields in force, sometimes decimating an entire field when they break down stalks to get at ripening ears. The animals can also damage fruit trees and grape arbors by climbing to get at hanging fruit, breaking branches and knocking arbors to the ground.

Although poorly designed for chasing down prey, raccoons consume animal flesh whenever they can get it. The carnivorous portion of their diets typically includes more invertebrates than vertebrates. Crayfish, grasshoppers and other insects, small rodents, frogs, birds, and hatchling turtles are components of the raccoon's diet. Essentially, any small animal that can be taken with little effort or danger is prey. Carrion may also be eaten, but not with the same regularity or in the same volume as by coyotes or other scavenging species.

Raccoons are also known for their habit of washing foods at the edges of waterways, a practice alluded to by its species name, "lotor," which translates to "the washer" in Latin. The purpose behind this practice was once a mystery, but is now known to be a sorting process in which the animal uses its extraordinarily sensitive fingerlike toes to separate inedible matter from its foods. Whereas many animals must simply swallow small prey bones and all, the raccoon can pick out and remove the parts it doesn't want to eat.

MATING HABITS
Raccoons become sexually mature at 1 year, but males will probably not breed until 2 years because they need to establish their own territories first. Mating season begins in late January and extends through early March, peaking in February. Populations in the far south may begin mating as early as December. Males travel to females from as far away as 3 miles, attracted to them by pheromonal scents. Mating doesn't normally occur immediately, but is preceded by several days of courtship during which males den with females.

Once impregnated, females reject further sexual overtures and males go on their way, often to find another receptive female. Female raccoons are believed to take only one mate per breeding season.

After a gestation period of 60 to 70 days, females retire to a secluded leaf-lined den, typically in a large hollow tree or under its roots, or sometimes in dry culverts and other man-made shelters. There the mother will give birth to litters of four to eight cubs in April or May, with larger litter sizes indicating healthy, well fed females. Cubs weigh about 2 ounces at birth, and come into the world blind, deaf, and almost naked (altricial). Young open their eyes at 3 weeks and begin to move about the den. At 2 months they leave the den to explore, but remain close to the safety of its entrance because raccoon cubs are prey for most carnivores and predatory birds. During this delicate stage in their development the mother may move her cubs to an alternate den, carrying them one at a time by the nape of their neck. If a larger predator threatens, she will push her young up a tree, then follow them, much like a black bear. If caught by surprise or cornered, the female will defend her litter viciously enough to discourage most carnivores.

By 3 months the cubs will have been weaned, and will begin foraging on their own for insects and other small food animals. The family remains together throughout the summer and following winter, but separates before the next spring mating season, when the mother will probably mate again. Males typically leave first, setting off to find their own territories, followed by female siblings who will likely take mates of their own in the coming breeding season.

BEHAVIORISMS

Except for mating and rearing young, raccoons are solitary creatures. The species is generally thought to be nocturnal, but in wild places where there are no humans or, especially, dogs, the animals may be seen foraging and hunting along shorelines at any time of day.

Raccoons are not true hibernators, but during periods of extreme cold or snow the animals may lay up in a den for a week or more until the weather breaks, living off a normally thick layer of body fat while conserving energy. Denned raccoons are normally alone, but mothers and cubs will den together, and courting pairs may stay together for up to one month prior to breeding.

Raccoons have highly developed tactile senses, and some researchers believe the sense of feel in their forepaws may be several times more acute than that of humans. What is known for sure is that raccoons possess the tactility needed to locate and catch snails, crayfish, and other underwater foods by feel alone. Along with that extraordinary sense of feel, a raccoon's handlike forepaws can grasp, pull, and tear with strength sufficient to pry open clams and remove the carapaces of crayfish, or even hatchling turtles.

An ability to grasp also makes the raccoon a good climber. Large smooth-barked trees like beech and sycamore can sometimes resist the animal's relatively dull claws, but rough-barked trees like maple, oak, and white pine are easy for it to climb. Raccoons lack the agility to pursue prey through treetops the way a fisher or pine marten can, and generally climb only to escape enemies. On rare occasions the animals have lost their grip and fallen, but are able to survive long falls of 30 feet or more with little or no injury to themselves.

Procyon lotor is also an adept swimmer, and frequently takes to the water to escape threats, especially when pursued by hunting dogs. They rarely swim unless motivated by danger, however, because coon fur lacks the repellent oils contained in the fur of aquatic mammals, and their coats become heavy when saturated. If a hunting dog should pursue a raccoon into water, the raccoon is notorious for turning and climbing onto the dog's head, holding it underwater with its own weight and sometimes drowning the dog.

Chapter Seventeen

SQUIRRELS *(SCIURIDAE)*

Sciuridae is the family of squirrels, and is represented in North America by sixty-three species that include such diverse animals as marmots, chipmunks, and tree squirrels. The family name is Latin for "shade tail," an allusion to the long bushy tail of tree squirrels, but is actually a misnomer where short-tailed ground squirrels like prairie dogs and woodchucks are concerned.

Physical characteristics common to all squirrel species include having four toes on the forefeet and five toes on the hind feet. All are plantigrade, or flat-footed, with elongated hind paws that resemble human feet. All are rodents, with chisel-shaped upper and lower incisors that are adapted to gnawing and cutting wood or vegetation, but most will also dine on an occasional insect or small animal if the opportunity arises.

The ubiquitous gray squirrel. LAURA PERLICK/USFWS

Gray Squirrel *(Sciurus carolinensis)*

Best known of the tree squirrels among human hunters, the gray squirrel has served as a food staple for as long as there have been people in the New World. In the days of colonial America it was common to refer to any long gun that was .45 caliber or smaller as a squirrel gun, which demonstrates how important a role this tree-dwelling rodent played in the lives of pioneers.

Although the eastern gray squirrel has been selected to represent larger tree squirrels in this book, the species has several very close cousins living throughout the forested areas of North America, and all of them share similar diets, mating, and behavioral traits. The same can be said of the larger fox squirrel *(Sciurus niger),* which shares almost exactly the same range as the gray squirrel.

GEOGRAPHIC RANGE

Sciurus carolinensis occupies the eastern half of the United States to the Mississippi River, ranging as far south as Florida and eastern Texas, and north to the southernmost edge of Canada. Introduced populations also exist in Italy, Scotland, England, and Ireland, where the squirrels have thrived to the point of becoming a serious pest species.

HABITAT

Sciurus carolinensis requires trees in its habitat, and will not be found in prairies, deserts, or in rocky places that lack tall trees in which to forage, make dens, and to escape predators. The ideal habitat includes undergrowth and ground plants, and ready access to drinking water. Larger fox squirrels prefer a mixed habitat of conifers and hardwoods; smaller red squirrels are found in mostly coniferous forests.

PHYSICAL CHARACTERISTICS

Mass: 1 to 1.5 pounds.
Body: Elongated and well furred. Short legs; rounded head with short muzzle; small round ears. Body length is 16 to 20 inches. No difference in body size between the sexes.

Some notable differences occur in skull size and fur color between gray squirrel populations in the northern part of the species' range and those in the southern. From north to south there exists a decreasing cline in skull size, although mandible sizes and dental arrangements remain unchanged. Also, individuals in the south tend more toward a gray coat, while populations in the north are more often black in color, better suited to life in a cold climate.
Tail: Well furred; less rounded (more flat) along its top than in other tree squirrels. Length 8 to 10 inches, or about 50 percent of body length. The tail functions as an umbrella in rain and hot sun, and helps keep its owner warm while sleeping in cold weather.

TRACKS

Gray squirrels have four toes on the front feet, five toes on the hind. Tracks of front feet are rounded, 1 to 1.5 inches long; tracks of hind feet are elongated, 2 to 2.5 inches long.

Track pattern much like that of a rabbit, but markedly smaller. Hind feet print ahead of forefeet, leaving a pattern like two side-by-side exclamation points (!!), indicating the hopping gait common to all tree squirrels. Total length of track pattern is 7 to 8 inches. Distance between track sets indicates gait: 10 inches for a casual hopping pace, 24 inches at an easy bounding run, 36 inches or more when the animal is fleeing danger.

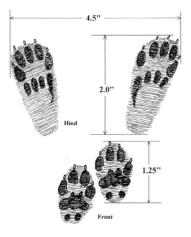

Gray squirrel tracks

SCAT

Pellet-shaped, dark brown to black, 0.25 inch in diameter. Pellets often exhibit a thin "tail" of rough plant fibers on one end, indicating more fibrous browse. Roughly one dozen pellets per scat deposit, more or less, depending on the size of the squirrel.

COLORATION

There are two distinct color phases in *S. carolinensis.* Populations that live in forests consisting all or mostly of beech trees tend to be gray, matching the smooth bark of the trees they inhabit. Those living among dark-barked trees like maples and oaks are mostly black, especially in the northern part of the range. Both color phases exhibit a grizzling of whitish guard hairs along the dorsal parts. The ears and underbelly are often lighter in color than the body. Albinism is uncommon, and doesn't occur at all in the colder northern latitudes, but albino colonies exist in southern Illinois,

Squirrel scat

New Jersey, and South Carolina. The fox squirrel is larger, with a reddish pelage; the red squirrel is much smaller with a brown to orange coat and white underparts.

Helping to explain the variation in fur colors are studies that have shown black squirrels experience 18 percent less heat loss than gray squirrels in temperatures below freezing, along with a 20 percent lower metabolic rate, and a nonshivering (thermogenesis) capacity that's 11 percent higher than in grey individuals.

SIGN

Beechnut husks; opened shells of acorns, walnuts, hickory nuts, and other nuts. In autumn, leafy nut-bearing twig ends are frequently found beneath food trees, the cut ends showing a neatly clipped, stepped bite left by the squirrel's sharp upper and lower incisors. Small patches of disturbed soil scattered atop the forest humus reveal where nuts have been buried in shallow holes for winter storage. In winter, hardpack snow will be pocked with holes, about 6 inches in diameter, where a squirrel burrowed diagonally downward to retrieve a buried nut, often leaving a spray of darker soil around the entrance.

A sure sign that squirrels have been feeding on acorns—clipped branch tips.

VOCALIZATIONS

Chirping barks are frequently heard from territorial males, especially during the autumn and early spring breeding seasons. Alarm calls consist of short clucking barks that humans can usually imitate well by sucking a cheek repeatedly against the molars on one side of their mouths. The intensity of a squirrel's alarm is gauged by the frequency of the barks: A fast chattering denotes immediate danger, becoming less frequent as the source of alarm recedes.

LIFE SPAN

Average lifespan in the wild is about 12.5 years, but one captive female lived to more than 20 years of age.

DIET

Gray squirrels feed mostly on nuts and seeds, with acorns, chestnuts, and other storable nuts being among the favorites. Tree buds make up a large part of the diet in winter and early spring, along with nuts that were cached in shallow holes the previous autumn. In summer the diet includes plants, grasses, and flowers. Pine and cedar nuts and buds are also eaten, but not as much as with other tree squirrel species, and mushrooms are sometimes nibbled on. Although mostly vegetarian, gray and other tree squirrels are also known to eat insects, tree frogs, and an occasional bird egg, with predatory habits being more common during times when nut crops are poor. Deer bones and antlers are gnawed on to wear down the squirrel's constantly growing incisors, and to get at the calcium and other minerals contained in them. Crops like wheat, and especially corn, are favored foods, making the squirrels a pest species in some agricultural areas.

Legend has it that gray (and fox) squirrels remember where they bury each nut, but in fact the squirrels possess an extremely acute sense of smell that can detect cached nuts by their odors, even under a foot of snow. Not all of these buried nuts are found, however, and during good years more nuts are buried than are needed to supply an animal's food requirements. In either case, a number of buried nuts go unretrieved each year, and many will take root to become new trees. In this way squirrels contribute to the expansion and health of their own habitats, carrying nuts to germinate in places where they couldn't have otherwise been spread.

MATING HABITS

Gray squirrels, like all tree squirrel species, typically have two mating seasons per year, one from May through June, and a second from December through February, with populations in the northernmost parts of the range entering the mating season as much as 1 month later. Males older than 11 months are drawn to pre-estrus females by the scent of sexual pheromones about a week prior to mating, and may come from as far away as half a mile. The testes of mating males become greatly enlarged prior to mating, increasing in mass from their nonbreeding weight of approximately 1 gram to as much as 7 grams at the peak of their heat.

Females may breed as young as 6 months, especially where population densities are low, but most mate at 15 months, and remain fertile for about 8 years. Estrus is indicated in the female by an enlarged pink vulva that makes it easier to identify her sex; males and females appear nearly identical during nonbreeding months. The vulva is typically swollen for just 8 hours, and the vaginal cavity is closed except during estrus.

Territorial battles between males are common and noisy during the mating seasons, with contenders battling sometimes furiously on the ground and in the trees. Embattled males are often so preoccupied that they become easy prey for carnivores. In areas where populations are high or females are scarce, the males of gray and other tree squirrel species have been observed actually biting off the testicles of competing males.

Once paired, copulation is short, generally lasting less than 30 seconds, after which mates go their separate ways. Males will attempt to breed again with as many partners as possible, but mated females will breed with other partners only until they become pregnant, which they appear to realize instinctively. After being impregnated, females form mucus plugs within their vaginal cavities to block further entry by sperm, and reject further sexual advances.

Gestation lasts an average of 44 days, with two to four kits born in an elevated, leaf-lined nest in a hollow tree. Young are born naked (altricial) but whiskered (vibrissal), each weighing about 4 ounces. Newborns nurse almost constantly for the first 7 weeks, and their mothers remain with them in the nest except for short outings to eat, drink, and relieve themselves. During the brief periods when the young are left alone they may fall prey to raccoons, weasels, and predatory birds (especially small owls), which are capable of entering the den opening. But nursing female squirrels will fight viciously in defense of their offspring, and predation is usually minimal. Still, a mother never wanders far from her young, and her territory may shrink by as much as 50 percent while her young are suckling.

During the nursing period, mother squirrels may move their young to different nesting locations as the situation demands. In cold months the nests are always in an enclosed den, but in warm weather young may be nursed in an open, dish-shaped nest of sticks and leaves located in the crotch of a high tree limb. By 10 weeks of age the young have become identical to adults and are weaned, after which the family separates and mothers provide no more maternal care. Adult size and mass are reached at 9 months.

BEHAVIORISMS

With the exception of flying squirrels, which are nocturnal, all tree squirrels are active during daylight hours (diurnal), with peak activity occurring about 2 hours after sunrise, and 2 to 5 hours prior to sunset, depending on the season. They avoid activity during the heat of the day in summer, resting on loafing platforms made from sticks and leaves and located in overhead branches. Unlike maternal nests, loafing platforms are flatter (less concave) because they don't have to contain youngsters that might fall out of a nest with lower sides. Loafing platforms are often indicative of the builder's age, with the more haphazardly constructed usually being made by younger, less-experienced animals.

Male and female gray squirrels are virtually identical in color and size, but the activities of an individual can provide clues to its gender. Generally, males are more active in autumn and winter, when food, territory, and mates motivate them to be alert for competitors and more defensive. Females tend to be more active during the summer months, when they must regain the energy lost while rearing the previous spring's litter, and put on fat needed for the autumn mating season.

While a number of sometimes widely differing estimates have been made of how much acreage is required to support a healthy population of gray squirrels, how large or small a territory must be is ultimately determined by the availability of resources. A single city block can be home to a half dozen of the animals so long as sufficient food, water, and trees are available, and in urban parks, where squirrels receive regular handouts from humans, population densities may be even higher.

In fact, urban and residential areas have proved so attractive to gray squirrels that a small pest removal industry has sprung up in response to their invasions of attics, ventilation ducts, and other places that bring them into conflict with human populations. The problem has become severe among transplanted populations in Great Britain, where gray squirrels are ranked second only to the Norway rat *(Rattus norvegicus)* in terms of property destruction.

Despite their status as pests in some areas, gray and other squirrels have a strong following among wildlife enthusiasts, and squirrel watching has become nearly as popular as bird watching. Gray and fox squirrels are also very popular with small game hunters, and represent millions of dollars in revenue for state governments and the sport-hunting industry each year.

Woodchuck *(Marmota monax)*

Largest of the squirrel family, the woodchuck and its close relatives, the yellow-bellied marmot, hoary marmot, and Olympic marmot, are ground-dwelling burrowers that lack the bushy tail associated with tree squirrels. This species gets its common name from the Cree Indian word *woochuk,* which the tribe used to describe all marmots. But the woodchuck retained it because its burrows are most often found near forests.

The woodchuck is the predominant marmot species in North America. STUART MONK/LICENSED BY SHUTTERSTOCK.COM

Probably best known as the "groundhog" that emerges from hibernation each year on February 2 to predict when winter will end, the woodchuck is the most populous marmot species in North America. Because nearly all of its habits and characteristics are shared by other marmots, the information given here about woodchucks is generally applicable to all marmot species.

GEOGRAPHIC RANGE

The range of *M. monax* extends from the Atlantic coast to the Pacific coast, across North America. In the north distribution extends in a line from New Brunswick, across the southern shore of Hudson Bay, through the Yukon Territory and into central Alaska. The southern boundaries extend from Virginia to Arkansas, and then northwest to British Columbia. Being burrowers, they are not found above the Arctic Circle, where permafrost prevents digging, although more than a decade of study has shown that the permafrost is receding, which may cause woodchucks to expand their range northward.

HABITAT

Like other marmots, woodchucks prefer open areas where they can bask in the sun, but are almost never far from the forests that give them their common name. Burrows excavated under the roots of large trees provide good protection from digging predators like bears and wolves, while tall trees permit a quick escape for woodchucks caught by surprise on the ground, or serve as elevated observation posts.

High ground with good drainage is a necessary component of the woodchuck's habitat, especially in northern regions that experience potential flooding from snowmelt in spring.

Like any animal, marmots require a source of drinking water nearby, but their excavated dens, which may extend underground as far as 25 feet and have as many as six outlets, must be in earth that remains dry year-round to a depth of at least 5 feet.

PHYSICAL CHARACTERISTICS

Mass: 4.5 to 14 pounds, with larger individuals occurring in the north. Males are slightly larger and more muscular than females.

Body: Chunky and stout, with short powerful legs well adapted for digging. Body length is 16 to more than 32 inches. Skull is broad and flat on top, flanked on either side by small roundish ears. The woodchuck's incisors continue to grow throughout its life span, and if they aren't worn down properly the upper and lower matching pairs can grow past one another (malocclusion), where they may continue to grow until the jawbones are pierced and eating becomes impossible.

Tail: 3.5 to 9 inches long. Well furred but not as bushy as a tree squirrel's, about 25 percent of body length.

TRACKS

Woodchucks have four toes on the forefeet, five toes on hind feet. The rudimentary first digit of the forepaw is covered by a flat nail; the other three digits terminate in curved claws that are useful in digging. The hind foot has five elongated and clawed digits that show clearly in most tracks. Front track is about 2 inches long; the hind track is usually 2.5 inches, but 3 inches or more on soft ground where the entire heel prints. Straddle is 3.5 to 6 inches; walking stride, in which hind feet print on top of or slightly ahead of front tracks, is 3 to 4 inches. In the running stride, which may be as fast as 10 miles per hour, hind feet print ahead of forefeet, which print individually behind and between them. The distance between track sets is about 14 inches.

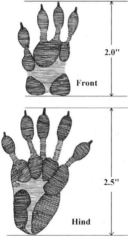

Woodchuck tracks

SCAT

Elongated and irregular in diameter, usually tapered at one or both ends, with plant fibers in evidence. Dark brown to black in color, lightening with age. Length is 2 to more than 4 inches.

COLORATION

Dark brown to nearly black along the dorsal region and sides, interspersed with coarser guard hairs that are banded in alternating red and yellow, and tipped with white. The underbelly is more pale. Head and feet are much darker. The tail is dark-colored, much shorter in comparison to tree squirrels. There is one annual molt, occurring during late May to September, which begins at the tail and progresses forward. The feet are black and plantigrade. The woodchuck's long incisors are white or nearly white, lacking the dark yellow pigmentation of other large rodents like porcupines and beavers.

SIGN

Burrow entrances 10 to 14 inches in diameter dug into knolls and hillsides, sometimes beneath the roots of standing trees, and occasionally into and under a hole in the trunk of a standing hollow tree. The woodchuck also possesses three nipplelike anal (perineal) scent glands that secrete a musky odor, and trees, stumps, or other prominent objects around den entrances will often be scented.

VOCALIZATIONS

Woodchucks are often vocal, particularly when alarmed, which explains the nickname "whistle pig." The alarm cry is a single loud, shrill whistle, often preceded by a squirrel-like bark. The call used to attract mates, to warn intruders impinging on territory, or issued by mothers calling young to the safety of the burrow, is a loud whistle followed by a less piercing call, which ends with a series of softer whistles that cannot be heard except at close range. Teeth grinding, chattering, and even doglike growls are common when woodchucks are cornered by a predator.

LIFE SPAN

Young woodchucks are preyed on by most carnivores and predatory birds, but those that reach adulthood may live up to 6 years in the wild, or up to 10 years in captivity.

DIET

Woodchucks are mostly herbivorous grazers, preferring clover, alfalfa, plantains, grasses, and most succulent ground plants during the summer months, but subsisting for short periods on the bark and buds of wild cherry, sumac, and other shrubs in early spring, before favored food plants are available. Poplar, cottonwood, and aspens are of particular importance because they provide food in the form of bark, buds, and leaves throughout the woodchuck's active time of year.

Like most sciurids, woodchucks and other marmots will also eat an occasional bird egg, grasshopper, snail, or small tree frog, and probably the young of most small rodents. These minor predations appear to be opportunistic in nature. Marmots aren't known to eat carrion, but they will gnaw on shed antlers and bones for the nutrients contained in them.

Because the geographic range and habitat of the woodchuck encompass most of the richest farming areas in North America, this species more than any other marmot has incurred the ire of farmers. Land cleared for planting provides good habitat, and crops like alfalfa, clover, wheat, and especially corn are relished by woodchucks, which can eat in excess of 1.5 pounds per animal per day, breaking down and killing plants while they feed.

In late summer, the woodchucks begin to feed more urgently. Each animal needs to gain about 25 percent of its body weight in a layer of fat that will insulate and sustain its body through the winter. During this period, before winter snows send it into its burrow, a woodchuck becomes especially territorial and protective of the food resources the territory contains. Trespassers, especially yearlings wandering in search of their own territories, will be decisively driven off as green food plants become more scarce with shortening and cooling days.

MATING HABITS

Breeding takes place in early spring, usually within 2 weeks of when the woodchucks emerge from hibernation in late March or April. Adults are normally solitary, but the territories of adult males will typically overlap those of the several females whose territories surround their own. This arrangement, which is seen in most animals, permits established males to make contact with receptive females without trespassing into the territories of other males. When two males do compete, the battles consist of boxing matches in which both contenders stand erect on their hind feet, slapping and biting one another until the weaker animal withdraws.

Females are believed to be monoestrous, and take only one mate per breeding season. Males stay in a mate's den for about 1 week—the only time these normally solitary animals are social—before leaving to seek out another female. In April or May, after a gestation period of approximately 32 days, females give birth to litters of one to nine naked and blind young, with five being the average litter size. Newborns weigh about 26 grams, and measure about 4 inches long.

Females have four pairs of teats and nurse their young from a standing position, staying with them almost constantly for their first 2 weeks. At 3 weeks, the young begin crawling about inside the den, and at 4 weeks they open their eyes. By 5 weeks, the young woodchucks are fully active and begin exploring around the den entrance, going only a short distance and scurrying back inside if the mother issues an alarm whistle.

Young woodchucks are weaned at 6 weeks, but may remain with their mother until July or August, when she forces them to disperse. Yearlings must find or excavate their own burrows after leaving their mothers, and will hibernate alone in their first winter. Females will probably mate on emerging from their dens the following spring, but competition may force young males to wait until the next spring, after they've established their own territories.

BEHAVIORISMS

Woodchucks are the most solitary marmot species, and both genders are generally hostile, or agonistic, toward one another on meeting. Battles are usually of short duration and relatively bloodless, but established adults will not tolerate trespassers. Reports of several individuals sharing a den stem from observations made during the short mating period, when males occupy the dens of their mates, or of nearly grown offspring denning with their mother.

Being diurnal, woodchucks are most often observed during the day, although some have been known to become partly nocturnal if harassed by humans. The stereotypical image of this species is that of an animal standing erect, forelimbs held tightly to the front of its body, as it surveys the surrounding area. While that posture is common for animals that have been alerted to possible danger, woodchucks prefer to spend most of their time on all fours, foraging and feeding. When not feeding, the animals are fond of sunbathing and cleaning their fur in the open, but never go far from the den entrance.

If alarmed, a woodchuck will quickly retreat into its den, turning to face outward once inside. This is a defensive position from which the marmot can bite and claw with surprising ferocity should a predator attempt to dig it out. The sharp incisors and viciousness of a large woodchuck defending itself is adequate to convince most predators, including badgers and coyotes, to seek easier prey, but black and brown bears are often successful in digging them free.

Like most burrowing animals, a woodchuck's den always has at least one, and sometimes as many as five, escape exits that are several yards from the main entrance, but that may be of limited value when the animal digging inward is a large bear. Bears, like badgers, are often accompanied by a coyote when digging into dens; the coyote stands guard over an escape hole while the bear digs, waiting to snap up the den's occupant if it pops out. This cooperative tactic is effective when the prey is a smaller ground squirrel, but a large marmot may prove to be more than a coyote can handle, and if a woodchuck can fight its way to a nearby tree, it will probably escape both enemies. None of the marmot species are agile climbers, like their tree squirrel cousins, but all can climb trees well enough to escape most predators, if they get a head start.

Like other marmots and ground squirrels, the woodchuck is a true hibernator, spending the cold winter months in a comalike slumber within a grass-lined sleeping chamber deep inside its den. The animals enter the den to hibernate prior to the first permanent snowfall, usually in late November in the north, and in December in the southern part of the species' range. Once inside and asleep, the marmot's body undergoes remarkable physiological changes: Its body temperature falls from a normal 97 degrees Fahrenheit to 40 degrees, and its heart rate slows from about 100 beats per minute to just 4 beats per minute. It remains in this state until warming days cause it to emerge in April, although its deep slumber appears to become lighter as spring approaches.

The animals do not ritually step out of their dens to see if they cast a shadow on February 2, but large gatherings of humans, like the annual Groundhog Day festival held in Punxsutawney, Pennsylvania, usually create enough commotion to awaken a hibernating woodchuck. This bit of American folklore, which coincides with Candlemas Day, probably has its roots in an Old World belief that sunny skies, which allowed the European badger *(Meles meles)* to see its shadow, heralded another 6 weeks of wintry weather.

Chapter Eighteen

BEAVER (CASTORIDAE)

Beaver (Castor canadensis)

This uniquely American aquatic rodent has played an important role in the development of North America. Its luxurious water-repellent fur was in great demand in Old World society for more than 200 years, until overtrapping exterminated the species in much of its original range. The original top hat, known colloquially as a "beaver," was a symbol of prosperity among gentlemen in Europe and Great Britain before silk supplanted beaver skin as the construction material of choice.

The demand for beaver pelts was also responsible for building a number of financial empires, some of which still exist. The Hudson Bay Company, the British East India Trading Company, and Sears–Roebuck all owe their beginnings to trade in beaver pelts.

The characteristic V-shaped wake of the beaver, which is often followed by a SLAP! of the tail as the beaver dives underwater for safety.

GEOGRAPHIC RANGE

Nearly exterminated in the 1800s, the beaver is one of North America's greatest wildlife success stories. Today, thanks in large part to lack of demand for their furs, beavers are found throughout North America, except in the desert Southwest. To the north, *C. canadensis* ranges across Canada from the Atlantic coast to the Pacific coast, from south of Hudson Bay into Alaska, with the range ending south of the Arctic Circle. The species' southern range extends to the northeastern border of Mexico.

HABITAT

Beavers can live in almost any habitat that provides fresh water to a depth of at least 5 feet (deeper is preferred) year-round, with sufficient trees and shrubs to provide food and building materials for lodges and dams. Small rivers and streams are dammed to create ponds that beavers can meter to remain at a constant level suitable for their habitation, and these ponds also provide habitat for many other species, including fish, reptiles, amphibians, waterfowl, and other aquatic mammals. Larger streams and lakes also make good beaver habitat. If their waters are deep enough, resident beavers will forego building dams or lodges, instead excavating dens into the shoreline, where they're known as "bank beavers."

PHYSICAL CHARACTERISTICS

Mass: 45 to more than 60 pounds, with the largest beaver recorded weighing 109 pounds.
Body: Rodentlike, with a stout body, short legs, and a humped back. Beavers have a comparatively small round head with a short round muzzle and small round ears. They have the ability to voluntarily seal their noses and ears while swimming underwater, and have a clear eyelid to protect their eyes from debris. Like all rodents, beavers have large central incisors that are always growing, and must be worn down constantly through gnawing to prevent malocclusion. Beavers keep them trimmed by gnawing bark.
Tail: Tails are fur-free, broad, and flat, covered with large black scales. No other animal possesses this paddle-shaped tail, which has evolved to serve as a rudder while the beaver is swimming. Length is 11 to 18 inches. Muskrat and nutria are similar in body shape, but are much smaller and have slender, more ratlike tails.

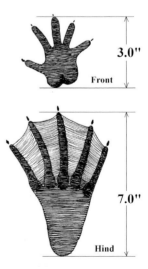

3.0"

Front

7.0"

Hind

TRACKS

Beavers have five toes on all 4 feet, although the innermost small toes may print lightly or not at all. Forefeet are about 2.5 inches long. Hind feet are about 6 inches long, elongated, and black, with widely spread toes connected by webbing. Front and hind feet normally print side-by-side in pairs, with forefeet usually printing to the outside of hind

Beaver track; front and back foot

prints, sometimes overlapping slightly. Distance between paired front and hind tracks averages about 4 inches. Webbing of hind feet may not be visible in tracks on ground harder than wet mud.

SCAT

Cylindrical, of uniform diameter, usually 1.5 to 2.5 inches long. Always found along shorelines. Beaver scat is distinctive and easily identified because it contains chips of wood and bark. Color is dark brown to black when fresh, becoming gray and sawdustlike, crumbling easily, after only a few days.

COLORATION

The body and head are covered with thick brown fur. Webbed feet on all four limbs are black, and the flat paddle-shaped tail is black. Long gnawing incisors are amber to orange in color due to pigmentation in the enamel.

SIGN

Most obvious are beaver dams and lodges. Dams are made of intertwined sticks and mud, are usually 2 to 3 feet wide, and span the width of rivers and streams. Lodges are tepee-shaped (conical), also constructed of sticks and mud. They rise to a height of 5 feet or more at the top, and are always sited in water. Entrances to lodges are always below the water's surface. Bank beavers—those living in larger rivers and lakes—may not build lodges or dams, and the entrances to their excavated burrows will also be underwater.

Another obvious beaver sign are "cuttings," trees that have been toppled by beavers gnawing through their trunks. The cut is V-shaped, leaving stumps that are conical, like a sharpened pencil. Most trees are smaller softwoods, especially poplar, aspen, and birch saplings 4 to 6 inches in diameter, but trees more than 2 feet across have been felled. From a distance these felled trees appear to have been cut with an axe, but closer observation reveals twin gouges made by the rodent's incisors. Felled trees will never be far from water, usually within 100 yards.

Beaver sign on the ground includes obvious, well-used slide troughs at shorelines, where tree branches used for construction and as food are dragged into the water. Near these slides there are often territorial scent posts, made from twisted tufts of long grasses that carry a strong musky odor deposited from the beaver's perineal (anal) glands.

VOCALIZATIONS

Normally silent, beavers are capable of making a number of typically rodentlike sounds that include a variety of chirps and chattering. When threatened, the feisty beaver may screech, chitter, and hiss. Perhaps the most notable call that I've heard personally is the high-pitched cry used between a pair of new mates to keep tabs on the other's whereabouts; this call is probably best described as a monotonal treble "beeeeeeeee," that lasts 2 to 4 seconds.

Although not a vocalization, the most commonly heard noise made by beavers is the tail slap made when a swimming animal is alarmed. This smacking noise is created by raising the flat tail above the water's surface, then bringing it down hard to make a resounding noise that warns other colony members to submerge. The individual making the alarm may also submerge, but an alpha beaver might remain on the surface to further scrutinize the source of its alarm.

LIFE SPAN
About 8 years.

DIET
Beavers are strict vegetarians, and there is no record of them eating any type of animal matter. At all times of year, most of the diet consists of young, tender bark from saplings and shrubs. Felled trees are stripped of their branches by the beavers' powerful incisors, then the bark is gnawed off and eaten, and finally the cleaned sticks are transported for use in construction of dams or lodges. Smaller diameter sections are gripped in the beaver's handlike forepaws and rotated as it is stripped of free of bark, much like a human eating corn on the cob. Large branches are gnawed as they lie on the ground.

Summer foods also include ground plants like plantains, young sedges, and the sprouts of most shoreline (riparian) plants. The thick rootstocks of pond lilies are also favored, although the crisp flesh is bitter to a human palate. Some leaves, especially those of deciduous softwoods, are eaten as well, along with buds and tender twig ends.

In autumn, when ground plants begin to die off, beavers begin storing food for the coming winter by pulling branches underwater and anchoring their gnawed ends in the mud, where they remain refrigerated and fresh during the frozen months. During the long winter, when the surfaces of ponds are likely to be covered by a nearly impenetrable shell of thick ice, the animals may not surface at all, retrieving food from the underwater larder as needed and swimming back into the lodge with branches clenched firmly between their incisors. Inside the lodge, the limbs are stripped free of bark, which is eaten and the woody cores are discarded by pushing them back into the water.

Most mammals lack the digestive system needed to reduce tough plant cellulose to a form from which usable nutrients can be extracted as food, but beavers have a digestive sac, called a cecum (pronounced SEE-come), located between the upper and lower intestines, the purpose of which is to do just that. Inside the cecum are colonies of microorganisms that break down plant tissues so that their nutrients can be absorbed and assimilated as the mass passes through the lower intestine. Chips of wood and fibers that cannot be digested are passed into the colon, where they scrape that organ clean and help to maintain the animal's rectal health.

MATING HABITS
Beavers of either sex reach puberty at about 18 months, but, like most social or pack animals, only the alpha, or parent, pair are permitted to mate within a colony; grown offspring must leave to establish their own territories before breeding. Parent pairs typically mate for life, unless one of them is killed, and will occupy the same territory throughout their lifespans. When the founding pair is gone, their lodge and pond are taken over by another pair, usually the original pair's offspring, and the cycle continues.

Mating takes place within the lodge from late January through February, often with young from the previous year present. Gestation averages 14 weeks, with litters of one to eight kits (usually five) being born during a period between late April and June (the earlier births occurring in more southern parts of the species' range). Kits weigh about 1 pound at birth, and enter the world fully furred, with eyes open and incisors already erupted. Newborns can swim immediately, and usually take to the water through their lodge's exit hole less than an hour after birth.

By the time newborns are 1 week old, they will have begun exploring the waters around their lodge, always under the watchful eye of at least one adult. Mothers continue to nurse their young inside the lodge for about 30 days, but as they grow and spend more time outside, both parents provide attention and care. Older offspring, who remain with their parents for 2 years before striking out to find their own mates and territories, also provide care and protection for their younger siblings, and all adults serve as rafts for young beavers when they become too tired to swim.

Despite receiving some of the best parental care in the animal world, a few beaver kits end up as food for a variety of predators. The speedy river otter is especially skilled at preying on beaver young, which helps to explain why otters are nearly always found where there are beavers. But ospreys, large pike, and even alligators will take a small kit if the opportunity presents itself.

By the end of their first summer, the yearling kits may weigh in excess of 15 pounds. The older siblings that helped to raise them, now 19 months old, will probably leave the parental lodge in late July or August to find their own mates and territories, but females may remain with the parents for another winter.

BEHAVIORISMS

Beavers remain active for as long as winter weather permits, and in the southern parts of their range they may continue to forage and work throughout the winter. In the north, where snow and sometimes bitterly cold temperatures make swimming above water an impossibility, resident beavers might not be seen until spring thaw. If the ice is thin enough to be broken from below, the animals might be seen feeding on shore, or occasionally even playing on the frozen surface. But the dead of winter in snow country is a poor time to observe beavers.

Beavers are nature's own construction engineers, second only to humans in their ability to change an environment to meet their needs. On seeing a beaver habitat for the first time, it's common for human researchers to comment that the animals' felling of nearby trees has wrecked that area, but the reverse is actually true. In damming a stream to create the deep water needed to ensure that the entrances to their lodges or bank dens will always be underwater, inaccessible to most predators, the beavers inadvertently turn a stream into a pond that benefits nearly every other animal in the area. Deer, elk, and moose feed on the abundance of water plants growing along that pond's shores; fish that couldn't otherwise survive in a smaller flowing stream find ideal habitat in the pond's deeper waters, and waterfowl of all kinds nest in the cattail forests at the pond's edge. Nearly every species in any given habitat gains from the richness a beaver colony brings to the environment.

Unfortunately, as both *Homo sapiens* and *Castor canadensis* continue to expand their numbers and range, the two species run afoul of one another with increasing frequency. Owners of resort cabins and investment properties do indeed suffer financial loss from the beaver's cutting of white birch trees along riverfront tracts, as well as the loss of real estate that is flooded by the damming of streams.

Timber companies dislike beavers because their ponds sometimes flood, and subsequently kill, large numbers of commercially valuable lumber trees. Everyone complains when roadways are flooded, and submerging electric or gas lines has a negative impact on the municipalities those utilities serve. With fur prices too low to entice trappers into performing the hard labors required to operate a trapline, civil authorities find themselves in the unenviable position of controlling beaver numbers by trapping, poisoning, and shooting them, and by destroying their dams.

Chapter Nineteen

MUSKRATS (*ARVICOLINAE*)

This New World aquatic rodent is often identified with more destructive terrestrial rodents, especially the Old World's Norway rat *(Rattus norvegicus)*, which has plagued human populations since biblical times. In fact, the muskrat is not parasitic on humans the way Norway rats are known to be, nor is it a vector of the numerous rat-borne diseases that have historically plagued humans. Confusion between the two species stems from a tendency for both rodents to inhabit urban waterfronts, where the harmless 4-pound muskrat is often mistaken as a gigantic specimen of the 1-pound Norway rat, or the even smaller black rat *(Rattus rattus)*.

Historically, the muskrat has played an important role in the commercial development of North America. Its soft water-repellent fur is still in such demand that approximately 10 million of the animals are trapped each year, and its very tasty flesh was once sold under the name "marsh rabbit."

GEOGRAPHIC RANGE
Considered Nearctic, the muskrat is found in swamps, marshes, and wetlands across North America from south of the Arctic Circle to the Gulf Coast and the Mexican border. Early in

The muskrat is found in swamps, marshes, and wetlands across North America. R. TOWN/USFW the twentieth century, muskrats were introduced to northern Eurasia, where populations appear to be thriving.

HABITAT

Muskrats are found only in wet environments, particularly in places having at least 4 feet of water year-round. Preferred locations are marshes, where water levels remain steady and most of the species' favorite foods are found in abundance. The animals shelter in excavated bank burrows whose entrances are generally underwater; these burrows may extend inshore at an upward slant for several feet, terminating in an enlarged chamber.

PHYSICAL CHARACTERISTICS

Mass: 1.5 to more than 4 pounds, sometimes larger in the north.

Body: Ratlike, with a humped back, short legs, and a long unfurred tail. Body length is 16 to 24 inches. Head is larger than that of true rats, with a blunt, squarish muzzle and small round ears.

Tail: Triangular: flat on the bottom and sides; ridged on top. Unfurred, black, and covered with small scales. Length is 7 to 12 inches, or about 50 percent of body length.

TRACKS

The muskrat has five long and widely spread toes on all four feet. The innermost toes of the front and hind feet are offset from the other four, almost thumblike. Webbed hind feet are elongated and plantigrade, similar to a human foot, but the heel portion may not print, resulting in tracks that can range from 2 to 3 inches long. Foreprint is 1 to 1.5 inches long. Straddle is about 3.5 inches; stride is about 3 inches. Hind tracks usually print behind, and sometimes overlap, foreprints. The long tail may leave serpentine drag marks between tracks, sometimes broken where the animal raised its tail.

Walking in Snow   Running in Mud

Muskrat tracks, shown walking in snow and running in mud, are always found near water.

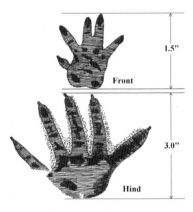

Front   1.5"

Hind   3.0"

Muskrat tracks

SCAT

Distinctive and easy to identify. Deposits typically consist of curved pellets that are connected in side-by-side fashion, and usually left on logs, flat rocks, or other prominent places where they serve as obvious territorial markings. Color is brown, with a fine sawdustlike texture. Individual pellets are 0.5 to 1 inch long.

COLORATION

Dorsal area is dark brown, lighter brown on the sides, with a grayish underbelly; the underbelly is darker in winter than in summer. There will often be a small dark patch on the chin. The tail is black and scaly.

Muskrat scat

SIGN

Most obvious are the muskrat's feeding platforms, sometimes called nests or rafts. These irregularly round platforms are composed of reeds, horsetails, and cattail stalks placed atop stumps and logs at the water's edge, sometimes in the water. Platforms are often flattened, indicating that they've been used frequently, and may be covered with clipped grasses and other edible vegetation, small opened clam shells, and crayfish carapaces. Freshly cut grass blades and reeds floating near the platform also indicate recent use.

Smaller platforms of cut grass stems, usually mixed with mud and found on shorelines, are territorial scent posts, marked with musky secretions from the muskrat's perineal (anal) glands. These scent posts are nearly always made by territorial males, seldom by females.

VOCALIZATIONS

Muskrats are normally silent. When threatened or alarmed, the muskrat can squeak, chatter, or emit a high-pitched bark.

LIFE SPAN

About 4 years.

DIET

Muskrats are primarily vegetarian, with an efficient digestive system that can break down coarse cellulose into usable nutrients. Webbed hind feet propel them forward and backward with equal ease when swimming on or below the surface, and one individual was reported to have spent 17 minutes underwater. Voluntary skin flaps close the nostrils and seal the mouth behind their chisel-like incisors, allowing the animals to bite off submerged plants without taking water into their mouths or noses.

In summer the animals feed on grasses, sedges, plantains, cattail shoots, wapato, wild rice, and a wide variety of other aquatic and shoreline vegetation. When winter snows make green plants unavailable, muskrats forage underwater for watercress, cattail roots, and wapato tubers, bringing foods onto the ice through body-size plunge holes that are smaller than those made by river otters.

Despite a preference for vegetables, muskrats routinely eat the flesh of other animals. Freshwater clams are a common component of their diet in any season, but frogs, earthworms, dragonflies, waterfowl eggs, and young snakes are among the prey eaten by this opportunistic rodent.

Whatever the diet consists of, a muskrat normally consumes a daily volume of food equal to about 33 percent of its body weight. This high metabolic rate keeps the rodents busy finding food through most of their active day. It also occasionally causes them to run afoul of farmers, as they have been known to enter planted fields through irrigation ditches to feed on crops.

MATING HABITS

Muskrat populations in the southern part of the species' range can breed year-round, with females giving birth to as many as five litters per year. Northern populations mate only in the summer months, between March and August, birthing two to three litters per year, depending on latitude and the availability of warm weather.

Males are more territorial than females, but unless overpopulation forces them to be protective of mates and habitat resources, there are seldom fights between them. When there are territorial disputes, they're usually limited to brief wrestling matches and nips from the combatants' sharp incisors, ending as soon as the weaker animal withdraws.

Males are drawn to females by pheromonal scents. The drive to mate prompts them to leave their own territories, which typically overlap the territories of several females. Males remain with mates for 2 to 3 days, denning with them until the female becomes pregnant and spurns further advances, then leaving to find another mate if there is one nearby.

After a gestation period of about 30 days, females give birth to an average of six young, although litter sizes may be as high as eleven if mothers are particularly well fed and healthy; larger litter sizes have been observed more often among northern populations. Young are born in a grass-lined birthing chamber at the end of the mother's tunnel-like burrow, where few predators can detect or reach them. Muskrat kits enter the world covered with fine dark fur, but are blind and helpless, weighing about 22 grams each.

Mothers nurse their litters almost constantly for the first 8 days of their lives. The muskrat kits grow quickly, and by 10 days they begin leaving their mother's burrow to swim and dive around its underwater entrance. After 30 days the young are weaned and driven away by the mother, who may have already become pregnant again while she was nursing them.

Emancipated offspring may not travel far to establish their own territories, depending on population densities and availability of resources, giving rise to the belief that muskrats sometimes live in colonies. In reality, each of the animals exists individually, without cooperation from others. Adult size is reached between 6 and 7 months of age, with females reaching puberty first. Male yearlings probably leave to establish their own territories, although inbreeding is probably common.

BEHAVIORISMS

Because muskrats are prolific breeders during warmer months, they often live relatively harmoniously in large groups, each with its own small territory. Territorial size is determined by the abundance of food and other resources, and when populations become large enough to burden these resources, territorial disputes increase both in frequency and feroc-ity. Adolescents are forcibly driven off, and there have been instances of cannibalism.

Muskrats may be active at any time of day or night, with peaks occurring at dusk and dawn. Adolescents are sometimes seen traveling far from water as they search for new ter-ritories, but most sightings are near or in water. With poor hearing and weak nearsighted vision, the animals are often easy to approach and observe, so long as the observer remains downwind and moves slowly, utilizing cover whenever possible.

On land muskrats move slowly, with a running speed of about 8 miles per hour. This causes them to remain close to the water's edge, and to be especially alert when feeding atop their waterborne rafts. Major aerial predators include ospreys, owls, and hawks, while bob-cats, coyotes, and otters take many as well. Mink are known to invade maternal chambers from their underwater entrances to prey on newborns, but only surreptitiously, because a mother muskrat defending her young is too dangerous an opponent for the small weasel. Young raccoons will sometimes attempt to dig downward into nesting chambers if they can detect them by scent, but most learn to abandon this practice because their labors usually net only an evacuated burrow.

Despite having a naked tail and lightly furred feet, muskrats are able to withstand sub-freezing temperatures and long periods in cold water because of a physical adaptation known as "regional heterothermia," which allows the temperature of their extremities to remain just above freezing without suffering cell damage. The animals' warm, fine fur retains most of their body heat even underwater, and a layer of fat beneath the skin further ensures that loss of warmth is minimal. In especially cold weather, muskrats retreat into their underground burrows, sometimes laying up there for as long as a week, until warmer temperatures return. The burrow's underwater entrance remains unfrozen during these periods, permitting resi-dents access to underwater foods, and giving them an exit through which to relieve them-selves without fouling the fastidiously clean den.

Muskrats, usually youngsters, sometimes incur the wrath of farmers by denning inside drain pipes and irrigation tiles, plugging them with their nests of grasses and reeds. The problem isn't generally widespread or serious, and is easily prevented by covering pipe open-ings with steel mesh that is fine enough to prevent entry.

Porcupine (*Erethizon dorsatum*)

The single species of North American porcupine has similar counterparts throughout the world, demonstrating the viability of its defense mechanism. All are lumbering, heavily built rodents that have adapted to ward off faster and stronger predators with a covering of highly modified hairs interspersed in the fur on their backs and tails. These modified hairs, or quills, have evolved into stiff, sharply pointed needles with ends covered with minute barbs. The porcupine's genus name, *Erethizon,* is Latin for "He who rises in anger," an allusion to this species' natural defense.

Because predators have almost universally evolved to kill food animals via hard physical contact using teeth and claws, these quills provide the porcupine and its relatives with a shield that few can penetrate without suffering serious, sometimes fatal injuries to themselves. A carnivore with a mouthful of firmly embedded quills can no longer eat, nor does it have the means to extract them, and most will suffer a serious infection. A few predators,

The porcupine is the slow-ambling oddity of the north woods. NATIONAL PARK SERVICE

most notably the fisher, have learned to flip porcupines onto their backs, exposing the unquilled underbelly, but even the fisher suffers an occasional injury.

GEOGRAPHIC RANGE

The common porcupine is native to boreal North America in Alaska and across Canada south of the Arctic Circle to Labrador. Its range covers the western half of the United States, southward from Montana through New Mexico, and into northern Mexico. In the eastern half of the United States, porcupines are found only in the northernmost regions, covering most of New England, northern Michigan, northern Wisconsin, and northeast Minnesota.

HABITAT

Porcupines are found primarily in coniferous forests, but will spend part of the year in deciduous woods while seasonal foods are available. Preferred habitat is mixed forest consisting of pine, hardwoods, softwoods, and a variety of ground plants, but nearly every environment in which porcupines are found includes tall trees and a source of fresh water nearby. There have been reports of porcupines frequenting riparian (riverfront) areas in mountainous regions, and even denning in rock crevices, but they are never far from woodlands that provide food, shelter, and refuge from enemies.

PHYSICAL CHARACTERISTICS

Mass: 8 to 40 pounds, with the largest specimens occurring in the north.
Body: Rodentlike, with a humped back and short legs. The dorsal region and, especially, the tail are covered with coarse hairs and approximately thirty thousand hollow, barbed quills

Porcupines are often observed in trees.

that can be voluntarily detached on contact, but not thrown. The longest quills occur on the rump and tail, the shortest on the neck; there are no quills on the underbelly. Body length is 25 to 37 inches. The head is small in proportion to the body, and round, with a short muzzle, flat face, and small round ears. Prominent yellow-orange incisors are ever-growing and must be kept from growing past one another (malocclusion) through constant gnawing. **Tail:** Large, round, and clublike; heavily covered with quills. Length is 6 to 12 inches.

TRACKS

Porcupines have four toes on the forefeet, and five toes the hind feet. Toes are long and articulated, each tipped with a heavy, slightly curved claw 0.5 to nearly 1 inch long. Front track is 2 to 3 inches long, including claws; hind track is 3 to 4.5 inches long, including claws. Tracks are elongated and plantigrade (flat-footed), with thick, distinctive, pebble-textured soles. At a walk, the porcupine's usual gait, hind prints register ahead of foreprints, occasionally overlapping. In snow the porky's wide, low-slung belly often drags, leaving a trough that can obscure tracks. In sand, tracks may also be obscured by the heavy tail, which typically swings back and forth, leaving striated broomlike markings.

SCAT

In winter, porcupines leave curved pellets with a sawdustlike texture, much like the muskrat's, but not connected. Pellets are dark brown, each about 1 inch long, and distinguishable by a small groove running lengthwise along the inside radius.

In spring, when the diet changes from woody fare to green plants, pellets are often shorter, with more

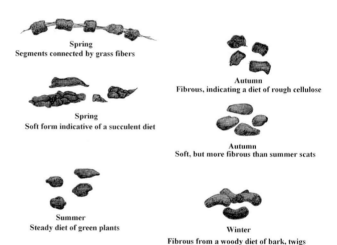

Spring
Segments connected by grass fibers

Autumn
Fibrous, indicating a diet of rough cellulose

Spring
Soft form indicative of a succulent diet

Autumn
Soft, but more fibrous than summer scats

Summer
Steady diet of green plants

Winter
Fibrous from a woody diet of bark, twigs

Porcupine scat

squared ends, and are connected together by grass fibers like a string of beads. Other forms seen from spring through autumn include formless, misshapen segments, still usually deposited as individual pellets, and showing evidence of plant fibers.

COLORATION

Most porcupines are covered with coarse gray hairs, but some may be brown, or even black. The unquilled belly is lighter in color than the back and sides. Hollow quills are black-tipped with whitish shafts.

SIGN

Most obvious at all times of year are porcupines' winter gnawing on smooth-barked pines, especially near the trees' tops, that leave irregular patches of exposed wood. In winter, when porcupines feed almost exclusively on pine bark and buds, there are usually scatterings of needle-bearing twig ends lying on the snow under the trees that serve as food sources (red squirrels also nip off cone-bearing twigs from spruces and hemlocks). Den openings at the base of hollow trees generally have large accumulations of winter scat pellets about their entrances. Bones and antlers of large animals, especially deer, are often gnawed to obtain the minerals in them, leaving gouges much larger than those made by squirrels that do the same. Look for gnawing in processed lumber too, especially on wood that has been treated with varnish, which the porcupine may actually eat in quantity because of its salt content.

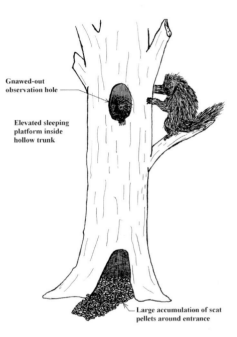

Gnawed-out observation hole

Elevated sleeping platform inside hollow trunk

Large accumulation of scat pellets around entrance

A porcupine den in a hollow tree.

VOCALIZATIONS

Porcupines are usually silent, even when cornered. Most vocalizations are heard during the autumn mating season, when males may grunt, squeak, and sometimes snort while in pursuit of mates.

LIFE SPAN

Up to 8 years.

DIET

Like beavers, and unlike most rodents, the porcupine is entirely vegetarian. In early spring, before most ground plants are sprouted, the animals climb high into poplar, aspen, and cottonwood trees to feed on their sticky, fleshy buds. During this brief lean period, buds of willow, staghorn sumac, beech, and most other trees and shrubs are eaten as well, but those in the poplar family seem to be favored.

From spring through summer, the porcupine's tastes turn toward more succulent green plants. Young grasses and sedges, plantains, sprouted beechnuts, cresses, mustard, chicory, dandelions, and other greens are only a few of the plants that make up *E. dorsatum*'s varied summer diet. As summer progresses into autumn, the diet expands or changes to match ripening fruits like serviceberries, blueberries, wild cherries, and other nuts or fruits.

When winter snows return and again make ground plants unavailable, porcupines begin looking to the trees for sustenance. Like rabbits, they will sometimes feed on bark stripped from sumac, cherry, and dogwood, but unlike those terrestrial bark-eaters, porcupines can climb with ease into the tallest trees to reach the most tender bark and twig ends.

Most preferred in winter are pines, especially white pines, and a single large tree may be occupied by a porcupine for several weeks at a time. Preferred portions include the smooth green bark at the top and at the ends of branches, bud ends, and young twig ends. Unfortunately, these feeding habits have made the timber industry look unfavorably on porcupines, whose winter gnawings can kill commercially valuable trees by "girdling" them with a belt of stripped bark that encircles the trunk.

Another feeding habit that causes friction between porcupines and humans is the animal's tendency to eat any wood that has traces of salt in it, including perspiration-soaked tool handles, plywood boats, decks, and wooden siding or shingles on rural houses. In one instance, legendary tracker Olas J. Murie described an outing in which he was forced to leash a half dozen prorcupines that persisted in gnawing at his canoe by looping cord around their necks and tying them to a tree until morning. The salt-loving rodents can cause considerable damage and expense, but are dissuaded easily by metal siding and concrete foundations.

MATING HABITS

Female porcupines may mate as young as 6 months of age, but competition will likely prevent males from breeding until they are 18 months old. The testes of male porcupines descend into scrotal pouches between late August and early September, and spermatogenesis peaks during October.

Mating occurs from October through November, and during this time, males may travel several miles to court prospective mates, and are likely to be vocal, especially when several eligible bachelors pursue a single female into a large tree while squabbling with one another over which of them should breed her. Male porcupines are seldom violent toward one another, and never use their quills on their own kind, but these arboreal pursuits can be dangerous if a shoving match among the upper branches causes one of the contestants to fall to the ground from a great height. Males that are pushed from a tree branch and survive the fall will withdraw to seek out a mate elsewhere.

Females are generally passive in the mating ritual, waiting for males attracted by their pheromonal scents to come to them. Courtship is mostly the male's domain, and consists of much squeaking and grunting, an odd hopping dance, climbing trees with the female, and marking her with urine. Females remain in estrus for just 12 hours, so time spent between mates is brief. If a female fails to become pregnant within that period, she will come into heat again (polyestrous) in another 25 to 30 days.

A longstanding jocular answer to the question of how spiny porcupines engage in sex has been "carefully," but in fact mating occurs in the same manner as other animals. When the female is ready, she voluntarily brings the quills along her back downward and holds them flat against her body, then raises her tail over her back, exposing her unquilled underside, as well as her genitalia. The male then mounts her from behind in conventional fashion.

After mating, a mucuslike plug forms in the female porcupine's vaginal cavity to prevent further entry by sperm, and she loses interest in mating again. Her mate will set out to find another receptive female before the breeding period ends, and takes no part in the rearing of offspring.

The porcupine's gestation period lasts approximately 30 weeks, which is very long for a small mammal, and probably includes a period of delayed implantation, although no data has been established to support that. Pregnant females give birth to a single pup (twins are rare) in April or May within a den that's usually located inside a standing hollow tree, but sometimes in a rock crevice. Young are precocial, born fully quilled and with eyes open, but the quills are soft and do not harm the mother. After being exposed to open air for about an hour, the newborn's quills harden, and the youngster becomes a smaller duplicate of its mother.

In captivity, mother porcupines have been observed to suckle their young for periods spanning several months, but youngsters in the wild are able to subsist on vegetation within 2 weeks, so nursing in a natural environment is probably much shorter. My own encounters with young porcupines found living alone in the wild have convinced me that adolescents as young as 1 month are fully capable of caring for themselves. Under normal conditions, young porcupines may accompany their mothers for 5 months or more, and females may mate with the same male their mothers bred with in the next autumn. Young males tend to wander off in search of their own territories during their first summer of life.

Porcupine populations rise and fall in cycles of roughly 12 years. The typical cycle consists of decline that extends for a period of 2 years, followed by a rise in numbers over the next 10 years.

BEHAVIORISMS

Porcupines are normally solitary (except for the autumn mating season), but they rarely show territorial aggression toward one another. In particularly harsh weather, several adults may take shelter in the same cave, roadway culvert, or outbuilding crawl space to wait out a storm, with no apparent animosity between them. When fair weather returns, the animals separate and resume their solitary lifestyles.

Porcupines do not hibernate, but during the winter months pregnant females especially seek out a den in which to give birth or take shelter from bad weather. These dens, which may be vital to an animal's survival, are used regularly throughout the winter, and are defended against usurpers, although ownership is rarely challenged and battles over possession are never violent.

Unlike other animals, which keep their dens and nests fastidiously clean, the entrance to a porcupine den is always marked with scat pellets—sometimes a small mountain of them if the den has been used repeatedly for several winters. When the den is inside a hollow standing tree, there is usually a ledge inside where the animal sleeps, 10 feet or more above the ground, and this platform is often partially or entirely constructed of scat pellets compressed to a hard surface under the resident porcupine's weight. Just above this elevated platform there will be a small observation hole gnawed through the tree's shell, and a sharp-eyed hiker can often spot the porcupine who lives there peering out to watch him or her pass by.

In summer porcupines rarely shelter in dens, but escape biting insects and the heat of day on a thick branch high in a tree, where they can be spotted from afar as an uncharacteristic large bump. They don't build nests the way squirrels do, preferring to rest in the open, the heavily quilled tail and rump pointed toward the tree's trunk, in the direction from which predators must approach. This simple strategy is proof against bobcats, raccoons, and most other climbing carnivores, but the fisher is able to clamber past the porcupine along the underside of the branch to emerge in front of it, thereby gaining access to its unprotected head.

Many species that are thought to be nocturnal have adopted that habit to avoid contact with humans, but porcupines prefer to forage at night, even in places where there are no people. Just before sunset they emerge from dens or elevated resting places to forage for food plants on the ground.

Only the most hungry or inexperienced predators chance tackling a foraging porky, but if one does, the porcupine points its tail end toward the enemy, turning as the predator circles to keep its most potent armament toward the adversary. Given an opportunity, the porcupine will escape by climbing out of reach, but a predator foolish enough to press its attack will be rewarded with a slap from the heavily barbed tail.

Along with timber companies that dislike *E. dorsatum* for the havoc they raise by foraging in pine trees in winter, farmers consider them a destructive nuisance of corn crops and orchard trees, homeowners resent their gnawing of wooden structures, and many dog owners learn to hate them for the injuries their quills inflict on pets. To others, the porcupine is almost revered: It's one of the few, and sometimes the only, species that a lost and hungry woodsman can catch on foot, and humans are the only predator that can kill the spiny animal with impunity—a sharp blow across its nose from a club does the job. Native Americans use the animals' quills to adorn ornamental birch-bark boxes, which today fetch a good price in gift and souvenir shops.

Nine-Banded Armadillo *(Dasypus novemcinctus)*

Let's take a moment to ponder the nine-banded armadillo. There is no mammal remotely like it anywhere in North America. The armadillo has no need for sharp quills, choking scents, or long, swift legs to escape its many predators. The species has followed a path as passive as its waddling and rooting, developing an armor of hard (ossified) plates that protect it from all but the most determined or desperate predators. Spanish conquistadors, with their own breastplates and tough battle-proven armors, provided the common name in the early sixteenth century. These early adventurers called the creature the *armadillo,* or "little armored man." The Aztec Indians, perhaps more attuned to the natural world and wildlife, named it *Azotochtli,* or "turtle rabbit."

A note of caution: *Dasypus novemcinctus* is the only mammal beside humans that suffers from lepromatous leprosy. There is growing evidence that armadillos could transmit the disease to humans. Researchers and naturalists should exercise caution when handling armadillos, or when working around their scats and dens, to avoid the possibility of contracting leprosy.

The nine-banded armadillo has expanded its range dramatically over the past century. JOHN AND KAREN HOLLINGSWORTH/USFWS

GEOGRAPHIC RANGE

Armadillos are found from Mexico to Peru and northern Argentina in the south, and on the islands of Grenada, Tobago, and Trinidad. In the United States, armadillos are found in Texas, Louisiana, Missouri, Florida, with the range extending northward into most of Oklahoma and Arkansas, and eastward across the southern portions of Mississippi, Alabama, and Georgia.

Armadillos have been moving steadily northward since they were first recorded along the Rio Grande in 1854. No one knows exactly how the species is making such a successful shift to different habitats and climates: Global climate change, landscape-scale modifications due to livestock grazing, and the extermination of major predators are all probably contributing and interrelated factors. Scientists have predicted that armadillos will be found as far north as Virginia by 2050 or before. There are many related species of armadillos, from the tiny screaming hairy armadillo of Argentina (no larger than a man's hand) to the seventy-pound "tatou" or Giant Armadillo, of tropical Colombia.

HABITAT

Nine-banded armadillos have proved remarkably adaptable to a variety of habitats, from the sand and sagebrush of Texas to the bayous of Louisiana and the piney woods and hills of Alabama. Fresh water and an abundance of insects for food seem to be the only requirements. So far, armadillos have proved capable of thriving in any habitat where winters are not too severe.

PHYSICAL CHARACTERISTICS

Mass: 6 to 17 pounds. Males are about 10 percent larger than females.

Body: Stocky with short, powerful legs for digging and burrowing. The most notable physical characteristic of nine-banded and other armadillos is their armor—leathery pebbled skin and ossified dermal plates on their backs, sides, tails, and the tops of the head. The overall impression is that of a turtlelike carapace, divided into three distinct sections: a scapular (shoulder) plate, a pelvic (hip) plate, and a series of hinged telescoping bands around the abdominal section. These bands are connected by flexible, hairless skin, with the anterior edge of each abdominal band overlapping the next band to form an unbroken shield. The nine-banded armadillo can have seven to as many as eleven abdominal plates, with the greater number of plates occurring in specimens in the northern parts of the species' range (where individuals tend to grow larger).

The underbelly has no plates or ossified armor, but is covered in a tough flexible skin that still provides some protection from predators, and from the thorns of the thickets where the armadillo seeks safety. Body length is 24 to 32 inches.

The armadillo has a narrow, spearlike head and a piglike snout designed for rooting through soil. Dentition is primitive. Its frontal jaw has no canine teeth, no incisors for cutting. Simple, peglike molars have single roots and do not develop enamel. An armadillo's ears are leathery, pointed, and piglike, 3 to 6 inches long.

Tail: 9 to 15 inches long, covered by 12 to 15 overlapping segmented rings.

TRACKS

Armadillo forefeet have four digits, the hind feet five, each with center toes much longer than the outermost toes. The innermost toes of the front and hind feet are much smaller and more offset than the others, helping to identify left and right tracks. Thick, strong digging claws are evident in tracks, which in dry sand can be mistaken for deer tracks. Forefeet are about 1.5 inches long, hind feet about 2.5 inches long.

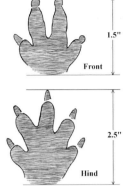

SCAT

Irregular, sometimes elongated, but often round and marblelike, consisting largely of clay and sand ingested as the animal feeds on insects; 1 to 1.5 inches long.

Armadillo tracks are a common sight on the sandy backroads of the rural Deep South.

COLORATION

Gray, yellowish, or brown. Lightly furred with long grayish hairs, especially on the hind legs. Scapular and pelvic plates slightly darker than the abdominal rings, with raised pebbled surfaces appearing as whitish dots against a darker background.

SIGN

Look for areas of rooted-up soil and leaves, anthills dug up and scattered, rotting logs or other vegetation torn apart.

VOCALIZATIONS

As nine-banded armadillos root and snuffle for food, they maintain an almost constant grunting and snorting that is unmistakable.

LIFE SPAN

About 8 years.

DIET

The nine-banded armadillo is an omnivorous opportunist. Whatever can be rooted or dug up is consumed, from insects to small amphibians and reptiles, baby birds and bird eggs, mice, and carrion. Roots and berries are eaten when encountered. Like the peccaries with whom the species shares much of its range, the armadillo spends its days rooting in the soil and searching under logs and rocks for insects. An acute sense of smell and powerful foreclaws for digging make it a very successful forager.

By voracious and constant foraging, an adult armadillo eats an estimated 200 pounds of insects per year, controlling the population of many potentially harmful insect pests. Among the favorite foods are ants—an armadillo can eat more than forty thousand ants in a single meal, and among the ants eaten are the red imported fire ant *(Solenopsis invicta)*, which is recognized as one of the more destructive invasive species in the modern United States.

MATING HABITS

Mating occurs in late July and early August. Although little is known about the mating process, the home range of a male armadillo probably overlaps that of several females. Males find receptive females through pheromones in urine or scats and mate with as many different females as possible during the brief season.

After mating, male and female armadillos return to their normal mode of solitary existence. Successfully mated females undergo a delayed implantation of the fertilized egg that lasts up to 4 months, to ensure that the mother is healthy enough, and can find enough food, to carry and birth a litter of young. Unlike other female mammals, an armadillo's egg is not spontaneously aborted if the mother is weak or starving. There have been incidents in which a mated female carried a single egg in stasis for 2 years before becoming pregnant. No wonder the nine-banded armadillo has so successfully expanded its range and numbers!

If conditions are favorable, a female's fertilized egg will attach to her uterine wall and begin to develop by November. The single egg will divide into quarters and begin growing four genetically identical embryos of the same sex. This unique reproductive phenomenon has made armadillos a preferred lab animal for medical research requiring identical subjects as an experimental constant.

Early in the 17-week gestation period, gravid female armadillos seek out areas with ample food and water and create extensive dens, excavated as deep as 15 feet into a cutbank or beneath the roots of a tree, with a small opening of no more than about 8 inches in diameter. The terminus of the den is a grass- and leaf-lined nesting chamber, in which, usually during March or April, the mother will give birth to the quadruplets. The young are born with eyes open and fully formed, and within hours are able to walk about in the safety of the nesting chamber and the den. Their armor starts out very soft but will slowly harden, and will not provide adequate protection against predators until after they are weaned, usually at the age of 4 to 6 weeks.

At that age, the little armadillos can follow the mother out of the den, scurrying along behind as she teaches them how to forage, all the while eating as much as she can to rebuild her fats and strength after 6 months of pregnancy and nursing. The quadruplets remain with their mother until July, when she usually abandons them to find another male for mating. The young armadillos will reach sexual maturity at 1 year old, and will find mates of their own at around 18 months.

BEHAVIORISMS

Nine-banded armadillos are most likely to forage at dawn, twilight, or at night. But this preference seems to be more related to temperature than to a preference for darkness. Having no fur and little fat for insulation, an armadillo must operate within a narrower range of temperatures than almost any other mammal. Prolonged exposure to freezing temperatures will kill them, as will the hot summer sun of the desert or prairie. The deep burrows that they are so adept at digging are perfect for waiting out periods of freezing weather, but because armadillos do not hibernate, it is believed that they will be limited in their eventual range to regions where periods of freezing weather are relatively short.

In regions of extreme heat and open country, armadillos likewise resort to deep earthen burrows for shelter, and follow a crepuscular or nocturnal schedule. In shaded forests, especially where there are plenty of creeks, springs, or swamps for water, armadillos can be seen actively foraging throughout the daylight hours.

Another trait that makes armadillos unique among mammals is an almost complete absence of territoriality. The humble and energetic armadillo lacks any interest in the kind of crippling territorial violence indulged in by wolves or raccoons. On the contrary, small groups of armadillos, often of the same sex, will often share a den, and there have even been reports of individuals sharing their dens with other species without conflict. Such behavior is extraordinarily rare among mammals.

From looking at the structure of an armadillo, most observers assume that the animal will curl tightly into a heavily armored ball when threatened, an assumption that probably comes from familiarity with the common "pill bug" or "roly-poly" (a wood louse of the genus *Armadillidium*) that resembles the mammal. Such defensive behavior is occasionally observed. But more frequently, an armadillo will try to escape a hunter or predator with a surprising burst of speed that can approach 15 miles per hour. Cornered, an armadillo will dig like a badger, burrowing as deeply as possible and wedging itself in its tunnel so tightly that it cannot be extricated.

Many people who have observed the steady movement of nine-banded armadillos into new habitats wonder how the animals cross rivers and other bodies of water. The answer adds yet another bizarre level of sophistication to this seemingly primitive creature: If a stream is relatively narrow, the armadillo simply ambles into it and walks across on the bottom, remaining submerged for as long as five minutes. If the body of water is too wide to cross in that fashion, the armadillo will actually inflate its intestines with enough air to provide buoyancy and start swimming.

Rabbits (genus *Sylvilagus*) are sometimes confused with hares (genus *Lepus*), but there are a number of physical traits that distinguish the two. Rabbits are generally smaller, with shorter ears and less powerful hind legs. Hares are more at home in open areas, where they escape predators by outrunning them, while rabbits prefer brushy habitats where they can hide. Hares give birth to fully furred young in relatively open places, while rabbit newborns are born naked in a sheltering burrow or nest, and require a more prolonged period of maternal care. Both are prolific breeders, with reproductive rates adapted to counter heavy predation from numerous carnivores.

Despite some physical similarities these animals are not rodents, as once thought, but members of the order Lagomorpha, a group that includes the even more rodentlike pika. One defining difference between lagomorphs and true rodents is a second, smaller and shorter pair of incisor teeth directly in back of the chisel-like upper incisors, which serve as a kind of cutting board when the jaw is closed. This dental arrangement gives the animals a very sharp, scissorlike cutting action when nibbling fibrous sedges, permitting them to chop tough cellulose into very fine pieces that digest more easily.

Lagomorphs are also remarkable in that males carry their scrotums ahead of the penis, instead of behind it, a characteristic seen in no other mammals except marsupials.

Currently there are eighty species of lagomorphs worldwide, all of them categorized in thirteen genera belonging to two families, Leporidae (rabbits and hares) and Ochotonidae (pikas). Native populations of lagomorphs are found on all continents except Antarctica, southern South America, and Australia, although introduced populations of rabbits in Australia have thrived and have long been part of that continent's ecosystem.

Snowshoe Hare (*Lepus americanus*)

Also known as the "varying hare" because individuals in the northern parts of its range grow a white coat in winter, the snowshoe hare gets its common name from oversize hind feet that give it greater weight displacement in the deep snows and muddy marshes that are the species' preferred habitat. One of the smallest hares, the snowshoe "jackrabbit" is a vital prey species for many carnivores, especially the lynx and bobcat.

GEOGRAPHIC RANGE

Snowshoe hares inhabit the northern United States from New England through New York, as well as in Michigan, northern Wisconsin, northern Minnesota, and northern North Dakota. To the south, their range extends only along mountain ranges that are snow-covered in winter, along the Cascade range to northern California, along the Rockies to Colorado, and through West Virginia and Virginia along the Allegheny and Appalachian mountain

Snowshoe hares are brown in the summer and turn white at the start of winter in snow country.

ranges. To the north, snowshoes inhabit nearly all of Canada and Alaska south of the Arctic Circle. Perhaps notably, the snowshoe hare's northern range butts up to, but rarely overlaps, that of the arctic hare *(Lepus arcticus)*, with a precise demarcation line between the ranges of the species.

HABITAT

Unlike rabbits, which tend toward thickets and prefer to hide from danger, snowshoe hares prefer more open areas where they can rely on powerful hind quarters and large feet to carry them out of reach of predators at speeds in excess of 25 miles per hour. Relatively open bogs, marshes, and swamps are preferred during daylight hours, but at night the hares venture out to feed in even more open areas, like fields and meadows, river and lake shorelines, aging clear-cuts, and roadside ditches.

PHYSICAL CHARACTERISTICS

Mass: 2 to more than 4 pounds, less than half the weight of larger hare species; about the same weight as an eastern cottontail rabbit, with which the snowshoe shares much of its range.

Body: Rabbitlike, with a humped back, long, powerful hind legs, disproportionately long and wide hind feet. Body length is 15 to 20.5 inches. Head is round, the muzzle blunt, with large eyes at either side of the head. Ears are shorter than those of most other hares to lessen loss of heat in cold temperatures; ear length is roughly 3 inches. Males, called "bucks," are slightly smaller than females, or "does," which is unusual among most mammals, but typical among leporids.
Tail: Dark gray to black on top, whitish below, 1 to 2 inches long.

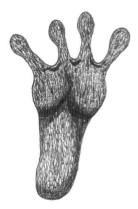

TRACKS

Four toes on the front and hind feet. Forefeet are comparatively round, 1.5 to 2 inches long. Hind feet are very large, with widely spread toes, 3 to 4.5 inches long. In winter, tracks may be obscured by a heavy coat of fur on the underside of the foot. Hind feet print ahead of forefeet at a casual hop, leaving a track pattern that looks like paired exclamation points (!!), similar to those of a fox squirrel but much larger. A set of all four tracks measures 10 to more than 16 inches. Distance between track sets may be more than 15 feet, with longer leaps denoting a faster pace.

The snowshoe hare's back feet are perfectly designed for fleeing from predators across the surface of snow.

SCAT

Typical of all rabbits and hares; generally marble- or egg-shaped, occasionally acorn-shaped, with spherical forms usually indicating a diet of drier, less succulent vegetation. Diameter is about 0.5 inch. Color is usually dark brown when fresh, becoming lighter colored and more sawdustlike with age. Scat pellets are generally found in groups of a half dozen or more.

COLORATION

Snowshoe hares are brown in summer, slightly grizzled, with a darker dorsal line and longer fur than the cottontail. The underside is whitish, the face brown, the ear tips black. Often has a white patch on top of the head. At the start of winter in snow country, the animal's coat turns entirely white except for the black tips on the ears. Snowshoes in Washington and Oregon normally don't exhibit this photoperiodic color change, remaining brown all year, and in the Adirondack Mountains there is a population that remains black (melanistic) all year.

Under normal conditions, snowshoe hares are known for their seasonal molts. The winter molt usually begins in November as a patchy, mottled coat of white spots that become larger until the animal is completely white, a process that takes about 70 days to complete. It's interesting to note that snowshoes possess two separate sets of hair follicles, one of which grows only white hairs, and the other set growing the brown and gray hairs of the summer coat. Color phases are regulated by daylight, not temperature, which during abnormally warm winters can result in white hares with no camouflaging snow on the ground.

Snowshoe hare scat

SIGN
Typical of all rabbits and hares: Sign includes stripped, barkless shrubs like sumac, dogwood, and willow during the winter months. Neatly clipped grasses and ground plants in summer. Trails are often regularly used and well packed; trails in snow may be packed to a depth of more than 1 foot, permitting high speed travel in troughs too narrow for predators to use.

VOCALIZATIONS
Snowshoe hares are normally silent. Mothers purr to young while nursing. Newborns whimper and whine. Most remarkable is the high-pitched alarm cry, a prolonged squeal that is normally heard only when the hare has fallen into the grip of a predator. In all cases the calls of a hare are generally lower toned than those of a rabbit. When battling over territory, two hares may growl and hiss. Also heard occasionally is the thumping of a hind foot being pounded repeatedly against the earth, especially when the animal suspects danger but can't locate its source; this is an attempt to entice a predator into revealing itself.

LIFE SPAN
Few snowshoe hares die of old age, but become prey to a host of predators as soon as their reflexes slow. Many don't reach adulthood. Average life span is 3 or 4 years.

DIET

The snowshoe hare's diet is more broadly varied than other leporids, but normally vegetarian. The animals graze on green grasses, vetches, asters, jewelweed, wild strawberry, pussytoes, dandelions, clovers, and horsetails, as well as the buds of aspen, poplar, birch, and willow. In winter, snowshoe hares forage on buds, twigs, bark, and the tips of evergreen twigs. If plant foods are scarce they may eat carrion, and have been known to raid traps baited for carnivores to get at the meat in them.

A notable trait among leporids is their need to reingest feces to thoroughly digest them. Because much of the vegetation a hare or rabbit eats is comprised of tough cellulose, and because most of the animals' digestion processes are contained in the lower gut, foods must be eaten and digested twice to extract all the nutrients from them. As with cud-chewing ruminants, this practice, known as "cecal fermentation," permits animals to quickly ingest food plants from a place where feeding may be hazardous, then retire to a safer location where foods can be completely digested at their leisure.

Despite being considered food by so many carnivorous species, snowshoes are among nature's best survivors, a fact that can be seen in the lack of fat on their bodies. With a broad diet that encompasses almost every type of vegetation, as well as carrion when times get hard, hares have little need to carry food reserves on their bodies. But they do need to maintain a body that's as lean and muscular as possible to escape fleet-footed predators like the coyote. Mountain men of old, for whom hares and rabbits were a staple winter food, often found themselves suffering from "rabbit starvation" by winter's end, a sometimes serious form of malnutrition that forced their bodies to consume muscle mass in lieu of fats.

MATING HABITS

Breeding season for the snowshoe hare runs throughout the summer months, beginning in March, when the males' testicles descend, and extending through August, when the testicles retract and become dormant. Males pursue females by following their pheromonal scents, frequently congregating around receptive does in groups.

Mating contests between breeding males resemble boxing matches, in which both contenders rise on their hind legs and bat at the muzzles of one another with sharp-clawed forefeet. If one of the combatants is knocked onto his back, the powerful, clawed hind feet are used to kick and scratch against an adversary's underside. Despite the apparent ferocity of these battles, they usually end quickly, when the weaker animal withdraws, and are seldom seriously injurious to either party.

Snowshoe does are polyestrous, coming into heat whenever they aren't pregnant throughout the summer months, and both genders engage in sex with different mates almost indiscriminately (polygynandrous). This seemingly lascivious behavior helps to ensure that these prolific breeders have a strong, widely varied gene pool.

Gestation takes about 35 days, with litters of two to eight fully furred precocial young typically birthed in a makeshift nest atop the ground, but sometimes in the recently abandoned burrow of a fox or coyote. The young hares are able to run within 2 hours of birth, and begin feeding on vegetation in their first day. Mothers nurse their litters for about 30 days, but will probably become pregnant again before the young are weaned. Adult does may birth as many as four litters per summer, and newborn females may begin mating almost as soon as they've been weaned. The species' rapid reproduction rate makes it resistant to heavy predation from the many meat-eaters that hunt it, and makes it unlikely that snowshoe hares will become a major concern for conservationists.

BEHAVIORISMS

Snowshoe hares are solitary animals, but population densities are often high enough to force them to live together. Under ideal conditions, an adult's territory may encompass as much as 18 acres, but when populations peak, the amount of land an individual can claim may shrink to a fraction of that size.

Actual population densities may range from one to as many as ten thousand individuals per square mile, with numbers typically increasing steadily for a period of about nine years, then drastically falling off in the following year. Direct causes for this sudden decline, which appears to be a normal phenomenon within this species, include sudden epidemics of pneumonia, severe fungal infections, salmonella, and tularemia. The root cause of these plaguelike illnesses is most likely malnutrition brought on by depletion of food resources. A secondary effect of the snowshoe's cyclic decline is a sudden decline in populations of lynx, which relies heavily on hares in its own diet, about one year later.

Notably, the greatest fluctuations in snowshoe hare populations occur in northwestern Canada, and the least in Colorado's Rocky Mountains. Explanations for this phenomenon include greater diversity among predator and prey species in warmer regions, while colder climates tend to be less varied, resulting in relationships between hunter and hunted being more critically symbiotic.

Lepus americanus isn't classified as nocturnal, but the hares do show a reluctance to be active in sunlight. In clear summer weather the animals are most likely to feed and breed during the hours between dusk and dawn, but may also be seen foraging at midday when skies are overcast or rainy.

Snowshoes have very good directional hearing, a keen sense of smell, and large protruding eyeballs positioned at either side of the head that permit them to detect approaching danger. But they tend to freeze, relying on their natural camouflage for protection, unless a predator's body language reveals that it has seen them. When a hare does run from danger, it zigzags through underbrush at high speed, changing directions instantly to make itself hard to follow visually as well as physically. Like white-tailed deer and rabbits, the hares rely on a maze of trails, each scented with frequent scat deposits, to confuse even the most acute sense of smell.

Although they run fast and erratically enough to outmaneuver predators in thick cover, snowshoe hares must escape quickly because they tire after a few hundred yards, while their main enemies can maintain top running speeds for a mile or more. When a hare begins to slow from exhaustion, it will freeze and remain motionless, hoping to go undetected by its pursuer. At this point the hare is in real danger if the predator sees it, and is likely to be caught. If open water is nearby, a hare in imminent danger will probably try to swim away.

On warm summer evenings, snowshoe hares, like rabbits, are frequently seen rolling about on the gravel shoulders of rural roads. These dust baths are taken to loosen shedding fur and to help dislodge fleas and mites. The animals sometimes engage in this behavior in the early morning, but most dust baths are taken in the evening because more parasites are contracted while the hares are sleeping during daylight hours.

Eastern Cottontail Rabbit *(Sylvilagus floridanus)*

Immortalized by nursery school fables and songs like "Here Comes Peter Cottontail," this is the most common and most recognized member of *Sylvilagus*, the genus of rabbits. Like all rabbits, it differs from its close cousin, the hare, by having shorter, more rounded ears, a generally smaller body, and shorter, less muscular hind legs. Also, like other rabbits and unlike hares, the cottontail is a fast short-distance runner that prefers to elude its enemies by seeking out thick cover, rather than outrunning them across open terrain.

Because the cottontail is so common, and because its physical traits, behaviorisms, and diet are generally representative of every rabbit species around the world, it has been selected to represent all members of genus *Sylvilagus* for the purposes of this guide.

The familiar eastern cottontail rabbit has shorter ears than its cousin, the hare. LEWIS GORMAN/USFWS

GEOGRAPHIC RANGE

Cottontails have the widest distribution of any rabbit in North America. To the north, the species ranges to the Canadian border, spreading across it only a few miles in southern Manitoba and Quebec. Except for Maine, the cottontail's range covers all of the eastern United States from the Atlantic coast to North Dakota and south to Texas, extending through Mexico into Central America and northwestern South America. In the west, cottontail populations are found along the Rocky Mountains and from Mexico through eastern Arizona and into Nevada.

HABITAT

Perhaps the most adaptable of all lagomorphs, the eastern cottontail seems to be at home in almost any brushy or forested environment that provides a source of drinking water and plenty of cover in which to hide. Historically, the eastern cottontail has inhabited deserts, swamps, coniferous and deciduous forests, and rain forests. Currently, the eastern cottontail seems to prefer "edge" environments, areas between woods and open terrain including meadows, orchards and farmlands, hedgerows, and clear-cut forests with young trees and brush. The eastern cottontail's range extends into that of six other rabbit species, and six species of hares, although, like all rabbits, it prefers less open terrain than hares do.

PHYSICAL CHARACTERISTICS

Mass: 2 to more than 4 pounds.
Body: Typically rabbitlike, with a high rounded back, elongated ears that are 2 to 3 inches long, muscular hindquarters, and long hind feet. Head is rounded, with a short muzzle, flat face, and large dark eyes located at either side. Body length is 14 to 18 inches.
Tail: Brown on top, fluffy cotton white below. Length is 1.5 to 2.5 inches.

TRACKS

Cottontails have four toes on all four feet. Forefeet are nearly round; 1 to 1.5 inches long. Hind feet are elongated; 3 to 4 inches long. Claws generally show prominently in tracks.

SCAT

Pelletlike, usually spherical or egg-shaped, sometimes flattened discs, usually less than 0.5 inch in diameter. Color is usually dark brown, becoming lighter and more fibrous-looking with age. Pellets often deposited in groups of six or more.

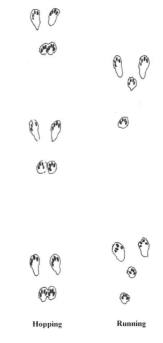

Hopping   Running

This is the track pattern of the cottontail rabbit.

COLORATION

The brown, grizzled coat is interspersed with gray and black hairs, generally uniform over the back, sides, top of the tail, and head, except for a reddish patch on the nape of the neck. The bottom of the tail is white and cottonlike. Ears are black-tipped. The underside is lighter; buff-colored. Cottontails undergo two molts per year: The spring molt occurs from mid-April to mid-July, and leaves a short summer coat that's predominantly brown; from mid-September through October, the brown coat is shed for a longer and warmer grayish winter coat.

SIGN

Neatly nipped-off flower and plant stems. Smooth-barked shrubs stripped of bark down to the cambium layer show where rabbits browsed in winter. Oblong "forms" of pressed-down grasses, snow, or sand where a rabbit lay down for an extended period of time while resting or sleeping.

VOCALIZATIONS

Cottontails are normally silent. Vocalizations include a bleating distress call intended to startle a predator into hesitating briefly and giving a rabbit the chance to flee. Bucks (males) chatter and squeal loudly during and immediately after copulation. Nursing does purr while suckling young, and sometimes emit sharp alarm barks if an intruder approaches too closely to their litters.

LIFE SPAN

Up to 5 years, but generally no more than 2 years because of heavy predation.

DIET

The eastern cottontail is believed to be strictly vegetarian, with roughly 50 percent of its summer diet consisting of green grasses, and the balance comprised of wild strawberry plants, clovers, alfalfa, and a broad variety of other ground plants. Its double row of upper incisors allows it to chop tough cellulose fibers into fine clippings that are easier to digest.

In habitats where winter snow makes ground plants unavailable, the cottontail diet turns to more woody browse, especially the smooth bark of saplings and shrubs like redosier dogwood, staghorn sumac, rose, lilac, and young poplar, birch, and aspen. They also eat the buds and tender twig ends of most trees, including pines and cedars. Deepening snows actually work for the rabbits by allowing them to reach higher up to get at bark and twigs that were previously inaccessible. Like other rabbits and hares, digestion of these tough plant materials is made possible by a process called cecal fermentation, a variation of the cud-chewing process seen in ruminant species. With cecal fermentation the mass of ingested plant material passes completely through the digestive system, where it's partially broken down, and is expelled through the anus as green pellets. The predigested pellets are then eaten and passed through the digestive system a second time, where the cellulose is completely broken down and nutrients extracted for use by the rabbit's body. Although repulsive to humans, cecal fermentation, like cud-chewing, permits rabbits and hares to quickly eat plant foods in places that are inherently dangerous for them, then retire to a more secure location to complete the digestive process.

Although generally considered nocturnal, cottontails may forage at any time of day in places where they feel safe. In summer, they tend to sleep away the head of the day in cool underground burrows and sometimes in shaded brushy thickets. But the colder temperatures and increased energy needs of winter often force them to forage throughout the day in that season. In every season, feeding activities are somewhat crepuscular, peaking in the 3 hours after sunrise, and again in the 2 hours after sunset.

MATING HABITS

Like all rabbits and hares, cottontails exhibit remarkable reproductive powers—an indication of their status as food for so many species of meat-eaters. As with other lagomorphs, cottontails reach sexual maturity at 2 to 3 months of age, and many of those born during the summer-long mating season are likely to mate before the coming autumn. In fact, an estimated 25 percent of the rabbits born in a summer are the offspring of juveniles who are themselves less than 6 months old.

The start of mating season coincides with the spring molt, when adults begin shedding their grayish winter coats for brown summer coats. The onset of breeding is also influenced by lengthening days, warming temperatures, and the availability of green foods. Bucks, whose testicles are retracted and inert during the winter months, become sexually ready in mid-February, although does aren't normally ready to breed until mid-March. This interval gives adult males time to seek out prospective mates. Both genders remain sexually active until late August or September, with mating season ending earlier in places where winters come earlier.

Like other rabbits and hares, cottontail does are polyestrous, accepting a number of mates throughout the summer mating period, and birthing as many as four litters in a single season. There is no lasting bond between mates, and each go their separate ways after breeding. This seemingly promiscuous breeding habit helps to ensure a varied gene pool.

Prior to mating, cottontails perform a curious courtship ritual in which a buck chases a doe until she tires and eventually turns to face him. The pair then rise on hind legs and spar briefly with their forepaws, after which both crouch on all fours, nose to nose, and the male jumps straight upward to a height of about 2 feet. The female replies by jumping upward herself, and both rabbits may repeat the action several times. The exact purpose of this jumping behavior is uncertain, but is probably used as an indication of the fitness of each animal to mate.

After being impregnated, does spurn further advances from males. Gestation lasts an average 30 days, at the end of which the mother-to-be retires to a sheltered burrow or hutch, which may be an abandoned fox den, a natural enclosure under the branches of a fallen tree, or sometimes under the floor of an outbuilding. There, in a grass-lined nest that has been further insulated with fur nipped from the mother's underbelly and from around her four pairs of nipples, she gives birth to four or five—sometimes as many as eight—naked and blind (altricial) young. Newborns weigh about 1 ounce (25 to 35 grams), and require almost constant care. The young grow fast, gaining more than 2 grams per day, and by 5 days have opened their eyes.

By 2 weeks of age, the young are fully furred and have begun to venture outside the nest to feed on vegetation. At this point the mother is nursing them only about twice a day, and may have already become pregnant with her next litter. Weaning occurs at about 20 days, and the young rabbits, who may have become intolerant of one another, disperse. Those born in spring or early summer are likely to sire or birth their own litter—perhaps two litters—before the mating season's end.

BEHAVIORISMS

Eastern cottontails are popular with sport hunters, who typically use dogs to flush and pursue them into shotgun range. Rabbit meat is very palatable, making them an even more desirable target. Although not a long-distance runner, an adult cottontail can exceed 18 miles per hour through thick brush, leaping 12 feet or more, and instantly changing direction by as much as 90 degrees. The flaw in their escape habits, which are often effective against predators, is that the animals tend to run in a circle, coming back to cross their own trails and thereby confusing the noses of wild carnivores. Human hunters have learned to exploit this habit by using dogs to chase rabbits back to where they stand, waiting to shoot them.

Cottontails are also a staple of the fur trade. The rabbit pelt is silky and thick, and tanned pelts are often sold in backcountry gift shops. Rabbit fur is also used as the trim around boot tops, parka hoods, and mittens, and sometimes as an entire fur coat. Rabbit fur isn't water repellent or as long-lived as beaver, ermine, or mink, but it is plentiful, inexpensive, nice to the touch, and there is a market for skins.

Cottontails are not well liked by farmers, gardeners, or landscapers. Their summer feeding habits and reproductive capacities can result in tremendous damage to crops, while winter browsing of shrubs and fruit trees makes them a pest in golf courses and orchards. The problem is often exacerbated, or even caused, by a historical reluctance to permit the cottontail's natural enemies to live near human habitation.

Except for brief mating encounters during the summer mating season, eastern cottontails are solitary animals that tend to be intolerant of one another. The sizes of their territories are dependent on food and other resources, but generally encompass between 5 and 8 acres. Males, which normally claim larger territories than females, tend to extend their claims to include the territories of local does during the summer.

Nearly every predator large enough to kill a rabbit considers the cottontail prey. Hawks, owls, and eagles hunt them from the air, skunks and other weasels prey on the young in their burrows, bobcats pounce on them from hiding, and the speedy coyotes chase them through the underbrush. A rabbit's best defense is freezing against or under camouflaging foliage, where a predator can't see its body, and creating a maze of seemingly random trails can make finding it by scent very difficult at best. Nevertheless, most cottontails won't survive into their third year. Fortunately, reproductive rates are high enough to ensure that this species is unlikely to be threatened by overpredation.

Chapter Twenty-Three
OPOSSUMS *(DIDELPHIDAE)*

This family of the order Didelphimorphia, or pouched mammals, is represented in North America by only one species, the Virginia opossum. Marsupials are distinguished from most mammals by giving birth to live but mostly undeveloped young after an average gestation of about 2 weeks. The helpless still-embryonic young, which are typically a half-inch long, make their own way from the mother's womb to a skin pouch on her belly, inside which there are nipples. There they nurse until old enough to travel with their mothers. There are more than 250 species of marsupials worldwide, most of them occurring on the continent of Australia.

Virginia Opossum *(Didelphis virginiana)*

The opossum is North America's only marsupial, although several marsupial species occur in South America, and it's something of a dichotomy. With fifty sharp teeth (more than any other animal on the continent), and a diet that consists mostly of animal flesh, it might be

The humble Virginia opossum is one of North America's most common animals. USFWS REFUGE STAFF

classified as a carnivore, while its prehensile tail, lemurlike eyes, and semi-opposable thumbs might seem to qualify it as a primate.

GEOGRAPHIC RANGE

Opossums are found throughout most of North America, from Central America and Mexico in the south, throughout the United States east of the Rocky Mountains into southwestern Ontario, and in California. As noted by Olas J. Murie in 1954, opossums are highly adaptable, spreading to the West Coast of North America in the late 1800s, and into northern Michigan in the 1980s. When North America was first colonized by Europeans, opossums didn't occur north of Pennsylvania.

HABITAT

Opossums are found in a variety of environments, but prefer swamps and marshes. They frequent roadsides in this type of habitat to feed on car-killed animals, and often visit dumpsters at campgrounds.

The opossum is poorly suited to cold climates because its nearly hairless tail, nose, and ears are subject to frostbite. Nonetheless, opossums now live in regions that experience sometimes bitterly cold winters, and in these places they've learned to take shelter in abandoned burrows or other relatively warm places for days at a time.

PHYSICAL CHARACTERISTICS

Mass: 4 to more than 14 pounds at maturity, with the largest animals occurring in northern latitudes.

Body: 12 to 20 inches from nose to rump. Shoulder height is 4 to 8 inches. Stocky build, about the size of a house cat, for which it's sometimes mistaken. Strikingly pink nose with long whiskers. Small rounded ears. Eyes are large and close-set, denoting excellent night vision and good depth perception.

Tail: 10 to 20 inches long; nearly naked and ratlike; responsible for the common but mistaken belief that opossums are members of the rodent family. The tail is prehensile, meaning that it can function as a working limb, allowing its owner to curl it around objects and hang from it. The tail also may be important for helping to subdue prey animals.

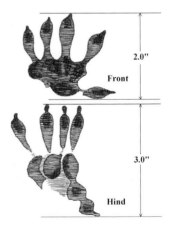

TRACKS

Front prints are about 1.5 inches long, with five toes, usually splayed, with bulbous tips and claws showing in tracks. The fifth toe is distinctively long and thumblike, pointing inward at the perpendicular or to the rear. Hind prints are 2 inches long, with four toes pointing forward with bulbous tips, claws showing. The fifth toe is distinctively long and   Opossum tracks thumblike, pointing inward at the perpendicular or to the rear. Hind prints are 2 inches long, with four toes pointing forward with bulbous tips, claws showing. Straddle is about 4 inches; walking stride is about 7 inches. Tail drag leaves a serpentine pattern in soft soil or snow.

SCAT

Segmented, 1 to 2 inches long and about 0.5 inch in diameter. Segments often connected by fur or plant fibers, black to brown in color, often with berry seeds in evidence.

COLORATION

Body fur ranges from grizzled black to gray to nearly white in the northernmost part of the opossum's range. Face is nearly white. The ears are darker than the face, tipped with white. The tail is pinkish gray. The nose is pink.

The opossum's shuffling gait leaves a characteristic pattern in soft mud or sand.

SIGN

Seldom seen because opossums aren't territorial, but nomadic. Usually consists of debris from scavenged garbage or carcasses that have been fed on, and could easily be mistaken for sign left by other small carnivores.

Opossum scat

VOCALIZATIONS

Opossums are mostly silent. Hisses and squeals are made when threatened, or when engaged in mating battles.

LIFE SPAN

7 to 8 years in the wild, depending very much on predators and human hunters.

DIET

Although best known as carrion eaters, opossum diets encompass virtually anything that can be metabolized as food. They do indeed consume road-killed deer and other animals, sometimes even living inside a large carcass for days at a time, but opossums are also adept hunters, able to prey on snakes, mice, frogs, tadpoles, and a variety of insects.

Fruits and vegetation when in season also make up a large portion of the opossum diet. Wild berries, especially blueberries, are preferred foods, but the animals are fond of farm crops like sweet corn, apples, and pears. In winter, when plant foods become hard to find, opossums may take up residence in rural barns, where they not only feed on stored grains but also prey on rats and mice.

MATING HABITS

The mating season for opossums lasts from January to July, occurring earlier in southern latitudes and later in the north. In warmer climes females may have two, sometimes three, litters per year. Mating is typically initiated by the males, which are attracted to females by pheromonal scents. Fights between males are common during this period, marked by screeches, hissing, and sometimes violent battles.

Because male opossums have a uniquely forked penis, there is an old myth about how they copulate through the females' noses. In fact, mating is performed in the same way as it is in most other species, with males mounting females from behind.

After copulation the pregnant female rejects any further solicitations, and the male moves on to find another receptive mate. The female retires to make a nest in a suitably secure crevice or abandoned burrow. After a brief gestation of 12 to 13 days, a litter of about eight blind and hairless young are born, each the size of a small bean. The young immediately make their way to the mother's fur-lined marsupial pouch, where each fixes itself to one of her eleven to thirteen nipples. The young remain fixed to the nipple for the next 60 days, after which they leave the pouch and travel about with the mother by clinging to her tail and back. By 100 days the youngsters are no longer dependent on their mother, and leave to find their own ways in the world. Females typically mate in their first year.

BEHAVIORISMS

Opossums are primarily nocturnal, sleeping away the daylight hours in a variety of secluded places that range from abandoned animal dens to outbuildings, crawl spaces under homes, and derelict automobiles. At dusk they emerge to forage and hunt for food, returning to a secure bedding spot at sunrise, but not necessarily to the same place they spent the previous day.

They are not social animals, with males being especially aggressive toward one another, and it's rare to see two or more adults together. When opossums are seen in a group, the animals are virtually always newly emancipated litter mates that are finding their bearings before going separate ways.

Opossums have adapted well to humans, raiding garbage cans and dumpsters, living in barns and outbuildings, and even invading occupied homes from time to time. Both sexes can act very aggressive when cornered, hissing loudly and showing their pointed teeth, but only the largest of them will consider an actual confrontation with animals of equal or larger size. If a show of ferocity fails to discourage an enemy, the animal will live up to its name by "playing 'possum": falling onto its side, eyes tightly closed, pretending to be dead, often urinating and defecating to enhance the image. The act is so convincing that opossums in this state have been petted (although this is never recommended) without breaking character.

Opossums differ from other species by being true nomads, traveling from one food source to another and never claiming a territory. Because of that, and because much of the opossum diet is made up of carrion, they are potential vectors of many diseases like rabies and tularemia, and are prime suspects in the rampant spread of bovine tuberculosis among white-tailed deer.

Despite their scavenging habits and human prejudice, opossums have historically been of value to people. The flesh is edible and usually considered quite good by those who can overcome their bias, while pelts have served as garment trim, and fur as paintbrush bristles. Opossums have also served as lab animals for scientific research, in part because they're relatively intelligent, and because they don't evoke the same sympathetic response from animal rights advocates as more attractive species.

Chapter Twenty-Four

TERRESTRIAL BIRDS

This chapter deals with bird species whose lives are spent mostly on the ground. These include turkeys, ruffed grouse (or partridges), woodcocks, ravens, and chickadees. The birds selected for inclusion in this section represent only a small number of the species that fall into this category, but they are some of the most commonly tracked birds in North America, both by hunters and birdwatchers.

American Wild Turkey (*Meleagris gallopavo*)

If Benjamin Franklin had his way, the symbol of the young United Sates would not have been the fierce and sometimes carrion-eating bald eagle, but the noble and intelligent wild turkey, which had fed the pioneers who carved hardscrabble settlements from the raw and seemingly endless wilderness. Franklin's nomination of the wild turkey as the national symbol was unsuccessful, but this beautiful, stealthy bird of the deep forests remains a national icon nevertheless.

An icon, perhaps, but not one that was always treated well. Between 1776 and 1920, unrestricted hunting had extirpated wild turkeys from eighteen of the thirty-nine states

The American wild turkey remains a national icon to this day. STEVE MASLOWSKI/USFWS

where they had once been so common. Fewer than one hundred thousand remained in all the United States. Strict game laws, relocation efforts, and public support for recovery of the birds resulted in one of the most successful rebounds of a native wildlife species in history: By 1959, the population of wild turkeys was estimated at a half million birds. Estimates made in 2010 indicate a population of around 7 million, occupying forty-eight of the fifty states. Further expansion of numbers and ranges may be limited by deforestation and other loss of habitat due to an increasing human population, but the wild turkey is now an icon of successful wildlife management, and treasured by hunters and wildlife watchers alike.

GEOGRAPHIC RANGE

Since recovery, the species is found from the western and southern United States to the Atlantic seaboard and New England, and far north into eastern Canada There are six recognized subspecies within this vast range, with one additional subspecies, the ocellated turkey, found in Central America.

The two most common subspecies of wild turkey in the United States are *Meleagris gallopava silvestris*, the eastern wild turkey, and *Melagris gallopava merriami*, or Merriam's wild turkey, found throughout much of the West. *Silvestris* is distinguished by a brown-tipped tail, rump, and back feathers, while *merriami,* perhaps due to its more open western habitat, has feathers with tan or even whitish tips.

HABITAT

Wild turkeys are able to thrive in a variety of habitats, including mixed forests, grasslands, agricultural areas, orchards, and on lakeshores. Thickets where the bird's broad wingspan is a hindrance to escape are avoided. The turkey's natural predators, bobcats, coyotes, and foxes, find the big birds easy prey in such places. Suitable habitats always include tall, usually deciduous, trees with widely spaced branches for safe night-time roosting.

PHYSICAL CHARACTERISTICS

Mass: 7 to more than 22 pounds. Weight can vary considerably depending on the time of year and the availability of preferred foods such as acorns.

Body: Heavily muscled and powerful. Adult males, known as toms or gobblers, have a dark, iridescent body, a reddish naked head, a "wattle" consisting of fleshy lobes hanging down from the chin, and a "caruncle," a wartlike fleshy projection on the forehead. Thick reddish legs have dark-colored fighting spurs projecting rearward about halfway up. Adult males, and occasionally females, have a breast tuft, or "beard," extending outward from the breast, typically growing longer as the bird ages. These beards are made up of hairlike feathers called mesofilophumes, and are prized as trophies by hunters. An adult male in his prime stands about 48 inches tall.

Adult females (hens) and adolescents (jennys and jakes), are smaller and duller-colored than adult males, lack breast beards and spurs, and have grayish heads. The back of the neck is feathered. An adult hen turkey is considerably smaller and lighter than a tom, standing about 36 inches tall.

Tail: Dramatically long, extending nearly to the ground when walking. The gobbler's habit of raising its tail upright and fanning it widely during the spring mating season has inspired awe in wildlife artists, hunters, and just about every person who has ever witnessed it. Tips of the tail feathers are light brown, followed by a black band, with narrow alternating black and brown bands extending to their bases.

TRACKS

Turkeys have three toes. The longer center toe extends straight forward, with the shorter toes on either side symmetrical and angled outward and forward. Claws are normally evident in tracks. In mud or other good tracking mediums, the thick segments of toes are obvious, typically with four segments in the outer toes, and five segments in the center toe. Rear toe generally prints as a round dot behind center toe, between the outer toes, but in snow or mud the entire rear toe may be visible. Tracks are about 4 inches long.

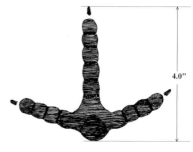

4.0"

Turkey track

SCAT

Varies according to season. In winter, when foods are drier, scats tend to be cylindrical, unsegmented, and slightly curved, with one end rounded, the opposite flat. Dark brown, greenish, or black in color. Length up to 3 inches, diameter usually less than 0.5 inch. During the spring and summer, when much of the turkey's diet consists of green plants, scats become softer and more variable in shape. Typical forms range from nearly spherical to flattened discs that are sometimes layered, similar to a cow pie, but about 1 inch in diameter.

COLORATION

Because turkeys have such sharp eyesight and good color vision, much of the communication between them is visual. The brilliant head and wattle of a dominant male in spring serves to attract females, while at the same time warning competitors that a territory has already been claimed. Fortunately, most of the turkey's most dangerous predators are color-blind, while even large birds of prey, which can see colors, find the big bird too massive to be considered prey.

SIGN

Invariably, roosting birds spatter the forest floor with numerous scats. Large deciduous trees are preferred for roosting, and those that have been used regularly by flocks of turkeys will have scats of varying ages beneath them, with the oldest and whitest scats being visible from a distance. Such roosts are also marked by feathers that fall to earth during the birds' nightly preening sessions.

Because turkeys tend to travel in flocks that may number more than a dozen birds, their foraging habits tend to leave obvious sign of their passing. Scratchings, loosened soil, flattened and disturbed grasses, and displaced leaves are all signs that turkeys have been around.

VOCALIZATIONS

Extensive and varied and sometimes almost constant, from hollow clucking sounds to low chirping to the distinctive gobble of mating adult males.

LIFE SPAN

Up to12 years. The first year of a young turkey's life is extraordinarily dangerous, with mortality estimated at 50 percent.

DIET

Turkeys are omnivorous and opportunistic. They generally forage in groups, scratching the earth underfoot with their clawed toes to expose edible plants, seeds, grubs, and insects. The species also eats blueberries and other fruits in season, and will crack the husks of acorns with their strong beaks to reach the fleshy nut inside.

Wild turkeys forage during daylight hours, and seek secure roosting places at night. They are especially active in the early morning, after descending from their roosts. Although occasionally seen in the open during the midday hours, most turkeys seem to prefer the shade and protection of forested areas until late afternoon and early evening, when they are often seen in farm fields, open meadows, and grasslands.

Turkeys do not migrate, but change habitats, areas, and food sources according to the season. Each region offers its own preferred winter forage—from cedar berries in the Midwest to acorns in the South to waste grain in farm fields, flocks will zero in on the feed that will best bring them through the winter.

MATING HABITS

Sexual maturity is attained at 10 to 11 months. Females will often mate in their second spring, but young toms are usually prevented from mating by aggressive older males until they reach their third year. The mating season can stretch from February through April, and extends into May in the northern extremities of the birds' range.

At the onset of the mating season, sexual readiness is indicated when the naked heads, wattles, and caruncles of mature toms take on brilliant hues of red and blue. Males become especially bold, frequenting open areas, from roadside meadows to hay fields, where they act out a dramatic display, tails fanned out, strutting, and gobbling loudly enough to be heard for more than a mile.

The display can be shockingly effective in attracting mates. Hens may come from as far as 2 miles away to gather in harems for successful toms. Harems as large as one hundred individuals have been recorded, although most mating flocks number about twenty.

Dominant gobblers will gather and hold as many hens as they can protect from the attention of other males, herding the harems from behind, often with their tails fanned. The wings are held slightly away from the body, and a strutting walk is employed to make the gobbler look as large as possible. Harems may include adolescents, and even young jakes are tolerated so long as they don't try to usurp the dominant tom's authority. The dominant tom will be the only male in the flock to mate, and he will attempt to breed every receptive hen in the harem before the season is through.

When challenged, dominant toms square off with fanned tails and outspread wings, and stalk around one another, displaying a hyperaggressive body language. If neither contender is discouraged the contest becomes a battle, with both toms flying at one another, feet extended and spurs raking. The spurs, tipped with a hard, sharp claw and often more than an inch long, are the tom's main weapons. Spurs are primarily stabbing instruments, used for jabbing with a downward motion when the owner flies upward and descends on top of an opponent. As natural weapons go, they aren't very effective, and most of a gobbler's real power lies in the bludgeoning force of its blunt and powerful wings. As with most wild species, mating battles are seldom more than mildly injurious to either party.

After copulation, gestation takes about 18 days. Hens leave the flock to lay an average of eight eggs (clutches numbering as many as fifteen eggs have been reported) in simple nests on the ground, usually no more than a leafy depression sheltered by overhanging shrubs or boughs, or under the branches of a fallen tree. Wild turkey eggs are about 50 percent larger than chicken eggs, with most measuring more than 3 inches long. Shells are beige in color.

Predation on eggs is minimal, despite the rudimentary nests. Though abundant, predators like raccoons, skunks, and ermine find an enraged turkey mother too dangerous, and although nesting hens must leave their clutches periodically to feed during the warmth of the day, they do not leave them for long. Incubation of eggs takes about 28 days. Hatchlings (poults) are precocious, and within days are able to follow their mothers. As soon as possible the mother and the little poults will seek out and rejoin the main flock, where a dozen or more pairs of eyes will be on constant lookout for danger, and the chances for survival are greatly enhanced.

BEHAVIORISMS

The turkey is a wary bird with keen eyesight and good hearing, able to detect most predators at a distance. When pursued, adults can run in excess of 10 miles per hour. Although they cannot fly great distances, turkeys can fly at remarkable speeds—up to 55 miles per hour, even in relatively dense forests.

In September or October, turkeys gather in wintering flocks of several males and sometimes more than twenty females. There appears to be no animosity between adult males at this time, with no time or energy wasted on strutting or other displays. Individuals in the fall are generally silent unless the flock gets separated. The lean and freezing winter is coming, and the turkeys concentrate on eating to the exclusion of all else.

Since their numbers have recovered and exploded, wild turkeys have become the most popular game bird in the United States, and the sale of turkey hunting licenses and permits brings in millions of dollars each year to state wildlife agencies. This revenue, and the popularity of turkey hunting, help conservation efforts for all wildlife by prompting governmental and sporting organizations to preserve, purchase, or create habitat where turkeys and numerous other species can thrive.

Ruffed Grouse (Partridge) *(Bonasa umbellus)*

Ruffed grouse are the most widespread of the grouse family, which also includes sage hens, prairie chickens, and ptarmigans. All members of the grouse family prefer a four-season environment where winters include snow. None are migratory. The scientific name *Bonasa* means "like a bison" in Latin, which probably alludes to this bird's stout physique and the manelike collar of feathers that both genders can voluntarily "ruff" outward to make themselves look larger to an adversary.

Many hikers have been startled by a ruffed grouse "exploding" from the bush.

GEOGRAPHIC RANGE

Ruffed grouse are a northern species, ranging all the way to the Arctic Circle, and encountered from Newfoundland west across Canada to Hudson Bay and on to central Alaska. They inhabit rural areas from New York State to northeastern Minnesota, and extend south all the way to the Allegheny and Appalachian Mountains of Tennessee, Virginia, and north Georgia.

Their range also includes the Rocky Mountains and the Cascades down into northern California. All of the places where ruffed grouse are found will be places where winters are snow covered.

HABITAT

Ruffed grouse prefer coniferous or mixed forests and are rarely seen in purely deciduous forests. They tend to avoid fields and other open areas. The ideal ruffed grouse habitat is overgrown, sheltered from wind, and canopied enough to be shaded at all times of day. The species generally avoids human habitation.

PHYSICAL CHARACTERISTICS

Mass: 2 to 3 pounds.
Body: This handsome, stoutly built bird stands approximately 18 inches tall. The ankle (tarsus) is partially feathered on both legs. Its namesake ruff of feathers around the neck, larger on males, can be erected when the bird is excited or agitated to make it appear bigger than it is. A white stripe extends from the base of the beak, around the eyes, to the rear of the head. The top of the head is partially crested with about three short, upright feathers that angle backward.
Tail: Wedge-shaped, wider at the end and tapering inward toward the body, consisting of roughly twenty broad feathers that have wide black bands at their outer ends and are tipped with gray. Males fan their tails dramatically, much like a strutting tom turkey, to attract females during the mating season.

TRACKS

Tracks usually show three toes, with longest center toe extending straight forward, flanked on either side by shorter toes extending forward and outward at symmetrical angles. On softer soils and in snow, the rear, grasping toe will print lightly and partially behind the three forward toes; on firmer soil the rearmost toe might not print. Forward toes exhibit three obvious segments per toe. Tracks are about 2 inches long (discounting rear toe), like miniature versions of the wild turkey track.

Ruffed grouse track

SCAT

Winter scats are usually brownish and elongated, of even diameter throughout their lengths, and crescent-shaped. One end will normally be flat, the opposite end rounded. Ruffed grouse scat is similar to that of a wild turkey, but usually less than half the size at about 1 inch long, and nearly always found in dense woods that turkeys tend to avoid.

Summer scats tend to be softer, less pelletlike, revealing a more succulent diet of greens and insects. Color is generally black or dark brown, usually with a chalky white (calcareous) substance at one end, sometimes throughout.

COLORATION

Ruffed grouse exhibit two distinctive regional color phases: A red morph occurs in the Appalachian range and in the Pacific northwest, while the gray morph is predominant in the

Cascades and Rocky Mountains. Both color phases have the same black collar (the ruff), a wide black band at the end of the tail, and a light-colored breast speckled with darker horizontal crescent shapes, with an almost scaled appearance on the wings and back.

SIGN

Scats beneath cedar, hemlock, and spruce trees. An accumulation of scats of varying ages mark a ruffed grouse's habitual perch on a favorite observation log. Green pine needles, pieces of poplar buds or catkins, and cedar nut husks often litter the ground beneath trees where partridges have been feeding.

VOCALIZATIONS

Low clucks and chirps often lost in the din of other, more distinctive bird songs. Extraordinary and unmistakable, the trademark drumming sound made by territorial males during the spring mating season is the harbinger of true spring. This drumming sound is made by beating the wings rapidly against the breast while standing atop a wide downed log. The sound has been likened to that of a two-stroke engine that sputters but refuses to start, and many have mistaken it for the noise made by a poorly tuned chainsaw.

LIFE SPAN

About 3 years.

DIET

An adult ruffed grouse makes full use of the abundant seasonal fruits of the forest, including strawberries, serviceberries, blueberries, and wild cherries. The sugar-rich blossoms of these trees and shrubs are also eaten, as are tender shoots of early grass.

Insects make up a large part of the warm season diet, and a ruffed grouse will eat them wherever they are encountered, from moths to grasshoppers, crickets, grubs, and ants. Young chicks too small to fly and forage in the trees focus particularly on insects, using these protein-rich foods to grow quickly.

During winter, grouse feed on withered berries and winter buds. Many shrubs and trees produce preleaf sprouts by midwinter, providing grouse with a plentiful diet of tender buds from river willow, cedar, beech, and other shrubs or trees.

MATING HABITS

Ruffed grouse breed throughout April and May, although a warm spring might cause males to advertise for mates as early as mid-March. Chicks born the previous spring may take part in their first mating season at about 10 months of age. The mating season appears to be initiated mostly by a photoperiodic response to lengthening days, although warming weather undoubtedly plays a part as well.

Male ruffed grouse advertise their desirability by standing atop an item that is elevated, usually a downed log or large stump, and "drumming:" beating their wings rapidly against the breast to produce a sound similar to that of a small piston engine. Such elevated drumming posts (most are less than 4 feet high) make the sound audible from more than a mile, as well as offer males a good view of the surrounding terrain. Receptive females approach the drumming post, and copulation normally takes place on the ground within a few yards.

Adult male partridges (roosters) frequently compete for prime drumming stations, particularly in areas where there are numerous females. Battles among male grouse are mostly bloodless shoving matches, with competitors flying at each other to try and knock the other off of a drumming post. A few feathers may fly, but the loser pays only by having to find another, usually inferior, place to drum and strut and fan.

After mating, male and female ruffed grouse separate, the male to find another mate, if one is available. The eggs grow quickly inside the female, and after a gestation period of 1 to 2 weeks, she begins laying them, one per day, in a bowl-shaped ground nest constructed of grasses, twigs, and pine needles. Clutches average about eleven eggs, and when all have been laid, the female sits on them almost constantly until they hatch, about 24 days later.

Attrition of eggs and hatchlings can be very high. Cold spring weather, especially combined with rain or late snows, can kill embryos within the eggs and freeze unfeathered hatchlings. Even though mothers attempt to locate their nests in places that are inaccessible to raccoons and larger egg-eaters, predation is a constant threat.

Chicks are fed a diet of mostly insects by their mothers for the first month, after which they begin foraging near the nest site under their mother's watchful eye. A high protein diet

Ruffed grouse nests are made from grasses, twigs, and pine needles.

of bugs causes the young birds to grow quickly. At 10 weeks all surviving chicks can forage on their own, as well as fly away from danger. At this point the mother's obligations are at an end.

BEHAVIORISMS

The most memorable, and probably the first, encounter a typical hiker has with ruffed grouse is a startled reaction to the bird's explosive and noisy eruption from cover. Partridge have an instinctive tendency to sit tight until a potential enemy has approached to within just a few feet, then burst into flight with a sudden loud flapping of wings. This effective defense uses the bird's very good camouflage to conceal it from sharp-eyed predators. Then, if a predator approaches too closely, the grouse's violent blast from cover nearly always guarantees a short head start while the enemy recoils involuntarily.

Except for the spring mating season, ruffed grouse are solitary birds. Males especially seem to claim territories, but there are almost no disputes beyond mating season, and territorial boundaries are respected. Drumming from territorial males helps to reinforce the peace, and may continue well past the mating season, through the month of June.

Despite its popularity as a game bird, the ruffed grouse is not endangered, although populations in some areas dipped noticeably in the late 1990s. More dangerous to ruffed grouse populations than hunting is destruction of the species' natural habitat. Logging of large tracts of forest ensures that grouse will neither mate nor live there.

American Woodcock (Timberdoodle) *(Scolopax minor)*

This member of the sandpiper family *(Scolopacidae)* is highly sought after by birders and sport hunters alike. Often confused with the common snipe, with which it shares most of its range, this migratory bird prefers wet, overgrown woodlands and mostly dry swamps, while true snipes frequent open shorelines.

GEOGRAPHIC RANGE

A true native, the woodcock is unique to North America, where its range covers all of the eastern states to a rough line extending from Minnesota south to eastern Texas. To the north, woodcocks are found in southeast Manitoba, and eastward along the southern borders of Ontario and Quebec. The woodcock is among the world's great wandering birds—a few individuals are reported to winter on islands in the Caribbean Ocean.

HABITAT

Damp, mostly deciduous woods and overgrown thickets, where moist soil with moderate to low acidity provides an abundance of earthworms. Mating birds seek out small meadows and glades surrounded by forest in spring. Nesting areas include coniferous and mixed forests that provide good cover, as well as older clear-cuts or logged areas. Despite being classed as a sandpiper, this shorebird is an inhabitant of deep woodlands, although never more than a mile from a source of open water.

Even though it is in the sandpiper family, the woodcock prefers to nest in clear-cut or logged areas. RICHARD BAETSEN/USFWS

PHYSICAL CHARACTERISTICS

Mass: 4 to 10 ounces; adult females about 10 percent larger than males.

Body: The American woodcock is short and stout compared to the closely related snipes, with a thick body, comparatively large rounded head, and very short neck. It's also distinguished from other sandpipers by three large blackish bands that run across the top of its head, instead of the lengthwise stripes found on snipes. Large brown eyes are set far back on the skull to provide good rearward vision. The slender, sharply pointed bill is specialized for probing into soil, and measures 2 to 3 inches long. Body length is 10 to 12 inches from tip of beak to end of tail. The wings are broad and rounded, spanning 17 to 19 inches when spread.

Tail: Very short and wedge-shaped, 2 to 2.5 inches long, and composed of 12 narrow feathers that taper to rounded ends.

TRACKS

Prints show three forward-pointing toes, and one rearward-pointing grasping toe that angles to the inside, enabling the bird to grasp small branches when perched. Rear toe prints lightly in soft soil, and sometimes not at all. Track length is 1.5 inches, discounting the rear toe.

SCAT

Seldom seen, but most likely to be found on the ground beneath low shrubs. Typical form is cylindrical, rounded at one end, slightly crescent-shaped. Dark brown to nearly black in color. Diameter is about 0.125-inch; length up to 1 inch. Because the diet is mostly earthworms, scats usually lack seeds and vegetable matter.

COLORATION

Woodcocks are brown, buff, and black, which makes the bird almost invisible in its woodland habitat. Wing feathers give the appearance of black scales when folded against the sides. A narrow dark band extends from the front of the eyes forward to the base of the beak. Legs are tan to gray. Woodcocks are monomorphic: Both sexes exhibit the same patterns and colors.

SIGN

Woodcocks are secretive and leave little sign of their presence. During the summer molt, feathers that have been discarded under low-growing shrubs and bushes can sometimes be found. A close examination of leaf litter below these bushes will often show evidence of having been disturbed where the bird probed for earthworms.

VOCALIZATIONS

The most common vocalization, heard in the spring and early summer in northern forests, is a nasal beeping sound. The call has been described as an unmelodious "peent" that lasts for about 1 second. This call is usually issued from males attempting to attract females during the spring mating season, but apparently serves as a territorial claim in summer, as well.

More commonly heard than a vocalization is the tremolo whistling of the woodcock's wings in flight. With each downbeat of the wings, the flight feathers emit a high-pitched whistle that is especially heard by hikers or hunters who approach a quietly sitting bird closely enough to cause it to burst into flight.

During the spring mating season, males fly straight up into the sky for 200 to 300 feet, making this same, much more pronounced *woo-woo-woo,* free fall earthward a hundred feet or so, then repeat the process. For anyone who has ever heard and seen this courtship display in the twilight of the springtime woods, it is unforgettable.

LIFE SPAN

3 to 4 years on average.

DIET

An estimated 50 to 90 percent of the woodcock's daily diet consists of earthworms, but numerous other insects are eaten as well, including beetles, moths, flies, centipedes, and the larvae of most insects. Because the woodcock is a ground forager, nearly all of the insects it eats are on the ground or under leafy humus; flying insects are not a large part of its diet.

Woodcocks are extraordinary earthworm hunters, able to sense minute movements under the ground. The long, sensitive beak is kept in contact with the earth almost constantly. An earthworm moving within several inches of the woodcock creates vibrations that are detected through the bird's beak, and the bird makes an unerring stab beneath the forest duff to grasp the worm before it can escape underground. If no movement is detected, a woodcock may stamp the ground with one foot to incite lethargic worms into motion, all the while keeping the tip of its sensitive beak in contact with the earth. And although there's no data to confirm this, it seems apparent that woodcocks also possess an acute sense of smell, and are able to narrow their searches for worms through odors.

Woodcocks also eat some vegetation, particularly seeds, grass sprouts, and buds in early spring when they migrate northward. Earthworms and insects are preferred in any season, but if warm weather arrives late in the woodcock's summer habitat and these creatures remain dormant, vegetation can suffice until temperatures rise.

MATING HABITS

Woodcocks reach sexual maturity at 10 to12 months. Courtship and nesting span the warm weather months, from spring to early fall, beginning as early as late February in southern latitudes and as late as May in the northernmost regions. Mating is preceded by a northerly migration of sometimes large flocks of these normally solitary birds. Males may begin courting during that migratory flight, but like salmon returning to a natal reach of river, breeding takes place only after the birds have reached the forests in which they were born.

Woodcocks are territorial, with males and females staking out territories in their winter and summer ranges that they'll continue to use throughout their life spans. The species is among the most nonviolent of animals, and there's no record of either sex battling over territory. Females seem content to nest within as little as 50 yards of one another, and can sometimes be seen foraging for worms in such close proximity that it makes them appear as if they are companions. Males who find themselves in competition for the same territory resolve their disagreements with puffed-up displays and excited chirps, but never fight.

Male woodcocks assume the most active role in mating, and their advertisement for mates is one of the most intriguing in all the bird world, even though most courting is done in the dark of night. On reaching their summer range, males find a clearing, sometimes referred to as a "singing site," where they can fly upward and descend freely, with no interference from an overhead canopy. There, the male begins his display by flying 200 to 300 feet upward on wings that make a high-pitched twittering sound when flapped rapidly. On reaching the apex of his flight, the woodcock falls or glides earthward to a height of about 100 feet, then rises again on twittering wings. Between aerial displays, males rest on the ground and utter their distinctive "peent" cries.

Receptive females are drawn to the male's courting display from a mile or more distant, initially by the distinctive whistling of its wings, then, as she draws closer, by his silhouette against the sky. The pair engage in a brief courtship in which the male again plays the most active role, peenting and occasionally flying upward for several yards on twittering wings. Copulation generally occurs within an hour, then the female leaves and the male returns to its display. There is no lasting bond between mates, and both will likely breed with several partners over the course of the summer.

Impregnated female woodcocks withdraw to their own, usually heavily wooded territories almost immediately after mating. Courtship may continue for those not fertilized, but those whose eggs have begun to develop will seek out a suitable nesting site.

Like turkeys and grouse, female woodcocks are ground-layers, making rough nests of leaves and debris directly atop the forest floor, always behind or under covering foliage and usually in a place that's difficult for most predators to access. Inexperienced mothers may lay their eggs directly atop the forest floor if the weather is warm.

Gestation is quick and eggs are laid within a week or so of mating. The usual clutch size is four gray-orange eggs that measure about 1.5 inches long. Incubation lasts about 21 days. Newborn woodcocks are walking around the nest within hours after hatching, but they cannot feed themselves for the first 3 to 4 days, and must be fed earthworms by the mother. By 4 days the hatchlings begin feeding themselves with small insects and plant sprouts, and will begin probing for earthworms with their long beaks. By 30 days the young are nearly fully grown, disperse to find their own territories, and join the long-distance wanderings of their kind.

BEHAVIORISMS

The American woodcock is a normally solitary bird that is most active at dusk and dawn (crepuscular). Woodcocks spend the sunlight hours sleeping in shaded undergrowth, usually on the ground, where their mottled camouflage makes them virtually invisible. When darkness falls, the birds leave their seclusion to probe the forest floor for earthworms and night crawlers.

The woodcock's large eyeballs give it exceptional night vision, and their placement near the rear of the head provides a field of view that permits a woodcock to see movement from behind, a valuable ability for birds that spend much of their time facing downward. Being primarily nocturnal, the woodcock's greatest danger comes from above, usually in the form of hunting owls. Terrestrial predators, especially foxes and bobcats, also prey on woodcocks, but it appears that relatively few birds are taken by these carnivores.

Like the ruffed grouse, most of a woodcock's defense against predators lies in the mottled camouflage pattern of its feathers, and in an instinctive reluctance to reveal itself. When approached by a potentially dangerous animal (including a human), the birds remain almost frozen under shading foliage, virtually invisible to even the sharpest eye. When the predator is mere feet from its hiding spot, the woodcock bursts from cover in a flurry of twittering wings that startles the enemy into hesitating for the brief second it needs to become safely airborne.

Escape flights seldom cover more than 100 yards before the woodcock again settles into an obscure hiding place, a habit also seen in ruffed grouse. This method of escape is effective against animal predators (and saves valuable calories for the birds), but human researchers and sport hunters can exploit it by noting in which direction a woodcock flew, then very slowly following, knowing that the bird has landed within a few dozen yards.

Woodcocks have been referred to as "timberdoodles" by hunting magazine writers, but this moniker rightfully belongs to the closely related common snipe *(Gallinago gallinago),* whose marshland habitat frequently overlaps that of the true woodcock. The name alludes to the corkscrewing flight pattern used by flushed snipes, whose spiraling escape over relatively open marshes is designed to make them a difficult target for hawks that are adept at plucking prey out of the air. The woodcock's forested habitat doesn't require such evasive maneuvering, and in fact often prohibits such aerobatics. A woodcock often flutters while flying away from an enemy, but isn't known to employ the corkscrew flight used by snipes.

Common Raven (*Corvus corax*)

Largest of the family Corvidae, which also includes crows, magpies, and jays, the raven ranks among the smartest bird species in the world, arguably second to the smaller American crow *(Corvus brachyrhynchos)* in terms of social structure and a rudimentary language. This innate intelligence has made both crows and ravens popular in zoos and as pets, where some individuals have even been trained to speak simple human words like "hello." Some cultures have revered these birds enough to incorporate them into their heritages—a spread-winged raven was once the icon painted on the sails of ships belonging to the Scottish clan MacDougall.

The raven's historical range was once broader than it is today, but for centuries the big, bold birds were easy targets for farmers who blamed them for crop damage, and for varmint hunters who eradicated them for sport. Today ravens enjoy legal protection in many states, and the species appears to be rebounding.

GEOGRAPHIC RANGE

Ravens seem to be capable of adapting to a wide variety of climates and habitats. They are common around most of the world, especially in the Northern Hemisphere, where they range well above the Arctic Circle. Ravens are native to northwest Europe, Great Britain, the shorelines of Greenland, Iceland, northern Scandinavia, central Asia and the Himalayas, northwest India, Iran, northwest Africa, the Canary Islands, and through Central America south to Nicaragua.

In North America the species is found throughout Canada and Alaska, throughout the western states, along the Rocky Mountains southward into Mexico. It is absent throughout all but the northernmost eastern states, except along the Appalachian Mountains, where it extends southward to Georgia.

Intelligent and raucous, ravens have a complex language of their own.

HABITAT

Ravens are partial to cooler climes where winters include at least some snowfall. The birds are capable of withstanding extreme cold, and it is probably not coincidental that the rugged, cold habitats that ravens seem to prefer are places where humans are sparsely populated.

Suitable raven habitats will include elevated places where females can nest well aboveground, out of reach of most predators. In mountainous terrain, rocky crags and cliff faces are used for nesting, but it appears that most prefer to nest in the tops of standing trees, particularly conifers.

PHYSICAL CHARACTERISTICS

Mass: 1.5 to 3.5 pounds, with heavier individuals occurring in the north.

Body: The raven is the largest of the all-black birds, standing 24 inches or more. An adult raven is roughly 50 percent larger than the closely related common crow. Wingspan is about 46 inches. The all-black bill is comparatively larger than the crow's, with the upper side covered with short black nasal feathers about halfway out from the head. As befits a bird that relishes extreme cold, the neck, and especially the throat, are more thickly feathered than the crow's. Female ravens tend to be roughly 10 percent smaller than males.

Tail: Wedge-shaped and much longer than that of the crow, extending nearly to the ground, sometimes dragging when the bird is walking.

TRACKS

The raven's three thick, segmented toes face forward. The center toe is longer than outer toes; one toe faces rearward, used for grasping. Forward-facing toes are less splayed than in some species (like the turkey), with less of an angle between the outer toes and the center toe. The rear toe is usually in line with the center toe, not offset as in crows and many other species. Claws are exceptionally long in comparison to most nonpredatory species,

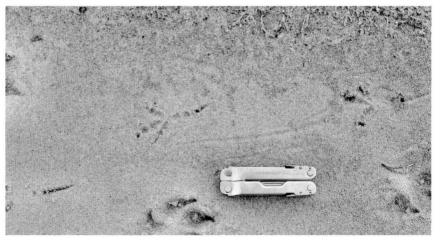

Raven tracks

measuring up to 0.5 inch, and normally showing in tracks. Track length (excluding claws) is about 3.5 inches from tip of rearward toe to tip of center forward toe.

Although they are extraordinary fliers, ravens tend to walk from one place to another with a strutting gait that might be described as almost cocky. This unique gait leaves a staggered line of left and right tracks, evenly spaced, and all pointing forward—as opposed to the pigeon-toed (inward pointing) or duck-footed (outward pointing) tracks of many other species. Distance between left and right tracks averages about 6 inches, with a narrow straddle of about 2 inches between the left center toe and right center toe. Note that rear toes tend to drag as the bird steps forward, leaving scrape marks behind them, and revealing the bird's habit of angling the forward toes upward as it walks.

When taking flight, ravens, like most birds, prefer to get a running start that consists of a series of hops in which paired left and right tracks print closely together, but have a space of 2 to 3 feet between pairs. Tracks tend to point forward, not angled, and rear toes seldom leave scrape marks.

SCAT

Varied according to diet. Most often watery and formless. Solid scats will be typically dark brown or blackish, unsegmented, evenly cylindrical in shape, and curved. Diameter is less than 0.5 inch; length ranges from less than 1 inch to more than 2 inches. Solid scats are often indicative of a poor diet that lacks good nutrition and moisture. Scats turn white as they dry with age.

A more succulent diet of fresh carrion and other animal flesh results in a semiliquid scat form that's most often found beneath trees and other elevated perches. These splattered scats may be up to 2 inches across, and usually have a mucuslike consistency, with traces of yellow or white. Occasionally there will be more solid segments included, as well as insect legs and carapaces in summer.

COLORATION

All-black feathers and bill. Legs and feet are unfeathered and black. Feathers are oily and appear iridescent, making the bird appear almost purplish in bright sunlight.

SIGN

Accumulations of scat under roosting trees, especially obvious atop snow. Molted or discarded all-black feathers under roosting trees, especially in summer. In winter, wingtips often brush against snow when the bird is taking flight, leaving imprints of flight feathers as well as a good indication of wingspan; the same phenomenon may be seen on dusty roads and sandy shorelines.

VOCALIZATIONS

Classified as a songbird by ornithologists, ravens are among the loudest and most vocal of birds, and have long been a favorite subject for researchers of avian behavior. However, the species' numerous calls, which range from the familiar croaks and caws to short whistles and clucks, remain mysterious. It's commonly accepted among ornithologists that both ravens and crows have at least rudimentary languages, but the process of defining them is a work in progress.

The most commonly heard call is a croaking "awwk" that keeps members in touch with others of the same flock. A call used to alert others to the presence of food is a higher-pitched and less hoarse "ock."

A less common raven vocalization consists of a repeated clucking sound that has sometimes been mistaken for the mating call of a male grouse. This sound, which a human can imitate by placing the flat of the tongue against the upper palate, then sucking it abruptly downward, is a hollow cluck, almost a popping noise. The call is usually in two stages, a lower-toned cluck followed by a slightly higher-pitched one, but different combinations are sometimes used. The call apparently relays a message, but is often issued from lone ravens perched on a low branch, and its exact meaning has yet to be determined.

Another raven call that often goes unidentified or misidentified is a hollow whistle that sounds much like the noise humans make by blowing across the mouth of a glass soda bottle. The exact meaning of this call has yet to be determined, but it seems to be uttered mostly in the early morning, and by lone individuals perched overhead.

LIFE SPAN
About 6 years in the wild.

DIET
Ravens are broadly omnivorous and opportunistic. Like the related crows, jays, and magpies, ravens are expert scavengers of carcasses, but all Corvidae are versatile feeders that can subsist on nearly any digestible organic material.

Like all sophisticated scavengers, ravens possess extraordinary eyesight and good color discrimination, which allow them to see dead or dying animals from great distances. A very long beak filled with olfactory receptors gives a raven the ability to detect the spoor of blood from several miles distant. Of all the birds, only the turkey vulture *(Cathartes aura)* has a more acute sense of smell.

Ravens are conspicuous consumers of roadkill, and are frequently observed dining on carrion provided by motorists. Smaller roadkills, like squirrels, are simply carried off in the birds' claws to be eaten in a quieter, safer location. Deer and other animals too large for transport sometimes draw large congregations of intensely squabbling ravens and crows, although rarely both at the same time because ravens are loath to share a bounty with their smaller cousins. Roadkill is particularly important to the birds, because large animals killed by cars are often split open, making the meat accessible to a bird that does not have the power or the tools to reach it otherwise.

It is for this reason—the difficulty in opening a carcass—that ravens maintain a crucial and symbiotic relationship with coyotes and wolves, and will advertise the presence of large dead animals to these more powerful carnivores by circling above a fresh carcass making a cacophony of croaking calls. While waiting for the larger carnivores to respond to the display, ravens busy themselves eating a carcass's soft parts—eyeballs, nose pad, and around the anal cavity. As the wolves or coyotes arrive and tear into the bounty, the birds will yield the now-opened carcass. After the larger carnivores have eaten their fill, the ravens descend to peck the plentiful remaining flesh from nooks and crannies inaccessible to teeth. It's a sure bet that wolves keep an eye on ravens, just as ravens keep an eye on wolves. Note also that knowledgeable ranchers who need to dispose of winter-killed cows or calves will split the hides with a knife, allowing the birds to clean up the carcasses.

Large dead animals that are in places too open to attract big carnivores may remain inaccessible to ravens until decay has set in. Rotted flesh isn't generally eaten, but fly and insect larvae, beetles, and other invertebrates that feed on decayed organic matter can make up a large portion of the roadway raven's diet.

Although not known as skillful hunters, ravens have a predatory side. Raids on the eggs and the newborns of smaller nesting birds, especially those that nest on the ground, are fairly common, and ravens will make meals of hatchling turtles in early summer, as well as eat snakes, frogs, mice and voles. The birds can often be seen foraging in meadows for grasshoppers and mice, following a farmer's hay swather to pick up fleeing or injured rodents, or hopping about freshly plowed fields for earthworms. Few small animals are excluded from the diet of this opportunistic hunter. In some areas, predation of ravens on the young of endangered species, like desert tortoises and least terns, has caused them to be considered pests.

Ravens are also fond of fruits and seeds. Raspberries, blueberries, and most other berries are eaten in season, but the birds dislike having their vision hampered by the dense foliage of a berry thicket, and will often fly up into nearby trees to survey the surrounding area for danger. More favored are fruiting trees, like crabapple, serviceberry, and wild cherries, which allow ravens an unrestricted view while they feed. Corn fields are sometimes plundered, and cobs carried off in the birds' feet to a safer, more open feeding spot. Ravens and crows also incur the wrath of farmers by eating seeds from freshly planted fields.

Like most species in family Corvidae, ravens are known to carry off and stash foods in elevated larders that range from cracks in cliff faces to holes in standing trees—and even in church bell towers. It doesn't appear that foods are cached for long-term storage, but rather to provide a safe place for them to be retrieved and eaten in the short term.

This tendency to cache items also extends to nonfood objects. Ravens and, to a lesser extent, crows, are known for stealing small shiny objects, like watches, marbles, and even coins, then flying off with them clutched in their feet to stash in an elevated cache, which might also be used for storing food. The purpose behind this theft behavior isn't known, but has been well documented.

MATING HABITS

Sexual maturity is attained at 11 to 12 months. Mating takes place from late February through early March, later in the north than in the south. It appears that breeding season is initiated by several factors, including lengthening days, warming temperatures, and probably pheromonal scents emitted by receptive females.

Both males and females become territorial at the start of breeding season, driving off other ravens of the same gender, and becoming generally intolerant of all larger birds within their claimed domains. Males tend to pursue females, and their territories are generally sited to overlap those of several females, even though both sexes are typically monogamous, accepting only one mate per breeding season.

Courtship between prospective mates is a ritualized affair of elaborate displays and dances. The female indicates her readiness to breed to an attendant male by crouching low to the ground and extending her wings, their tips drooping to the ground, in a posture of submission. The male struts around her, breast and neck feathers ruffled to make himself look as large as possible. If the male is an acceptable mate, the crouched female raises her tail, exposing her genitalia, and shakes it rapidly. The male then mounts her from behind in typical bird fashion, pressing her to the ground and holding her in a submissive position while covering her outspread wings with his own. Copulation lasts less than a minute, and may be repeated several times before the pair fly off together.

Mated pairs are highly territorial, defending their clutching area from intruders through-out the summer, and often longer. Both mates participate in building a broad dish-shaped nest, about 3 feet in diameter, constructed of large sticks encasing a more densely inter-twined wall of smaller sticks. The bowl of the nest is lined with feathers, fur, grass, and other soft materials. The raven's larcenous nature and innate intelligence sometimes result in nests that are lined with socks and small articles of clothing stolen from clotheslines, while the nest walls may include wire, plastic drinking straws, string, or other suitable man-made objects.

The raven's best known nesting places are rocky ledges on high cliff faces, out of the wind, but other equally elevated and sheltered locations are also used. Just as nesting ravens recognize the utility of an object like a soft sock or towel, they are quick to utilize suitable man-made structures for construction platforms. Raven nests are found atop power poles, farm silos, microwave towers, and even on the roofs of abandoned cars. In forested country, the birds often nest at the tops of tall pines, especially those standing in open marshes, where terrestrial predators simply cannot get at them.

Pregnant females begin laying their eggs almost immediately after their nests are com-pleted, within about 10 days of mating. Clutch sizes average four to five blue-green, brown-spotted eggs, each about 3 inches long. Eggs are incubated by the female, although some reports claim that males may sit on the eggs for short periods when their mates leave to drink and feed. Males also bring their nesting mates food.

Raven eggs hatch after an incubation period of about 18 days, in late March to early April. Similar in size to chicks of the domestic chicken, hatchlings are born naked in the south, and covered with a fine fuzz in the north. Both parents care for the young, bringing them insects and scraps of meat.

Young ravens learn to fly at about 8 weeks, and leave the nest with their parents. Adolescents can be differentiated from their parents by being slightly smaller. They also lack the blue-black iridescence of an adult, especially around the head and shoulders. Parents and young remain loosely together throughout the summer and following winter, with the family growing progressively less cohesive as the young ravens approach maturity. Yearling ravens leave their parents to establish their own territories and to find their own mates the following spring.

BEHAVIORISMS

Ravens are complex birds, which historically led to some disagreement about their habits and behaviors among ornithologists and amateur observers alike. Much remains unknown. Adult birds are indeed solitary, but only until they find mates. Mated pairs probably remain together for life, yet widowed mates will rarely remain alone past the next spring mating season, and a widowed parent of immature nest-bound young will probably find a new mate to help raise the offspring soon after losing the parental mate.

Although described by some authorities as being solitary in nature, ravens are most often seen in flocks that can number fifteen birds or more. The explanation behind this seeming contradiction is that only unmated adults in search of their own territories are solitary. Mated adults tend to remain together throughout the year, probably until one of them dies, and the bond between parents, offspring, and siblings seems to diminish very little as the birds age.

The primary reason that related ravens flock around a carcass is to create an intimidating show of force to discourage other ravens, and even eagles, from attempting to appropriate their food. Bald eagles and other large raptors have little to fear from individual ravens, and in fact consider them prey, but a half dozen or more ravens gathered at a deer carcass is more trouble than even a pair of eagles can contend with. Though unable to engage an eagle in individual combat, the ravens persist in harassing the raptor by jumping in from all sides to peck at it. Unable to enjoy its spoils, the eagle invariably abandons the carcass to find a more peaceful meal elsewhere. That same tactic works against smaller carnivores, like foxes and opossums, but is not used against coyotes or wolves, which ravens rely on to tear through the tough hides that their own beaks can't penetrate.

Historically, ravens have been persecuted by humans for superstitious reasons. Edgar Allan Poe's narrator in the immortal poem, *The Raven,* refers to the bird as "devil" and "demon," and even the legendary John James Audubon incorrectly accused the raven of preying on lambs. Prompted by these myths, by depredations on crops, and perhaps subconsciously unnerved by the raven's bold curiosity and obvious intelligence, farmers in the New World did what they did to most wildlife for over a century: They made a point of shooting the birds on sight (as they did with other members of family Corvidae, and all raptors). By the first quarter of the twentieth century, this once common species had all but disappeared from much of its historical range in the eastern United States. Today raven numbers are rebounding, especially in the western states. Many eastern states still classify them as endangered or threatened.

Black-Capped Chickadee (*Poecile atricapillus*)

This tiny but endearing bird has long been a favorite among birders. Chickadees have been described as the toughest birds in the forest, because while eagles, hawks, and other species known for their fierceness flee south to warmer climes come winter, the little chickadee remains, energetic and seemingly cheerful, in the coldest, most hostile weather.

Black-capped chickadee. DONNA DEWHURST/USFWS

GEOGRAPHIC RANGE

Black-capped chickadees are unique to North America, where they occupy central and western Alaska and can be found throughout Canada. In the western United States, the species ranges south as far as northern California and Nevada, and through the Rocky Mountains as far south as New Mexico. In the eastern and central United States chickadees are found as far south as Indiana and New Jersey.

HABITAT

Black-capped chickadees prefer open deciduous woodlands, but are not uncommon in mixed or mostly coniferous forests, cedar swamps, or among willow and dogwood thickets along riverbanks and lakeshores. Many sources list them as being most common at the edges of forest and field, but this may be due more to the number of observers in those places than to the actual number of chickadees living there.

PHYSICAL CHARACTERISTICS

Mass: About 3 ounces.

Body: Black-capped chickadees are easily recognized by their short, plump bodies, solid black caps and bibs, and white cheeks. Standing height is 5 to 6 inches; wing span is 6 to 8 inches. Beak is proportionally short, about 0.25 inch long. Sexes are alike in color and size. The black-capped is difficult to differentiate from the Carolina chickadee, whose range slightly overlaps that of the black-capped at the southeastern edge of the latter's range, except that the true black-capped chickadee's breast bib is more irregular along its lower edge.

Tail: Proportionally long; dark gray.

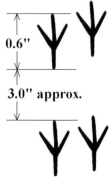

Chickadee tracks

TRACKS

Chickadee tracks are tiny and very faint even in snow or mud, due to the lightness of the bird. Three toes point forward; the center toe is slightly longer than the outer toes; the outer toes are arrayed at outward-pointing angles to either side. The rear toe typically points straight backward; used for grasping. Track length is about 0.5 inch, discounting the rear toe. Black-capped chickadees hop rather than walk, leaving paired side-by-side tracks with 3 to 4 inches between pairs.

SCAT

Difficult to find, but usually on the ground below branches where the birds perch. Solid form is cylindrical and blackish when fresh, rapidly becoming white as it ages. Length is about 0.125 inch; diameter is about equivalent to a number 2 pencil lead.

COLORATION

Black skull cap, black bib, white cheeks, a greenish-gray back, with streaks of white and black. Wings and tail are dark grayish; flanks are buff-colored. Upper wing feathers have white edging.

SIGN

Seed husks, and sometimes discarded feathers, on the ground below perches. Chickadees leave little evidence, but the birds' energetic activity level and vocal nature usually make their presence obvious.

VOCALIZATIONS

Black-capped chickadees have a range of vocalizations that are used to communicate not only among themselves, but apparently with grosbeaks and other small bird species commonly seen feeding with chickadees. To a casual listener the calls sound simple, but researchers have found them to be surprisingly complex and languagelike, encoded with information on identity and recognition of other birds, as well as predator alarms and gathering calls. The call for which chickadees are best known suggests its common name: "dee-dee-dee-dee." Its song consists of two or three whistled notes, the first higher in pitch, described as "fee-bee-ee."

LIFE SPAN

Chickadees live an average of 2.5 years in the wild, although birds up to 5 years old aren't uncommon. Life spans very widely: The oldest wild black-capped chickadee on record lived 12 years and 5 months.

DIET

Black-capped chickadees are omnivorous, feeding on most forest-dwelling insects, their larvae, and spiders, many of which are snapped up as the birds hop about on the trunks of rough-barked trees like oak, ash, and white pine. Fat-rich grubs and caterpillars are especially preferred during the birds' breeding season. Insects make up roughly 70 percent of their diets during the summer months, making the chickadees important in controlling mosquitoes and other pests. Because chickadee communities tend to be large in their suitable habitats, this species' impact on the numbers of parasitic and agricultural insect pests can be significant.

During the growing season, flowers, fruits, and seeds make up the other 30 percent of a chickadee's diet. Summer plant foods include nectar-rich flowers, numerous seeds, and many types of berries, including serviceberry, blackberry, goldthread, rose hips, and blueberries. Chickadees have also been observed eating waxy berries like soapberry and the autumn fruits of poison ivy. Chickadees play an important role in dispersing undigested scat-borne seeds throughout their habitats, helping many plants to propagate.

In winter, chickadees eat seeds of cattails, cedars, and dogwoods, as well as the tender bud ends of river willow, pines, and most other trees, sometimes hanging upside down from twigs as they feed. Hibernating spiders and insects are plucked from recesses in the bark of trees.

Chickadees also eat carrion when they can get it, especially in winter. Many hunters have noted that their skinned and hanging deer are a major attraction for chickadees, which focus most of their attention on plucking away at the tallow, or fat, rather than meat. They can also be seen cleaning the bones of larger prey brought down by carnivores.

MATING HABITS

Black-capped chickadees generally reach sexual maturity at about 12 months, although it's believed that some females born in early spring may mate late in the same breeding season in which they were hatched. Mating extends from April in the south to early July in the north, and adults mate only once each year. Chickadees probably do not possess a keen sense of smell, so mating is most likely triggered by warming weather and lengthening days, and less by the pheromonal scents that drive other birds and mammals.

Male and female chickadees are typically already paired from the previous autumn. Unpaired males and females are drawn to one another through vocalizations, which studies suggest are complex enough to be considered a form of language. Courtship appears to have no discernable ritual, but consists of much flitting around one another. Mating competitions between breeding males are brief and limited to shoving matches in which contenders vie for possession of a perch.

Once paired, mates retire from the rest of the flock to find a nesting site, usually inside a standing hollow tree or a knothole in a large dead branch. Females do all of the nest building, while their mates bring them gifts of food. Nests are constructed of grasses, animal fur, feathers, and pine needles.

Fertilized females begin laying as soon as the nest is completed, with clutch sizes ranging from five to ten roundish, marble-size eggs with white shells and red-brown spots, especially around their larger ends. Both mates watch over the nest, but only the female sits on the eggs, leaving for brief periods that seldom exceed 5 minutes to drink and relieve herself. Incubation time is a short 12 days, and chicks are born blind and naked (altricial). They grow quickly on a diet of insects brought to them by both parents.

By 9 days the chicks will have grown feathers, and by 16 days they'll have learned to fly. Both parents continue to feed them a high-protein diet of insects until the young are 3 to 4 weeks old, at which time they are able to fend for themselves.

BEHAVIORISMS

The black-capped chickadee is a social bird except during the breeding season. During the spring-summer mating season, pairs withdraw from their flocks to incubate and rear young, joining the flocks again between May and August, depending on latitude.

Before and after the breeding season, black-capped chickadees exhibit some of the most intensely social behavior in the animal world, gathering together in flocks that may number in the dozens. Further adding to the size of a chickadee flock are numerous similar-size but unrelated bird species that fly, feed, and often roost—but are not known to interbreed—with the chickadees. These friends of the chickadee include grosbeaks, nuthatches, warblers, vireos, and small woodpeckers. Aside from an occasional squabble at bird feeders, there seems to be no animosity between the different species, and it's thought that this communal behavior, like schooling fish, provides safety from predators by making it difficult to isolate a single individual from the confusion of a large flock.

Probably due in large part to its flocking behavior, the chickadee suffers relatively few losses from predation. They make a difficult target for the usual bird predators—forest-dwelling owls and hawks, red squirrels, arboreal snakes that prey on eggs and hatchlings, and occasionally a pine marten or fisher that sneaks up on a nighttime roost. Almost entirely diurnal, chickadees have relatively poor night vision, but their habit of sleeping on small-diameter end twigs, where vibrations from an approaching predator can be felt, ensure that the tiny birds aren't easy prey at any time of day or night.

Black-capped chickadees do not migrate, and individuals prefer to remain within as small an area as possible, sometimes living their entire lives within just a few acres. This quality has helped to endear them to bird lovers, because chickadees remain in the same territory throughout the coldest winters, and are regular visitors to bird feeders.

Chickadees' metabolisms slow while sleeping in cold weather, and their body temperatures drop slightly, much the same as a hibernating mammal. This phenomenon doesn't appear to have an effect on the birds' ability to react to danger, but it does serve to conserve energy. Despite this ability, subzero weather is said to be the greatest killer of chickadees, which frequently die of hypothermia while roosting.

Chickadees are not threatened, and their numbers are at healthy levels throughout the species' range. Continued logging of forested habitat, with subsequent loss of nesting sites, is the biggest threat to populations of *P. atricapillus*.

Chapter Twenty-Five

SHORE AND WATER BIRDS

This section deals with bird species whose lives are spent mostly or entirely around water. These include geese, swans, ducks, herons, cranes, bitterns, and many species of hawks and eagles. The water birds selected for inclusion in this section represent only a small number of the species that fall into this category, but they are some of the most important species, from an ecological standpoint.

Great Blue Heron (*Ardea herodias*)

One of the most magnificent shorebirds, the great blue heron is an icon of marshlands throughout North and Central America. The great blue heron is a migratory species, wintering and breeding during the summer months in northerly climes, then migrating to warmer regions with their young before the snow falls. A less migratory all-white subspecies, the great white heron, is found almost exclusively in shallow shoreline habitats around the Florida Keys. In places where both white and blue heron populations meet, an intermediate subspecies, Wurdemann's heron can also be found.

The great blue heron is known as a solitary watcher and king of the marsh birds. FRANK MILES/USFWS

292 THE COMPLETE TRACKER

GEOGRAPHIC RANGE

The great blue heron breeds throughout North America, Central America, the Caribbean, and the Galapagos Islands. A migratory species that dislikes snow and ice, the great blue heron moves northward in spring to breed and live along waterways on the Pacific coast of southern Alaska, throughout the southern half of Canada, and across all of the lower 48 states. Other populations and individuals can be found in Mexico and Central America. With the approach of cold weather, blue herons and their grown young fly south to winter in warmer regions that extend from coastal Canada up to Nova Scotia, in the southern half of the United States, in Mexico, and into South America. In winter, heron populations that remain in more northern regions are concentrated around the Pacific and Atlantic coastlines, where temperatures are warmer due to latent heat from the oceans.

HABITAT

The great blue heron's natural home will always be at the edge of a body of water: rivers, lakes, beaver ponds, marshes, saltwater tidal creeks, surf, the shorelines of the Great Lakes. Smaller streams are sometimes frequented, but these are nearly always the tributaries of larger bodies of water nearby.

Herons, like most large stilt-legged shorebirds, take flight more slowly than smaller birds, and they prefer a running start of several steps. An observer will note that they tend to avoid overgrown shorelines where willows, dogwoods, and other tall shrubs inhibit freely spreading their wings, which extend to a span that can exceed 6.5 feet. Most herons will be seen in relatively open shallows with a low curtain of cattails or reeds for cover, places where escape from predators is most likely to be easy, and where most of the heron's favorite prey can be found. These carefully selected hunting grounds are a species-rich soup of the aquatic food chain, from other water birds to otters and frogs and microorganisms.

PHYSICAL CHARACTERISTICS

Mass: 4.5 to more than 5.5 pounds.

Body: This is the largest heron in North America, standing 38 to 54 inches from its large feet and long, comparatively spindly legs to the top of its black-crested head. The skull crest consists of two blackish stripes that extend from the eyes at either side of the head back to the nape of the neck, and terminate in black, upward-curling plume feathers. Wing span is from 66 to 79 inches. The daggerlike bill is about 8 inches long. The graceful and elongated neck is carried in an S-shape, even when in flight. A line of almost shaggy-looking plume feathers extends along the spine from neck to tail.

Genders are identical in appearance, though males are usually slightly larger than females. Juveniles resemble adults but lack the crest, and instead have a dark gray to black cap extending from the nape, across the top of the head, around the yellow eyes, to the top of the characteristically rapierlike bill. Juveniles also have a dark upper bill, rust-colored edging on the back and wing feathers, and lack the mane of long plume feathers that encircle the adults' lower necks.

Tail: Comparatively short, squared at the end, with a blackish tip.

TRACKS

Blue heron tracks are impressively large. They are four-toed, with three toes pointing forward, and one gripping toe pointed rearward. Total length, from tip of the rear toe to tip of the center front toe, is about 6.5 inches. Note that the outermost front toes of either foot are widely splayed from the inner two toes, which are held nearly parallel to one another. A track with a splayed outer toe that points left was made by the left foot, and vice-versa.

SCAT

Right foot

Blue Heron tracks

Sometimes cylindrical, dark brown when fresh, 0.5 inch in diameter, about 1 inch long. More often scats are semiliquid, mucuslike spatters among shoreline grasses, sometimes with evidence of fish scales, but are often indistinguishable from those of other large shorebirds.

COLORATION

A white crown stripe extends front to back across the skull, bordered at either side by a black plume extending from behind the eye to the back of the neck. Blue-gray back, wings, and breast, often appearing all-gray from a distance. Brownish patch under the leading edge of both wings, black patches at elbow wing joints. Flight feathers are black-tipped, contrasting against wing centers and against a spinal tuft of gray-blue plume feathers when the wings are folded. Long gray neck, sometimes marked with rusty brown, especially in younger birds. The breast streaked with white, black, and red-brown. The bill is yellowish. Legs are brown, sometimes dyed green from wading through algae; thighs may be marked with brown. Eyes are yellow, round, and striking.

SIGN

Cattail and other reeds pushed aside, leaving a trail of foliage displaced by the bird's large body. These trails are often marked by blue-gray feathers snagged as the heron pushed through the foliage.

VOCALIZATIONS

The great blue heron is less vocal that most members of its family, usually going about its business in silence. The most common call between mates is a hoarse, low-toned, and relatively quiet croak, similar to that of a raven. A guttural "rawk" sound is made when the bird is distraught, and sometimes while it's in flight. When disturbed near its nesting site, a parent of either sex may utter a nasal "rawnk" that sounds similar to the call of a Canada goose.

LIFE SPAN

About 7 years.

DIET

Although generally thought of as a daylight operator, blue herons also frequent shorelines at night, especially on warm, moonlit nights when many of the birds' prey are particularly active and the lunar glow creates an advantage for the predator. A typical heron spends about 90 percent of its day hunting for food in the shallows.

The great blue heron's hunting technique is effective and relatively simple. Able to wade shallows more than a foot deep without getting its feathers wet, the heron spends most of its waking hours standing motionless in the concealment of a reed marsh. If no prey wanders within the bird's reach, it may move to a new location with slow, stealthy steps, placing each foot softly to avoid disturbing food animals and fine silt that can swirl up in clouds and obscure the bottom. Perhaps because of their shapes, neither movement of the heron's legs nor the silhouette of its body against the sky seems to disturb the smaller animals that make up most of this species' diet.

Prey includes small fish of about 4 ounces, crayfish, snails, small clams, frogs, snakes, and small rodents. Because most of these creatures are crepuscular in their habits, herons and other shorebirds tend to be most active in the twilight hours of predawn and dusk.

Larger prey is captured with the heron's long, sharply pointed bill, which shoots forward, propelled by unwinding the springlike S shape of the bird's neck. The target is impaled with unerring accuracy. The prey is then thrown straight upward into the air with a toss of the head, where it slides free of the tapered bill and is caught in the heron's wide open mouth on the way down. Prey animals tossed into the air are caught headfirst nearly every time, which generally neutralizes their biting ends, and orients small fish so that their spiny fins will lie back and down as they slide into the bird's gullet. It's an impressive process, but not entirely without its hazards. In a few instances, herons have choked to death when fish became lodged in their throats. But the vast majority of the time, great blue herons are superbly skilled at skewering and flipping prey into their gullets.

Smaller prey, like snails and small clams, are held down with one of the heron's large, strong feet, and pecked or pried at with its bill until the shell's occupant has been consumed. Besides being an effective stabbing weapon and a good pry bar, the heron's long pointed bill can serve as needlenose pliers, reaching through chinks in natural armor, including the carapaces of turtles small enough to be gripped and held by one foot. Crayfish are pecked apart to get at the meat beneath their carapaces; freshly molted softshell crayfish are simply swallowed whole. Snakes are pecked on the head until they die, then swallowed whole like a string of spaghetti.

Most small creatures lie within a great blue heron's dietary bounds, but the birds will also eat seeds and tender sprouts found around their shoreline habitats. Like other carnivores, herons appear to require at least some of the nutrients and vitamins that can obtained only by eating plants.

Like otters, blue herons and their cousins are popular and convenient scapegoats whenever a favorite fishing hole becomes depleted of game fish. But the reality is that great blue herons seldom, if ever, seriously impact wild fish populations (though as noted below, they can be serious pests at fish hatcheries and aquaculture operations). As in most natural predator-prey dynamics, the birds tend to take the weakest and the least cautious of the prey base, making the species they prey upon stronger and more likely to survive in the long run.

MATING HABITS

Solitary by nature, blue herons gather to breed at different times, depending on the latitude in which they live. Some adults, including chicks born the previous spring, may remain in southern latitudes year-round, and these populations begin mating early, from November through April. In the northern parts of the species' range, where herons and other shorebirds don't live during the winter months, breeding is delayed until after the birds arrive at their summer habitats, with most mating occurring from March through May in the coldest climes. The instinct appears to be triggered mostly by warming, lengthening days in the north, but the heron's long bill probably endows it with an acute sense of smell that permits it to locate responsive mates by pheromonal scents, too.

Blue heron mating territories vary in size with the environment—wooded lakes, for example, have smaller areas of open shoreline—but a strong male heron will try to claim as much open space as it can hold from competitors, including claiming any females whose territories overlap his boundaries. Even so, claims are generally moderate: Territories seldom exceed more than 3 or 4 acres.

Disputes between breeding males are resolved with a display of stalking one another, stiff-legged and with feathers fluffed outward to make each bird appear larger. If one of the contenders doesn't concede, the two may fly at one another, feet clawing, sometimes stabbing with their beaks. Territorial battles are seldom more than mildly injurious to either party, and less able males move on to find less well-defended territory. Females are regaled with dances that consist of a male leaping straight upward to a height of 3 or 4 feet, wings outspread, then fluttering back to earth. These mating displays aren't as ritualized as those of the whooping crane, but they're no less spectacular to watch.

Mated herons often stay together throughout the breeding months, with more polygamous behavior observed in areas where there are fewer males than females. Males aren't remarkably paternal, but they do sometimes sit on the eggs while their mates take a break, and they will defend nesting sites from small predators. Nests are extremely large, dish-shaped platforms of intertwined reeds, lined with softer pine needles, cattail fluff, grasses, and feathers. Overall diameter may exceed 6 feet. Nests are often constructed atop secure, dry, grass hummocks above standing water, and concealed by a forest of bulrushes and cattails. Herons will sometimes also build extensive nests in the higher branches of big trees near their hunting waters. These nests consist of a bowl-shaped rough outer wall of sticks, cushioned on the inside with an insulating layer of softer materials. The tree nests may be more difficult to defend from raptors.

As the size of the nest indicates, great blue heron eggs are roughly 50 percent larger than a chicken egg. Females begin laying eggs in batches every two to three days until an average clutch size of three to seven pale blue eggs is reached. Larger clutch sizes occur more frequently in the north, a natural adaptation to counter increased mortality from predation and cold. Both parents, but especially the mother, incubate the eggs and defend the nest site.

After an incubation of 28 days, the eggs hatch. Heron chicks are semi-altricial, born with eyes open and covered with pale gray down. For their first 7 weeks, they are clumsy and easy prey. By 9 weeks, the chicks will usually have gained sufficient strength and feathers to fly short distances.

Both parents provide food for the chicks, with voles and mice making up most of the hatchlings' diet in many cases, followed by fish, insects, and snakes. Parents also provide aggressive protection against predators until the young reach 10 weeks of age and about 2 feet in height, when the rapidly growing herons can fly and feed themselves. By summer's end, the young will have mostly or entirely dispersed to seek out their own territories.

BEHAVIORISMS

While great blue herons are solitary by nature, except for the breeding months, neither are they especially intolerant of one another, except during the breeding months. In habitats where food and other resources are abundant, adult males may forage the same shoreline with only a few yards between them. In some especially good habitats, heron populations can increase to a point where some biologists consider them colonies.

Places where great blue herons can make a nuisance of themselves include fish hatcheries and rearing ponds, where fry and small tank-raised fish are easy prey. Commercial and governmental fish hatcheries generally defeat the birds by covering their stock tanks with a roof to lessen the amount of sunlight striking the water in them, or by adding a roof of light fencing. Pond owners try to discourage herons by placing heron decoys, flags, and other scarecrows around their shorelines.

The great blue heron, with its dull-colored feathers, was mostly spared the late-nineteenth century slaughter that almost eradicated the nation's flamingos, egrets, cranes, and other herons, as plume hunters overharvested feathers to adorn women's gaudy hats. The heron's numbers have never fallen as low as its more brightly plumed brethren. Today, like those more endangered species, the great blue heron is protected by the United States Migratory Bird Treaty Act, and it seems to be thriving in most parts of its range. In some of the heron's migration paths, collisions with power lines have become a leading cause of mortality, prompting the installation of a series of orange, basketball-size spheres on the wires to make them more visible to the birds. For the most part, today, the great blue heron faces only one major threat, and it is one shared by all wildlife: the rampant draining and destruction of wetlands for development, agriculture, and other uses.

Sandhill Crane (*Grus canadensis*)

With their great size, strange vocalizations, and grace on both the wing and on foot, sandhill cranes are perhaps the most charismatic of North America's large shorebirds. Standing as large—or larger, depending on subspecies—than the great blue heron, sandhills also make astounding annual migrations, flying hundreds of miles north each spring to summer breeding grounds, then flying with their grown young south to warmer regions before winter snows set in. Adults wear a distinctive cap of short reddish feathers that make them unlikely to be confused with any other species.

One of the great wildlife comeback stories of the century, the impressive sandhill crane once again fills the skies with its wild voice.

Sandhills are closely related to the whooping crane *(Grus americana),* which has long been an endangered species. Both birds wear a red skullcap, but the adult whooping crane is marked by a black triangular stripe extending rearward from its eyes, and by all-white plumage.

GEOGRAPHIC RANGE

During the summer months, sandhill cranes range as far north as Alaska's northern coastline, throughout the northern half of Canada, and into Michigan, Wisconsin, and northeastern Minnesota. To the west, their range extends southward along the Rocky Mountains, and west to Oregon. Notably, the Pacific coast is devoid of sandhill cranes to a distance of at least 100 miles inland.

In winter, sandhills and their grown young return to winter habitats along the southern border of the United States, ranging from Florida to California and southward into western Mexico. Populations have been reported as far south as Cuba, and as far north as Siberia. In spring, before the full heat of summer sets in at their southern wintering grounds, the cranes fly hundreds of miles north to mate, incubate, and rear the next generation in a cooler climate. It is a journey that has fascinated the earthbound human species ever since Herodotus described it in the fifth century BC.

Sandhills feed at the water's edge.

HABITAT

Sandhill cranes are always within walking distance of a freshwater shoreline. Active by day, they're most often seen frequenting fields and meadows in search of insects and rodents. By night the cranes retire to a nearby shoreline, often in the same marsh where they nest, to sleep and keep eggs or young warm through the chill of darkness. Sandhill cranes tend to avoid dense forests, where trees and vegetation inhibit spreading their wings, and they prefer to live well away from human habitation.

PHYSICAL CHARACTERISTICS

Mass: 8 to 9 pounds, with larger individuals occurring in the south.

Body: Sandhill cranes are heavy-bodied, with long necks and legs, and the long rapierlike bill typical of herons and cranes. Body length from tip of the bill to the claws averages between 4 and 5 feet. Wings are about 22 inches long; total wingspan is 5.5 to more than 6 feet. Males and females are indistinguishable, except that males are normally slightly larger.

Tail: Long, drooping grayish feathers about 1 foot long (sometimes called "the bustle") that hang downward, presenting an almost ragged appearance when the bird is standing erect.

TRACKS

Prints show three forward-pointing toes, each tipped with a claw that measures about 0.5 inch long. Middle toe is longest, at 2.5 to 3 inches, and points straight forward. Outer flanking toes point forward at outward angles from the center toe. The single rearward-pointing toe is about 1 inch long, is located higher up on the ankle, and doesn't print in tracks; this short toe also prevents sandhills from roosting in trees like blue herons. Tracks may be mistaken for those of a wild turkey in meadows where both species forage, except that the tracks of the more terrestrial wild turkey tend to be slightly longer and more robust, with obvious segmentation, whereas the delicate toes of the far-flying crane are more slender and lack obvious segments.

SCAT
Often indistinguishable from that of other large birds with similar diets, especially great blue herons, except that sandhills tend to forage in dry meadows and fields, while most shorebirds remain near water. In solid form scats are cylindrical, dark brown when fresh, roughly 0.5 inch in diameter and about 1 inch long. Scats are often semiliquid spatters among meadow grasses where the cranes hunt, sometimes with evidence of insect parts.

COLORATION
Sandhill cranes are easily identifiable by their bright red skullcaps, which cover the tops of their heads from the base of the long bill, around the

Sandhill crane tracks are unmistakable.

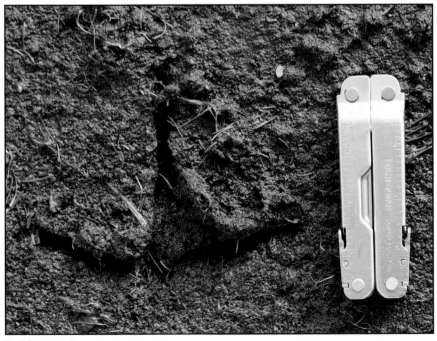
Sandhill crane track

eyes, and halfway to the rear of the skull. Directly below the red cap are cheek patches of near-white that contrast with the gray feathers covering the rest of the body. Wing and tail feathers are edged with darker gray to nearly black. Older adults also tend to become stained with a brown color on their wings and back, the result of algae and minerals in the shoreline waters where they nest and sleep.

Juvenile sandhills have wing feathers tipped with brown, and an all-brown head and neck. They do not grow their red skullcap until sometime in their second year. Sandhill cranes in juvenile plumage are virtually indistinguishable from juvenile whooping cranes.

SIGN
Depressions in tall grasses where the cranes have sat down, football-size or larger. Discarded large grayish feathers in grassy areas are a reliable indication of sandhill cranes.

VOCALIZATIONS
Unmistakable high-pitched staccato cooing sound that can carry great distances. Heard most often from marshy shorelines, or from groups of cranes passing overhead, sometimes at high altitude, in night or day. Heard especially in early spring, when groups of migrating birds are establishing territories and advertising for mates. Other voices in the same timbre include a short "awwk" that serves as an alarm, and a more prolonged version that indicates greater fear or agitation.

LIFE SPAN
20 years or more in the wild.

DIET
Like other herons and cranes, sandhill cranes eat an omnivorous diet that consists of mostly animal matter, but also includes seeds and young vegetation. Like a super-size version of the woodcock, sandhills use their long bills as probes to unearth and find worms and insects, but also as spears for impaling small rodents, snakes, and frogs. The sandhill is a capable fisher, but prefers to spend its daylight hours foraging in open fields, rather than along shorelines where it might need to compete with great blue herons.

In northern latitudes especially, vegetation and berries form a large part of a sandhill's diet. Their long bills are used to winnow seeds, to nip off young grass and other shoots, and to pluck sugar-rich berries. During the spring migration, when flocks of cranes travel northward to summer mating grounds, their arrival often coincides with the spring planting season, and many farmers complain that sandhills eat the seeds from their freshly planted fields.

MATING HABITS
Sandhill cranes are sexually mature in their second year, but some individuals, especially males, may be forced by competition to wait longer before breeding. The most active breeding ages are between 2 and 7 years.

Most sandhill cranes are migratory, leaving wintering grounds in warmer latitudes in spring, before the heat of summer, and flying several hundred to more than 1,000 miles to reach the northerly latitudes where they were born. Mating season begins immediately after the birds arrive in their summer habitat, preceded by a brief period in which males fight mostly ritualistic territorial battles that appear to involve little more than flying at one another with flailing wings and outstretched feet. Although cranes spend most of their days on dry land, preferred nesting territories are always at the edges of or near marshy shorelines.

After territories have been established, usually between mid-March and early June, depending on latitude, the much-described rituals of mating begin. Like its close relative the whooping crane, the sandhill male woos a prospective mate by jumping high into the air, wings outstretched to make his size appear more impressive. At the apex of his leap, he turns and flutters to the earth. These leaps are accompanied by extremely loud staccato cooing. Dances may continue for an hour or more, until the female becomes enthralled enough to accept the male, or leaves to find a more suitable mate. Frequently the female will dance as well, but most displaying is done by the male.

After mating, crane pairs set to work constructing a nest. A few incidents of sandhills nesting on dry land have been reported, but nearly all nesting sites are along remote shorelines with standing water and emergent (surface-growing) vegetation that includes bulrushes, cattails, and hummocks of rough grasses. Large grass hummocks, or "deadheads," that stand well above water are favored nesting spots not only for cranes, but for most waterfowl.

Nests are constructed from sticks, reeds, and grasses assembled from the surrounding area, and consist of a walled platform, up to 6 feet across, in the center of which is a smaller egg cup that has been lined with softer grasses, cattail fluff, and down feathers. Time from start to completion is about 7 days. Sandhills sleep in nests at all times of year, including males.

Expectant female cranes begin laying a clutch of one to three eggs, usually one per day, as soon as the nest is completed. Eggs are long and oval, about 4 inches in length, with dull brown shells that are irregularly spotted with rust-colored markings. Incubation begins as soon as the first egg is laid, and both parents assume responsibility for sitting on them, as well as for defending the nest against raccoons and other egg-eating predators. Males sit on the nests only during daylight hours; from dusk to dawn, all incubation is done only by the female.

After an incubation of about 30 days, the young hatch on a staggered schedule of one every 2 or 3 days. Chicks emerge almost ready to take on the world. They begin wandering from the nest as soon as 6 hours after hatching, even swimming for short distances, under the wary vigilance of one or both parents. The first hatchling will bully its younger siblings, so parents use their own bodies to keep chicks from fighting. Chicks are fed a diet of mostly insects for their first 30 days, after which the mother feeds them bits of their own broken eggshells, probably for the nutrients they contain.

At this point the parents begin leading their offspring away from the nesting site to teach them the hunting skills they'll need in coming years. The family returns to the nesting site each evening, often calling loudly to one another as they settle in to sleep in relative safety among the marshes. By their fifth week, chicks will have become strong fliers, but both parents continue to look after their brood for about nine months, separating just prior to the migratory flight south.

Established pairs may reunite each breeding season for several consecutive years. But the strong family bond shown during the summer months dissipates once the birds have migrated to their southerly wintering grounds. Yearling chicks may remain with their mothers for a month or more in winter, but will normally have become independent before the spring flight north.

BEHAVIORISMS

Adult sandhill cranes 2 years and older spend three-quarters of each year with mates and offspring, and are only solitary for the roughly three-month period spent in their winter habitats. Although considered among the most migratory of birds, not all sandhills feel the need to fly hundreds or thousands of miles each year, and many do not. Distances traveled between warm wintering grounds and cooler summer habitats vary considerably; for every crane that flies from western Mexico to the Arctic, another may simply shift a few miles from a lowland swamp to a mountaintop lake. Most individuals tend to return to the places where they were hatched.

During annual migrations, sandhills flock together in survival groups, relying on numbers to discourage predators that prey on the young especially. These groups are not cohesive, and upon reaching the summering or wintering grounds, the birds establish individual territories.

Like most heron and crane species, sandhills are diurnal by nature, sleeping through the night on large, dry nests concealed within marshes. The birds are most active during the twilight hours of dusk and dawn, when small rodents that are their prey are traveling to or from foraging places, and when most cold-blooded reptiles, amphibians, and insects are sluggish. On hot summer days, the birds may retreat from the open places where they hunt to the cooler breezes of their nesting marshes, standing silently for hours, often on one leg in typical crane fashion, and feeding on an occasional frog or snake.

Unlike the whooping crane, the current US population of seven hundred thousand sandhill cranes isn't considered to be threatened, though three subspecies, the Mississippi sandhill, the Cuban sandhill, and the Florida sandhill, have not fully recovered from the mass slaughters of the eighteenth and nineteenth centuries and remain protected by law. Today, many farmers in the American Midwest complain that the iconic cranes, brought back from the brink of extinction, are simply pests that create economic hardship by cleaning their fields of newly planted grain.

Sandhill cranes are legally hunted in three provinces of Canada, parts of Mexico, and in Texas, Kansas, and eleven other states along the birds' migratory flyway. At the time of this writing, state game agencies were debating whether to have hunting seasons for cranes in Wisconsin, Kentucky, Tennessee, and other states. Modern, regulated hunting does not pose a threat to the species, and money from license sales may contribute to habitat protection efforts, but the hunts remain controversial even as they become more popular, spawning a market for crane calls, crane decoys, and guided crane hunts.

Ornithologists say the real threats to the crane population now lie in the overuse of water along the critical Central Flyway (especially on the Platte River near the Sand Hills of Nebraska, for which the birds are named) by industries and agriculture, and in the ongoing

conversion of wetlands and open spaces to urban sprawl and industrial agriculture operations. Associated threats, such as mycotoxins from moldy waste grains left behind in farm
fields, are annual causes of mortality in cranes.

Canada Goose *(Branta canadensis)*

One of the most common and easily recognized birds on the North American continent, the
Canada goose is loved by many for its beauty and intelligence, and loathed by more than a
few for its eagerness to occupy human habitat, graze valuable crops, and empty its bowels
prolifically in inconvenient places.

There are four recognized subspecies, *B. canadensis occidentalis, B. canadensis hutchinsii,
B. canadensis minima,* and *B. canadensis leucopareia,* all of which are smaller than the true
Canada goose *(B. canadensis canadensis)* but share its distinctive markings. In general, indi-
viduals are larger in southern populations, and breasts are darker in western populations.

GEOGRAPHIC RANGE

Canada geese are native to and found throughout North America, with specific subspecies
being more regional. The larger, pale-breasted *B. canadensis canadensis* is found mostly in
the eastern portions of North America, while the equally large, brown-breasted *B. canadensis
occidentalis* inhabits the west. The smaller, pale-breasted *B. canadensis hutchensii* is found in
central and western Canada. *B. canadensis minima,* as its name implies, is the smallest of
the Canada geese, and is found in western Alaska. *B. canadensis leucopareia* of the Aleutian
Islands is threatened, and is distinguished from *B. canadensis minima* by its larger size, paler
breast, and, often, its wider white neck ring. All subspecies tend to winter in southern parts
of North America, then fly north in spring to mate and raise the next generation. This
migratory habit has been artificially changed in many locales by humans, who feed waterfowl throughout the winter months and make it unnecessary for flocks to travel south in
search of food.

The prolific and widespread Canada goose has become the bane of golf course managers everywhere.

HABITAT

Every goose habitat (as well as the habitat of their duck cousins) includes a relatively large body of open fresh water—usually a lake or pond, or large, slow-moving rivers—where the birds can escape or avoid terrestrial predators by swimming into deep water. In midsummer and in their southerly wintering grounds, Canada geese are often seen swimming along the shorelines of larger bodies of water, including the Great Lakes. But nesting areas will always be along the marshy shorelines of, usually, smaller lakes and beaver ponds, where cattails and reeds provide cover, grassy hummocks provide dry nesting sites, and calm shallows hold an abundance of edible aquatic vegetation.

Like most large birds, including herons and turkeys, the terrestrial portion of Canada goose habitat will always be in open places, where spreading their large wings won't be inhibited by trees or undergrowth. Grassy, open meadows along shorelines are especially preferred.

PHYSICAL CHARACTERISTICS

Mass: Slightly more than 2 pounds for *B. canadensis minima,* smallest of the subspecies, to more than 19 pounds for *B. canadensis canadensis.*

Body: Large, heavy body with massive breast muscles and a long, comparatively thin neck. Females tend to be slightly smaller than males, although both genders share the same colors and patterns. Short, stout legs are positioned close together under the bird's body, causing it to waddle as it walks and belying the grace that is evident as soon as it takes to the air. Feet are large and webbed. The flat bill is lined around its outer edges with teethlike projections, called lamellae, that are used for cutting grass and other stems that serve as food. Wings are long and very strong, spanning 50 to more than 65 inches when spread.

Tail: Short, black-tipped, terminating in a blunt point. Seen from above while the bird is in flight, the tail exhibits a white semicircle just forward of its black tip.

TRACKS

Prints are three-toed, with thick webbing extending from the tip of one toe in a semicircle to the tip of the next. Webbing normally shows in tracks, with the heaviest impressions being made by the longest center toe, which points straight forward, and the outer flanking toes, which also point forward, but at outward angles from the center toe. Track length is about 4 inches; width from the end of the outermost toe to the tip of the innermost toe is about 4 inches. Walking track pattern exhibits an extreme toe-in (duck-footed) stride, in which all toes point inward. Stride length from one track to that made by the opposite foot is about 6 inches.

Note that Canada goose tracks are very similar to those of the smaller ducks and the larger swans, with the only obvious difference being one of size and stride length. A typical large duck (i.e., a mallard) leaves a track roughly 3 inches in length, with a stride of about 4 inches. A mute or trumpeter swan has a very large track that can exceed 6 inches, with a longer stride of 9 inches or more.

Canada goose track

SCAT
Cylindrical, with a consistent diameter from one squared (flat) end to the other, occasionally with a larger bulbous form at the end that was excreted first. Diameter is about 0.5 inch; length up to 3 inches but often shorter. Color is typically olive-brown when fresh, becoming darker with age. Grass and other plant fibers, clipped short by the goose's toothed bill, are usually obvious in fresh deposits. Dimensions given are for the largest of the Canada geese, and vary downward in size for the smaller subspecies.

COLORATION
Branta canadensis have a black neck, bill, head, legs, and feet. A white patch, sometimes called a chin strap, extends from behind the eye, then under the chin just rearward of the bill, and to the rear of the opposite eye. The upper body and back are brownish-gray, with a whitish breast and underbelly (breast is brown in the western subspecies *B. canadensis occidentalis*). The smaller subspecies *(B. canadensis leucopareia and B. canadensis hutchensii)* have a distinctive white ring around the base of the neck, just above the breast. Wings are brown, with darker tips. These color patterns are unique to the Canada goose and its subspecies, making it unlikely to be confused with any other bird.

SIGN
Flocks of geese often gather in open, grassy areas, especially during migratory flights, and the grasses in these places can be clipped nearly to ground level as large numbers of birds feed on them. Such places may exhibit a trampled look from having been walked over by many flat, heavy feet. These places are usually well marked with scats.

The bane of the golf course, Canada goose scat has become a fact of life around lakes and rivers in many urban areas.

VOCALIZATIONS

Varied. Historically described—and oversimplified—as a honk, only the high-pitched call of migrating Canada geese in flight accurately matches that definition. When nesting, the call between mates might be described as a high-pitched "rrrawwnk." The call of an agitated or threatened goose is a rapidly repeated "awnk-awnk-awnk," which becomes quieter as the source of agitation withdraws. Like swans and ducks, geese can also make a loud hissing sound, heard especially when the birds are attempting to drive off intruders during the mating and nesting seasons.

Calls of the Canada goose (and also ducks) are normally heard only during daylight hours. An exception occurs during the spring hatching season, when the nested birds, eggs, and hatchlings may be threatened by nighttime predators such as bobcats, coyotes, or otters.

LIFE SPAN

The reported maximum life span in captivity is 28 years. Typical life span in the wild is 8 years or more.

DIET

Canada geese are mostly herbivorous, although there have been accounts of the birds eating grasshoppers and other small insects. On land the birds eat a variety of plants, including most grasses, plantains, dandelion shoots and flowers, and wild strawberry plants and fruits. Most types of nontoxic berries are eaten when in season and when in proximity to the birds' feeding areas—they never venture into woods or brushy places where they cannot open their wings and take flight to escape danger.

Despite having no true teeth, Canada geese are able to snip free small, more easily digestible sections from rough grasses and stems using the serrated, teethlike, lamellae that border the outer edges of their bills. By pinching leaves and stems in the bill, then pulling with a quick jerk of the head, geese are able to cut free small mulchlike snips of rough vegetation, which digest more easily than do longer blades of grass or stems.

Aquatic plants also make up a large part of the Canada goose diet, especially during the nesting season when parents prefer to remain close to their eggs. Pondweed, pond lily, and water lily leaves are eaten, along with tender cattail sprouts, wapato, and freshwater seaweeds. As the summer progresses and plants begin to mature, most types of seeds are eaten, including wild rice and grass seeds of all types.

A notable characteristic displayed by geese and ducks while feeding on aquatic vegetation is the tail-up posture assumed when plucking plants from the bottom of shoreline shallows. By tipping their bodies 90 degrees, with tails pointing skyward and heads underwater, the birds are able to extend their long necks to reach food growing on the muddy bottom. Sometimes this feeding method is observed with lone geese or ducks, but most often there will be a pair or more, which take turns foraging underwater while the companions remain upright and alert for potential danger.

MATING HABITS

Canada geese, like ducks, swans, and other migratory waterfowl, breed in the spring, returning to the same waterways where they were born. Mating begins as early as March in southern latitudes, and as late as June in the northernmost parts of the species' range. Individuals born the previous spring are sexually mature, but may not mate until they are 2 years old if competition is strong. Fortunately for the geese, there exists an almost even ratio between geese (females) and ganders (males), and adults of either sex take only one mate per season, so breeding rivalries are less common than in some waterfowl species.

Mating rituals are a much pared-down version of those of cranes or other water birds. When two males find it necessary to compete for a female, the contest consists mostly of hissing and flying at one another with outspread wings that are used as bludgeons. Battles are of short duration and neither contender is likely to be injured. When the vanquished suitor withdraws, the winning male approaches the female with head down, its neck outstretched and undulating from side to side.

Most older geese arrive at their breeding habitats already paired with a mate. Sometimes the pairs will have joined during the flight north, but the majority of adults will be with the same mate they had the year before, and perhaps for several years prior to that. Some biologists believe that Canada geese mate for life, but an adult whose mate is killed by hunters or predation will find another mate prior to or during the following breeding season.

Copulation between Canada geese is unusual in that it takes place on the water, and the female may be partially or wholly submerged during the act, held underwater by weight of the male when he mounts her from the rear and covers her body with his own. For this reason, perhaps, coitus is quick, lasting only a few seconds.

Choice of a nesting site is at the female's discretion; her mate simply follows where she leads. Likewise, the male takes little part in actually building the nest, and his role is generally limited to offering bits of reeds and grasses to his mate. Preferred nesting sites are on a raised point surrounded by water, especially grassy hummocks, snags of felled trees, and occasionally atop a muskrat house. Nests tend to be quickly made, simple affairs, usually little more than a rounded depression in the grass formed by the female's large feet and heavy body. In one unusual instance, a particularly inexperienced goose tried nesting atop a raised platform that had been constructed for ospreys, 15 feet above the surface of a beaver pond.

Females begin laying eggs within a day or so of mating, laying one egg about every 36 hours until a clutch of two to as many as nine eggs have been deposited in the nest's center. Eggs are slightly larger than a large chicken egg, measuring almost 4 inches long, and are cream-colored. Mothers partially cover their clutches with an insulating layer of down feathers plucked from their own breasts, which helps to keep the ova from becoming too cool or too warm, and the eggs are turned regularly to ensure even exposure all around.

Ganders remain close by during the nesting period, but don't take part in incubating the eggs. When the sitting goose leaves to feed or relieve herself, the gander's job is to guard the nest against predators. Smaller egg-eaters, like foxes, skunks, and crows, are chased away by loud honking and the male's bludgeoning wings. Larger carnivores like coyotes are led away on a "wild goose chase," in which the gander pretends to be injured and entices predators away from the nest by flopping pathetically and giving the impression of being easy prey.

After an incubation period of 25 to 28 days, the eggs begin hatching. Despite having been laid as many as 3 days apart, all eggs begin hatching within 24 hours. Hatchlings break free of the shell using their single egg tooth, and by the end of 48 hours, all goslings have freed themselves. Hatchlings are born covered with downy yellow coats that are marked with patches of green-gray atop the back and neck. Their legs, feet, and bills are blue-gray, but grow darker as the birds mature.

Goslings are able to swim within hours after hatching, and leave the nest with their parents immediately, usually on the same day they are hatched. The young are imprinted on their mother, and follow her wherever she leads, while the father generally follows behind. The goslings grow quickly, and by summer's end have become slightly smaller replicas of their parents. In autumn, the entire family joins with other groups of migrating geese to form the large flocks seen flying southward each year. When the flocks return to their northern summering grounds the following spring, goslings will have reached full adulthood and will seek out their own mates.

BEHAVIORISMS

The best known characteristic of the Canada goose is the distinctive V-shaped formation of a migrating flock. These flocks, which may number more than thirty birds, are made up mostly of families that have been making the same annual migratory flights to the same places for many generations. By flying together in large groups over long distances, which may span more than 1,000 miles, the geese find safety in numbers when they land in a strange place to spend the night each evening.

A primary benefit of flying in the trademark V formation is that it creates a slipstream behind each bird, beginning with the foremost—and generally the strongest—gander, who leads the flock. This arrangement permits every bird following the leader to "draft" behind the goose immediately in front of it, much the same as race car drivers employ the vacuum generated by the vehicle in front of them to lessen the amount of fuel their own cars expend while maintaining the same speed. Drafting permits adolescents and less-strong geese to keep pace with the most powerful individuals, while at the same time ensuring that the long flight is much less taxing on flock members than it would be if each big bird was making the same trek alone.

Although Canada geese flock only during annual migratory flights, individuals are seldom seen alone. The birds aren't social in the same way that turkeys are, and don't tend to live their lives as members of large groups, but mated pairs typically remain together throughout each year until one of them dies, and parents look after their broods through most of the youngsters' first year of life.

The wariness of wild geese, particularly those of the smaller subspecies, results from the near-constant threat of predation. Geese at every stage of their lives fall victim to predators, from carnivorous mammals to the alligators and snapping turtle of their southern winter habitats. Large pike have been observed eating goslings, and hawks, owls, and eagles kill them whenever they can. Raccoons, skunks, opossums, and ravens are known for preying on unhatched eggs whenever they can avoid the bludgeoning power of an irate parent's wings, while bobcats especially make a habit of patrolling spring nesting grounds at night, when the geese are effectively blind.

Nested geese are seldom preyed on during the day, when their keen hearing, eyesight, and the panoramic field of vision provided by placement of their eyeballs at either side of the head permits them to see approaching danger from the air or ground (ask any human hunter who has tried to stalk a flock of geese feeding in a farm field). In most nesting habitats, Canada geese are too large and strong to be successfully attacked by predators in the daylight, and the birds' aggressive defense of nests and hatchlings is sufficient to discourage most carnivores, even those as large as a coyote. An interesting behavior exhibited by nesting mothers is their tendency to lie flat, neck outstretched atop their eggs, when they spy an approaching enemy, thus lowering their conspicuous (and vulnerable) heads and necks below a predator's line of sight, and allowing their mates to lead it away on the proverbial wild goose chase.

Another threat to nesting populations of Canada geese comes from swans, particularly the much larger and notoriously aggressive Asian mute swan *(Cygnus olor)*. Introduced to the United States as a replacement for dwindling populations of native trumpeter swans *(Cygnus buccinator)*, the mute swan's powerful physique makes it the terror of most wild predators. The mute swan is now firmly established around the Great Lakes region and along the northern Atlantic seaboard. An aggressively territorial species, these swans are able to displace native ducks and geese from their historic nesting areas. The presence of mute swans also inhibits the return of native swans, which has caused wildlife authorities to consider eradicating them from the Great Lakes region.

Although protected from spring hunting under the 1918 Migratory Bird Treaty Act, and again by the imposition of autumn bag limits in 1960, the Canada goose in general has never been threatened. The smaller Aleutian subspecies was once listed as endangered by the US Fish and Wildlife Service, after populations were reduced to just eight hundred birds by the introduction of a nonnative fox in 1967, but good recovery efforts and steadily increasing numbers caused them to be moved to threatened status in 1990, and the danger appears to have passed. In 2001, the U.S. Fish and Wildlife Service the Aleutian Canada Goose population had rebounded to thirty-seven thousand individuals.

Canada geese populations in general have increased to the point of making them serious pests along many urban and suburban waterways. In some places, flocks that can number in the hundreds leave large volumes of scats, a quantity sufficient to create bacterial infestation of land and water, including the fungal infection known as "swimmer's itch." Adding to the problem are goose populations that have abandoned migration and become year-round residents in areas where people don't want them, such as on golf courses and in city parks. In all instances the troubles are caused, or at least exacerbated, by humans themselves, because Canada geese inhabiting remote northern waterways are not overpopulated, nor do they remain through the winter. Canada geese, like deer, squirrels, and numerous other species, have learned to occupy territories close to human habitation because wild predators have been exterminated, and because many well-meaning people create problems by feeding wildlife or providing a year-round source of easy nourishment in other ways.

Chapter Twenty-Six

PREDATORY BIRDS

While most species of birds can be considered predatory, some are exclusively, and extravagantly, so. Eagles, ospreys, hawks, and owls make up a large group of hunting birds whose diets consist almost entirely of the flesh of other animals. All are strong, fast fliers with very keen eyesight, have powerful feet with sharp talons evolved for gripping prey, and have hooked beaks designed to tear flesh from bone. Most are diurnal, when the asset of powerful vision can be used most effectively. Owls, with their silent wing beats and wide, night-seeing eyes, are among the top predators of the nighttime forests and fields. The bald eagle and the osprey are famed for their abilities to snatch fish from water, while the Cooper's hawk can snatch songbirds from the air, and the peregrine falcon can kill ducks on the wing at 180 miles per hour, a speed once thought reserved for men in fighter planes.

Bald Eagle (*Haliaeetus leucocephalus*)

The bald eagle is a symbol of fierce independence and strength, and has been the national bird of the United States since 1872. Benjamin Franklin had argued that the national bird should be the uniquely American wild turkey, stating that the bald eagle was a bird of poor moral character because of its habit of stealing food from other predatory birds. Franklin was right, both in his observation about the habits of eagles and on the fact that the turkey had played a much more important role in the forging of a new nation by providing food for early pioneers. But the peaceful and earthbound turkey just didn't evoke the same image of strength and pride as the bald eagle.

Despite being the emblem of the United States, the bald eagle was nearly extirpated in America by the widespread use of the insecticide dichlorodiphenyltrichloroethane (DDT) in the mid-twentieth century. DDT spread through the food chain to bald eagles and other accipiters, where it caused females to lay eggs that had weak shells, or sometimes no shells at all, cutting reproduction to almost zero. By the time the United States banned DDT in 1972, the bald eagle's numbers had fallen from an estimated fifty thousand individuals to about eight hundred breeding pairs in the lower 48 states. Enactment of the Endangered Species Act in 1973 prompted a concerted, and ultimately successful, recovery effort. As of 2011, the bald eagle has been taken off the Endangered Species List altogether, although it is still protected by law, and numbers are estimated at between thirteen thousand and sixteen thousand individuals in North America. It remains such a potent symbol that lawmakers, fearful that people would kill the newly recovered birds for trophies or religious objects, have made the possession of eagle feathers and other body parts illegal.

The bald eagle is an extraordinary predator, an efficient fisher, and a powerful flier.

GEOGRAPHIC RANGE

The bald eagle is native to North America and was once common from central Alaska through Canada and in the United States, as well as southward to the Mexican border and the Gulf of Mexico.

HABITAT

Bald eagles seem to be able to live anywhere on the North American continent where there are adequate nest trees, roosts, and feeding grounds. Suitable habitats include temperate forest, rain forest, prairie, desert, and mountains. Being especially capable fishers, open water and a reasonably healthy fishery are necessities in every bald eagle habitat, whether it is a big river, a lake, or the ocean.

PHYSICAL CHARACTERISTICS

Mass: 6.5 to 14 pounds; females typically larger than males.
Body: Males are 30 to 35 inches long; females are 34 to 43 inches long. Legs are feathered half way down the tarsus. Wing span may exceed 7.5 feet. Sexes are identical in plumage.
Tail: Moderately long, 6 to 8 inches, slightly wedge-shaped.

TRACKS

Bald eagles have massive tarsi (feet), short and powerful grasping toes, and long talons. The talon of the hind toe is used to pierce vital areas while the prey is held immobile by the front toes, and is powerful and highly developed in all eagle species.

SCAT

Typically birdlike, but larger than that of most birds. Solid form is irregularly cylindrical, dark brown in color, usually white at one end, sometimes bulbous at one end, about 3 inches long and less than 0.5 inch in diameter. Alternately, scat may be massed in form, sometimes nearly liquid. Look for undigested fish scales, fur, or feathers.

COLORATION

Bald eagles aren't bald; the term is an abbreviation of the word "piebald," which describes a spotted or patchy color pattern, especially in black and white. The adult bald eagle's dark brown body—which

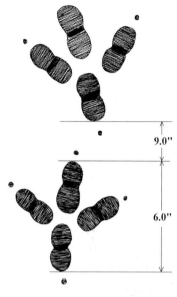

Bald Eagle tracks

can look black against the sky—stands in stark contrast to the white feathers of its head, neck, and tail. The long, hooked bill is yellow, as is the cere (the fleshy swelling at the base of the upper beak). Eyes and feet are yellow as well; legs are yellow and unfeathered.

Immature eagles are irregularly mottled brown and white until 4 or 5 years of age but, like adults, their feet and legs are bright yellow. Eyes are darker yellow or brown; the bill and cere are dark gray.

SIGN

Large, brushy nests at the tops of usually dead standing trees. The ground around these nesting trees is typically scattered with a variety of feathers, fish fins and scales, and small bones and fur.

VOCALIZATIONS

Best described as a screeching whistle that's often heard while the bird is in flight. Eagles can also croak or squawk, much like a crow.

LIFE SPAN

Approximately 15 years or longer in the wild; up to 50 years in captivity.

DIET

Bald eagles are strict carnivores. Best known as fishers, eagles swoop down onto the waters of a lake or large river to snatch shallow-swimming fish in their powerful, hooked talons, then fly off with the prize to feed at leisure on some lofty perch. Although not so skilled at catching fish as its slightly smaller cousin, the osprey *(Pandion haliaetus)*, the eagle is larger and stronger, able to carry away fish and other prey weighing in excess of 8 pounds.

In fact, the eagle's large size can work against it while fishing. Ospreys and smaller hawks that share the waterways found in every bald eagle habitat are better suited to catching blue-gills, perch, and young bass, which aren't easy targets for an eagle's large feet. This has led to the larcenous behavior that Benjamin Franklin found so objectionable, in which an eagle waits for a smaller, more nimble cousin to capture a fish, then steals that fish for itself—or, as the Odawa Indians say, "The osprey catches the fish that an eagle eats."

Despite its prowess and fame as a fisher, the bald eagle is an efficient hunter of other prey as well. With the "eye of an eagle," this raptor can spot a foraging rabbit from more than a mile distant, then swoop down onto the unsuspecting prey at a diving speed of nearly 200 miles per hour—or about the same speed as a World War II fighter plane. When just a few yards above the target, the eagle applies the brakes by spreading its wings wide to catch air like a parachute, and, with a bit of luck, lands directly atop its next meal with sharp-clawed talons that pierce the prey's body with a viselike grip. In fact, not every strike results in a kill, but with the power to take hares, muskrats, young beavers, and most other small animals, the eagle usually finds sufficient opportunity to keep itself and its young well fed.

Other birds also serve as eagle prey. Smaller species, like blue jays and red-winged black-birds, are too tiny and quick, but ducks, immature geese, swan cygnets, and the occasional young heron or crane are taken if the opportunity presents itself. Often these prey birds are taken with the swooping attack while they are on the water or ground, but bald eagles are agile enough on the wing to take most shore- and water birds out of the air, too. Crows and ravens are also frequent victims: When these birds see an eagle, they often gather in a tree whose branches prevent the eagle from diving upon them, and caw loudly to alert one and all of the mighty hunter's presence.

Other prey favored by eagles include large snakes, especially water snakes and cotton-mouths, small alligators, and large bullfrogs. Carrion is sometimes eaten, especially in win-ter, and eagles are occasionally seen feeding on road-killed deer, but the birds generally prefer to hunt or steal fresh meat.

MATING HABITS

Bald eagles become sexually mature at 4 years, but may not mate until age 5. In the northern part of the species' range, mating takes place between mid-February and mid-March, but in the south eagles may mate until August. Mating appears to be initiated by the female, who typically approaches a suitable male with ducking gestures of her head. The ritual that follows is suitably extraordinary. Both eagles take to the air, flying up to an altitude of several hundred feet, usually over water, then turn toward one another and lock their talons together. With feet locked in this manner, both birds free-fall nearly to earth before relinquishing their grips and flying upward again to repeat. The precise reason for this activity is unknown, but it appears to be a test of strength and agility, to determine if the male is physically strong enough to be a candidate for mating. The male must be able to keep up with the female as she flies upward, and his eligibility to mate—as well as his personal safety—demands that he have strength enough to recover from the free-fall.

If a male is deemed acceptable, the receptive female repeats the head-down gesture, raising her tail and presenting her cloaca (genital cavity) to the male. The male then mounts her from behind, with his talons closed into fists to protect her from being harmed by his claws. The male maintains his position atop her by pressing his closed fists firmly against her sides, gripping her body tightly between his feet during copulation. As with most bird species, intercourse is completed within a few seconds.

Historically, bald eagles have been thought to mate for life, although it appears that may not be true in all cases. What is certain is that mated pairs will remain together for at least as long as it takes to rear the next generation. Immediately after mating, the pair seeks out a suitable nesting site high in a large tree (usually a conifer), or on a cliff ledge. The site is always near open water. Nests consist of a rough outer shell of interwoven sticks, with a softer interior lining of grasses, moss, fur, and feathers. Newly constructed nests measure about 6 feet in diameter by about 1 foot deep.

Pairs that have mated in previous years may use the same nest for many years, building onto it with each passing year, so the size of a nest is indicative of the number of generations that have been reared there. Some very old nests have reached huge dimensions, measuring more than 20 feet across, 10 feet deep, and weighing in excess of 1 ton. Providing a nest isn't toppled by wind, or doesn't crush the tree onto which it's built, it will continue to be used year after year, sometimes by succeeding generations who were themselves hatched there.

Impregnated females occupy the nest as soon as it's finished, laying their first creamy white 5-inch-long egg within about 3 days, usually in late March or early April. The female will lay another every 1 to 3 days thereafter, until a clutch of usually two, but sometimes three, eggs has been deposited.

Incubation of the eggs is performed mostly by the female, and exclusively by her at night, while her mate sleeps in a nearby tree. After an incubation period of 35 to 42 days the eggs begin to hatch, with the first-laid hatching first, and the siblings hatching every 2 or 3 days thereafter in the same order in which the eggs were laid. By mid- to late June, all eggs will have hatched.

As you might expect from such birds, sibling rivalry is fierce and sometimes violent. The eldest hatchling is typically the largest, and will try to steal food from its younger and smaller nest mates. Parents will not intervene, leaving the younger chick to fend for itself in a real example of survival of the fittest. In a clutch of two, both eagle chicks will probably survive to the fledgling stage, but a third chick's odds of survival are greatly decreased.

Feeding duties are performed by both parents, and one will always be nearby when the other is away hunting. Hawks, and especially ravens, that might prey on the chicks are driven off vigorously, and predation on eaglets is virtually nil. By 60 days of age, the chicks will have become fledglings, and will fly short distances with their parents. Parents will continue to hunt for and feed their brood for an additional 30 days, when the eaglets will have become educated enough and strong enough to fend for themselves. The family remains together until autumn, when the offspring strike out to establish their own territories.

BEHAVIORISMS

Native only to North America, the bald eagle is as big as, or slightly smaller than, the golden eagle *(Aquila chrysaetos)* of Eurasia, North Africa, and North America. But it is no less a predator. Stories of eagles carrying off small children and lambs are probably groundless, but the big raptors have often incurred the wrath of farmers—and a few pet owners—by occasionally snatching up small dogs, cats, chickens, and rabbits.

Bald eagles are migratory only by necessity; if they possess access to open water, they will remain near their summer nesting sites year-round. Those in the north that don't have access to open water in winter fly to southern latitudes, or to coastlines where waters remain unfrozen enough to permit fishing. In northern latitudes, where small mammals and other prey remain plentiful, adults will sometimes remain all winter, even though lakes and rivers are frozen.

Young eagles that have been recently emancipated from their parents are, as a rule, wanderers, and they may remain wanderers for years, or until they find a mate and have their own offspring. Such juveniles have been known to travel more than 1,000 miles in search of new habitat, territory, or a new pool of eagles from which to seek a mate.

Eagles rarely fly at night, but the reason has less to do with lack of night vision than with air currents. Like vultures and other long-winged raptors, bald eagles prefer to glide rather than fly, because gliding requires less energy. Thermal updrafts, which these birds rely on to hold them aloft for hours at a time, are normally present only during daylight hours, when a warming sun causes heated air to rise. For that reason, most eagles are seen on the wing between dawn and dusk.

An unusual behaviorism among eagle mates is their occasional tendency to copulate outside of the mating season. Except for humans, sexual intercourse for pleasure alone is virtually unheard of in the animal kingdom, and some biologists believe that this behavior might be related to the strong bond that exists between eagle mates.

Today, the bald eagle remains the symbol of strength and courage that America's Founding Fathers believed it always would be. It's still the main icon of the Presidential Seal of the United States, and among most Indian tribes it's still the messenger that carries prayers to the Creator. Its curious, ferocious, utterly untamed habits, discovered over decades by researchers and careful observers, rather than dispelling the mystery that surrounds this fierce creature of the skies, have had the unique effect of making the raptor yet a more powerful symbol of freedom and integrity and the wonder of life on earth. The Native Americans, and the Founding Fathers, chose well.

Chapter Twenty-Seven

SNAKES AND TURTLES

Snakes *(Serpentes)*

Perhaps among the most hated animals on the planet, snakes seem to embody the dark, dangerous, uncontrollable secrets of nature for many human beings. No other animal has inspired so much myth or so many stories throughout human history, few of them positive, and few of them recognizing the keystone role that snakes play in the health of the ecosystems where they live.

All snakes are carnivores; all have evolved sophisticated and effective ways of catching and killing prey. The constrictors clamp onto their victims with hooked teeth in reasonably powerful jaws (they don't chew, so they don't need the muscles of a wolf or cat), while embracing the prey with strangling coils that tighten every time the animal exhales. Venomous species are equipped with sharp teeth, or fangs, that pierce a victim's skin and inject a usually fatal dose of poison. The thousands of nonvenomous snakes have a variety of techniques for catching their food: Many simply strike, hold, and begin to swallow.

All snakes are cold-blooded, hairless, and legless. They travel primarily by using muscles in their scaled undersides to push backward against the earth in succession, propelling their bodies forward in a smooth, slithering motion. They cannot crawl backward but they don't need to; their long, extremely flexible spines permit them to change direction, and even double back on themselves. Many species spend their lives, or large parts of them, above the ground in the branches of trees, safe from terrestrial predators, eating insects and birds, even monkeys. Other species are aquatic, coming up for air occasionally, at home among the fishes and the turtles. Still others live distinctly terrestrial lives, and some of those, such as the American coachwhip or the racers, are among the fastest reptiles in existence.

One characteristic shared by all snakes is a relatively slow metabolism. A large meal such as a cottontail rabbit for an adult eastern diamondback rattlesnake, a toad for a hognose snake, or, to go to an extreme, a small pig for an anaconda, can last a snake

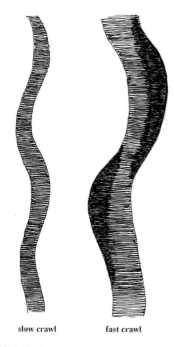

slow crawl   fast crawl

Snake tracks

for several weeks. Snakes also, especially in temperate climates, spend a lot of time managing their body temperatures by sunning or moving to shade.

Among the most secretive of animals, even the most venomous or largest species of snakes prefer to avoid humans altogether, not surprising given the history of humans killing snakes, often for no good reason, at almost every opportunity.

Common Garter Snake *(Thamnophis sirtalis)*

In most parts of the United States, the garter snakes—and there are thirteen subspecies of them—are the most commonly encountered snake. They are diurnal, live in woods and fields, and often hunt near or in water for frogs, crayfish, minnows, and other small prey.

The common garter snake is found across North America. The thirteen subspecies include the red-sided garter snake *(Thamnophis sirtalis parietalis)*, found in the West from northern Mexico all the way to the Yukon; the blue-striped garter snake *(Thamnophis sirtalis similes)*, unique to northern Florida; the maritime garter snake *(Thamnophis sirtalis pallidulus)*, found in Maine; the New Mexico garter snake *(Thamnophis sirtalis dorsalis)*; the Texas garter snake *(Thamnophis sirtalis annectens)*; the valley garter snake *(Thamnophis sirtalis fitchi)*; the California red-sided garter snake *(Thamnophis sirtalis infernalis)*; and the San Francisco garter snake *(Thamnophis sirtalis tetrataenia)*.

GEOGRAPHIC RANGE

The common garter snake is found throughout North America. The garter snake is the only species of wild snake found in Alaska, ranging farther north than any other North American reptile. Absent only from the arid Southwest, the common garter snake is native from Texas and Florida to Canada.

The common garter snake is found in many parts of the United States in many different color variations and habitats. It is an efficient predator, as seen here, and may be the most cold-adapted snake species on earth.

HABITAT

The common garter snake is highly adaptable and can survive the cold better than any other North American snake. It may be the most cold-adapted snake on the planet. Although never very far from water, this snake is common to a wide variety of habitats, including hardwood and pine forests, marshes, drainage ditches, and even suburbia. Its importance in controlling rapidly reproducing populations of mice, rats, and insect pests is well known, so much so that garter snakes are one of the few snake species not subject to random persecution by humans.

PHYSICAL CHARACTERISTICS

Mass: A graceful, slender snake, sometimes becoming stouter and heavier with age, but never approaching the stoutness of vipers or common water snakes.
Body: Most commonly 18 to 24 inches; may attain lengths of up to 4 feet.
Tail: Tapered to a thin point; color patterns go all the way to tail tip.

TRACKS

Undulating grooves left in loose sand and forest debris

SCAT

Watery with varying mixes of black, white, and brown. The snake often excretes an odorous mix of fluid from its anal glands and feces as a defense against predators.

COLORATION

All garter snakes have lateral stripes of white, yellow, green, blue, orange, or red against a darker background that ranges from black, to dark green or brown. Despite this wide variation within the species, it can be distinguished from other *Thamnophis* species by the location of the lateral stripe, which is always limited to the second and third rows of scales up from the ventral scales. There is usually a double row of black spots between the lateral stripes. Distinguishing between the many subspecies of *Thamnophis* requires a detailed field guide.

SIGN

Shed skins during the summer months.

VOCALIZATIONS

The snakes are generally silent. The common garter snake can make a low hissing sound when threatened, but this is rare.

LIFE SPAN

Maximum life span in captivity has been 14 years. In the wild, life span depends upon the density and types of predators in the habitat. Garter snakes are eaten by everything from domestic cats to birds and other snakes.

DIET

Varies according to habitat. These snakes feed on earthworms, grasshoppers, frogs, toads, birds, and rodents that are small enough to be swallowed. Fish and tadpoles are readily consumed. Having no fangs or venom, *Thamnophis sirtalis* uses stealth to ambush prey, usually snatching it by the head with a very fast and accurate strike. With its head engulfed, the prey animal struggles less as it's held in place by the small serrated teeth that line the snake's jaws. Light constriction is also used to immobilize prey as it is slowly swallowed whole. Digestion may take several days.

MATING HABITS

Like many successful species that are subject to heavy predation, common garter snakes are extremely prolific. They are also ovoviviparous, bearing live young that are incubated from fertilized eggs carried in the mother's lower abdomen. Sexual maturity is reached at 1.5 years in males, 2 years in females. Mating occurs in spring, just after the snakes emerge from hibernation in April or May, depending on climate. Males emerge from hibernation first, and immediately begin to congregate around the den entrances of females, where the males emit pheromonal scents to advertise their willingness to breed. Male garter snakes are polygynandrous, or promiscuous, and will seek out another mate as soon as they've finished breeding a female. Female snakes have the ability to store a partner's sperm, ejecting it if a more suitable mate comes along.

After mating, females go about their business of hunting and hiding over a gestation period of 2 or 3 months. Locating a reasonably safe place to give birth, the female will bear from fifteen to fifty young, depending on the mother's size and health. Baby garter snakes receive no care from the mother after birth.

BEHAVIORISMS

Like most snakes, garter snakes tend to be most active during the day. When the evening chill sets in they take refuge under whatever shelter is available. With the coming of morning, they move to places where the sun's warming rays help them regain a normal body temperature of about 30 degrees centigrade. As the sun rises and makes the ground at these basking places too hot for comfort, the snakes once again seek more shaded spots.

Common garter snakes are very sociable, although they also tend to spend much of their time alone during summer. When two snakes meet they communicate with one another through a system of chemical scents, called lipids, that are exuded through their skins. These pheromonal scents are used by breeding snakes to advertise both their availability and their gender, although it appears that male snakes can be endowed with female lipids that cause other males to court them by mistake. Lipid-borne pheromones also help garter snakes track one another when they gather together prior to hibernation in the fall.

When the fall weather turns cold, garter snakes will often to congregate in a single large burrow below the frost line, where the small amount of body heat generated by their numbers helps to keep all of them safe from freezing before spring returns. It appears that the trails used by garter snakes are well established and permanent around mating and denning places, because the same routes are followed by newborn snakes when they leave the den, and are used again by the young to return to the den prior to hibernation.

With a top speed of about 3 miles per hour, garter snakes are easily caught by predators. When cornered they may coil into striking position like a viper, and may hiss. When handled they often bite, but these bites produce little more than a few small holes and scratches on human skin. Perhaps most effective against humans is the garter's ability to exude foul smelling chemicals through its cloaca.

Garter snakes are popular as pets, and some biologists warn that over-collection of the snakes for that market has caused a decline in their numbers that could one day become serious for this environmentally important predator and prey. That problem seems especially likely to occur in the north, where denning snakes gather together in larger numbers, and are more easily collected. One subspecies, the San Francisco garter snake, was placed on the Endangered Species List in 1967.

Corn Snake (*Elaphe guttata*)

One of the most beautifully patterned North American snakes, the corn snake is a member of the genus *Elaphe* and also known as the red rat snake. These snakes are nonvenomous, but larger individuals are capable of inflicting a painful bite when handled. The orange-colored eastern variation is sometimes mistaken for a copperhead *(Agkistrodon contortrix)*, though the corn snake is much more elongated and slender than its venomous cohort, and its habits are very different. A somewhat less colorful subspecies, the Great Plains or Emory's rat snake *(Elaphe guttata emoryi),* occupies the western portion of the range, from northern Mexico up through Texas and as far north as Nebraska.

Because of their striking appearance and well-known habit of focusing their predation on rats that infest barns, corn snakes do not suffer quite the level of persecution that other snakes do.

Because of their similar coloration, corn snakes are often mistaken for their venomous cousin, the copperhead.

GEOGRAPHIC RANGE

Eastern corn snakes are found in the eastern United States from southern New Jersey south through Florida, and west into Louisiana and parts of Kentucky. The species appears to be most abundant in Florida and the southeastern United States.

HABITAT

Open woodlands, rocky hillsides, and farms. Throughout their range, corn snakes may be far more common in areas of human habitation, especially in barns, older houses, and abandoned dwellings and outbuildings, than they are in less disturbed forests. This is because their favorite prey species—rats, mice, and smaller birds—are more abundant, and more easily caught, in these places. Ideal corn snake habitat would look like this: Corn or soybean fields bordered by tree lines, with blackberry vines reclaiming an abandoned farm yard, a slowly falling-down chicken coop, and a large two-story barn still used for storing bales of hay, farm equipment, and various barrels of animal feed that attract rats. A spring-fed cattle trough full of fresh water completes the picture.

PHYSICAL CHARACTERISTICS

Mass: A relatively slender snake. Weight is usually less than a pound; occasionally a snake weighs in excess of 4 pounds.
Body: Attains a maximum length of about 6 feet.
Tail: Slender, patterned to the tip.

TRACKS

Undulating grooves left in the surface of loose sand or mud on dirt roads and trails.

SCAT

Seldom seen, but small elongated blobs that are black and white, with varying shades of brown or gray.

COLORATION

Corn snakes are nonvenomous, but mimic venomous species like the copperhead in coloration, ranging from orange to brownish-yellow, with large, black-edged red blotches down the middle of the back. On the belly there are alternating rows of black and white marks that make it resemble an ear of Indian corn, and these are believed to have been the origin of this species' common name. Considerable variation occurs in the coloration and patterns of individual snakes, depending on their age and the region. Hatchlings are more subdued, lacking the brighter coloration and contrasts found on adults.

SIGN

Shed skins during the summer months. Skins retain the snake's markings, but without coloration.

VOCALIZATIONS

Corn snakes are generally silent, but may hiss if cornered. They are among several species that will vibrate their tails rapidly when alarmed. In dry leaves or grass, the vibrating tail makes a sound very similar to a buzzing rattlesnake.

LIFE SPAN

Corn snakes have lived up to 23 years in captivity, but their life span is generally much less in the wild due to predation.

DIET

Hatchlings tend to feed on small lizards and tree frogs, while adults feed on larger prey like mice, nesting birds, and roosting bats. Their many small, inward curving teeth don't kill prey, but serve to hold it securely while the corn snake, a powerful constrictor, wraps its coils around the prey's body and suffocates it. Smaller, less dangerous prey is swallowed alive.

MATING HABITS

Corn snakes mate from March to May, earlier in southern climes than in northern. Impregnated females deposit a clutch of roughly twenty eggs from late May to July in carefully selected rotting stumps, mounds of decaying vegetation, or other hiding places that have a moderate amount of moisture and will remain around 80 degrees Fahrenheit for the incubation period. The eggs are abandoned soon after they're laid. The eggs hatch after about 60 days. Corn snake eggs hatch from July through September, earlier in the north than in the south. Hatchlings are about 3 inches long at birth and attain maturity in about 2 years.

BEHAVIORISMS

Corn snakes are active both day and night so long as temperatures allow, and are more nocturnal than many North American species. They are excellent climbers, and some individuals are almost arboreal. All will ascend trees to capture birds, and raid nests for eggs and hatchlings. Old barns and outbuildings are favorite hunting and resting territories, and one explanation for the corn snakes' name is that it was commonly seen in corn cribs, seeking mice and rats. Corn snakes also hunt voles, moles, and other burrowing rodents underground. Despite its striking colors and impressive size, the relatively common corn snake has proven difficult to study due to its secretive nature, and much remains to be learned about its habits.

Corn snakes are not an endangered species, but they are listed by the state of Florida as a species of special concern because they face habitat loss in the lower Florida Keys. Although the pet trade at one time posed a potential threat to the corn snake, captive breeding programs have reduced the number of corn snakes caught in the wild and sold for pets.

Eastern Hognose Snake (*Heterodon platirhinos*)

One of the most clownish and truly odd North American snakes, the hognose is short, stout, and named for the characteristic turned-up nose that it uses for digging and burrowing in search of shelter and prey.

The genus *Heterodon* consists of three distinct North American species, *H. platirhinos,* the eastern hognose, *Heterodon nasicus,* the western hognose, and *Heterodon simus,* the southern hognose. All three species share the classic hognose characteristics of dramatic threat behaviors, feigning death, and other oddities. Historically, people have been fascinated and frightened by the hognose, and it is known throughout its range by intimidating names such as "spreading adder," "puff adder," and others that indicate its dangerous nature. Add to its bizarre behavior the fact that some of its color phases, and its stout body structure, look very much like the venomous copperhead, and you have a snake that most people will either kill or leave very much alone. Ironically, the hognose is among the shyest of snakes, and seldom even attempts to bite in self-defense.

GEOGRAPHIC RANGE

As its common name suggests, the eastern hognose is found throughout the eastern United States, ranging from southeastern South Dakota to Texas, and eastward to the Atlantic seaboard from southern New York to Florida. The southern form is found along the coastal plain beginning in the Carolinas and sweeping down along the Gulf of Mexico as far west

The hognose snake uses its upturned nose to burrow into loose soil or sand. GERALD A. DEBOER/LICENSED BY SHUTTERSTOCK.COM

as western Mississippi. The western hognose inhabits prairie and badlands habitats from Canada to west of South Dakota and northern Mexico.

HABITAT

The hognose is a burrowing species and seeks out areas of loose soil or sand. In the case of the eastern variety, the hognose prefers open woodlands where its primary prey, toads, can be hunted in the leafy debris of the forest floor.

PHYSICAL CHARACTERISTICS

Mass: Stout; an exceptional adult can weigh in excess of 4 pounds.

Body: Up to 3 feet long, occasionally larger. All species are short, thickly built snakes with a pointed, upturned snout and a wide neck. The anal scale plate is divided into halves. Although considered nonvenomous as far as humans are concerned, the hognose possesses a pair of enlarged teeth at the rear of the upper jaw that do inject venom into prey as it's being swallowed. These teeth are used to puncture toads that inflate themselves as protection against being swallowed, and they give the genus its name, *Heterodon,* which translates to "different tooth" in Latin. The location of the teeth also mean that a human must insert part of his or her anatomy fully into the back of the snake's mouth to receive a venomous bite—a difficult exercise indeed.

Tail: Blunt, patterned to the tip.

TRACKS

Serpentine grooves in dry sand, unusually wide in comparison to other snakes of similar length.

SCAT

Seldom obvious, but mucuslike elongated blobs of black, white, and varying shades of gray and brown.

COLORATION

The eastern hognose exhibits an extraordinary variation in colors and patterns, sometimes even appearing as a dull black or dark gray snake that looks nothing at all like the brightly patterned yellow and tan individual that may live in the same area. In some eastern individuals, the body shape, upturned nose, and distinctive behavior are the best identifying characteristics. Some herpetologists believe that this variation is due to the species' status as a relatively new member of the hognose genus, and that the snakes haven't yet evolved a permanent camouflage color scheme. Western hognoses are more consistent—a light brown with mahogany blocks down their backs. At first glance, the western hognose is almost indistinguishable from the prairie rattler *(Crotalus viridis)* that often shares its habitat. The southern hognose is not as varied as the eastern, ranging widely in colors but not in patterns. Its patterns are very like those of the pygmy rattlesnake *(Sistrurus miliarius)*, which lives in similar habitat, varies widely in color, and has an almost identical body structure. Such mimicry works in the hognose snakes' favor in the case of all predators except for humans.

SIGN
Shed skins with keeled (ridged) scales that are usually arranged in rows of twenty-five scales.

VOCALIZATIONS
Hognoses are generally silent, but may engage in loud hissing when cornered. They are much more vocal than most snakes. Vibrates the tail against dry leaves and debris to imitate the buzzing of a rattlesnake.

LIFE SPAN
10 to 15 years, although many are killed as prey in their first year.

DIET
Hognose snakes eat toads, frogs, mice, salamanders, and small lizards. The hognose is especially immune to the toxins excreted through the skin of toads, and is, in fact, one of the few species of snake that makes toads a large part of its diet. After unearthing denned toads from their daytime burrows with its snout, the hognose swallows them head first. The toad's natural defense is to inflate its body by gulping in air to prevent itself from being swallowed, but a pair of venom-producing teeth located at the rear of the snake's upper jaw are adapted to circumvent that defense by puncturing the toad and deflating it. Once deflated and paralyzed by venom, the toad becomes relaxed and easy to ingest. Enlarged adrenaline glands in the snake's body also help it to resist the bufotoxins secreted from the toad's parotid glands and warts.

MATING HABITS
Little data has been established about the hognose snake's mating habits or reproduction, making it an ideal candidate for field research.

Eastern hognose snakes generally mate between May and June, depending on temperature and latitude, but those living in southern regions, where temperatures remain warm year-round, may mate again in August or September. There is no discernable bond between mates, and both go their own ways after breeding. Eggs are laid in late June or July. Females seek out natural depressions or secluded holes in soft sandy or loamy soil, depositing a clutch of whitish, thin-shelled eggs that are ovoid in shape and measure about 1.25 inches long. Clutch sizes appear to relate to the mother's physical size and state of health, and may vary widely in number from four to as many as sixty eggs. After laying her eggs, the mother abandons them.

Kept warm by sun-heated earth, the eggs hatch after a gestation of 50 to 65 days, most of them in August or September. Unusually, incubating eggs actually grow during the gestation period, resulting in relatively large hatchlings that may be from 6 to 10 inches long. Although generally lighter in color than adults, the hatchlings are duplicates of their parents.

Young hognose snakes spend much of their time in hiding. Garter and other snakes prey on the hatchlings, as do opossums, skunks, ravens, and numerous predatory birds. Toads that are eaten by adult hognose snakes will also prey on hatchlings.

BEHAVIORISMS

Hognose snakes are best known for their threat displays and defensive behaviors when confronted by a predator or danger. If escape is impossible—or will expose the snake to more danger—it immediately coils like the rattlesnake or copperhead that it much resembles. The tail vibrates furiously, and in dry grass or leaves creates a convincing buzz. Lacking the actual threat of a rattler's venom, the hognose relies on charade. It flattens its already wide body and spreads its neck like a cobra, waving its head back and forth while hissing loudly. It will strike repeatedly and aggressively, but a close observer will notice that it does so with its mouth closed. If this fails to frighten away the threat, the hognose will suddenly begin to writhe violently, feigning convulsions, and will sometimes excrete a foul-smelling fluid from its anal glands. It flips onto its back, writhing unabated; its mouth opens, its purplish tongue extends and lolls in the dirt. It becomes still, a very effective imitation of death except for one weakness—if turned right-side-up, the snake will quickly flip onto its back again. Left alone, after a few minutes the snake will cautiously right itself and crawl away. Of course, such defensive displays vary according to individual snakes, but many hognoses will act out the whole scenario as described above.

Eastern and western hognose snake populations are stable in many parts of their range but the southern hognose is in decline and may already be extinct in Alabama and Mississippi. Reasons for the decline may include predation of hatchlings by the red imported fire ant, but habitat destruction is probably primary. The southern hognose, like the gopher tortoise and North America's largest snake, the indigo, is associated with the longleaf pine forest habitat that has been reduced by as much as 98 percent over the past 200 years. Restoration of longleaf habitat is underway in many parts of the coastal South, which may help the southern hognose avoid extinction.

Eastern Diamondback Rattlesnake (Crotalus adamanteus)

Considered by many to be the most dangerous rattlesnake in North America, the eastern diamondback lives up to its reputation: 40 percent of the people unlucky enough to receive a fully envenomed bite from this showy and deeply impressive predator do not survive. Unlike its close cousin the western diamondback *(Crotalus atrox),* which prefers open mesquite country and spare desert places, the big—up to 8 feet long—eastern diamondback lives in palmetto thickets and deep, junglelike forests where encounters with humans are often at close range and a complete surprise. This jungled country has made the eastern diamondback a more fearsome snake in another way as well: To make sure that prey is anchored before being lost in the thickets, *Crotalus adamanteus* has developed a potent venom that includes both the standard tissue-dissolving hemotoxic poisons of other rattlers and a fast-acting neurotoxin (nerve toxin) like that of the Old World cobras. Such a venom kills the cottontail rabbit fast. It's also responsible for the grim statistics that pertain to human bite victims.

Caution is the watchword for living, working, hunting, or hiking in the home of the diamondback, whether east or west. In some cases, diamondbacks will announce their presence with a warning buzz from their rattles, but the snake is as likely to remain silent and hope that a threat passes by. Travelers on foot in diamondback country are advised to carry a long

Caution is the watchword for living, working, hunting, or hiking in the home of the diamondback, whether east or west.
RUDY UMANS/LICENSED BY SHUTTERSTOCK.COM

walking stick to poke into hidden spaces and along trails before they walk through, and to be sure that dogs and children are well tended.

GEOGRAPHIC RANGE

The eastern diamondback inhabits coastal lowlands from southeast North Carolina south through Florida and its keys, and westward to eastern Louisiana.

HABITAT

Eastern diamondbacks prefer well-foliated environments, including dry swamps, palmetto groves, and pine forests. The species is seldom found in wet swamps or marshes, but may inhabit dry shorelines. Despite having an apparent aversion to water, these snakes have been reported swimming in the shallow waters of the Atlantic as they travel between islands off the Florida coast.

PHYSICAL CHARACTERISTICS

Mass: Usually about 6 pounds, but may reach weights of more than 14 pounds.

Body: Up to 8 feet long, but average about 4 feet at maturity. Broad, triangular head with large sensory pits located below and between eyes, and nostrils in the upper jaw. Long, tubular fangs fold backward to lie flat against the upper palate.

Tail: White with black peripheral rings, and tipped with rounded, segmented rattles that are stacked atop one another in a rough cone shape. Each rattle is a remnant of the last scale left when the snake molted. End rattles may be broken on older individuals.

TRACKS
Serpentine undulations in sand and loose earth.

SCAT
An elongated mass of white, black, and brown.

COLORATION
A row of large dark diamonds with brown centers and cream-colored borders down its back. The ground color of the body ranges from olive to brown to almost black, depending on the habitat. The tail is usually a different shade, brownish or gray, and banded with dark rings. The head has a light-bordered dark stripe running diagonally through the eye. The young are similar to adults in color pattern.

SIGN
Shed skins, discarded broken rattles.

VOCALIZATIONS
The rattler is generally silent. The tail vibrates with a buzzing rattle when agitated.

LIFE SPAN
Up to 20 years.

DIET
Carnivorous. Primarily a nocturnal hunter, *Crotalus adamanteus* and its western cousin prey on small mammals, birds, reptiles, amphibians, large insects, and sometimes fish. Larger snakes may take larger prey, sometimes as large as a rabbit or muskrat.

Adapted to prey especially on small, warm-blooded animals, eastern diamondbacks and other pit vipers possess specialized thermally sensitive pits, located on the sides of the face, that detect minute differences in air temperatures, enabling the snakes to locate prey in darkness. Prey is also detected by scent using the forked tongue, which flicks outward almost constantly when the snake is actively hunting.

Once detected, prey may be stalked quietly by slithering in close. The snake then swiftly lunges forward with mouth open and fangs exposed. Ambush—lying in wait beside trails or food sources such as fruiting berry bushes—is also a common hunting strategy. Striking distance is up to 75 percent of the snake's body length, meaning that an 8-foot rattler may accurately strike its victim from as far away as 6 feet. Fangs are driven into a prey animal's body, and muscles contract to inject a dose of venom. Venom flow is controlled by voluntary muscles surrounding the glands where it is manufactured, permitting the snake to meter dosage in relation to the size of its prey. But target areas are not specific, and there appears to be no preference about where a bite is administered. Although fangs are sometimes broken off and remain in the victim, rattlesnakes can replace lost teeth up to four times per year, as reserve teeth are carried in the upper jaw.

After envenomation, prey animals are released, and the fangs return to their resting position against the upper jaw, ensuring that the rattler will not be injured by a still fighting, dangerous animal. The fleeing prey is quickly overcome by the effects of the venom. The neurotoxic component acts immediately to paralyze a stricken animal's heart and respiratory system, while hemotoxins break down blood vessels, causing acute internal hemorrhaging, and actually breaking down and softening the prey's tissues, making it easier to swallow and digest.

The effects of the venom varies according to the prey, where it is injected, and the physical condition of the rattler. In most cases, the prey runs only a few yards before collapsing. The snake follows, using its acute senses of smell and heat detection. The dead prey animal is swallowed headfirst and whole, a process that may take several minutes to more than half an hour, depending on the size of both animals.

The rattler will seek out a secure and hidden place nearby to wait out the long process of digestion. As with all snakes, this process is very slow but very efficient, assimilating bone, hair, and other body parts that would pass intact through the intestines of most predators. Two weeks or more may pass before the snake needs to eat again, and during that interval the rattler will remain almost sedentary unless disturbed.

The deep pine forests and palmetto lands of the South, where eastern diamondbacks live, usually have an abundance of rain, rivers, creeks, and springs, but the big rattlers require very little water to thrive, in part because of that hyperefficient process of digestion: most of the water they need is absorbed from the bodies of their prey. The only time a diamondback needs more water is during the seasonal molting of its skin, because the new skin loses moisture as it toughens. Anyone who has ever seen a big eastern diamondback in the wild that is freshly shed, with the brilliant patterns showing on the new skin, will never forget the sight.

MATING HABITS

Males and females reach sexual maturity at 3 years. Mating occurs in the spring, soon after adults emerge from hibernation. Ritualized territorial fights, or contests for mates, occur among male diamondbacks, consisting of a wrestling match where the two "combatants" entwine around each others' upper bodies in a contest of balance and strength. The snake that is consistently toppled retreats. Researchers say that such contests seldom if ever involve biting or using venom—a dose of venom requires a lot of physical resources to create, and rattlers and other poisonous snakes are careful to expend it only when the payoff is a large and restorative meal, or as a last ditch act of self-defense.

The female diamondback is passive during courtship, remaining almost inactive while the male slithers in jerky movements on top of her body, flicking his tongue continuously. Copulation occurs when the male forces his tail beneath the female's tail and she accepts the advance by raising her tail to allow insertion of his forked hemipenis. Intercourse typically lasts for several hours, with numerous resting periods between.

Gestation requires an average of 167 days. Diamondbacks are ovoviviparous—the young hatched from eggs carried within the mother's womb. The average brood consists of ten to twenty young. Newborn snakes are born both fanged and venomous, and remain with the mother for no more than a day before striking out on their own.

Born at the onset of autumn, the young snakes must immediately learn to hunt and find a suitable shelter—a gopher tortoise burrow is preferred above all other hibernation sites—in which to spend the coming winter. Predation on the little snakes is high, and most will fall prey to birds, lizards, toads, and other snakes. The young grow fast, gaining roughly 1 foot per year until reaching puberty (about 18 to 24 months), at which time they have little to fear from most predators.

BEHAVIORISMS

Eastern diamondbacks are quick to take a defensive posture when threatened, but often prefer to lie motionless in the hope that an enemy will pass them by without notice. Ironically, this passive reaction increases the danger they pose to humans, who might inadvertently walk closely enough to, or step on, the hiding rattler and panic it into striking. Again, a walking stick used to probe shadows where a snake might be hiding provides sufficient warning of a rattler's presence, and may prevent trouble.

Diamondback rattlesnakes are often touted as causing more fatalities than any venomous snake in North America, but the truth remains that bites are extremely rare: Out of 308 million people in the United States, seven to twelve may die each year from the bites of poisonous snakes. Bees and other stinging insects kill fifty to one hundred people annually. Of those who are bitten, many if not most are attempting to kill or play with poisonous snakes that could just as easily have been left alone. An old proverb states that the best way to avoid a coiled and buzzing rattlesnake is to take one step backward, which remains sound advice for anyone faced with any species of venomous snake.

The rattles that give diamondbacks and other rattlesnakes their name are actually the terminal scales of a snake's tail, left behind each time the growing snake sheds its skin. Rattles were once thought to be a means of communication between rattlesnakes, but it is now known that snakes are deaf to sounds, able only to detect vibrations through the ground. Instead, it appears that rattles evolved mainly as a means to avoid being stepped on by larger animals.

The frequency at which the rattles are shaken indicates the owner's level of fear: A slow shaking, like that of a maraca, is used to alert potentially dangerous animals to the snake's presence. Rattling increases in frequency as the snake's level of agitation increases, until the sound becomes a buzzing at about fifty cycles per second. This latter sound, which has been described as cicada-like, or like the sizzling of bacon, is always accompanied by a coiled body that presents an enemy with a smaller target, and a tongue that flicks rapidly to gather as much scent as possible from the surrounding air.

A successful predator in its own right, the eastern diamondback, like snakes around the world, also serves as prey for a number of fellow carnivores. Hatchlings are eaten by toads, frogs, larger snakes, many species of birds, and even ants. Individuals up to 3 feet in length are preyed upon by hawks, owls, and eagles. Some coyotes appear to have a limited immunity to venom that permits them to kill and eat rattlers. Other than humans, it is pigs, both wild and domestic, that are most dangerous to snakes of any size or kind. Swine are especially resistant to snake venoms, and any serpent unlucky enough to attract the attention of a pig is almost certain to be killed and eaten.

Diamondbacks inhabit regions where winters are short and fairly mild, but they, like other rattlers, become dormant during the coldest months of the year. The snakes will sometimes gather in communal dens, called hibernacula, which may be found under abandoned buildings or under the roots of big trees, in the burrows of gopher tortoises or other animals, or anywhere that is sheltered enough to provide protection from extreme cold. The snakes don't actually hibernate during this period, but gather together in a lethargic mass that uses little energy, and helps to keep all of its members warm enough to survive until warm weather returns in March or April.

While the eastern diamondback rattlesnake was not considered endangered as of 2011, it is listed by the US Fish and Wildlife Service as a "Species of Special Concern." This status gives the species no legal protections, and it may soon need them. Continuing destruction of diamondback habitat from housing and other development is forcing the reptiles to occupy increasingly smaller areas. Added to this, many people still have a kill-on-sight response to rattlesnakes, even those encountered far from human habitations, which is steadily decreasing the number of diamondbacks in the last places where they can exist. Only time will tell if human beings will make room for this magnificent predator.

Turtles *(Testudines)*

All turtles and tortoises belong to the order *Testudines,* which includes all reptiles that have a hard, plated carapace over a bony shell on their backs, and a hard, plated underbelly called a plastron. Tortoises spend their lives on land, have vegetarian diets, and are equipped with flat feet that are better suited to walking and digging. Turtles spend most of their lives in or near water, have webbed feet adapted for swimming, and pursue a more carnivorous diet.

Like all reptiles, turtles are considered to be cold-blooded animals, but at least one species, Blanding's turtle *(Emydoidea blandingi)*, has been observed swimming under the ice on frozen ponds. All turtles and tortoises are hatched from eggs that have been buried in soft soil, then abandoned by their mothers.

Northern Snapping Turtle *(Chelydra serpentina)*

The northern snapping turtle is the dominant aquatic carnivore in almost every body of water that it inhabits. In size, this species is second only to the alligator snapping turtle *(Macroclemys temminckii)* of the southeastern United States. But the northern snapping turtle makes up in adaptability for its second place in bulk and mass—except for the painted turtle *(Chrysemys picta)*, the northern snapping turtle is the most widespread turtle species in North America.

Snapping turtles, and the northern snapper especially, also differ from most turtles and tortoises by having a carapace and plastron that are too small for the animal to retreat into completely. Whether the too-small shell is the cause or the result of this species' legendary ferocity when cornered on land is a matter of conjecture, but an adult northern snapper has little need to fear any animal except humans.

The northern snapping turtle is the dominant aquatic carnivore in almost every body of water it inhabits.

GEOGRAPHIC RANGE

Chelydra serpentina's northern range extends from southern Alberta eastward to Nova Scotia. To the south, the species' range covers all of the United States from the Rocky Mountains eastward to the Atlantic coast, and along the Gulf of Mexico into central Texas.

HABITAT

Freshwater lakes, streams, ponds, and rivers. This species much prefers slow-moving or still waters, especially backwaters, sloughs, and oxbows of major rivers with mud bottoms and plentiful aquatic vegetation for hiding, ambushing prey, and hibernating.

PHYSICAL CHARACTERISTICS

Mass: Snapping turtles attain weights of 70 pounds, but typically weigh 35 to 40 pounds at maturity.

Body: A comparatively large head that cannot be completely withdrawn under the carapace. Carapace length is up to 19 inches. Powerful jaws and a hooked beak. The long neck is normally kept retracted, the skin on its upper surface covered with bumpy projections (tubercles). Legs are thickly built and powerful, covered with scaly skin and tubercles, and terminating in large, webbed feet with strong claws. The plastron is small, but sufficient to cover the vital organs in the belly.

Tail: Nearly as long as the carapace, thickly muscled, and covered along its top with saw-toothed keels. Reminiscent of an alligator's tail.

TRACKS

The turtle has five toes on forefeet, four toes on hind feet, and each toe is tipped with a thick, sharply pointed claw. Tracks are generally not perfect, but show scrape marks where the foot slipped as the turtle's heavy body was pushed forward, usually with claw marks evident. Tracks tend to print individually, without overlap, and in pairs, hind print behind front print. In soft mud or sand, the carapace drags intermittently, leaving a shallow trough. The tail also drags, leaving a serpentine channel between tracks. Straddle is variable, depending on the turtle's size, but always comparatively wide because of the snapper's plastron. Stride is also variable, depending on size, but equates to roughly one half of the carapace length.

SCAT

Misshapen and with a jagged, uneven surface. Color varies somewhat with diet, but usually dark brown or black. Adult scats are generally 1 to 1.5 inches long. Scats are usually deposited in water, but may be found along shorelines and on large partially submerged logs where the turtle basked.

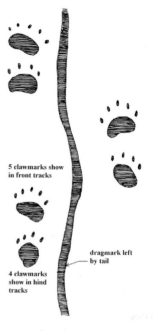

5 clawmarks show in front tracks

4 clawmarks show in hind tracks

dragmark left by tail

Snapping turtle tracks

COLORATION

The shell ranges in color from dark brown to tan and can even be black in some individuals. Snapping turtle necks, legs, and tails have an olive or yellowish color, with the head being a darker shade. The plastron is white or yellow.

SIGN

In late spring or early summer, look for narrow excavated holes, or large disturbances in sandy soil where egg-laying females buried a nest. Trails of flattened grasses near shorelines indicate a snapper's passing. Clouds of silt under stream banks mark where a snapping turtle buried itself in mud after being alerted to an observer's presence.

VOCALIZATIONS

Turtles are nearly always silent unless cornered on land. When threatened, the turtle may hiss and snap its jaws.

LIFE SPAN

Unknown, but at least 40 years. Attempts to determine a snapping turtle's life span have been unsuccessful, and in some cases the turtles have outlived the people studying them.

DIET

Snapping turtles are omnivorous, and opportunistic to the extreme, consuming large amounts of aquatic and shoreline vegetation, as well as carrion, and nearly any small animal that comes within reach of their powerful jaws. Part of the snapper's ability to occupy such a vast range of climates and aquatic habitats is its ability to thrive on almost any available organic matter.

Northern snapping turtles are remarkably efficient predators. Unlike its larger cousin, the alligator snapping turtle, which lies in wait with mouth open wide and its pink, wormlike tongue waving as bait, the northern snapper relies on stealth and camouflage. Ambush of small fish, frogs, crayfish, or other creatures from a vantage point buried in muck or mud is a favored low-output/high-return snapper strategy. When a fish or other prey comes within range, the snapper's powerful jaws shoot out, powered by its long extendable neck, and its beak snaps shut on the prey's body. Small prey is swallowed whole, but larger animals are gripped tightly by the jaws while the turtle uses its strong, sharp-clawed forefeet to shred the body into smaller pieces. This snapping behavior appears to be an ingrained instinct, because captive turtles raised from hatchlings also lunge with their jaws, even at inanimate foods. The size of a snapping turtle's prey changes as it grows: Hatchlings subsist on insects, fish, and crustaceans, but large turtles have been witnessed snapping ducklings and goslings from the surface of shallow waters, along with snakes, frogs, and an occasional young muskrat.

Although an air breather with lungs, snapping turtles, like frogs, can absorb much of the oxygen they require through their skins while submerged in water. The snapper will ascend occasionally to the surface, linger for a breath or two, perhaps take some sun, then slowly fade back into the safety of the depths.

Snapping turtles grow continuously throughout their lives, with some very old individuals achieving a carapace length of 2 feet or more.

MATING HABITS

Male northern snapping turtles reach sexual maturity at age 5, and females at around age 7.

Mating takes place in April or May among most northern populations, but occurs as late as November in the Deep South. Sexual maturity seems to be dictated by size rather than strict chronological age, because individuals that are malnourished take longer to reach puberty, while well-fed snapping turtles breed earlier.

Mating season is initiated more by warming temperatures than by the calendar or the length of days, and an unusually cold spring will delay procreational activities. Because snapping turtles, like all turtles, incubate their eggs in an underground nest, it's imperative that the soil be warm enough to maintain a constant temperature between 60 and 70 degrees Fahrenheit.

Just how male and female snapping turtles are attracted to one another is still under study, but pheromonal scents contained in urine probably play a large part in drawing the sexes together. Females may not mate every year, but are able to carry live sperm from a previous mating within their reproductive organs for several years before laying eggs. This process of delayed implantation is seen in numerous other species, and is an adaptation that helps to ensure that females are physically strong enough to withstand the demands of bearing and birthing without draining their own bodily reserves, and perhaps losing both themselves and their broods.

Copulation generally occurs at or near the water's edge. Mating is fairly conventional, with males mounting receptive females from behind. The female, if she accepts the male's advances, pushes her long tail to one side and allows him to climb atop her carapace, where he uses his strong clawed forefeet to firmly grasp the edges of her shell. He then curls his own tail downward until their genitalia meet, and deposits his sperm within her body.

There is no lasting bond between snapping turtle mates, and as soon as a female is impregnated, she abandons the male. Precisely how long it takes for an egg clutch to fully develop within the female's body is dictated by her own state of health, but 3 to 4 weeks is about average.

When she's ready to lay her eggs, most often in late May or early June, a female leaves the water to find a suitable nesting place on dry ground, always well above the water table. Preferred nesting sites are in sandy soil along shorelines, but females have been observed laying eggs as far as a half mile away from open water, sometimes even crossing paved roads. Loose soil is an imperative, because nests are excavated by the turtle's strong hind feet to a depth of roughly 8 inches.

Nests begin as a broad, shallow hole wide enough to accommodate the female's rear, then abruptly taper to a narrow, downward-sloping tunnel about 2 inches in diameter. At the bottom of this remarkably consistent tunnel is an enlarged chamber that will contain the eggs.

When her nest is ready, the female settles her rear over the hole and begins laying her clutch of round eggs, a process that may take several hours. Each egg is about the size of a table tennis ball. Clutch sizes depend on the size of the female, averaging about forty eggs, but one clutch of more than one hundred eggs was recorded, laid by an exceptionally large turtle in Nebraska. Eggs are creamy white and covered with a flexible shell, again much like a table tennis ball, but softer. The flexible covering permits the eggs to roll down the tunnel-like nest opening and land atop one another without sustaining damage.

After depositing her eggs, the female refills the nest with loose soil and returns to the water. She may return to the same nesting site to lay eggs in subsequent years, but once deposited, each clutch is abandoned.

Attrition is very high on snapping turtle nests. Of the hundreds of eggs that may be laid within a single square mile of ideal nesting habitat, few will hatch. With a taste and texture very much like a small chicken egg, snapping turtle eggs are highly sought after by any carnivore. Strong diggers, like raccoons, skunks, badgers, and bears, take a heavy toll by eating whole clutches, and I've personally been guilty of eating a dozen fried snapping turtle eggs for breakfast while backpacking. Despite heavy predation, snapping turtle populations remain healthy, a testimony to the success of the species.

Most snapping turtle eggs hatch after an incubation period of about 9 weeks. Hatching will normally occur in late July or August, but a spell of unusually cool weather can delay hatching for much longer, sometimes even into the Indian summer days of September or October. The turtle hatchlings, only about one inch in diameter, tear free of their eggs using a typically reptilian "egg tooth" (also seen in snakes), which later falls off, and dig upward to the surface. For their first 2 weeks, the newborns carry a fat-rich yolk sac under their plastrons to give them a nutritional head start as they learn to forage for plants and insects.

Like hatchlings of every turtle species, young snappers make a tasty catch for every predator, from muskrats and snakes to a wide gamut of bird species. Instinct compels the little turtles to immediately head for water, where they'll find sanctuary from most terrestrial predators, and where their swimming abilities give them at least some advantage. But the world of the water is a predators' banquet, too. Hatchlings are readily eaten by large fish, varieties of water snakes, herons, otters, and larger turtles for their first 3 years of life. In waters with an abundant food supply, a good rule of thumb for growth is about 1 inch of length per year for the first 5 years. At 5 years of age, and with a typical length of as many inches, the snapper becomes a proven survivor, a predator in its own right, and safe from all but the largest and most tenacious enemies.

BEHAVIORISMS

No turtle species is gregarious, but northern snapping turtles are perhaps the least social of all. With the exception of brief sexual encounters during the breeding season, neither juveniles or adults of either gender are tolerant of one another. Territorial battles between snappers are common, but are seldom more than slightly injurious to either party. Lacerations from claws, and bites to the tail or hind legs of a retreating, vanquished adversary are common, but combatants seem reluctant to use their powerful jaws as effectively as they might.

The same consideration does not apply to other turtle species. As some researchers have noted, large painted turtles especially are frequently found decapitated along shorelines during the snapping turtle's spring mating season. These beheadings are the result of decidedly lopsided battles in which dominant painted turtles stood their ground against snapping turtles in disputes over territorial or nesting rights. Because the painted turtle heads are never found with the bodies, and are apparently eaten by the snapping turtles who bite them off, some have suggested that this practice might stem from "inefficient feeding behavior." The fact that decapitated turtles are typically found with their meaty legs and tails intact indicates that this behavior is most likely territorial.

In the water, snappers are retiring and secretive, yielding to any threat or challenge by seeking a hiding place. Swimmers need have no fear of them. Researchers and observers should note, though, that snapping turtles encountered on land can be very aggressive and are capable of delivering a memorable bite regardless of age or size. A turtle will likely stand its ground, and may even attack. With a top running speed of about 1 mile per hour, there's little danger of being overtaken by a charging turtle, but such aggression, combined with the snapper's obviously powerful jaws, can frighten any adversary into backing up long enough for the turtle to make it to the safety of the water.

Handling a snapping turtle is not recommended, largely because they are a known vector of salmonella bacteria. If research demands handling a snapper, the safest method is to wear heavy work gloves and to grasp it firmly at either side of the carapace, keeping hands, forearms, and other parts of the body away from its sharp claws, and especially away from its long, extendable neck. Be prepared for sharp jerking as the animal lunges backward for your hands, jaws snapping. Turtle hunters who take snappers as meat for the pot (turtle soup is a delicacy), or for sale to restaurants, recommend carrying the animal by its tail, but many researchers consider this method inhumane. However a turtle is handled, the handler should always wash his or her hands thoroughly afterward, and especially before eating.

INDEX